• Maps of the World •

MAP 0.1 ● The World's Geographical Borders

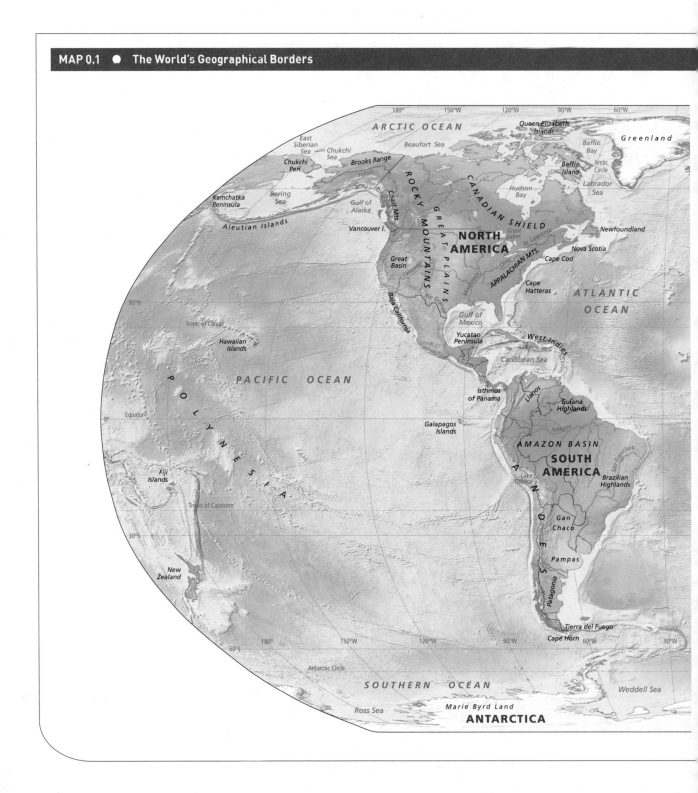

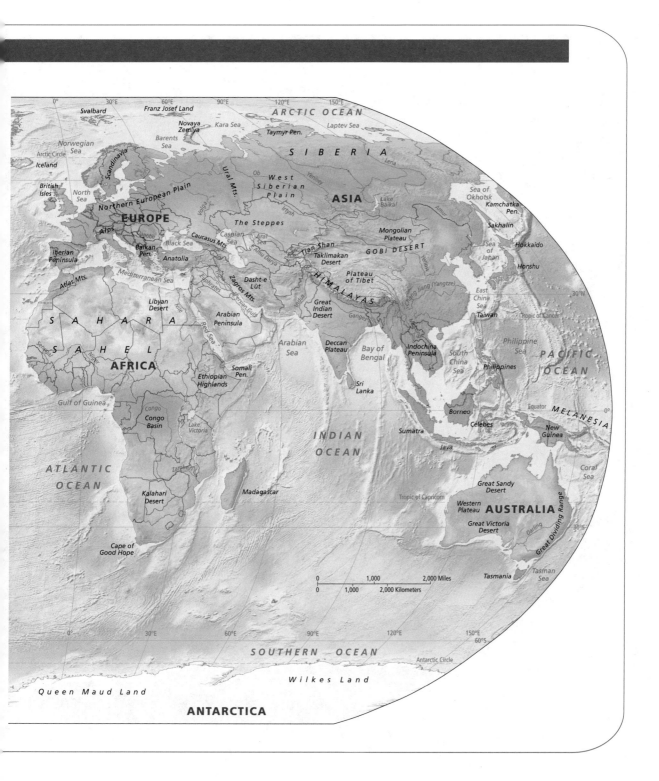

MAP 0.2 ● The World's Political Borders

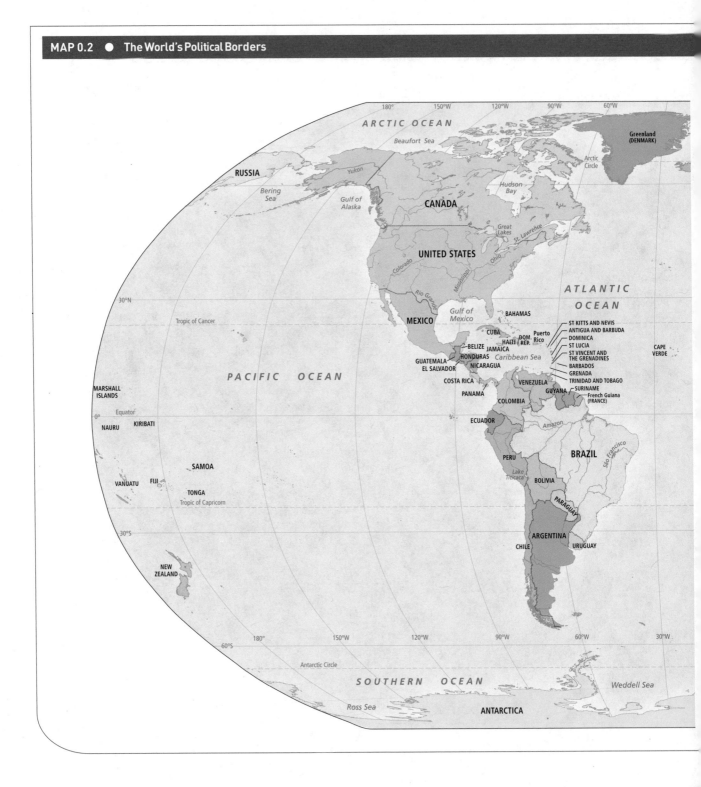

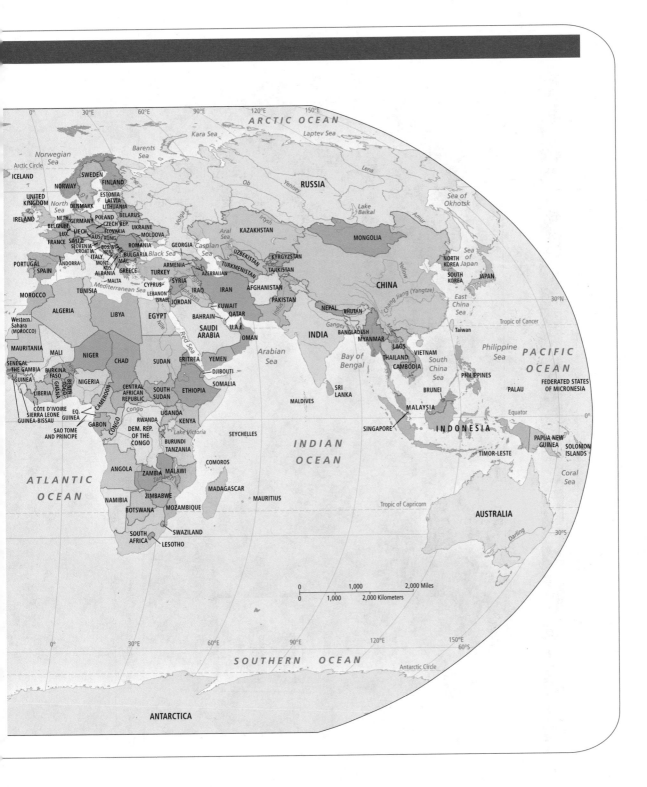

MAP 0.3 ● The World's Economic and Trade Borders

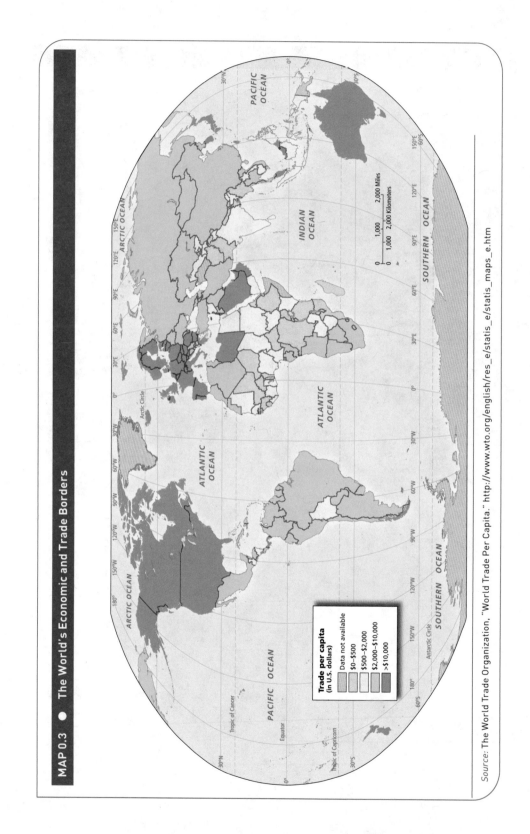

Trade per capita
(in U.S. dollars)

Data not available
$0–$500
$500–$2,000
$2,000–$10,000
>$10,000

Source: The World Trade Organization, "World Trade Per Capita." http://www.wto.org/english/res_e/statis_e/statis_maps_e.htm

MAP 0.4 ● The World's Social Borders

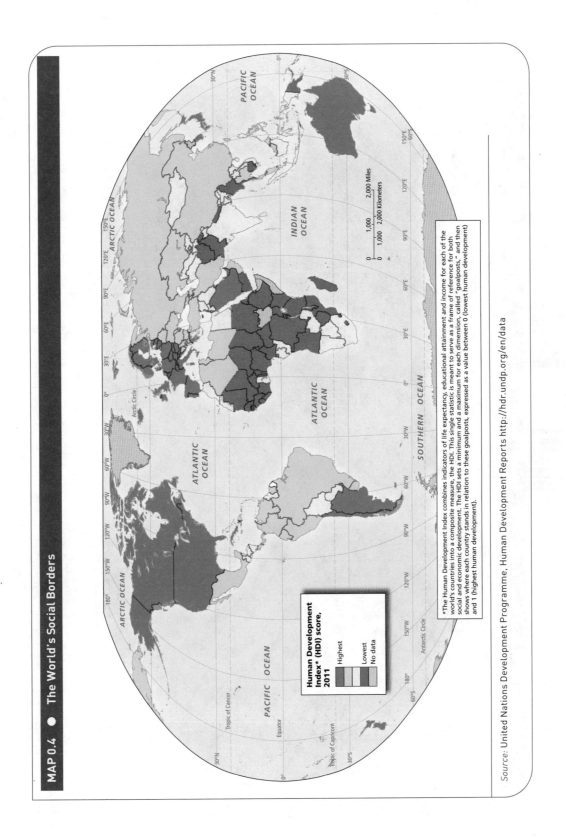

Human Development
Index* (HDI) score,
2011

- Highest
- Lowest
- No data

*The Human Development Index combines indicators of life expectancy, educational attainment and income for each of the world's countries into a composite measure, the HDI. This single statistic is meant to serve as a frame of reference for both social and economic development. The HDI sets a minimum and a maximum for each dimension, called "goalposts," and then shows where each country stands in relation to these goalposts, expressed as a value between 0 (lowest human development) and 1 (highest human development).

Source: United Nations Development Programme, Human Development Reports http://hdr.undp.org/en/data

MAP 0.5 ● The World's Cultural Borders

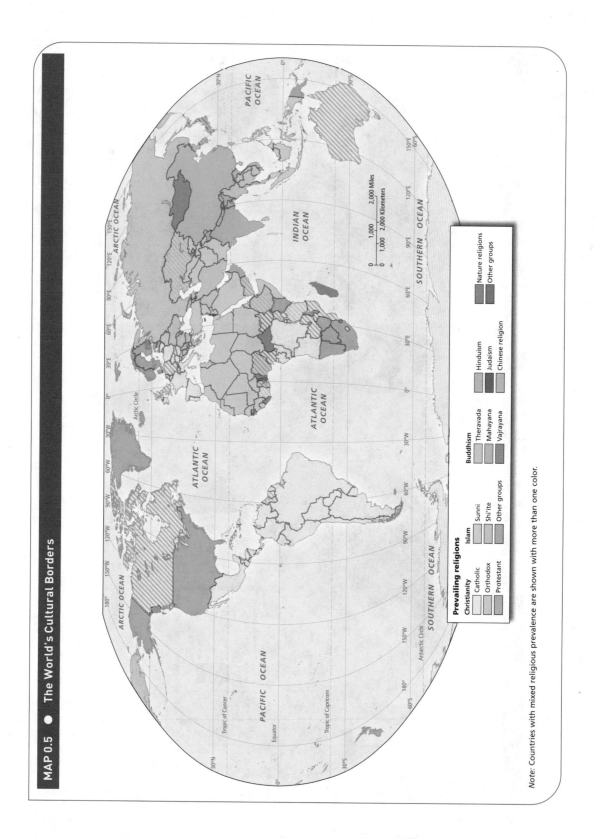

Prevailing religions

Christianity
- Catholic
- Orthodox
- Protestant

Islam
- Sunni
- Shi'ite
- Other groups

Buddhism
- Theravada
- Mahayana
- Vajrayana

- Hinduism
- Judaism
- Chinese religion

- Nature religions
- Other groups

Note: Countries with mixed religious prevalence are shown with more than one color.

Crossing Borders

Third Edition

To my wife, Elaine, for a lifetime of loving support, and to Rena, Chris, and Nathan

—Harry

With love to my husband, Steve, and our children, Perry and Madison

—Heidi

Sara Miller McCune founded SAGE Publishing in 1965 to support the dissemination of usable knowledge and educate a global community. SAGE publishes more than 1000 journals and over 800 new books each year, spanning a wide range of subject areas. Our growing selection of library products includes archives, data, case studies and video. SAGE remains majority owned by our founder and after her lifetime will become owned by a charitable trust that secures the company's continued independence.

Los Angeles | London | New Delhi | Singapore | Washington DC | Melbourne

Crossing Borders

International Studies for the 21st Century

Third Edition

Harry I. Chernotsky
University of North Carolina at Charlotte

Heidi H. Hobbs
North Carolina State University

Los Angeles | London | New Delhi
Singapore | Washington DC | Melbourne

FOR INFORMATION:

CQ Press

An Imprint of SAGE Publications, Inc.

2455 Teller Road

Thousand Oaks, California 91320

E-mail: order@sagepub.com

SAGE Publications Ltd.

1 Oliver's Yard

55 City Road

London EC1Y 1SP

United Kingdom

SAGE Publications India Pvt. Ltd.

B 1/I 1 Mohan Cooperative Industrial Area

Mathura Road, New Delhi 110 044

India

SAGE Publications Asia-Pacific Pte. Ltd.

3 Church Street

#10-04 Samsung Hub

Singapore 049483

Acquisitions Editor: Scott Greenan

Content Development Editors: Anna Villarruel, John Scappini

Editorial Assistant: Sarah Christensen

Production Editor: Bennie Clark Allen

Copy Editor: Laureen Gleason

Typesetter: C&M Digitals (P) Ltd.

Proofreader: Eleni-Maria Georgiou

Indexer: Mary Harper

Cover Designer: Rose Storey

Marketing Manager: Erica DeLuca

Printed in the United States of America

Library of Congress Cataloging-in-Publication Data

Names: Chernotsky, Harry Ira, author. | Hobbs, Heidi H., author.

Title: Crossing borders : international studies for the 21st century / Harry I. Chernotsky, The University of North Carolina at Charlotte, Heidi H. Hobbs, North Carolina State University.

Description: Third Edition. | Washington : CQ Press, DC. [2018] | Revised edition of the authors' Crossing borders, [2016] | Includes index.

Identifiers: LCCN 2017035915 | ISBN 978-1-5063-4692-2 (pbk. : alk. paper)

Subjects: LCSH: Technological innovations—Economic aspects. | Security, International. | Economic development. | International relations.

Classification: LCC HC79.T4 C4574 2018 | DDC 303.48/2—dc23 LC record available at https://lccn.loc.gov/2017035915

This book is printed on acid-free paper.

SUSTAINABLE FORESTRY INITIATIVE
Certified Chain of Custody
Promoting Sustainable Forestry
www.sfiprogram.org
SFI-01268
SFI label applies to text stock

18 19 20 21 22 10 9 8 7 6 5 4 3 2 1

• Brief Contents •

• Detailed Contents •

• About the Authors •

Harry I. Chernotsky is professor in the Department of Global Studies and served as founding chair of the department at the University of North Carolina at Charlotte. He has a PhD in political science from Rutgers University.

Heidi H. Hobbs is the director of the Master of International Studies program and an associate professor of political science in the School of Public and International Affairs at North Carolina State University. She has a PhD in international relations from the University of Southern California.

• Preface •

The proliferation of international studies majors at colleges and universities across the United States has created both a new frontier for understanding the world and a problem for those of us who are expected to identify the key concepts associated with these programs. We are asked to structure distinct disciplines into a coherent multidisciplinary major, where learning outcomes and objectives are most often in the eye of the beholder. Not only is this difficult intellectually; it is challenging administratively as well. International studies is the intersection of anthropology, political science, geography, culture, language, science, technology, art, health, and so many other disciplines. Historically, it has lacked an integrative framework. This eclectic scheme of organization is reflected in the way international studies has developed in colleges and universities. While the growth of majors and minors has been fueled by an increasing interest in all that is "international," it is the "studies" aspect that has varied from one academic institution to the next. As a result, it has become quite difficult to define a core curriculum.

This book addresses this challenge by providing a framework for students that is built on an understanding of the many borders that define the international system. In adopting this view, we are able to address the many different fields that constitute international studies and provide instructors with a starting point from which they can pursue their own disciplinary interests. The challenge for students majoring in international studies is less about what anthropology, political science, or sociology *is* and more about what each of these disciplines *does* to contribute to its understanding of the world.

Features

The various features we have included are designed to engage students directly with the material.

- The **How You Can Connect** feature encourages students to consider their own experiences, habits, and attitudes as they might relate to the issues under consideration, and to identify how they can take action on these matters in their own communities as well.

- The **Pro/Con** feature introduces students to the opposing arguments put forward with respect to a number of contentious global issues and is followed by probing questions that ask **Where Do You Stand?**

- The feature **What Can You Do with International Studies?** profiles some of our former students who have gone on to apply their studies through their activities and work in the field. It fits particularly well with our intent in Chapter 12, which surveys the array of educational, experiential, and career opportunities that await students of international studies.

Organization of This Book

The notion of global citizenship as an organizing concept for international studies is critical to our perspective. Whatever the focus of international studies may be at your college or university, we are dedicated to the belief that students must have a greater understanding of the world around them and the role they will play in it. This sense of cosmopolitanism will be critical as they navigate their daily lives and consider the range of career opportunities available to them. We have designed this work to provide a dialogue between academic frameworks and to include practical components that suggest how students can put an international studies degree to work. The book is organized to reflect these goals by including chapters on both the various disciplines that address international studies and the global challenges we must all confront. The book concludes with a how-to guide for students that offers suggestions for study abroad, internships, service learning, and future training. We hope it will serve as a road map for students to better understand the world and to become important actors in it.

New to This Edition

All of the book's chapters have been updated to reflect recent events and trends that amplify the material under consideration. Political developments that are significantly transforming traditional relationships and hot spots around the world are specifically addressed in Chapters 4 and 5. In Chapters 6 and 7, we examine in some detail the continuing evolution of the global economy and growing dissatisfaction with the consequences of globalization. The rise of nationalism and the persistence of religious and ethnic conflict is discussed in Chapters 8 and 9, while Chapters 10 and 11 explore various methods to promote cooperation to solve global problems.

This book offers several features that help students integrate the various perspectives on international issues and think about how to apply them. To that end, we have updated the **Understanding Cross-Border Conflict: How Can International Studies Help?** feature. It appears in six separate chapters and offers examples of particular conflicts that can be better understood by applying the multidisciplinary approach of international studies. We also include focused questions that invite students to think about how each of the approaches would help identify the key factors affecting possible solutions. To help readers better identify the major conceptual take-home points and provide a platform for review, we have included a revised set of **Learning Objectives** at the start of each chapter. We have also identified some additional resources and included them in the **To Learn More** sections at the end of the chapters. Finally, this edition includes **Turning Point**, a new feature that looks at critical junctures that have altered the course of selected global relationships.

Digital Resources

SAGE Edge for Instructors supports teaching by making it easy to integrate quality content and create a rich learning environment for students. Instructors can access these resources at **https://edge.sagepub.com/chernotsky3e**. SAGE Edge instructor sites include tools and elements such as

- **Test banks** that provide a diverse range of prewritten options, as well as the opportunity to edit any question or insert personalized questions to effectively assess students' progress and understanding

- Editable, chapter-specific **PowerPoint slides** that offer complete flexibility for creating a multimedia presentation for the course

- **Multimedia content**, including links to video, audio, web resources, and data that appeal to students with different learning styles

- An **instructor's manual**, which summarizes key concepts by chapter to ease preparation for lectures and class discussions

- A **transition guide**, which provides a chapter-by-chapter outline of key changes to the new edition

- A set of all the **graphics from the text**, including all the maps, tables, and figures, in PowerPoint, .pdf, and .jpg formats for class presentations

SAGE Edge for Students provides a personalized approach to help students accomplish their coursework goals in an easy-to-use learning environment; it features elements such as

- Mobile-friendly **eFlashcards** that strengthen understanding of key terms and concepts

- Mobile-friendly practice **quizzes** that allow students to independently assess their mastery of course material

- **Chapter summaries** with **learning objectives** that reinforce the most important material

- **Videos** and **multimedia content** that appeal to students with different learning styles

- Carefully selected **SAGE readings** to support and expand on the concepts presented in each chapter

Students can access these resources at **https://edge.sagepub.com/chernotsky3e**.

• Acknowledgments •

The broad nature of this subject matter has been difficult to capture in a text, and we are very grateful to the people who have played important roles in this process. First, we must thank Darin Van Tassell for his many intellectual contributions to the first edition, most notably that fated conversation in Starbucks that really laid out the borders theme we would subsequently adopt, as well as his work on Chapter 1. Thanks to those who have thoughtfully worked on the conceptualization of international studies and to the participants in the many International Studies Association (ISA) panels on this topic, especially Ann Kelleher, Rob Blanton, Barron Boyd, and Marijke Breuning. Thanks also to our academic homes, The University of North Carolina at Charlotte and North Carolina State University, which have supported us through this endeavor.

Pulling from so many disciplines has been challenging. The work of several teaching assistants in the Master of International Studies program at North Carolina State University has been critical, from the early days with Shirreef Loza, Lisa Sands Shelton, and Carl Booksing and on to include Sarah Cowles, Margaret Jackson, Chantell LaPan, Leah McManus, Chris Sawyer, Lesa Sexton, Mary Sloan, Shari Tate, and Nicole Zapata. Leah Gardner contributed significantly to the completion of the final manuscript and the development of teaching resources for the second edition. We thank our former students who contributed to the "What Can You Do With International Studies?" features, as well as the many students who have taken our classes and informed our decisions in crafting this work.

We are indebted to the editors and staff of SAGE and CQ Press for their support and assistance. We greatly appreciate the initial and continuing enthusiasm of Charisse Kiino for this project. It is contagious. We thank Elise Frasier for all her efforts on our behalf and for her invaluable contributions to the first and second editions. We are grateful to Sarah Calabi for her oversight of this work and to Laureen Gleason and Cate Huisman for their production work on the first edition and Veronica Hooper and Megan Markanich on the second. The editorial work of Anna Villarruel and Duncan Marchbank, as well as the production work of Bennie Clark Allen and Laureen Gleason, was essential for the third edition.

Finally, we are grateful to our families, whose support has been critical throughout this process. They stuck with us and encouraged us through the thick and thin of it all. We could not have done this without them!

Publisher's Acknowledgments

CQ Press is grateful to reviewers Daniel Allen (Anderson University), Lesley Daspit (University of North Carolina Wilmington), Michael Makara (University of Central Missouri), Bora Pajo (Mercyhurst University), and Anjali Sahay (Gannon University) for their editorial insight and guidance.

• List of Tables, Figures, and Maps •

Tables

Figures

Maps

1

Getting Your Global Bearings

Navigating the World

Don't panic.

—Douglas Adams's 1979 science fiction classic, *The Hitchhiker's Guide to the Galaxy*[1]

Learning Objectives

After studying this chapter, you will be able to do the following:

- Define the field of international studies.
- Describe the different kinds of borders that shape our understanding of the modern world and identify their main units of analysis.
- Understand the different stages of globalization.
- Explain the pros and cons of globalization.
- Explain the concept of citizenship and how it has changed over time.

You can't escape it. The world has become smaller as the food you eat, the clothes you wear, and the products you use come from all around the globe. Your own daily routines are closely connected to the world beyond your doorstep. As distances shrink and traditional borders become fuzzy, we have to approach the world in a new way. We have to learn to think differently. In Douglas Adams's science fiction classic, *The Hitchhiker's Guide to the Galaxy*, the protagonist, Arthur Dent, is thrust into a tour of the galaxy without warning. Overwhelmed by this new challenge, he is relieved upon receiving his Hitchhiker's Guide emblazoned with the words DON'T PANIC.

Anyone embarking on a journey to understand the world today might benefit from similar advice. You must embrace the many changes taking place, but you might want some help in planning your trip. What you really need to set you at ease is a "hitchhiker's guide to the global arena" that will provide a road map for the world of today and the people who inhabit it. This book will serve as that guide as it lays out the foundations of international studies and describes the knowledge, skills, and experience you will need to get your global bearings to navigate the world.

Navigating the world's borders has become increasingly easy with the emergence of new technologies—we can find our way through a completely new city with the touch of a screen. Still, most of us will face geographic, political, economic, social, and cultural challenges as we traverse these borders for the first time. Our job in this book is to introduce you to ways of approaching some of these new and potentially strange challenges. So, don't panic! This book will be your resource through the entire journey.

Toward a Working Definition of International Studies

The goal of international studies is to prepare students for meeting the challenges of a rapidly changing world. A working definition of **international studies** is "a field of inquiry that examines the broad array of human relationships that involve cross-border interactions." International studies is one of the fastest growing majors in the United States today—in large part because students and teachers alike recognize that we live in a rapidly changing landscape and know that we need a new set of tools to engage with it. The field is different from traditional studies of international relations and their narrower emphasis

international studies a field of inquiry that examines the broad array of geographic, political, economic, social, and cultural interactions and relationships that cross borders

This young woman works on her laptop while on a trip to Tibet.

iStock/Solovyova.

on politics in that it offers a unique and broader way to examine the challenges of a global world order. For instance, whereas a focus on politics helps us think about how countries around the world interact with one another, it does not tell us very much about how ordinary people are connected to or impacted by the world around them and how they, in turn, affect it.

As a course of study, international studies draws upon multiple disciplines and perspectives. These may include anthropology, business, communication, economics, geography, health care, history, languages, literature, political science, religion, and sociology. Relationships among these different disciplines are often hard to manage for academic institutions, but the changing nature of the international system and the ability to understand it requires looking at the world through these multiple lenses. Ultimately, international studies is designed to help students forge a new identity for themselves that is responsive to their environment.

Different Ways of Looking at the World's Borders

Each of these academic disciplines represents a different way of studying the world, focusing on a particular aspect as its unit of analysis. For our purposes, we can think of those units as making up different kinds of "borders," the features that most strongly define the various parts of any given system (see Table 1.1). Every day, you cross borders physically and intellectually. You leave your home to cross from street to street, city to city, state to state, or even country to country. In your classes, you look at the world through different lenses that guide your educational experience from art to science. As we look to understand the multiple dimensions of the international system from a variety of perspectives and vantage points, we will examine five major types of borders: geographic, political, economic, social, and cultural.

In the popular *Cosmos: A Spacetime Odyssey* documentary series, host Neil deGrasse Tyson says that our cosmic address begins on earth, then proceeds to the solar system, then expands to the Milky Way galaxy, and reaches all the way to the observable universe! Looking at earth from outer space, it appears as a peaceful blue globe distinguished by landmasses and bodies of water. Upon closer inspection, we can begin to identify rivers, deserts, and mountain ranges (see Map 0.1 in the color insert). These **geographic borders** affect how and where humans have settled and the degree to which they interact with one another. The academic field of geography studies these borders, measured by bodies of water, various elevations, and expanses of forest and desert.

Over time, these geographic borders have changed, shifted, expanded, and shrunk. Volcanoes, glaciers, earthquakes, and meandering rivers transform the landscape.

geographic borders borders that delineate the physical world (mountains, oceans, rivers, deserts, ozone) and affect how and where humans have settled and the degree to which they interact with one another

TABLE 1.1 ● The Borders of International Studies		
Type of Border	**Main Unit of Analysis**	**Primary Academic Field of Study**
Geographic	Physical earth	Geography
Political	States	Political science
Economic	Markets	Economics
Social	Class	Sociology
Cultural	Nations	Anthropology

Geographic borders are also altered by the environmental impact of melting polar ice caps, retreating wetlands, and expanding deserts. Furthermore, such borders have shifted because people increasingly live in large groups today, whereas they once did not. The valleys subject to monsoon flooding in Bangladesh and the converted deserts of wildfire-prone areas of southern California are examples of two such areas where large numbers of people now live.

While geographic borders may shift, they are still fairly simple to identify. The rest of the borders of international studies, however, are distinguished in a more nuanced manner. Looking at a modern map of the world (see Map 0.2 in the color insert), we see a series of recognizable lines and boundaries. These lines represent the **political borders** of the world. These political borders form states, critically powerful actors in the world today. Defined largely by governments in control within these boundaries, states remain a primary focus for students of international studies.

The sheer number of states is important to recognize as well. Today, there are almost 200 independent states. Only 100 years ago, roughly fifty states existed. By the start of World War II, there had been little change. Because the end of World War II brought incredible devastation to the European continent and consequently ended the formal trappings of colonialism, some thirty-six new states had come into existence by 1960. The existence of so many relatively new political entities itself is important to recognize, particularly when observing that these new political borders sit on top of—and often divide—very old cultures. The field of political science focuses on these important actors.

International studies involves much more than government members sitting around a table discussing issues of war and peace. Beyond political borders that form states, the existence of **economic borders**—those that form markets—is central to the relationships among states, nations, and individuals (see Map 0.3 in the color insert). Markets, or the exchange of goods and services within a given system, represent dynamic forces that provide almost everyone with the items they consume. As a result, the emergence of a global marketplace is driven not just by states but by other actors, such as transnational private corporations and individuals. The discipline of economics examines these borders and their effect on you and the international system.

Think about your morning routine:

> You may have woken up to the sounds of the alarm emanating from your Korean-made smartphone, checked your e-mail and social media accounts—Facebook, Twitter, Instagram, and Snapchat—gotten out of a bed that had been made with linens from Egypt or Malaysia, and struggled to get to the kitchen. Once there, perhaps you made a cup of Brazilian coffee or tea grown in Sri Lanka. You might have even had a banana from Costa Rica or an orange from Morocco. Next, you headed into the shower with the fixtures possibly made in Germany. Then, you slipped into your Levi's made in Vietnam, T-shirt made in India, and Converse made in China, and then headed for school in your Toyota, assembled in Kentucky. You stopped to buy gas, imported from Saudi Arabia or Venezuela, arrived on campus, and then searched for a parking space—a problem confronted worldwide!

Your ability to purchase goods across international borders has much to do with economic success, but access is not equal. Goods and services and the resources needed to produce them are not distributed evenly across the world's population—they go to those who can afford them and who have access to them. As a result, this uneven distribution and contact produces a divide along **social borders** (see Map 0.4 in the color insert). In other words, it separates people into different social classes.

political borders borders that delineate the governing entities of the world and that are distinguished on the basis of territory, population, governments, and recognition by others

economic borders borders that delineate the markets that promote the exchange of goods and services across the world

social borders borders that delineate the class divisions of the world that are formed by inequality of opportunity

John Moore/Getty Images.

A jogger and his dog run toward the US-Mexico border fence at its end in the Pacific Ocean on May 12, 2017, in Tijuana, Mexico. The border spans almost 2,000 miles, from the Gulf of Mexico to the Pacific Ocean, and is fenced for some 700 miles of its total length.

cultural borders borders that delineate the nations of the world that form identities in terms of language, religion, ethnicity, or a common historical experience

citizenship the duties, rights, privileges, and responsibilities of individuals to and in the community in which they reside

Karl Marx is the best known advocate of using class as an important means of analysis. His ideas were implemented by some of his most prominent followers—Lenin and Stalin in Russia and Mao in China—in the formation of governing bodies to oversee political states. But social divisions remained even in these proposed utopian societies. Such divisions are even more pronounced today along the north-south line formed by the equator, such that societies to the south of the equator, known as the Global South, are less economically viable than those to the north. The inherent structure of the world's political and economic systems creates a world of haves and have-nots that furthers class distinctions. Understanding these divides and the hardships they impose is part of the field of sociology.

The **cultural borders** that form nations constitute a related area and additional layer that must be considered. Nations can be defined in terms of language, religion, ethnicity, or a common historical experience. Such cultural distinctions provide us with some of the most important insights into the world's people. There may be some 200 different states, but there are more than 6,000 languages, dozens of global religions, countless folk religions, and hundreds of different ethnic groups (see Map 0.5 in the color insert).

Though governments decide who belongs or has membership (generally referred to as **citizenship**) in a state, it is largely up to individuals to determine their cultural identity. The language of international studies makes these distinctions between political and cultural borders confusing. The countries that are members of the United Nations (UN), for example, are referred to as *nation-states*; with this term, there is an implicit assumption that political borders and cultural borders generally coincide. But such is not always the case, and the African continent offers an excellent example. There are fifty-four African states and more than 300 distinct nations on the sub-Saharan African continent. Many of the problems surrounding the violence, leadership, and economic stagnation in that region must begin with the recognition that there are many new states that have been formed that split very old nations. Questions of identity and how they affect the international system are studied in the field of anthropology.

One of the striking characteristics of our world today is that its inhabitants routinely cross these borders, and it is largely the impact of technology and technological innovation that has transformed the relationship between individuals and their political, economic, and cultural affiliations. Perhaps best exemplified by the telecommunications revolution and the presence of the World Wide Web, these technological developments permit much of the world's people to be connected with one another in ways unimaginable until recently in history. In just over 100 years, the transition from horse and buggy to cars and planes made people more physically mobile, while communications, through radio and television, transformed society. In the twenty-first century, it is the access to smartphones, computers, and cloud technologies that is bridging geographic, political, economic, social, and cultural divides, particularly as the costs of these devices continue to shrink while their capabilities grow.

HOW YOU CAN CONNECT

You can define and establish your sense of personal identity through connections to your . . .

- country
- state, province, or local community
- religion
- language
- race or ethnic group
- gender
- some combination of all these identities

The Evolution of Globalization

The most popular way to understand what is happening in the world today is the concept of **globalization**, a buzzword that emerged during the latter stages of the Cold War and the ensuing interconnectedness of the international arena. Originally coined by Theodore Levitt in a 1983 *Harvard Business Review* article titled "The Globalization of Markets," it referred to changes in behaviors and technology that allowed companies to sell the same products around the world.[2] Today, the definition is much broader. Generally, the term is used to describe the political, economic, social, and cultural flows across the international system. It includes a broad range of interactions, from trade and financial relationships to the integrated communication networks that have developed to facilitate those connections.

There is still some controversy, however, as to the extent and impact of this connectivity. Some have argued that the most recent acceleration marks the beginning of the end of the current global system—that something even bigger than globalization is happening. They point to the emergence of a new era of **hyperglobalization**, as it has come to be called, with the progressive erosion of the borders that have differentiated national economies and sustained the centrality of nation-states. They argue that this development has resulted in a significantly altered environment, as defined by the following changes:

1. The nation-state is in steady decline and is now merely one of a growing number of players or actors on an increasingly multilevel world stage, where the practical limits to sovereignty have become more pronounced.

2. There are a growing number of issues that are global in scope and cannot be dealt with effectively by individual countries or even small groups of countries without some overarching system of global governance.

3. The mobility of capital has produced new patterns of finance and commercial exchange that do not necessarily correspond to flows that fit neatly within existing political borders.

4. The future will be marked by an increasing number of transnational interactions and institutions that will lead to a widening and deepening of integration processes—politically, economically, and socially.[3]

globalization the political, economic, social, and cultural flows across the international system; the term includes a broad range of interactions, from trade and financial relationships to the integrated communication networks that have developed to facilitate those connections

hyperglobalization the view that emphasizes the progressive erosion of the borders that have differentiated national economies and sustained the centrality of nation-states

A Buddhist monk on a trip to Angkor Wat takes a photo with his Apple iPad while his colleague talks on the phone. Increasingly, we are connected via technologies such as these, even in the most hard-to-reach areas of the world.

gross domestic product (GDP) the value of all the goods and services produced within a country

gross national product (GNP) the value of all the goods and services produced by a country's citizens, regardless of where they may be living

Not everyone agrees with this assessment. Skeptics point to the resiliency and political endurance of the nation-state system and the continuing capacity of states to regulate the global economy. While not disputing some of the important changes that are bringing disparate parts of the world closer together, these critics are less certain of the uniqueness or overarching significance of these developments. The expansion of trade and investment, they argue, is occurring within prevailing structures and continues to be shaped by existing borders. While more and more trade across the world is between transnational companies, trade balances are still measured on a country-to-country basis. In addition, the role of nationalism and other more restricted forms of identity in shaping relationships across the planet suggests potential limits to the cooperative spirit required to nurture and maintain global connections.

Similar patterns have developed previously, only to be strained or even severed due to emerging conflicts. The high levels of trade and investment that characterized the global economy of the late nineteenth century, for example, came to an abrupt halt with the outbreak of World War I in 1914. The volume of trade had risen sharply, with merchandise exports rising from 5 percent of the world's **gross domestic product (GDP)** in 1870 to 8.7 percent in 1913.[4] Merchandise trade represented 12 percent of the **gross national product (GNP)** for developed countries, a level unmatched until the 1970s.[5] Postwar efforts to revive the global economy and political order were hindered by lingering distrust and failure to devise an effective collective security system. A repetition of this pattern is certainly not outside the realm of possibility today, particularly in light of the efforts of some states to limit their international exposure following the global financial crisis of 2008 and the backlash against international exposure that has recently surfaced in the United States and parts of Europe.

The inconsistent patterns evident across the global political and economic arenas are reflected in what some have labeled the *third wave* of globalization theory.[6] This view, often referred to as the *transformationalist* perspective, emphasizes the complexity of globalization. Its proponents see globalization as an extended historical process that goes back as far as the early "globalizers" in the third century BCE who traveled the Silk Road trade route linking the Chinese and Roman empires. This initial wave was followed by a more pronounced period in the 1500s with the rise of European metropolitan centers and merchant classes. The activities of the Dutch and British East India trading companies marked the expansion of these centers into previously uncharted areas.

Transformationalists view the more recent trends that have been stimulated by major advances in technology as unprecedented in terms of their growth and intensity and as serving to alter fundamental political, economic, and social relationships. The lines between what is domestic and what is international have become increasingly blurred. The national origin of particular products, for example, may be difficult to discern given the multiple sources of inputs or assembly. This is portrayed quite vividly by business professor Pietra Rivoli, who follows the life cycle of a T-shirt from its origins in a Texas cotton field to its manufacture in a Shanghai factory and its eventual appearance at a used clothing market in Tanzania.[7] Similar challenges present themselves when it comes to music, food, and fashion, as they have become increasingly influenced by styles and tastes originating in many places.

Even as the sovereign authority of states has diminished and the world economy has become increasingly deterritorialized, third-wave theorists emphasize the importance of recognizing the uneven patterns of and different responses to these globalizing trends.[8] Nation-states still enjoy the legal right to sovereignty, while territorial boundaries maintain both their political and commercial significance, despite the fact that they may no longer serve as the "primary markers of modern life."[9] Crops are raised and goods and services are produced locally, and countries across the global economy tend to operate within regional contexts that often serve to limit contacts or integration outside those networks. While there are considerable and mutual stakes in sustaining these ties and relationships, their strength will be affected by the behaviors and policy choices of international actors.

Globalization: Winners and Losers

Given these disagreements and differing interpretations, it may not be so easy to get a clear sense of what globalization is all about. When you think about globalization, what is the first thing that comes to mind? Is it a generally positive or negative image? What do you consider the primary strengths and weaknesses of globalization? Who benefits from the increasingly connected world in which we live?

In fact, globalization has become a contentious process. While many argue that everyone benefits from these changes—as the saying goes, a rising tide raises all boats—that has not always been the case. Consumers may gain from access to more goods and lower prices, but they have become more vulnerable to political and economic fluctuations abroad. As economic interdependence moves the free trade economic model to a global arena, the private sector will succeed or fail as a result of its ability to compete. Moreover, competition is not simply domestic in nature but now involves everyone around the world. People are living and interacting with their global neighbors on a level unprecedented in human history, but they are apprehensive when such interactions are perceived as threatening their traditions and customs.

It is possible that overall standards of living can be improved through access to more goods produced around the world. In terms of purchasing power for everyday items, consumers benefit from global competition that can provide access to cheaper goods. Items once considered luxuries are now more widely available. Diversification of manufacturing can create jobs in places where there were limited opportunities before. For example, workers in China, Sri Lanka, Indonesia, and Mexico have benefited from these developments. The heart of this argument is that globalization promotes a better quality of life for a greater number of people.

An increasingly connected world has meant that more and more trade across the globe is between transnational companies, yet trade balances are still measured on a country-to-country basis.

Proponents of globalization further believe that it empowers individuals both economically and politically. Advances in communications and greater opportunities to travel and experience unfamiliar places, coupled with the heightened migration of people, increase people's awareness of many of the challenging issues facing the world. This recognition may serve as a catalyst in promoting cooperative and collaborative efforts at both the local and global levels.

While everyone in the world may be directly or indirectly affected by this new system, not everyone benefits equally from it. This reality has produced a backlash from people who feel frustrated by their inability to control their destiny. *New York Times* columnist and best-selling author Thomas Friedman talked about the difficulties societies may have in keeping up with globalization or adapting to its demands—what he referred to as a hardware/software type of problem—and went on to address reasons for broader social and political resistance to the process in his first book on globalization, *The Lexus and the Olive Tree.*[10] Ultimately, he came to label the policies that would be required to get with the globalization program and reap its benefits the "**golden straitjacket**," whereby a state would need to balance its budget, cut state bureaucracy, promote the private sector, and encourage free trade to compete effectively in the global market. Even in a Western-based, politically democratic, and relatively free trade economic environment, these objectives are hard to achieve.

golden straitjacket a term used by journalist Thomas Friedman to describe what states must do to participate competitively in the global market

For many of the less affluent people of the world, such objectives may not even be necessarily advisable. They see themselves as being left behind, as transnational corporations (TNCs) and other key agents of the globalization system manipulate their status in pursuit of their own economic interests. Consequently, this loss of economic control makes them susceptible to decisions that are made in faraway places that do not necessarily take local interests into consideration. This trend has prompted many to argue that while globalization may well expand the economic pie, it is also contributing further to the divide between the rich and the poor.

Examples of such antiglobalization forces abound in both developed and developing countries. Some opponents cite the transfer or outsourcing of jobs as manufacturing moves from traditional industrial countries to offshore locations. While relocation may create jobs where they did not previously exist, employment conditions are often questionable or unsafe, resembling the sweatshops of a bygone era. Furthermore, outsourcing is not limited to manufacturing.

One of the fastest-growing areas is in information technology (IT). It is estimated that approximately 43 percent of the companies in this sector engage in outsourcing activity.[11] India has been the prime beneficiary to date, owing chiefly to its large pool of trained professionals and relatively low labor costs. By 2017, three of India's largest IT services firms—Tata Consultancy Services (TCS), Infosys, and Wipro—employed a combined total of more than 740,000 workers.[12] The result is the creation of new jobs in other countries that are drawing people from rural areas to the city, contributing to the increasing urbanization of the world. As people move to the emerging megacities of Latin America, Asia, and Africa to take advantage of these jobs, living conditions for those at the lower end of the economic ladder are often below acceptable human standards. The problems of sanitation, inadequate housing, overcrowding, and serious health-care issues are pervasive.

Opposition to globalization has become more public and pronounced, resulting in large-scale protest demonstrations. One of the first was in late November 1999, when trade ministers from 135 countries assembled in Seattle, Washington, to launch a new round of global trade talks. Delegates to the World Trade Organization (WTO) meeting were greeted by tens of thousands of demonstrators who disrupted the proceedings. The "Battle of Seattle," as it was labeled, was a debate about more than trade. It turned into a broader discussion about globalization. Since that time, similar protests have occurred almost every time there has been a meeting of a major international organization associated with promoting the globalization agenda.

Globalization also has a significant cultural impact. It is difficult to protect what is unique about different cultures, and this has prompted the question as to whether the world is becoming too homogenized. This question is an important one for many people, particularly when they believe their traditional ways of living are threatened by forces that might erase their local identity.

In short, there is a feeling among those who question globalization that with the focus on competitiveness and efficiency, too little attention is given to the impact on the human condition. Despite the emphasis on cooperation and the growth of international organizations, there is a sense that the needs of many go unmet. While it may not be particularly useful to think of globalization as good or bad, it has become increasingly apparent that there have been winners and losers.

At what came to be called the "Battle of Seattle," Seattle police used tear gas to push back World Trade Organization (WTO) protesters in the city's downtown area. The protests delayed the opening of the WTO's third ministerial conference. Protests have since been staged at nearly every WTO conference.

What, then, might be the alternatives for those who do not see their interests served? Throughout history, states have turned inward when they thought the intrusion of the outside world would jeopardize their way of life. They have believed that minimizing contact would limit their vulnerability. China tried it twice. The first was during the fifteenth century under the Ming dynasty with the decision to ground all seagoing vessels to protect the Chinese base of knowledge. Later, under Mao Zedong in the 1960s, the Cultural Revolution was instituted to shield the country from outside forces that were deemed responsible for perverting the basic principles and ideology of the communist revolution. Iran moved to a more protectionist posture after the revolution in 1979 and the establishment of an Islamic republic. Under the leadership of Ayatollah Khomeini, Iran's government sought to sever all ties to Western influences to strengthen its Islamic hold on the country.

The United States also has a history of avowed isolationism (with the notable exception of its intervention in Latin America) that can be traced from the farewell address of President George Washington to the events following World War I. America was reluctant to enter World War I, and when it did, then president Woodrow Wilson characterized it as "the war to end all wars." Immediately thereafter, Wilson advocated the creation of the League of Nations to provide collective security for its members. His colleagues in the US Senate did not agree, however. When the Treaty of Versailles that ended the war and embraced Wilson's ideals came to them for ratification, they did not approve it.

In all these cases, and to varying degrees, isolation did not work. Today, China has adopted an open economic strategy while remaining tied to a closed political system. Its economic prowess is impressive, even as an extended run of annual growth averaging approximately 10 percent has come to an end. The country continues to expand at a rate of 6 to 7 percent, and its trade surplus remains strong.[13] Fear of outsiders, however, still remains. In contrast to the Great Wall of China that was built hundreds of years ago, an electronic wall has now been constructed that filters Internet content. Over time, Iran has rejected isolationism as well and is presently seeking to bolster its influence and prestige through its ongoing development of nuclear capabilities and engagement with the global economy. Despite domestic pressure to limit the US role in world affairs during the early twentieth century, the ensuing turbulence punctuated by the financial crash of 1929 and the rise of extreme nationalist political ideologies in Europe and Asia returned the United States to an activist role. Since that time, there have been periodic efforts to limit US international involvement; however, this commitment has remained intact.

Today, technological innovation, the integration of markets, and overlapping financial networks preclude effective isolation. Britain can vote to limit obligations by exiting the European Union (the so-called Brexit strategy), but its external entanglements and vulnerabilities do not disappear. We cannot build up the walls, disconnect the computers, cut the phone lines, take out the satellite networks, and turn off the TV indefinitely. There is an emerging set of challenges—more commonly known as **global issues**. They are global not simply because they are happening all over the world but because they transcend state boundaries and require a collective response. No single entity (government, TNC, nation, organization, group, or individual) possesses the ability to deal with, much less solve, these issues by itself. While this is not an exhaustive list, global issues include protection of the physical environment, terrorism, development of alternative energy, protection of human rights, growth in the human population, creation of wealth and alleviation of poverty, and halting the spread of weapons of mass destruction.

global issues challenges that transcend state boundaries and require a collective response; no single entity possesses the ability to deal with or solve these issues by itself

The difficulty of addressing these issues is compounded by the fact that they are experiencing exponential growth. The metaphor of the lily pond used by Lester Brown—borrowing from the philosopher Jean Boudin—illustrates the use of a riddle to teach schoolchildren the nature of exponential growth.[14] A lily pond contains a single leaf. Each day, the number of lily pads doubles—two leaves the second day, four leaves the third day, eight leaves the fourth day, and so on. If the pond is one-fourth full on Day 28, on what day is the pond half full? The answer is actually the next day—Day 29. It is completely full by Day 30, and the lilies will overflow beyond the pond after that, such that the resources of the pond will be tapped out, and the lilies will begin to die. By that time, the pace of growth and change is so great that there is no longer the capacity for a solution, and so it is for global issues.

Further, the growing interdependence of the global system compounds the difficulty in responding to these issues effectively. Governments and other actors can no longer disregard what happens in the rest of the world, as there is a growing reality that no one country has the capability to solve the world's problems. Issues have become linked from one country to another. The conceptual challenges are especially daunting if the goals are to minimize violence, maximize human rights, enhance social justice, and rehabilitate the environment. Advances in one area may have adverse effects on another. Such is the nature of the interdependent world.

The metaphor of a spider's web is also useful in conceptualizing today's global problems and challenges. Touch that web anywhere, even lightly, and it vibrates everywhere. Similarly, the reach of global problems resonates beyond any immediate environment. This book is not only an introduction to international studies and the different borders it crosses but an introduction to the global issues confronting the world today and the tools that must be employed to address them.

What are the tools we can use to understand global issues—to make sense of them and assess their impact? The first step is to clearly define the issue—what are the facts, data, and trends that define the issue? Who are the actors, and what are their perspectives? How can these different actors' views be reconciled to address global issues in an effective way that benefits everyone? It is frequently borders—political, economic, social, or cultural—that inhibit cooperation as self-interests are prioritized over a common good. As University of Chicago psychologist Mihaly

Personal photo by Elaine M. Chernotsky.

The lily pond in Giverny, France, that served as inspiration for the famous French impressionist artist Claude Monet.

Csikszentmihalyi has suggested, it is imperative to recognize the actual interconnections of causes and effects.[15] One example is the debate over the environment. As corporations use the Amazonian rain forests to generate wealth, subsistence farmers also are clearing them to survive. While these actions may be justifiable in the short term, they are contributing to the destruction of the world's vital oxygen supply. Experts estimate the following:

> We are losing 137 plant, animal and insect species every day due to rainforest deforestation. That equates to 50,000 species a year. As the rainforest species disappear, so do many possible cures for life-threatening diseases. Currently, 121 prescription drugs sold worldwide come from plant-derived sources. While 25 percent of Western pharmaceuticals are derived from rainforest ingredients, less than 1 percent of these tropical trees and plants have been tested by scientists.[16]

As suggested by this dilemma, the intricacies of our interconnected world are often difficult to master. Even as we may make considerable progress in addressing one set of challenges, we may aggravate other problems that we cannot afford to ignore. Collective action is required, but it is not always easy to attain.

The Changing Definition of Citizenship in a Global Era

The extent to which global issues come to our attention frequently depends on the individuals who champion them. What do pop star Katy Perry, rock icon and U2 front man Bono, Microsoft founder Bill Gates, entrepreneurial banker Muhammad Yunus, and activist Wangari Maathai have in common? All have taken it upon themselves to participate directly in efforts to protect the vulnerable, promote prosperity, or advocate for peace. For her work to protect and defend the rights of children across the world, Katy Perry was the recipient of the 2016 Audrey Hepburn Humanitarian Award of UNICEF (United Nations International Children's Emergency Fund). As a UNICEF goodwill ambassador, Perry has traveled widely to campaign on behalf of the needs of children and has added her voice to the drive to empower girls and to support those living with HIV/AIDS.[17] As cofounder of ONE, a global campaign to fight extreme poverty, Bono lobbies governments to take action. ONE's sister organization, RED, has partnered with global brands to raise awareness of health crises threatening large numbers of people around the world. It has generated more than $360 million through the Global Fund to Fight AIDS, TB, and Malaria.[18] The Bill and Melinda Gates Foundation is also changing lives through various initiatives to combat poverty and improve global health. As founder of the Grameen Bank in Bangladesh, Muhammad Yunus received the Nobel Peace Prize in 2006 for pioneering the microlending movement that provides loans to the poorest of the poor. Wangari Maathai of Kenya was awarded the Nobel Peace Prize in 2004 for her activities on behalf of the Green Belt Movement, an organization seeking to reduce poverty and protect the environment through community-based tree planting. She continued to work tirelessly to improve the lives of others until her death in 2011.

Wendy Maeda/The Boston Globe via Getty Images.

Many well-traveled individuals consider themselves to be members of a global community.

Understanding the contributions of renowned rock stars, bankers, and environmental-ists is one thing, but where do regular individuals fit in? What role can they play in the global community? Beyond having a framework for understanding the globalized world of the twenty-first century, we also need to make a personal connection to it. One way to realize this relationship is to take a fresh look at the idea of citizenship.

Traditional notions of citizenship date back to the time of the ancient Greek city-state and have focused on membership in distinctive political communities that are very much tied to a particular place. Since the mid-seventeenth century, that place has been the state. In return for certain protections and rights, citizens are expected (and often compelled) to assume responsibilities and obligations to the state. While not necessarily prevented from acting in venues or on behalf of ideals that might transcend the state, citizens may do so only if those actions are deemed consistent with state interests. Primary political loyalties and identities have been defined by a connection to a particular physical space and have been differentiated on the basis of territorial boundaries.[19] In the early days, the Romans came from Rome and owed their allegiance to their state and its leaders.

But people across the world are reconsidering these matters. Much of the turmoil that can be observed today can be traced, in part, to a fundamental rethinking of both indi-vidual and collective identity and belonging. In addition to an increasing number of states that cannot sustain themselves, such as Somalia and Sudan, the limited capacity of count-less others to fulfill various responsibilities to their citizens has added to the uncertainty.

People are also moving around the world at an accelerated and unprecedented rate. The United Nations has estimated there were 244 million international immigrants in 2015, up from 173 million in 2000. Refugees accounted for 19.5 million of the total, with more than half of these coming from three countries—Syria, Afghanistan, and Somalia.[20] The migra-tion phenomenon has touched every region of the world and has had considerable impacts (see Figure 1.1). Access to citizenship rights and privileges for noncitizens has become a controversial topic in many countries. Such challenges are exemplified by the European Union (EU), which has gone a long way toward redefining citizenship by extending entitle-ments available to citizens of member states residing elsewhere in the union—for instance, a citizen of France, one of the EU member states, can travel freely throughout Germany by virtue of both states' membership in the EU. The arrival of increasing numbers of refugees, asylum seekers, and displaced persons from outside the EU has produced considerable back-lash while producing new challenges that have proven difficult to resolve.[21]

Once again, the question of borders must be addressed. Matters of national or regional security fuel support for more exclusionary policies. Increasingly, there are relationships between people, ideas, and problems that are not defined or confined by existing borders. Consider the experience of Nathan, a young professional from Charlotte, North Carolina, working as an analyst at a major US financial institution. While sitting on his couch with his laptop in hand, Nathan is actively involved in the global microfinancing effort to assist budding entrepreneurs across the developing world. As noted earlier, this movement has been spurred by the work of the Grameen Bank and its founder, Muhammad Yunus. Nathan participates by interfacing with Kiva (www.kiva.org), a web-based organization originat-ing in San Francisco, to match aspiring businesspeople with prospective lenders across the globe. He is able to review the business plans and check the repayment records of potential recipients and to execute secure online loans. After a satisfactory first pass, which consisted of $25 loans to four separate borrowers, Nathan is considering a significant increase in his lending activities. He is also encouraging many of his friends to get involved.[22]

By his own admission, Nathan was drawn to this activity as an opportunity to broaden his experience and to sharpen his professional skills. He had also been affected by the extreme poverty he observed during a visit to Mexico and was looking for an outlet to address that concern. In his own way, Nathan is stretching the boundaries of his citizenship

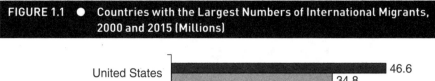

FIGURE 1.1 ● Countries with the Largest Numbers of International Migrants, 2000 and 2015 (Millions)

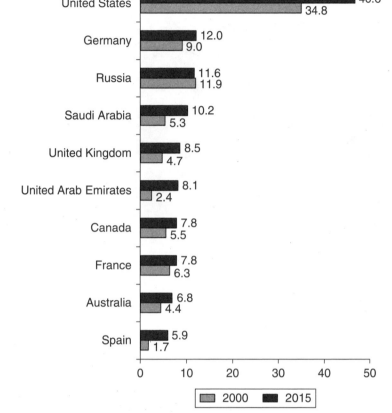

United States — 46.6 / 34.8
Germany — 12.0 / 9.0
Russia — 11.6 / 11.9
Saudi Arabia — 10.2 / 5.3
United Kingdom — 8.5 / 4.7
United Arab Emirates — 8.1 / 2.4
Canada — 7.8 / 5.5
France — 7.8 / 6.3
Australia — 6.8 / 4.4
Spain — 5.9 / 1.7

2000   2015

Source: From the United Nations, Department of Economic and Social Affairs, Population Division © (2015) United Nations. *International Migration 2015 Wallchart* (United Nations publication, Sales No. E.16.XIII.12), http://www.un.org/en/development/desa/population/migration/publications/wallchart/docs/MigrationWallChart2015.pdf. Reprinted with the permission of the United Nations.

by exploring new ways to express his connection to the world. He is not alone. The growing popularity of crowdsourcing or collaborative funding via the web through platforms like Kickstarter is a way to generate funds for important causes that builds on this interest in personal involvement in bringing about change. The example shown in Figure 1.2 is a project that transforms recycled smartphones into solar-powered listening devices to detect sounds, such as those coming from chainsaws, which suggest deforestation activity.

As Nathan and others come to grips with the realities of an increasingly interconnected world, the idea of global citizenship has gained popularity. What does it mean to be a global citizen? Nigel Dower suggests that **global citizens** are individuals who see themselves as members of a global community and who confront the challenges we face from a global perspective.[23] From this vantage point, global citizenship is about belonging and taking responsibility. Global citizens are seen as those with the knowledge, skills, and desire to act on behalf of a set of beliefs and ideals to bring about a more just and compassionate world.

global citizens individuals who perceive themselves as members of a global community; such people are aware of the wider world, respect and value diversity, and are willing to act to make the world a more equitable and sustainable place

FIGURE 1.2 ● **Kickstarter Rainforest Connection Project**

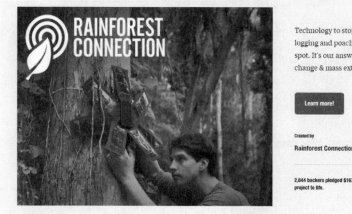

Source: Kickstarter, "Rainforest Connection—Phones Turned to Forest Guardians,"
https://www.kickstarter.com/
projects/topherwhite/rainforest-connection-phones-turned-to-forest-guar?ref=tag.

Oxfam, a British nongovernmental organization (NGO) noted for its extensive development and relief activities, has offered one of the more widely cited definitions of global citizenship. It defines a global citizen as someone who

- Is aware of the wider world and has a sense of their own role as a world citizen

- Respects and values diversity

- Has an understanding of how the world works

- Is outraged by social injustice

- Participates in the community at a range of levels, from the local to the global

- Is willing to act to make the world a more equitable and sustainable place

- Takes responsibility for their actions[24]

While advocates of global citizenship seek to encourage the acquisition of knowledge and skills to promote proactive involvement in dealing with the challenges of the world, their efforts have generated considerable controversy. Critics argue that the very notion of global citizenship is vague and does not really have much meaning to most people, particularly those who do not think of themselves in these terms and have no effective means to become engaged in these matters. Moreover, with no institution in place to confer such citizenship—no global organization that can say, "Congratulations, you're now a citizen of the world!"—the very idea is seen to lack serious practicality.

Others have not been so quick to dismiss the possibility of a growing interest in this new thinking; rather, they view global citizenship as problematic and have been quite pointed in their criticisms. Global citizenship, they suggest, can undermine the foundations of national citizenship. It provides a rationale for the strengthening of global institutions and forms of global governance that might threaten state sovereignty. Perhaps most disconcerting to critics, however, has been the notion that global citizenship emphasizes issues such as global social justice, the protection of human rights, and environmental conservation, which tend to promote a partisan political agenda. Opponents of a global identity resist an approach that elevates certain sets of values that may not necessarily correspond to the interests of all affected parties. The creation of organizations or institutions designed to impose policies reflecting these values, no matter how reasonable or lofty they might appear, remains the source of critics' concern.[25] Supporters of the global citizenship concept answer these detractors by noting the increasing number of issues requiring common approaches and mutually derived solutions. The development of plausible strategies, they argue, would benefit greatly from a generally acceptable ethic or set of values upon which to build cooperative action.

Discussion of this concept has been around for a while. The 1993 Parliament of World Religions offered a useful example of this approach. It suggested the need to adopt a global ethic that included a commitment to a culture of nonviolence, a just economic order, tolerance, and equal rights. Similarly, the 1995 Commission on Global Governance urged the inclusion of an ethical dimension that incorporated respect for the rights of all people and shared responsibilities to contribute to the common good based on the values of justice and equity.[26] At first glance, adherence to these principles might not seem particularly problematic. However, opposition has been significant. Critics have questioned the assumption that it is possible to identify some set of universally acceptable values or common obligations. Others have gone even further by charging that the presumption of a global ethic suggests cultural imperialism and does not account sufficiently for the different ways in which these ideals might be defined or applied in various societies around the globe.[27] A good example would be the debate surrounding what constitutes basic or universal human rights. This controversy illustrates the difficulty of moving forward to address the challenges that lie ahead.

Does the notion of global citizenship pose a threat to national interests and potentially undermine the foundation of our current international order? The world has been brought closer together through an expanding number of formal and informal networks as well as governmental and nongovernmental contacts. The destinies of people across the world have become more closely linked, and individual actions—no matter how limited or trivial they may appear—can impact others in profound ways. Our consumption of resources, our interface with the environment, our efforts to limit the costs of production, and our responses to those under siege will go a long way in shaping the world of the future.

It can further be argued that at least some of the controversy surrounding the idea of global citizenship stems from its terminology. For many proponents, a *global* citizen implies nothing much more than a globally oriented or globally minded person who is both sensitive to many of the effects of globalization and interested in some form of personal engagement. Rather than posing any threat or danger to commonly accepted forms of existing citizenship, this view offers the possibility for additional outlets for expression and action. Globalization has not rendered national citizenship obsolete. It may be seen as presenting avenues for the expression of multiple citizenships that reflect the different stages and venues—local, regional, national, global—that many people find themselves occupying these days.[28]

Broader acceptance of this mind-set might, at the very least, help guard against the extreme forms of ethnic nationalism that have characterized so many recent conflicts. It could also encourage a greater willingness to seek a commonality of purpose when approaching the many vexing problems that threaten the tranquility and security of the world. Martha Nussbaum, a leading contributor to the discussion of citizenship and a proponent of this more expansive view, strongly suggests the need for cosmopolitan education to enable us to realize this potential. She argues that it is critical to recognize our obligations to the rest of the world and forge a set of clear global values to make progress in solving problems that require broad-based cooperation.[29]

WHAT CAN YOU DO WITH INTERNATIONAL STUDIES?

Preparation for a Life Abroad

By Rachel Werz, International Studies Graduate, United States

Ten years ago, I was sitting in a class just like yours, wondering what international studies was actually about and what I could do with it in the future. International studies can be hard to pin down because it's so fundamentally interdisciplinary. I didn't realize it at the time, but now I believe that's its biggest strength.

As a freshman, I only knew I was interested in current events and wanted to study abroad. International studies helped me narrow and define my interests while still taking classes that contributed to my major. I took an anthropology class about Israel and Palestine, a history class about the Holocaust, and an Islamic politics course, and I participated in Model UN. Eventually, I discovered a passion for the Middle East and North Africa, studied abroad in Morocco, and graduated with a minor in Islamic Studies.

I don't think I could have explored my interests as much as I did if it weren't for international studies with its interdisciplinary nature. By letting me take courses on language, culture, history, and politics, international studies widened the lens through which I view the world, while at the same time making it seem like a smaller, more understandable place. Studying it gave me the confidence to navigate the world as a global citizen and prepared me for a life abroad.

Despite graduating during the recession, I felt like I was entering a world full of opportunities. Within a few months, I was leaving the United States with my future husband and a one-way ticket to Indonesia in my hand. As we explored a new continent together, we knew we wanted to find a way to stay. I started applying for ESL jobs in South Korea while traveling through Southeast Asia, using computers in hostels to fill out applications and having Skype interviews in the quietest Internet cafés I could find. Before long I found myself in Seoul teaching English at a private academy. It was there that I realized I actually enjoyed teaching and might be good at it. I spent my evenings working through an online TEFL certification course, applied for the Korean public school system, and was

Photo courtesy of Rachel Werz.

offered a job at an elementary school in a small city named Yangsan.

I had only intended to stay in South Korea for another year, but I found myself staying four more. What started as a "work-abroad experience" turned into a whole new life abroad. I got married, changed apartments four times, bought a car, paid my bills (even paid off my student loans!)—all the things you associate with "real life." I made a close group of friends from all over the world, went to their weddings, threw baby showers, and watched their babies when I wasn't busy. I attended training sessions to become the best teacher I could be, learned the Korean language after a lot of hard work and countless late night classes, and all the while pursued my hobbies, like spoken-word poetry and the local theater scene.

After almost six years of this, the decision to leave was extremely difficult. South Korea was our home. When people asked if we were "returning home," I didn't know what to say. Should I understand that as America, or South Korea?

During our last year in Korea, my husband and I were accepted into the Peace Corps, fulfilling a long-held dream for us both. Today we are training teachers in Indonesia, back where our journey first began six years ago. I feel like my education and experience have come full circle. I'm still in Asia, my new comfort zone, but now I'm dusting off my old Arabic books and teaching in a middle school madrasah in the most populous Muslim nation in the world. My dream of helping bridge the Muslim world and America, born in an international studies classroom ten years ago, is now my job.

HOW YOU CAN CONNECT

You can define your sense of citizenship and engagement on the basis of any of the following:

- becoming familiar with local issues
- participating in a national campaign
- adopting a cosmopolitan perspective that embraces different viewpoints
- some combination of the above

Where Do We Go from Here?

International studies must introduce the perspectives and competencies required to prepare for citizenship in the global community of the twenty-first century. This book responds to that need by addressing the following objectives:

1. It will enhance understanding of the issues, actors, institutions, cultures, ideologies, and policy instruments, as well as the relationship among them—all of which condition and affect the primary issues and events confronting the peoples of the world. In short, it will help readers understand the interdependent nature of the contemporary world.

2. It will provide an opportunity to develop an appreciation for how scholars, policymakers, and ordinary individuals living in various regions of the world understand and explain the various topics covered here and to consider and evaluate the impact of the various policies that have attempted to address these issues.

3. It will consider and evaluate alternative explanations and interpretations as to what drives the policy process and help the reader develop an awareness of the realities of the workings of the contemporary world we live in.

4. Finally, it will sharpen critical thinking skills, analytical abilities, and effective communication skills as a way to prepare for the changing definition of citizenship in a global era.

To achieve these objectives, this book will embark upon a journey that crosses the borders of the world and those that define international studies. Following this introduction, Chapter 2 delineates the geographical conceptualization of borders. The way physical borders have been understood and mapped has changed throughout history and colors the way the world is perceived. Today, more than ever, people are cognizant of planet earth as a finite resource and the challenges it faces. Chapter 3 provides the jump start to this trip by noting how technology has become the means for making border crossings more accessible for many while simultaneously dividing further those who are without the latest tools of innovation.

The next six chapters launch the trip in earnest, as the various borders to be crossed and the issues that confront them are introduced. For each of the borders that must be crossed, there is a group of challenges that must be addressed, and we take these up in alternating chapters. Chapter 4 introduces the political borders of the world and the nation-state system. The security of these borders is a critical concern and has frequently led to conflict. Chapter 5 examines the security issues faced by nation-states in terms of conflict and war, weapons of mass destruction, and terrorism. Chapter 6 defines the economic borders that have emerged over time, from barter economies to the transnational financial networks that operate around the clock today. The challenges facing economic interests—most notably in the areas of trade, investment, finance, and development—are addressed in Chapter 7. In Chapter 8, identity and the importance of social and cultural borders are examined. This section concludes with Chapter 9, which provides a closer look at the challenges to identity posed by the roles of religion, ethnic conflict, and fragile states.

We then take the journey beyond borders to look for areas of global cooperation. Chapter 10 explores the transformations that have occurred in recent years that promote a more global view of the world, including the expansion of international law and the proliferation of international organizations. Chapter 11 explores some of the issues that transcend borders and require a more global response—poverty, disease, and human rights—while also examining the possibility of global governance.

The journey ends in Chapter 12 with a road map for what you can do—where you can go from here. This chapter addresses the role individuals can play in this new global order and what students must do to connect to the world and become effective citizens. It includes an overview of the career opportunities that students can pursue to respond to the challenges presented throughout the book.

Chapters 2, 3, 4, 6, 8, and 10 define the borders; each chapter opens with a historical view of the subject matter and continues with a delineation of how various academic fields have grown to study the type of border being discussed. Prominent scholars who have shaped these fields are introduced, and each of these chapters includes a section where these scholars directly tell the reader about their perspectives: **In Their Own Words**. Chapters 5, 7, 9 and 11 discuss the challenges generated by the many borders that exist and close with a **What Can Be Done?** section. Six features in the book place the various borders and their challenges in a broader context and bring the chapters to life:

- **How You Can Connect** boxes found throughout the book offer suggestions on steps you might take to engage directly with your world.

- **Pro/Con** boxes, accompanied by **Where Do You Stand?** questions, outline controversial issues in crossing borders and invite you to take a position on global issues.

- **Understanding Cross-Border Conflict: How Can International Studies Help?** boxes explore critical global issues and the role the different borders of international studies can play in addressing those issues.

- **Turning Point** boxes address important milestones in the evolution of select issues that have considerable bearing on matters of security, prosperity, and identity.

- **What Can You Do with International Studies?** boxes showcase interviews with current and former international studies students from around the world reflecting on how international studies has led them to where they are today.

There is a popular saying suggesting that everything local is global, urging us to "think globally and act locally." The essence of this comment is embodied in international studies. It is not enough simply to acknowledge the linkages that exist; it is necessary to derive an action plan for individuals to embrace those connections not only for their own benefit but as citizens of an increasingly complex world. The goal of this book is to offer you a plan to do exactly that—to provide you with an intellectual map that will show you the many borders you must cross and the tools you will need to be an effective citizen of the world. As we said at the beginning of the chapter, "Don't panic!"

Key Concepts

citizenship 6	global issues 12	hyperglobalization 7
cultural borders 6	globalization 7	international studies 3
economic borders 5	golden straitjacket 10	political borders 5
geographic borders 4	gross domestic product (GDP) 8	social borders 5
global citizens 15	gross national product (GNP) 8	

To Learn More

Books and Other Print Media

Nayan Chanda and Susan Froetschel, eds., *A World Connected: Globalization in the 21st Century* (New Haven, CT: Yale Center for the Study of Globalization, A YaleGlobal Online Ebook, 2012).

This online book is a collection of more than 100 essays that have appeared over the past ten years on the YaleGlobal Online site that probe the critical questions facing globalization, grouped by topic areas from demography to diplomacy.

CQ Researcher, *Global Issues: Selections from CQ Researcher*, 2016 ed. (Thousand Oaks, CA: CQ Press, 2017).

This book is compiled annually by CQ Press and provides an in-depth look at current issues affecting the global arena. *CQ Researcher* is available online and can be accessed through many university libraries: http://library.cqpress.com/cqresearcher.

Nigel Dower, *An Introduction to Global Citizenship* (Edinburgh, UK: Edinburgh University Press, 2003).

This classic provides a theoretical and historical context for considering the idea of global citizenship and suggests how it may be applied in dealing with an array of current global issues.

Thomas L. Friedman, *The Lexus and the Olive Tree* (New York: Farrar, Straus and Giroux, 1999).

This best-seller, which is still widely quoted today, broke important ground in offering a comprehensive look at the dynamics of globalization and highlighting the tensions between the forces of change and the desires of some to maintain traditional ways of life.

Thomas L. Friedman, *Thank You for Being Late: An Optimist's Guide to Thriving in the Age of Accelerations* (New York: Farrar, Straus and Giroux, 2016).

Thomas Friedman's latest epic focuses on three forces—technology, globalization, and climate change—that are accelerating all at once and are transforming our lives in truly fundamental ways.

Jeffrey E. Garten, *From Silk to Silicon: The Story of Globalization through Ten Extraordinary Lives* (New York: HarperCollins, 2017).

This book explores the history of globalization by tracing the lives of ten people who changed the world through their activities.

Irene Langran and Tammy Birk (eds.), *Globalization and Global Citizenship: Interdisciplinary Approaches* (New York: Routledge, 2016).

This edited volume includes a series of informative essays that explore the idea of global citizenship in both its historical and contemporary contexts and how it affects one's identity and sense of belonging.

Peter Singer, *One World Now: The Ethics of Globalization* (New Haven, CT: Yale University Press, 2016).

Singer takes a look at some of the important challenges facing the world and addresses them from an ethical perspective. He makes a strong case for a global approach, arguing that these problems cannot be solved at the national level.

Ethan Watters, *Crazy Like Us: The Globalization of the American Psyche* (New York: Free Press, 2010).

Journalist Ethan Watters addresses an effect of globalization that has not garnered much attention—how the spread of American culture has resulted in the export of some of our psychological baggage (such as depression, posttraumatic stress, and eating disorders) to people in other parts of the world.

Fareed Zakaria, *The Post-American World: Release 2.0, Updated and Expanded* (New York: W. W. Norton & Company, 2012).

Indian American political commentator Fareed Zakaria, host of *Global Public Square* (*GPS*) on CNN, expands on his earlier version of this book to describe the shift in power in the world today away from the West to what he calls the "rise of the rest."

Websites

Center for Strategic and International Studies (CSIS), www.csis.org

A good primer on international issues, the CSIS website provides users with information on particular topics and regions as well as on international studies programs and leading experts.

Council on Foreign Relations, "Backgrounders," http://www.cfr.org/publication/by_type/backgrounder.html

These summaries provide background information on current issues confronting the world today.

Global Citizen, globalcitizen.org

This platform offers information about significant global issues and provides a pathway to action in addressing these challenges.

International Forum on Globalization, www.ifg.org

The International Forum on Globalization is an international organization that analyzes and critiques the effects of globalization on culture, society, politics, and the environment.

International Monetary Fund (IMF), "Globalization: A Brief Overview," https://www.imf.org/external/np/exr/ib/2008/053008.htm

The IMF provides an overview of globalization and then delves into specific issues with regard to the effects of globalization on finance, trade, and poverty.

State University of New York (SUNY) Levin Institute, "Globalization 101," www.globalization101.org

This website is a project of the Levin Institute in the SUNY system. It provides a very good overview of what globalization is and an in-depth analysis of a number of specific issues. It also includes a series of expert videos.

UNESCO Global Citizenship Education, http://www.gcedclearinghouse.org/

This is the clearinghouse for materials relating to a range of global issues that is part of the Global Citizenship Education program sponsored by the UN agency focusing on education, scientific, and cultural matters.

YaleGlobal Online, http://yaleglobal.yale.edu

The Whitney and Betty MacMillan Center for International and Area Studies at Yale University publishes this extensive online magazine, *YaleGlobal*, as well as scholarly articles and multimedia presentations by globalization experts from around the world.

Videos

Babel (2006)

Winner of the Golden Globe award for Best Motion Picture, Drama, this movie depicts a crosscutting set of events taking place in Morocco, Japan, and Mexico that highlight the global interconnectedness of world problems.

Globalization at a Crossroads (2011), https://www.youtube.com/watch?v=hTVgd1wUhW4

This is a concise documentary produced by Films for the Humanities & Sciences that highlights the debate over the impacts of globalization.

Issues in Globalization (2011), https://www.youtube.com/watch?v=XMVl8WG126c

This video focuses on environmental stability and the lives of textile workers in Bangladesh as a way to understand the tensions underlying globalization, by contrasting Western demands for goods with the lives of the people who make those goods.

Life 8 (2009), http://www.bullfrogfilms.com/catalog/l8.html

This is a sixteen-part series about the effects of globalization on people around the world. It is an excellent opportunity to see how the global economy directly impacts the lives of people. Programs from previous series are also available. Bullfrog Films also offers a wide selection of videos focusing on climate change, sustainability, and social justice.

Life in a Day (2010), http://movies.nationalgeographic.com/movies/life-in-a-day

From *National Geographic*, this documentary is unique in that it was created from 80,000 clips submitted to YouTube depicting daily life from 192 nations on July 24, 2010.

What Does It Mean to Be a Citizen of the World? (Hugh Evans, 2016), https://www.ted.com/talks/hugh_evans_what_does_it_mean_to_be_a_citizen_of_the_world

This brief yet compelling TED Talk by Hugh Evans of Global Citizen puts forward a strong case for personal engagement.

A World Without Borders (2016), https://iai.tv/video/a-world-without-borders?gclid=CPvmqMqGz9ICFU48gQodFCEKcA

This is an admittedly dry yet highly informative debate over the benefits of a borderless world offered by the British nonprofit Institute of Art and Ideas.

2

Point of Departure

Planet Earth

Our interconnectedness on the planet is the dominating truth of the 21st century.

—Jeffrey Sachs, Director, Earth Institute at Columbia University[1]

Learning Objectives

After studying this chapter, you will be able to do the following:

- Define the field of geography, and explain its key units of analysis and measurement.

- Identify the key challenges facing our physical world.

- Explain how population growth is affecting the world.

- Explain how food scarcity is affecting the world.

- Explain how energy shortages are affecting the world.

- Explain the impact human beings are having on the physical world.

As noted Harvard economist Jeffrey Sachs suggests, we are connected to planet earth in fundamental ways that are critical to our future. Everyone has responsibility for the earth as a common resource, and we all must work together to maintain it. It is a shared resource that represents a **global commons**, a natural asset of the earth that is available to all. Clean air, a healthy environment, and access to the oceans and outer space all fall into this category. But sharing this global commons requires that all people must use it in a responsible way to protect not only their individual interests but those of future generations as well.

global commons a natural asset of the earth that is available to all

Ecologist Garrett Hardin captured the tension between individual interests and shared resources in his famous essay, "The Tragedy of the Commons," first published in *Science* magazine in 1968.[2] Hardin posed a hypothetical scene in which a village of herdsmen shares a common pasture for grazing their sheep. If each herdsman adds a sheep, he alone will benefit from future sales, but the costs of grazing for that sheep will be shared by all. An individual herdsman will add sheep because he does not feel the negative effects by himself. The benefits to him are great, but everyone shares the negative impacts, so they are not as great on an individual level. The incentive, then, would be for each herdsman to increase his personal flock at the expense of the others. The ultimate result, however, would be overgrazing of the commons until there is nothing left and, hence, the tragedy of the commons. Hardin concludes his assessment with the sobering truth that following this logic will result in ruin: "Ruin is the destination toward which all men rush, each pursuing his own best interest in a society that believes in the freedom of the commons. Freedom in a commons brings ruin to all."[3] In the real world, we see the potential for devastation all the time in terms of finite resources, population pressures, and pollution, to name just a few examples.

The problem of the tragedy of the commons helps us focus on the issue of sustainable development. The term *sustainable development* can be traced back to the World Commission on Environment and Development, better known as the Bruntland Commission, convened by the UN General Assembly in 1983 to address growing concerns about the deterioration

This familiar National Aeronautics and Space Administration (NASA) image is the most requested photo of the earth, depicting it as a watery blue marble floating alone in a sea of space. Viewed this way, it is easy to see how important stewardship of our global commons is for our mutual well-being. In this chapter, we will explore a variety of other ways of looking at and understanding the earth—the starting point for our journey.

NASA and the National Space Science Data Center.

of the environment as a consequence of economic and social development.[4] The commission's 1987 report, *Our Common Future*, would provide what has become the most widely used definition of **sustainable development**: "Development that meets the needs of the present without compromising the ability of future generations to meet their own needs."[5]

How this concept has been addressed globally is critical to our understanding of the borders that we will cross. This chapter explores our connection to the earth as the starting point of our journey toward understanding international studies. First, the study of **geography** will be introduced as a way to understand the earth and the ways in which it is depicted through maps. Geography is the basis for our understanding of the planet. Human settlements are elementary units for us to understand ourselves. There are reasons why settlements spring up in some areas but not in others or why some flourish and some do not—underlying those reasons is geography. Some of the critical challenges that threaten our global well-being will then be examined: settlement patterns, population growth, food production, energy, and climate change. Finally, we will give you some ideas about what you can do to sustain the earth for future generations.

Getting Our Heads around the Earth: Geography as a Field of Study

Viewed from space, the earth appears as a physical mass marked by oceans, mountains, deserts, rivers, forests, and fields. From this perspective, it appears static, when in fact it is not. Over the course of time, the borders that have differentiated this mass have been changed by natural events, from continental drift thousands of years ago to more recent hurricanes, wildfires, earthquakes, tsunamis, droughts, and floods. The earth's physical attributes, such as where arable land or mineral riches or waterways are located, have to a large extent determined where people have settled and what they do. The fundamental challenge of geography has been that there is no one place where any of us can stand on the planet in order to observe the whole thing at once. It is also nearly impossible for any one person to conceive of all the ways in which people are connected to one another and to the planet. Our image of what the earth as a whole even looks like has changed radically over time and has been profoundly shaped by technological developments.

Scholarly attempts to understand the world in a meaningful way date back to the earliest philosophers. For starters, we owe the word *geography* to Greek scholar Eratosthenes, who was born around 275 BCE. Eratosthenes was very interested in writing and learning about the earth, and the term he coined for this activity came from the Greek language—*geo*, meaning earth, and *graphos*, meaning description.[6] His greatest accomplishment in this regard was the first scientific calculation of the circumference of the earth based on his observations of the sun.

One of the earliest scholars whose impressions had lasting effects was Claudius Ptolemy. Born sometime late in the first century CE, Ptolemy was of Greek origin but lived in Alexandria, Egypt. Two of the major texts he produced, *Geography* and *Almagest*, were efforts to map the world in a system of degrees that measured distances from the equator.[7] Relying on limited knowledge of the world, Ptolemy created a map that introduced the concepts of latitude and longitude (see Figure 2.1). While his calculations were off and much of the world was not known to him at the time, his contribution to measurement was significant and enduring.

The modern discipline of geography developed many years later in the mid-1800s. Alexander von Humboldt (1769–1859) was a German naturalist who is often called the "father of modern geography" for his contributions not only to an understanding of the physical world but also to the relationship of humans to their environment.[8] His great

---

sustainable development
"development that meets the needs of the present without compromising the ability of future generations to meet their own needs," as defined by the World Commission on Environment and Development

geography the study of the earth and its characteristics

FIGURE 2.1 ● Ptolemy's Map of the World

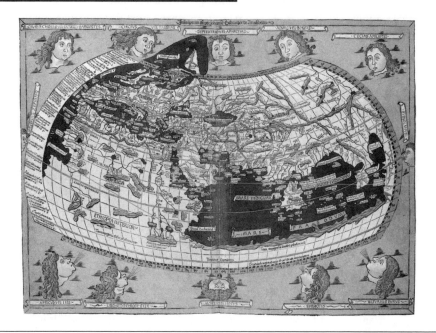

Source: "Claudius Ptolemy—The World" by Johannes Schnitzer, engraver. Claudius Ptolemy, cartographer. Scanned by Scott Ehardt from *Decorative Maps* by Roderick Barron. Licensed under public domain via Wikimedia Commons, http://commons.wikimedia.org/wiki/File:Claudius_Ptolemy_The_World.jpg#mediaviewer/File:Claudius_Ptolemy-_The_World.jpg.

work, *Cosmos*, was a multivolume examination of nature that included some of the first systematic observations about climate and its relationship to geography. Juxtaposing a review of ancient writings about the natural universe with the technologies emerging during his time, von Humboldt sought a scientific way to understand the earth.

Today, the discipline of geography is generally divided into two branches: physical geography and human geography. **Physical geography** refers to the study of the earth and its resources. **Human geography** refers to how humans interface with the physical environment and how political, economic, social, and cultural factors influence these connections.

The study of maps, or **cartography**, refers to how these physical and human borders are depicted. Maps can show **topography**—any of the earth's physical features, including mountains, rivers, lakes, and streams, and their relationships to one another in terms of location and elevation. They can also depict political borders, which are frequently influenced by topography but fundamentally drawn by people to serve political interests. Many modern states, for example, are the artificial constructs of former colonial powers and do not necessarily accommodate the diversity of interests and needs of their inhabitants. Another type of map can show economic distinctions, such as the location of resources and trade routes. Social and cultural division can also be depicted where ethnic and cultural identities overlap with political and economic borders. Even cooperation across borders can be mapped in terms of regional and international organizations.

Modern technologies have changed the field of geography and how mapping occurs. Geographic information systems (GIS) combine the power of computers with satellite imagery to produce new ways of understanding spatial relationships and include new technologies such as Google Earth and the global positioning system (GPS). These technologies

physical geography the study of the earth and its resources

human geography the study of how humans interface with the physical environment and how political, economic, social, and cultural factors influence these connections

cartography the depiction of physical and human-made borders

topography the depiction of the earth's physical features and their relationships to one another in terms of location and elevation

are able to utilize different kinds of information about geography, from physical dimensions to human interventions, to track changes in the environment.[9] As a result, they are able to give a much more comprehensive view of the earth and the changes taking place today than what was available before these systems were put into use. This is particularly critical in understanding some of the challenges we face. For example, the National Snow and Ice Data Center has used Google Earth to track changes in the polar ice cap over time.[10] Countries are also using GIS technology for more strategic purposes that include pinpointing the location of military installations, potential improvised explosive devices (IEDs), or even the whereabouts of suspected terrorists.

Technological innovation and our ability to better understand the world around us has made us more sensitive to the finite nature of the planet on which we live. This capacity to know more has also led us to be more conscious of the challenges that can affect everyone and are not specific to any one area on the globe. The earth is a finite resource, and our charge must be to extract and utilize the resources we need to sustain our lives while not inflicting undue harm that might threaten the sustainability of the planet itself. The historical record suggests that we have not done a particularly good job in this regard.

With its interdisciplinary perspective and approach, international studies can help us appreciate why we may have difficulty in effectively interfacing with our environment. Dealing with such issues as population management or climate change is not simply a matter of negotiating physical space or utilizing the tools at our disposal. Political considerations may constrain efforts to devise solutions, as they have in the case of finding suitable living arrangements for waves of refugees from Syria. When it comes to implementing policies intended to protect rain forests or limit unhealthy emissions, financing or other financially related factors can undermine the effort. As we have seen in parts of Africa and elsewhere, moreover, social and cultural traditions might frame resistance to vaccination programs designed to eradicate deadly diseases that know no borders. Our relationship with planet earth is a complicated one. The following sections address some of the challenges of managing resources and how they have been handled.

IN THEIR OWN WORDS
ALEXANDER VON HUMBOLDT

There dwells an irresistible charm, venerated by all antiquity, in the contemplation of mathematical truths—in the everlasting revelations of time and space, as they reveal themselves in tones, numbers, and lines. The improvement of an intellectual instrument of research—analysis—has powerfully accelerated the reciprocal fructification of ideas, which is no less important than the rich abundance of their creations. It has opened to the physical contemplation of the universe new spheres of immeasurable extent in the terrestrial and celestial regions of space, revealed both in the periodic fluctuations of the ocean and in the varying perturbations of the planets.[11]

Where We Live

As a starting point, it is important to understand that where people settle is not always a choice made freely. In that sense, the borders that shape where we live are human-made. People can be displaced by conflict and forced to flee their homes. They may have few or no options as to where they resettle and under what terms and circumstances, and they may end up having to live in inhospitable environments. Large refugee tent cities can grow up overnight in response to violence and sometimes continue to exist for years.

For example, the world's largest refugee camp, Dadaab in Kenya, is run by the United Nations (UN). It has supported those fleeing violence in Somalia for more than twenty years, but it is now running out of room.[12] People in these camps are susceptible to natural dangers, ranging from wild animals attacking small children who have invaded their environment to flooding from the annual rains. The temperatures in this area can soar well above 100 degrees Fahrenheit, and the camps offer the refugees' only hope for shelter, food, and water. Kenya's government moved to close the facility in 2016, thereby jeopardizing the survival of its residents, who would face repatriation to their home-

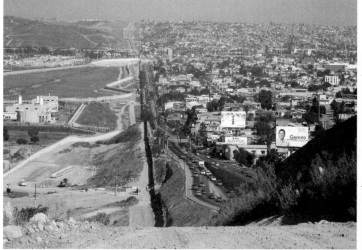

A small fence separates densely populated Tijuana, Mexico, right, from the United States in the Border Patrol's San Diego sector.

land. A Kenyan court blocked this plan in early 2017, however, citing its discriminatory and arbitrary nature. The saga continues as the government pursues an appeal of this decision.[13]

Economic pressures can also lead people to relocate to areas where they can find work but where human habitation is not sustainable over time. People lose their jobs and have to find alternative employment. They move to areas, often along borders, where factories have been built. Shantytowns are constructed with homes built from cardboard and any other spare materials that can be found. People are overcrowded in these areas, and there is often no electricity, no running water, and no way to manage sewage and waste. The result is a systematic degradation of the environment fostered by the need to meet the challenges of competition. Many of the communities hosting the manufacturing facilities or *maquiladoras* across the US border, in Mexico, exemplify these conditions.

Living and working in this type of situation can further deepen and aggravate social and cultural divisions. While those who move to cities for work frequently have rising expectations about their futures, they may easily find themselves relegated to marginal status. Particularly in many of the world's lesser developed countries, poverty is persistent, and the success that was so eagerly anticipated often goes unrealized. These conditions can last for generations, as there is no easy way out.

Finally, it is important to note that settlement patterns may be significantly influenced or altered by environmental considerations. The Internal Displacement Monitoring Centre of the Norwegian Refugee Council estimates that since 2008, an average of 26.4 million people have been displaced annually as a result of disasters. Climate-related and other events or circumstances account for 22.5 million of the total.[14] Disasters are not restricted to any particular area across the world, but their burdens often fall disproportionally on those impacted in the poorest regions, where management capabilities are more limited. Resettlement challenges are further complicated by the fact that environmental refugees are not generally covered under international provisions designed to assist displaced people. These refugees may have a particularly difficult time finding safe haven in places where the political backlash against migration has gained traction.[15]

Population Management

One of the underlying factors in perpetuating uneven development has been the rapid growth of the world's population. As more and more people come to inhabit the planet, protecting and managing shared resources becomes even more challenging.

Burgeoning populations are consuming natural resources at unprecedented rates. As a result, there is a delicate balance with the environment that must be considered. Whether intentional or not, the actions of this growing population have significantly impacted the earth, from the destruction of natural habitats and extinction of animal and plant life to the pollution of the atmosphere.

To put this growth in perspective, in just one minute, taking births and deaths into account, the population of the world expands by 148 people, with a growth rate of 2.5 per second.[16] This growth is uneven, such that the more significant increases often occur in those regions or countries that are least able to provide for the added numbers. The fastest rates are found across Africa, with the vast majority of that growth coming from the region's poorest countries.[17] Figure 2.2 shows the most populous countries in 2017 and their projected growth by 2050. In 2017, the top ten countries accounted for 57.9 percent of total world population; it is estimated they will account for 52.8 percent in 2050.

What are the factors that affect these disparities? There are several that can be examined. One of the most frequently cited is education. For example, in the largest, least educated, and most populous Indian state of Uttar Pradesh, the proportion of women using birth control is less than 30 percent, whereas the national average is 48.5 percent. Moreover, the average woman in this region will bear up to four children and be challenged to feed them.[18] Despite general declines in the overall birth rates for India, from six children per family to three, the population still grew by 1.24 percent from 2012 to 2016, and it is anticipated that India will surpass China in population by 2050.[19] Cultural values also continue to push births in the area, as the desire for a boy is great, and rural parents are still influenced by the need for large families to support them. Figure 2.3 suggests where the greatest growth in population is occurring—primarily in sub-Saharan Africa, as discussed later in the chapter—by measuring crude birth rate, which is the most commonly used indicator in determining population growth rates.

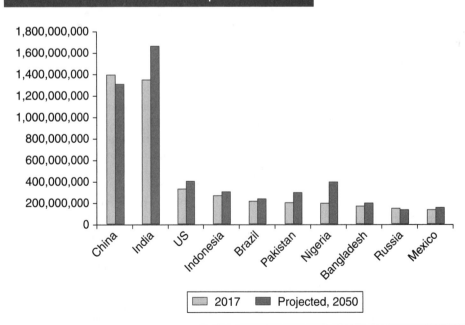

FIGURE 2.2 ● The World's Most Populous Countries

Source: Data are from internetworldstats.com, with data from US Census Bureau, www.internetworldstats.com/stats8.htm.

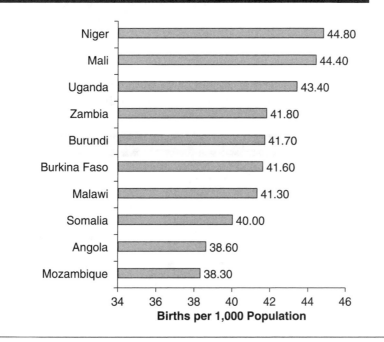

FIGURE 2.3 ● Countries with Leading Population Growth Rates, 2016

Country	Births per 1,000 Population
Niger	44.80
Mali	44.40
Uganda	43.40
Zambia	41.80
Burundi	41.70
Burkina Faso	41.60
Malawi	41.30
Somalia	40.00
Angola	38.60
Mozambique	38.30

Births per 1,000 Population

Source: CIA World Factbook, https://www.cia.gov/library/publications/the-world-factbook/rankorder/2054rank.html.

China has taken an interesting path in addressing this issue through its governmental policy of one child per family. Up until recently, only those families living in rural areas were allowed to have more children to support their agricultural needs. There was considerable criticism of this policy by human rights activists because of the limits it places on individual choice, as well as the unintended consequences that have occurred. Female babies were abandoned or even killed by Chinese parents who, like those in India, wanted a boy. This prioritization has resulted in a disproportionate number of males, which has both practical and political consequences. Many young Chinese men have difficulty finding wives, are underemployed, and often feel alienated from society. As a result, they are seen as a potential source of political opposition by the government. In response to these tensions, the policy was amended in December 2013 to allow a second child if one of the parents was an only child. The previous exception to the policy applied only if both parents were single children. In 2016, the government went further in revising its approach to counter this pattern by extending the right to bear two children to every married couple, so long as they are granted the required permit.[20]

A view of just a small section of the Dadaab refugee camp in Kenya; as of January 2017, it was home to 270,100 refugees, primarily from Somalia, with the majority (58.5 percent) under the age of eighteen.

UNHCR/Brendan Bannon.

These trends have additional implications. In China, families traditionally cared for their aging parents. Now there is a shortage of care providers due to an aging population and the strict controls that have been placed on reproduction. The number of Chinese people over age sixty-five is expected to triple by 2050, and the mechanisms for their care simply do not exist.[21] In contrast, many developing countries find themselves coping with a population that is very young (see Figure 2.4). The median age in Afghanistan is eighteen, and in Somalia it is just seventeen; in contrast, it is almost thirty-seven in the United States and forty in the United Kingdom.[22] The political unrest in the Middle East in the spring

FIGURE 2.4   ●   Population Distribution by Country, Age, and Gender

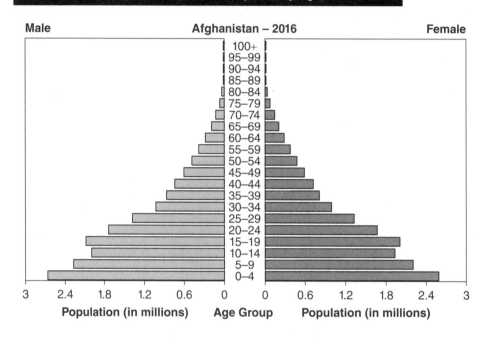

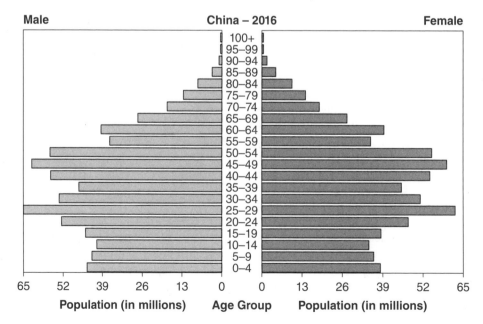

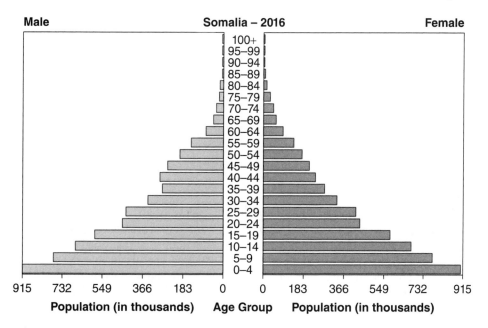

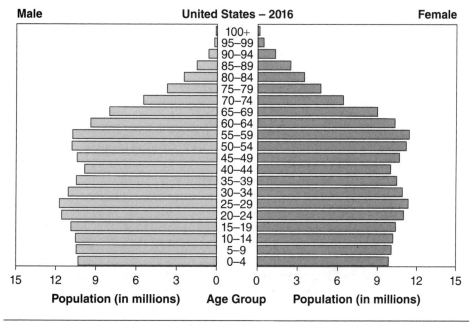

Source: CIA World Factbook, "Population Pyramids," https://www.cia.gov/library/publications/the-world-factbook.

of 2011 was led by youth, who represent a significant demographic shift. They are a new generation that has found innovative ways to communicate and bring about change.

Food and Hunger

Can the earth adequately provide for this growing population? Human efforts to sustain ourselves and to develop and progress have strained the earth's **carrying capacity**. In other words, our needs have placed considerable strain on the world's ecosystems, thereby

carrying capacity the earth's ability to meet the needs of its population threatening the global commons and suggesting the possibility of a potential tragedy, as envisioned by Hardin.

First and foremost, it is important to recognize that people require access to sufficient amounts of food and clean water to ensure their survival. This is the most basic physiological need of humans, as noted by psychologist Abraham Maslow when he delineated his hierarchy of needs in the 1940s. While Maslow identified five levels of needs (to be discussed more thoroughly in Chapter 11), critical to the point here is that the first level is the most basic—the need for food and water. Only once these bodily needs are met can people move up the pyramid to assure safety, belonging, esteem, and ultimately self-actualization.[23] Therefore, sustenance is critical to development, and the ability to produce enough food to provide for a growing population while protecting the environment poses great challenges.

The idea that population could exceed food supply is not new. Thomas Malthus (1766–1834), an English economist who was very interested in demographics, wrote of this possibility in "An Essay on the Principle of Population," first published anonymously in 1798 and later revised to include more detail. Malthus speculated that the growth of the world's population would be geometrical, compared to the production of food, which could increase only arithmetically.[24] This notion is referred to as the **Malthusian dilemma**. More recent interpretations have suggested that, in today's terms, what Malthus's prediction might mean is a population of more than 9 billion people by the year 2050, with agricultural resources significantly short of being able to provide for everyone.[25] There is simply not enough arable land to meet that need, according to Columbia University's Earth Institute, and even the best efforts could not recover lands that have been devastated by **deforestation** to allow for adequate agricultural production.

Appropriate use of the land is critical. Specifically, the production of food is closely related to geographic changes taking place, both natural and human-made. For example, natural disasters—from forest fires to drought—that destroy crops and render lands unviable are just one impediment to the production of food resources adequate to address the growing population. Environmental degradation through the overuse of arable land and fertilizers also has a negative effect. The challenges are not limited to production. The availability of food can also be impacted by war, due to the disruption of supply and distribution lines. Together, these factors play a considerable role in influencing both the price and safety of our food. A closer look sheds light on these concerns.

Despite Malthus's forecast, food production has increased over time, but the ability to feed a growing population has been undermined by other factors. The use of pesticides and chemicals designed to increase crop yields over the short term, for example, can have longer-term adverse effects on the soil. When the soil is damaged, there are consequences that can last generations. The greatest need is often found in the most unregulated developing areas where this damage occurs. There is still reason for some optimism. The UN Food and Agriculture Organization (FAO) reports steady progress in reducing hunger over the past ten years, with the overall number of undernourished people declining by 167 million. Current figures suggest that there are still 795 million hungry people in the world, however, with nearly 780 million of these living in the developing regions. India (194.6 million) and China (133.8 million) are the countries with the largest numbers of people affected, while sub-Saharan Africa is most impacted proportionally, with 23.2 percent of its population undernourished.[26]

Countries having difficulties facing these challenges are not able to produce enough food or adequately distribute food provided to them from other sources. Natural conditions such as drought may exacerbate the situation, as does the need to earn money through exporting much of the food that is produced locally. For example, the African country of the Democratic Republic of the Congo suffered from heavy rains in late 2015 and early

Malthusian dilemma the conflict inherent in the idea that the growth of the world's population increases geometrically, whereas the production of food can increase only arithmetically

deforestation the destruction of forest areas due to human actions or environmental factors

2016, resulting in the displacement of 40,000 people and significant damage to more than 5,000 hectares of crop land. In contrast, severe drought in Ethiopia affecting livestock and crop production has left more than 10 million people in need of food assistance.[27]

Hunger is not simply about not having enough food; it is also about nutrition. Those who endure hunger may not be starving but are suffering from undernourishment. Ultimately, the impact can be devastating and can result in death. The FAO, which monitors global food issues, refers to this condition as **food insecurity** and defines it as "a situation that exists when people lack secure access to sufficient amounts of safe and nutritious food for normal growth and development and an active and healthy life."[28] The Integrated Food Security Phase Classification (IPC) is a standardized scale that is used to measure the level of food insecurity by also factoring in nutrition and the extent to which livelihoods are affected.[29] It is estimated that chronic undernourishment and the lack of vitamins and minerals that result from it contribute to more than 5 million child deaths annually. *Undernourishment* is defined as dietary energy consumption that is continuously below the minimum requirement for maintaining a healthy lifestyle. Figure 2.5 identifies the countries with the greatest percentage of their populations suffering from undernourishment.

Why not simply send food to those in need? This is where political and economic considerations often intervene. There are many efforts to provide food aid, coordinated by both governmental and nongovernmental entities. Internationally, the UN World Food Programme (WFP) is a key actor in emergency food aid response. While welcomed, this aid is frequently hard to get to the people who need it most. Deliverability is limited by many factors. Perhaps one of the greatest inhibitors is conflict. The safe transportation and distribution of food in countries ravaged by war can be almost impossible due to the lines of battle or even the logistics of navigating vastly overcrowded refugee camps. This situation is particularly problematic in sub-Saharan Africa. Conflict in central Africa has resulted in

food insecurity the lack of secure access to sufficient amounts of safe and nutritious food for normal growth and development and an active and healthy life

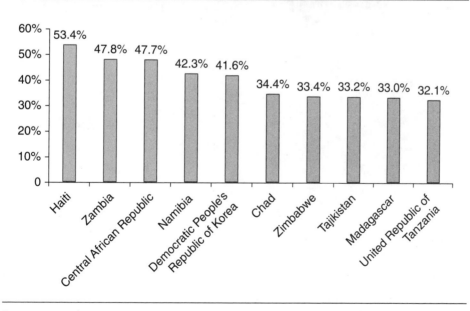

FIGURE 2.5 ● The World's Most Undernourished Populations (by Percentage), 2014–2016

Source: Food and Agriculture Organization of the United Nations, International Fund for Agricultural Development, and World Food Programme, *The State of Food Insecurity in the World 2015* (Rome: Food and Agriculture Organization of the United Nations, 2015), Annex 1, Table A1, http://www.fao.org/3/a-i4646e.pdf.

very large numbers of displaced people from the Central African Republic (CAR), estimated to be 420,000 in April 2016. As a result, 1.5 million of the total population of 4.6 million needs urgent assistance. In the Democratic Republic of the Congo (DRC), the numbers are even higher, with an estimated 4.5 million people affected by food insecurity in conflict-affected provinces. In South Sudan, the conflict that began in the capital city, Juba, in mid-December 2013 left 4.4 million people in need of emergency aid by 2016.[30]

The magnitude of the food insecurity crisis is reflected in the vast numbers of people in dire need of assistance. In 2015 alone, the WFP serviced 76.7 million people impacted by the ravages of hunger. While natural conditions such as drought or floods leave many in harm's way, it is interesting to note that the problem is often most acute in countries experiencing serious political turmoil. Figure 2.6 identifies the leading recipients of WFP food aid in 2015. Five major donors contributed approximately 68 percent of the funding for this work (the United States, the United Kingdom, Germany, Canada, and Japan).[31]

Cost is also a factor in limiting the supply of food to those in need. Food is a primary commodity, and commodity prices can vary widely. They are often not regulated in the same way that the prices of industrial goods are controlled. The FAO has reported a significant increase in costs over time. Prices spiked in 2008 due to the global financial crisis and again to even higher levels in 2011. They began to come down in 2014 and have continued to moderate.[32] Food prices are difficult to project, given the number of factors that can influence the availability of most commodities. In addition to growing demand and

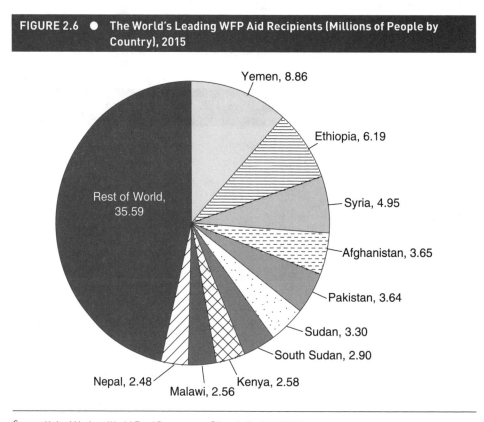

FIGURE 2.6 ● The World's Leading WFP Aid Recipients (Millions of People by Country), 2015

Source: United Nations World Food Programme, "Year in Review 2015."

http://documents.wfp.org/stellent/groups/public/documents/communications/wfp284681.pdf?_ga=1.23165372 4.2104839375.1489184066.

Note: The total for all countries served is 76.7 million.

natural conditions that might limit production, political volatility or even an uptick in investor speculation to manipulate markets can push prices upward. Figure 2.7 documents recent trends in food prices.

There are many ways to address these issues, most notably through international organizations like the FAO and the World Trade Organization (WTO). The FAO monitors food prices internationally and develops multiple paths to address hunger issues. The WTO has also addressed agricultural prices and the stability of the food supply over the course of many years but with little effect.[33] Agriculture has been an issue on the agenda of various rounds of WTO negotiations but with little progress due to the highly politicized nature of these concerns, particularly those relating to the rights of governments to subsidize their farmers and to manage production in ways that maintain higher prices for their food-related exports.

Scientifically, there are efforts to be more effective in food production through the utilization of genetically modified organisms (GMOs). The idea here is to use modern biotechnology for greater agricultural productivity. Crops can be made more resistant to pests and more nutritious through genetic manipulation. The fear about this modification, however, is that it may undermine natural biological processes and have a long-term harmful effect.[34]

Junior D. Kannah/AFP/Getty Images.

Congolese refugees, returning from Uganda, walk back home on November 1, 2013, in Bunagana, 99 kilometers from the eastern Democratic Republic of Congo city of Goma, at the frontier with Uganda. Fighting between Congolese rebels and the army has created massive instability and widespread food shortages throughout the country.

FIGURE 2.7 ● The Shifting Cost of Food

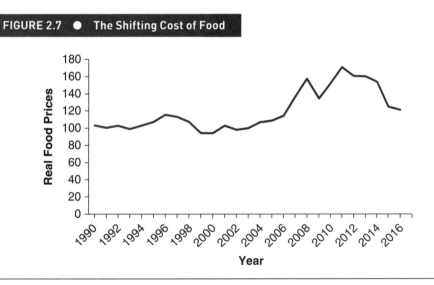

Source: Food and Agriculture Organization of the United Nations, "World Food Situation: FAO Food Price Index," http://www.fao.org/worldfoodsituation/foodpricesindex/en.

Note: The FAO Food Price Index is a measure of the monthly change in international prices of a basket of food commodities. It consists of the average of five commodity group price indexes (representing fifty-five quotations), weighted with the average export shares of each of the groups for 2002 to 2004.

Energy Security

Beyond the need for food and some of the consequences of efforts in this regard, the earth is also being compromised by lifestyle and consumption choices. The use of energy offers an important example of the dilemma. One of the key components of sustainable development is that it does no harm to future generations. The global demand for coal, oil, and other nonrenewable sources of energy taxes the environment and calls attention to the fragile nature of the world's resources.

Persistent demands for economic development have exacerbated this problem as the need for energy continues to grow. The world has relied extensively on oil for its industrial development, but the oil supply is limited. One alternative has been the development of nuclear energy. Although it was once popular with the United States, Japan, and parts of Europe as a source of cleaner and more efficient energy, there have always been concerns about its safety and potentially severe or even catastrophic human and environmental impacts. Among the more notable examples of the possible consequences were the nuclear plant meltdowns in the United States at Three Mile Island in Pennsylvania in 1979 and the far more serious malfunctions in Ukraine at Chernobyl in 1986, which had severe health implications for thousands of inhabitants and rendered a significant amount of surrounding land unusable and uninhabitable due to contamination. The more recent meltdowns in Japan resulting from the 2011 tsunami, however, may prove to be an important watershed in terms of support for nuclear energy, raising concerns over the safety of these production facilities. Not long after the Japanese tragedy, Germany announced that it would severely curtail its nuclear energy activities and move to phase out nuclear energy production by 2022. A number of other countries also indicated that they would review their policies.

Energy disasters are not limited to the nuclear arena and can affect both air and water supplies as well. The harvesting of natural resources for energy has had its own set of challenges and disasters. A gas plant leak in Bhopal, India, in 1984 killed 3,800 people and sickened several thousand.[35] The explosion on the BP *Deepwater Horizon* oil rig in the Gulf of Mexico in 2010 killed eleven workers and resulted in roughly 5 million barrels of oil spilled into the water.

The Human Factor: Contributing to the Problem?

In our efforts to sustain ourselves and to provide for our basic needs, we have both purposefully and inadvertently contributed to the degradation of our environment. Among the more significant ways this destruction has occurred has been through the progressive depletion of our rain forests, the desertification of arable land, the pollution of our water supply, and the compromising of our air quality. Perhaps the greatest of these impacts is in the area of global warming and the subsequent climate changes that are occurring around the world. A closer look at these actions illustrates their effect.

Approximately 31 percent of the earth's surface is covered by forest, but that figure is declining. It is estimated that roughly 46,000 to 58,000 square miles of forest are lost each year, the equivalent of 36 football fields every minute.[36] Population growth has contributed significantly to this loss of trees, as the clearing of forests provides opportunities for cultivating crops and grazing animals. The activities of commercial logging companies seeking to capitalize on the worldwide demand for timber have also added to this devastation. The consequences are significant not only for the destruction of the land but also the wildlife that resides there. Perhaps most important, trees play a critical role in maintaining the balance of the ecosystem by storing carbon. The removal of trees releases carbon, thereby contributing to global warming and climate change. While the rate of deforestation is slowing down, it is still considered by the FAO to be alarmingly high, with a net loss of approximately 3.3 million hectares per year between 2010 and 2015 and the most significant damage occurring in tropical areas. Table 2.1 identifies these declines by region.

A related consequence of human activities changing the landscape is **desertification**. This refers to the degradation of land in "arid, semi-arid and dry sub-humid areas" resulting from variations in the climate and human activities.[37] It is estimated that around 52 percent of land used for agriculture is moderately or severely affected, impacting 1.5 billion people.[38] Many of these victims are among the world's poorest. The results of desertification are less food production, increased downstream

Sri Lankans wait for relief items near a flooded road in Godagama, Matara, Sri Lanka, on May 30, 2017.

Tharaka Basnayaka/NurPhoto via Getty Images.

flooding, and reduced water quality. In Africa alone, soil erosion has reduced the grain harvest by 8 percent, while 65 percent of arable land and 30 percent of grazing land has been damaged.[39]

Similar problems exist for water—perhaps the most critical resource for human survival. Estimates suggest that globally, 663 million people lack access to safe water supplies, 1.5 billion people are affected each year by water-related disease, and 160 million children suffer from malnutrition related to water and sanitation.[40] As noted earlier, the quest for energy resources has frequently fouled water sources through oil spills and nuclear tragedies. Human activity has contributed to this pollution, from bodies of water being used as waste disposal sites for animals and trash to runoffs from agriculture and industry that bring toxic pollutants into the water supply. As a result, freshwater is becoming scarcer. This concern prompted a dispute between Ethiopia and Egypt in 2013, for example, when Ethiopia moved to divert a part of the Nile River to construct a hydroelectric dam. While the parties ultimately agreed to ensure that the project did not adversely affect countries downstream,

desertification the degradation of land in arid, semi-arid, and dry sub-humid areas resulting from variations in the climate and human activities

TABLE 2.1 ● The World's Forest Areas, 2015			
	Forest Area (Mill. Hectares)	Percentage of World Total	Net Annual Forest Change 2010–2015 (Mill. Hectares)
Africa	624	15.6	−2.8
Asia	593	14.8	0.8
Europe	1,015	25.4	0.4
North and Central America	751	18.8	0.1
Oceania	174	4.3	0.3
South America	842	21.1	−2.0
Total World	3,999	100.0	−3.3

Source: Food and Agriculture Organization of the United Nations, *Global Forest Resources Assessment 2015: How Are the World's Forests Changing?* (2nd edition, 2016). http://www.fao.org/3/a-i4793e.pdf.

UNDERSTANDING CROSS-BORDER CONFLICT

HOW CAN INTERNATIONAL STUDIES HELP?

The South China Sea

The South China Sea has emerged as one of the most contentious waterways in the world today. The disputes, which revolve around a number of critical issues and involve an array of pivotal actors, suggest how physical attributes can assume considerable economic and political importance. The sea is estimated to carry approximately $5.3 trillion in annual trade and is believed to contain the equivalent of around 11 billion barrels of oil and 190 trillion cubic feet of natural gas. For the United States and China, it also represents an important geostrategic test of wills with respect to power and influence across the Asia Pacific.

Map 2.1 offers a glimpse into the complexity of the challenge. In close proximity to numerous countries, there are competing claims to sovereign control of the South China Sea and the right to access and free passage. China has been particularly assertive in this regard. It has engaged in considerable land reclamation activities to bolster its alleged historical entitlements, including the actual creation of new islands in the Spratly Island group by adding sand to existing reefs and the construction of ports and military installations. For China, these are seen as legitimate steps to protect its security and consistent with its interpretation of prevailing international norms and standards.

Vietnam, the Philippines, Taiwan, Malaysia, and Brunei have all put forward their own competing claims. For its part, the United States has become increasingly entangled in the drama, periodically sending military ships and planes into the area under the guise of ensuring freedom of navigation and to constrain China. Tensions spiked in July 2016, when an arbitration panel under the auspices of the UN Convention on the Laws of the Sea ruled in favor of the Philippines in one of its territorial disputes with China. The proceedings were boycotted by China, which indicated it would not be bound by the ruling.

This is more than a localized set of skirmishes. The significance of the South China Sea extends well beyond the region. With its considerable resources and strategic location, the sea is a source of significant financial leverage and provides a means to promote and extend political security. Given the concerns of both China and the United States, the disputes can also influence the future direction of this most important relationship. With much at stake, a failure to reach some sort of accommodation could prove highly destabilizing for many years to come.

MAP 2.1

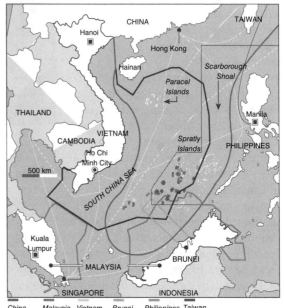

What is the role of crossing borders in resolving this issue? How can the cross-disciplinary focus of international studies help?

Questions:

- What role does geography play in adding to the intensity of this conflict?

- What are the political motives behind the actions of the countries involved in this dispute?

- What are the economic stakes for each of the countries engaged?

- Do social and cultural factors come into play?

- Can the international community play a constructive role in mediating the tensions?

Sources: Howard W. French, "What's Behind Beijing's Drive to Control the South China Sea?" *Guardian,* July 28, 2015, https://www.theguardian.com/world/2015/jul/28/whats-behind-beijings-drive-control-south-china-sea-hainan; "Understanding China's Position on the South China Sea Dispute," *ISDP,* June 2016, http://isdp.eu/publication/understanding-chinas-position-south-china-sea-disputes.

the protracted struggle suggests how the competition for access to water becomes highly politicized.[41] Across a highly volatile Middle East, some have suggested that future conflict may be as much about water as it will be about competing claims to the land.

Human activity has also damaged the atmosphere, perhaps irreparably. Air pollution from industrial output and the burning of fossil fuels, combined with the devastation of the rain forest, which naturally absorbs carbon emissions, has resulted in a situation commonly referred to as the **greenhouse effect**. While the release of greenhouse gases—that is, gases that trap heat in the atmosphere[42]—occurs naturally, the amount of these gases in the atmosphere has expanded significantly due to the burning of fossil fuels. As a result, the average temperature of the earth has increased. National Oceanic and Atmospheric Administration data suggest that 2015 was the hottest year on record to that point, with average temperatures across land and ocean surfaces 1.62 degrees Fahrenheit (0.90 degrees Celsius) above the twentieth-century average. The pattern persisted into 2016, with temperatures even exceeding those of the previous year and reaching another all-time high.[43] The effects are most evident in what has been termed *global warming*. For many years a controversial subject due to the unwillingness of some scientists and politicians to acknowledge its existence, global warming stems largely from the large-scale emissions of carbon dioxide and other greenhouse gases into the atmosphere. Figure 2.8 identifies the largest carbon dioxide emitters in 2015.

greenhouse effect the rise in the earth's temperature due to greenhouse gases that trap heat in the atmosphere

The Global Response

There has been an array of international efforts to address these issues, beginning with the Earth Summit in 1992. Organized by the UN Conference on Environment and Development (UNCED) in Rio de Janeiro, Brazil, this meeting brought together both governmental and nongovernmental actors in the largest gathering ever held on global environmental issues to adopt guiding policies that would slow down and perhaps someday eliminate pollution of the earth. Subsequent meetings would seek further agreements, such as the Kyoto

FIGURE 2.8 ● The World's Largest Carbon Dioxide Emitters, 2016 (Million Metric Tons)*

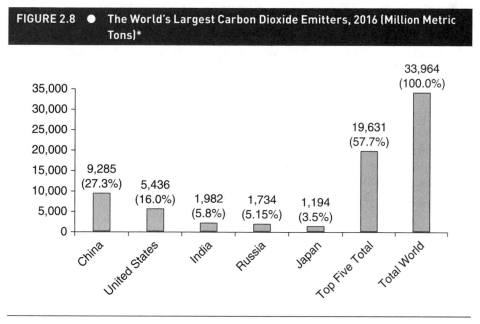

Source: U.S. Energy Information Administration, International Energy Outlook 2016, https://www.eia.gov/outlooks/aeo/data/browser/#/?id=10-IEO2016&sourcekey=0.

*Includes carbon dioxide emissions from consumption of petroleum, natural gas, and coal and from flaring of natural gas.

Protocol that was adopted in 1997 and went into effect in 2005. This accord marked an important breakthrough, as specific guidelines were developed to reduce greenhouse gas emissions. While developed countries committed to the lowering of annual carbon emissions, developing counties were exempted from the mandate, even as they were encouraged to engage. With few mechanisms available to ensure compliance, the results were limited at best, with the United States and China continuing to contribute heavily to the fouling of the atmosphere. Indeed, worldwide emissions actually rose nearly 40 percent between 1990 and 2009.[44]

In June 2012, the UN Conference on Sustainable Development met for the Rio+20 Conference to mark the twentieth anniversary of the 1992 Earth Summit. Delegates renewed their commitment to a common vision in the closing outcome document, "The Future We Want." But many issues remain. As the world's population increases and the burdens of maintaining the global economy mount, environmentally related pressures will persist. For developing countries, in particular, the task is magnified by the lack of resources to address these matters—even if there is the political will to do so. Without more directed activity to protect this global commons, we may find ourselves even further challenged to sustain ourselves.

Of particular concern are the effects of climate change. Following four years of negotiations, the 21st Conference of the Parties to the UN Framework Convention on Climate Change (referred to as COP21) was held in Paris in late 2015 in an effort to hammer out a comprehensive plan. The Paris Agreement, as it came to be known, was significant. In addition to reaffirming the goal of limiting the increase in global temperature to below 3.6 degrees Fahrenheit (2 degrees Celsius) and urging countries to further limit the rise to 2.7 degrees Fahrenheit (1.5 degrees Celsius) above preindustrial times, the accord was particularly noteworthy for getting countries to set national targets for reducing their greenhouse gas emissions. Although there would be no penalties for failing to reach those targets, the agreement contained provisions to enhance transparency as a means to encourage compliance. For the first time, developing counties committed contributions to achieve these objectives; developed countries reaffirmed their financial responsibilities.[45]

To take effect, the agreement would require approval by at least fifty-five countries accounting for no less than 55 percent of global emissions. In a major step forward, China and the United States affirmed their participation through a joint announcement in September 2016. These two countries alone generate close to 40 percent of total emissions.[46] While heralded by many as a potential game changer in the effort to counter climate change, COP21 was still limited in terms of its projected impact. National emission targets and financial commitments are not legally binding, thereby complicating efforts to sustain momentum and uniformity. On balance, the accord broke new ground in terms of its underlying approach and range of participation and in setting the framework for future deliberations.

In June 2017, however, President Donald Trump announced that the United States was withdrawing from the agreement, arguing that it placed a disproportionate burden on the country. While China and other key signatories indicated their intention to continue to abide by their commitments, this step was a considerable blow that called into question the ability to meet the projected targets. But the effort is not necessarily destined to fail. Under the terms of the treaty, the United States cannot actually exit until 2020. It is also interesting to note that, despite the rejection of the federal government, a number of US states and cities have expressed their plans to pursue policies that fall within the guidelines of the accord.[47]

An October 2016 deal that addresses hydrofluorocarbons (HFCs), chemical coolants used in refrigerators and air conditioners that add to the level of greenhouse gases in the atmosphere, built on the Paris deliberations. Although limited to one particular aspect of the global warming challenge, the agreement of more than 170 countries in Kigali, Rwanda,

PRO/CON

IS FURTHER OIL DRILLING GOOD FOR THE ARCTIC?

Pro

Kara Moriarty

President and CEO, Alaska Oil and Gas Association. Written for *CQ Researcher*, December 2016.

The Arctic is much more than a source of energy resources and natural beauty. It is home to thousands of Alaska Natives who understand the link between energy resource development, infrastructure needs and the vibrant ecosystem that supports a subsistence lifestyle. Not to mention, the Alaskans who live here overwhelmingly support developing our Arctic resources—more than 70 percent want to see more oil and gas development in the Arctic, including offshore.

The United States and Alaska are uniquely positioned to capitalize on the emerging opportunities becoming available in the Arctic, but they can do so only if vibrant private-public partnerships can flourish. As other Arctic countries like Russia rush to develop the Arctic for their own benefit, America is in danger of being left behind.

The Arctic desperately needs infrastructure as more activity comes to the region. Fortunately, companies that want to do business in the Arctic stand ready to spend the billions of dollars required to develop infrastructure. Oil and gas companies are experts at developing world-class infrastructure in sensitive environments. These companies regularly spend billions in Alaska building roads and bridges, health and safety facilities, search-and-rescue operations, airstrips and hangars and other facilities that improve the quality of life in a remote and underdeveloped part of the world. This infrastructure provides immense benefit to Arctic communities that would not otherwise enjoy such amenities.

As engagement in the Arctic becomes urgent, accelerating energy development will expand the nation's footprint in an area that is strategically important. The newly open waters are multiplying U.S. security concerns, prompting Coast Guard Rear Adm. Daniel Abel to state, "Just the amount of new open water I have to deal with is the size of 45 percent of the continental U.S."

The choice for the United States is whether to lead in the Arctic or sit on the sidelines and watch as other countries pursue the opportunities offered in the region. With one-third of the nation's oil and gas reserves, Alaska is poised to support Arctic development for decades and in turn continue to be an energy heartland to the United States. By using proven technology to safely and responsibly drill for oil and gas in the Arctic, America stands to benefit from economic growth, development of robust infrastructure and improved national security.

Con

Dune Lankard

Alaska Representative, Center for Biological Diversity. Written for *CQ Researcher*, December 2016.

I've been hearing about drilling in the Arctic all my life. For Native Alaskans, it's one of those discussions that never seems to end. But the truth is, there's no way to make drilling safe—and it's time to finally put an end to it.

More drilling will only push us deeper into the very climate crisis that's driving the tragic transformation of the Arctic, where sea ice has hit record lows and polar bears and ice seals that rely on that ice for survival face the very real prospect of disappearing forever. It's profoundly depressing to bear witness to what's happening in the Arctic because of climate change. We have a moral obligation to make sure it doesn't get worse.

If a major offshore oil spill occurred, there would be no way to clean it up. If you thought the 2010 *Deepwater Horizon* disaster was bad, imagine the same scenario in a place that's prone to hurricane-force storms, 20-foot swells, sea ice, frigid temperatures and seasonal darkness. In some cases the nearest Coast Guard facility is 1,000 miles away. Alaska, sadly, already knows the damage that the oil industry can do.

Prince William Sound has never fully recovered from 1989's *Exxon Valdez* oil spill, an event that changed my life and that of my Native Alaskan fishing community forever. I've been a commercial and subsistence fisherman for decades, so everyone should know that the herring have yet to recover from the spill.

An oil spill in the Arctic could destroy the livelihoods of the people who depend on a clean environment for hunting and fishing. The Arctic is a national treasure that supports a rich diversity of wildlife, but oil drilling and infrastructure would put caribou, polar bears, birds, whales, ice seals, salmon and the traditional communities that depend on them in harm's way. My brothers and sisters in Arctic communities are already being displaced by rising seas and depleted hunting and fishing grounds.

A recent study found that carbon emissions from current drilling projects would take us beyond 2 degrees Celsius of warming. And scientists have warned that all Arctic oil must be left untapped if we are to meet our climate goals. Arctic drilling just doesn't make sense—not for the planet and not for those of us who call Alaska home.

Source: Reed Karaim, "Arctic Development," *CQ Researcher* 26 (December 2, 2016): 989–1012. Retrieved from http://library.cqpress.com.

(Continued)

(Continued)

Where Do You Stand?

1. Is oil drilling a good option for generating money to promote Arctic development?

2. Are the potential environmental hazards worth the risk?

was especially noteworthy for its legally binding nature and its inclusion of specific time-tables and targets to replace HFCs with alternative coolants. While allowing for a more gradual implementation schedule for some of the world's hottest countries, the pact signals an important step in the continuing effort to counter climate change.[48]

Efforts to protect the environment may be complicated by the need to balance multiple and sometimes competing objectives. This has been evident, for example, in the discussion over development in the Arctic, a fragile ecosystem rich in vital resources. The "Pro/Con" debate regarding further oil exploration highlights the dilemma.

What Can You Do?

Even if nation-states cannot reach agreement on how to address these issues, the inter-connected nature of the environment necessitates that people recognize the global conse-quences of their personal actions. There has been considerable attention directed toward alternative and renewable energy resources since the oil crisis of the 1970s, when gas prices quadrupled due to the outbreak of war in the Middle East. These renewable sources include solar technologies, wind harnessing for energy production, and geothermal energy gen-erated from the heat of the earth. Progress has been slow and sporadic due to the cost involved and the reluctance of governments and major energy consumers to absorb that cost. While some progress has been made with regard to conservation, impacts are just beginning to be felt. Examples of conservation include the use of appliances with Energy Star consumption ratings, hybrid automobiles that use both gas and electricity, and fluo-rescent and LED lightbulbs.

The efforts of Ashton Hayes, a small English village outside of Liverpool, are instructive. Spurred by the initiative of a long-time resident, members of the community have under-taken a series of individual and collective steps to cut greenhouse emissions. They have installed solar panels and glazed windows to insulate their homes, have used clotheslines instead of dryers, and have even cut the number of airplane flights taken by residents. Recently marking the tenth year of the experiment, Ashton Hayes has reduced its emissions by 24 percent. About 200 cities and towns from across the world have been in contact with the residents of Ashton Hayes over the years, and a good number have adopted some of the many activities and techniques utilized by the small village.[49]

The success of these alternatives depends on the choices we as individuals can make that will have a positive impact on the environment and its sustainability for future genera-tions. Here are just a few examples of what you can do.

carbon footprint a measurement of the amount of greenhouse gases produced daily through the use of fossil fuels for electricity, heating and air conditioning, and transportation

With regard to energy, you can see how well you are doing by calculating your carbon footprint. **Carbon footprint** is a measurement of the amount of greenhouse gases pro-duced daily through the use of fossil fuels for electricity, heating and air conditioning, and transportation. The carbon footprint calculator that is shown in Figure 2.9 asks about your

FIGURE 2.9 ● Carbon Footprint LTD Website

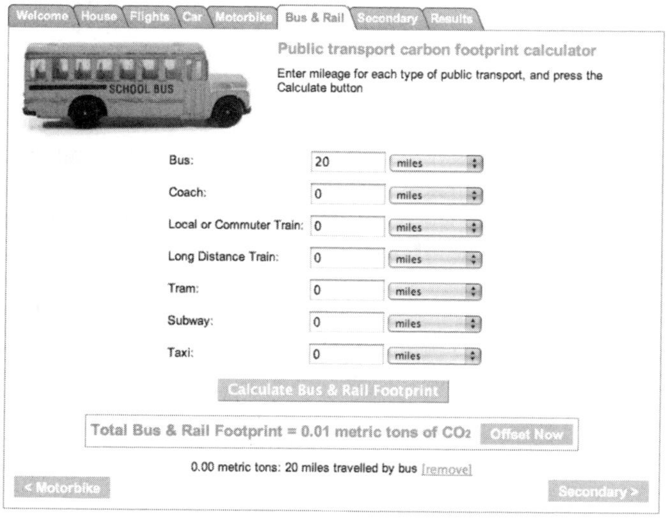
Welcome
House
Flights
Car
Motorbike
Bus & Rail
Secondary
Results
Public transport carbon footprint calculator
Enter mileage for each type of public transport, and press the Calculate button
SCHOOL BUS
Bus: 20 miles
Coach: 0 miles
Local or Commuter Train: 0 miles
Long Distance Train: 0 miles
Tram: 0 miles
Subway: 0 miles
Taxi: 0 miles
Calculate Bus & Rail Footprint
Total Bus & Rail Footprint = 0.01 metric tons of CO2
Offset Now
0.00 metric tons: 20 miles travelled by bus [remove]
< Motorbike
Secondary >

Source: © Carbon Footprint LTD, www.carbonfootprint.com.

use of natural resources to heat and cool your home, how you get around town, and even your food preferences to help you identify areas where you can reduce your impact on the global system.

Another way you can make a difference is to follow the three *Rs—reduce, reuse,* and *recycle. Reduce* refers to the amount of waste you generate, particularly in terms of disposable goods that cannot be recycled. According to the US Environmental Protection Agency (EPA), between 1960 and 2013, the amount of waste each person generated in the United States rose from 2.7 to 4.4 pounds per day. In 2013 alone, Americans produced 254 million tons of trash, while recycling and composting at a rate of 34.3 percent. This was considerably higher than the recycled rate of a mere 6.4 percent in 1960.[50] Particularly problematic is waste that is not biodegradable, and one of the more significant culprits is packaged goods. The challenge of managing waste is even greater for less developed countries that do not have adequate systems in place to handle this increased production. More and more, they find themselves buried in this waste, with no place to dispose of it.

One area of great concern is electronic waste. The UN Environment Programme (UNEP) estimates that nearly 42 million tons of e-waste is generated each year and that this figure will rise to 50 million tons in 2017. The United States (7.1 million tons) and China (6 million tons) lead the way, followed by Japan, Germany, and the United Kingdom. Estimated at around $19 billion, up to 90 percent of this waste is illegally traded.[51] With anticipated sales of electronic products rising significantly across the developing world, there are additional concerns about recycling and the hazards of e-waste disposal. By the year 2020, e-waste from old computers in China will increase by 200 to 400 percent, and in India it will increase by up to 500 percent. In addition, e-waste in the form of discarded mobile phones will be seven times higher than 2007 levels in China, and eighteen times higher in India.[52] The proliferation of hazardous waste can have not only serious environmental effects but health consequences as well. While there have been important efforts to develop national recycling programs, the road is not always a smooth one. In India, for example, recycle and recovery projects in large urban centers such as Bangalore and Mumbai often encounter political, social, and managerial challenges as they seek to raise awareness among locals and move forward with infusing state-of-the-art technologies and techniques that fit community needs.[53]

The second *R* stands for *reuse* as a way of reducing waste. The concept of reusable materials applies to salvaged goods from buildings that are torn down; these recycled goods are used to construct new buildings or reused in other ways. For example, the nonprofit organization Habitat for Humanity has established ReStore resale outlets in the United States and Canada that take donated home improvement goods and resell them; the proceeds support the construction of Habitat for Humanity homes in local communities.[54] Another example is playground safety surfaces that consist of rubber mulch made from recycled tires. There is a need for caution when utilizing these materials, however, due to evidence uncovered regarding potential health hazards to soccer goalies and others frequently and directly exposed to them.[55]

The success of these programs depends on the third *R*—recycle. Recycling allows materials that are considered waste to be transformed into usable items. It can be as simple as putting a plastic water bottle or newspaper in a recycling bin or purchasing goods made from recycled materials. It can include sharing with others through charitable donations of usable goods or simply swapping clothes with friends.

HOW YOU CAN CONNECT

You can reduce, reuse, and recycle by . . .

- using reusable grocery and shopping bags
- carrying a reusable water bottle
- riding a bicycle or some other nonmotorized vehicle when feasible
- taking public transportation or carpooling whenever possible
- installing LED bulbs in your home
- adjusting your thermostat to limit energy consumption

There is a challenge to recycling that occurs in developing areas, particularly among the urban poor—waste picking.[56] In many city centers, large numbers of people survive by salvaging recyclable goods from trash piles. One source suggests this is a way of life for as many as 15 million people, or 1 percent of the urban population in developing countries.[57] In Brazil, for example, these pickers account for as much as 92 percent of aluminum and 80 percent of cardboard recycling.[58] Children are heavily engaged in this process and the ones most directly at risk. The country has undertaken a national campaign supported by the World Bank that provides health care and gives parents a cash credit if their children attend school. The money compensates for the revenue lost from not having the children picking the waste.

What is clear from these observations is the interconnectedness of the environment and the responsibility everyone must share for it. Individual decisions will be an important first step, but a global response is really required. The need for sustainability and the reality that people are dependent on their physical environment to survive are critical factors to consider. Technology links people around the world and offers ways to work together on these issues. The next chapter, on technology, allows us to jump-start our trip across the other borders dividing the world today.

WHAT CAN YOU DO WITH INTERNATIONAL STUDIES?

Composting in India

By Rozita Singh, Sustainable Development Graduate, New Delhi, India

A few years back, I watched a documentary called *Don't Rubbish It*, and little did I know that the nine-minute documentary would shape my "interest area"—solid waste management. A minute or so in, the documentary was devoted to composting. It was then that I got to know about this lovely organization called Daily Dump in Bangalore (http://dailydump.org). The director, Ms. Poonam Bir Kasturi, has designed a series of products suitable for household composting. I fell in love with the three-tier *khamba* model—it was beautiful, could be kept anywhere (veranda or balcony), and what I liked the most was that it made composting so much easier!

As part of the British Council's Climate Champion Programme, I decided to take this up as my school project. It is part of the National Action Project (NAP), and I was selected to receive a grant. I became part of a group called Social Action Team under NAP, and though my fellow climate champions are based in different cities, we have taken up waste management as our agenda and are working toward it simultaneously from different places. Upon graduation, this activity led me to a job as a research associate in the Centre for Research on Sustainable Urban Development and Transport Systems at The Energy and Resources Institute (TERI) in New Delhi, India, working on urban climate resilience issues. I recently returned to graduate school in The Netherlands at Erasmus University to further my education on urban issues.

As urbanization increases, the problem of mounting garbage in the cities increases. With land fast becoming a scarce commodity, how long can we depend on landfills? The idea is to promote the habit of segregation at the source among the urban households in New Delhi, India. The technique is aerobic composting using terra-cotta pots designed by the Daily Dump organization (http://www.dailydump.org), which converts organic kitchen waste into manure in a very simple way. The intended outcome is to sensitize urban residents to the problem of increased solid waste generation and show them a sustainable solution to tackle the problem. Using the pots will decrease the pressure on existing landfills by offsetting the organic waste that currently constitutes roughly 60 to 70 percent of the total waste generated in an ideal

Personal photo by Rozita Singh.

household. My ultimate dream or mission is to convince the urban residents to adopt the practice of composting so that we handle our own waste responsibly.

I believe in the power of the "one"—the individual. As an eco-lover and graduate of a master's program in sustainable development practice, I feel that I should emulate the teachings of sustainable living. Moreover, this project is the perfect example of the three *R*s (reuse, reduce, and recycle). Turning your waste into compost is good for the environment and good for your soul. It is also a logical step because it doesn't make sense for organic waste to be sent to the landfill! On average, an urban Indian household generates 0.5 kg (1.1 lb.) of waste each day. When this mixed waste ends up in the landfill, it produces methane, a greenhouse gas. Do the calculation on how many emissions you can save by not sending this waste to the landfill, instead turning it into manure, which in turn could support green-belt development and develop carbon sinks.

If you would like to learn more, please visit me on my blog at http://come-n-post.blogspot.in. Happy composting!

Key Concepts

carbon footprint 44	food insecurity 35	Malthusian dilemma 34
carrying capacity 33	geography 26	physical geography 27
cartography 27	global commons 25	sustainable development 26
deforestation 34	greenhouse effect 41	topography 27
desertification 39	human geography 27	

To Learn More

Books and Other Print Media

Michael M. Andregg, *Seven Billion and Counting: The Crisis in Global Population Growth* (Minneapolis: Twenty-First Century Books, 2014).

Michael Andregg looks at the capacity of the planet to sustain a population projected to reach 10 billion people before 2050.

Thomas L. Friedman, *Hot, Flat, and Crowded: Why We Need a Green Revolution—and How It Can Renew America* (New York: Picador, 2009).

In this book, Thomas Friedman examines the global thirst for oil and its future environmental impact.

McKenzie Funk, *Windfall: The Booming Business of Global Warming* (New York: The Penguin Press, 2014).

Journalist McKenzie Funk brings a different perspective to the serious issue of global warming, examining how many people around the world have sought to cash in on the crisis and the very serious implications of these trends.

Al Gore, *An Inconvenient Truth: The Planetary Emergency of Global Warming and What We Can Do About It* (New York: Rodale, 2006).

Former US vice president Al Gore's famous book and documentary film of the same name trace the pattern of global warming and its consequences and were quite instrumental in heightening awareness of the challenges presented by climate change.

Ken Jennings, *Maphead: Charting the Wide, Weird World of Geography Wonks* (New York: Scribner Books, 2011).

Ken Jennings, the trivia expert who won seventy-four consecutive times on the television game show *Jeopardy*, explores the world of "map nerds," who, like himself, are obsessed with how geography is mapped.

Naomi Klein, *This Changes Everything: Capitalism vs. The Climate* (New York: Simon & Schuster, 2015).

Naomi Klein puts forward a forceful case for reducing greenhouse emissions, suggesting the need for innovative approaches that recognize how the market system has contributed to the severity of the climate crisis.

Elizabeth Kolbert, *Field Notes from a Catastrophe: Man, Nature, and Climate Change*, Rev. ed. (New York, Bloomsbury USA, 2015).

This update of Elizabeth Kolbert's 2006 classic on global warming puts forward a compelling case for addressing the many issues adding to the magnitude of the challenge.

Frances Moore Lappe and Joseph Collins, *World Hunger: 10 Myths* (New York, Grove Press, 2015).

The authors identify some of the more common myths that distract us from addressing the underlying factors contributing to the persistence of hunger across the world today.

Dan Smith, *The Penguin State of the World Atlas*, 9th ed. (New York: Penguin Books, 2012).

Dan Smith's book offers multiple ways of looking at the world through very different types of maps.

Websites

Earth: A Graphic Look at the State of the World, www.theglobaleducationproject.org/earth

This website is run by a Canadian nongovernmental organization (NGO) offering high-quality graphics, with a section called "Earth" related to environmental issues.

GRID-Arendal, www.grida.no

Based in Norway, GRID-Arendal is a center that collaborates with UNEP to communicate information and data about the environment. It features excellent data and maps.

National Aeronautics and Space Administration (NASA), Earth, www.nasa.gov/topics/earth/index.html

This website features data and information, including high-quality video, photos, and maps of earth-related science topics, including many interactive features and other visualization tools.

Population Reference Bureau, www.prb.org

This organization provides information about population, health, and environmental issues around the world and seeks to influence policy on these matters.

Rise Against Hunger, www.riseagainsthunger.org

This international hunger relief organization provides food and other forms of aid to some of the world's most vulnerable.

World Atlas, www.worldatlas.com

This is a good, user-friendly site that includes a considerable number of maps and information regarding social, economic, and environmental conditions for countries across the world.

Videos

Before the Flood (2016)

In this documentary film, producer Leonardo DiCaprio explores climate change and numerous ways in which it might be addressed. An accompanying website includes considerable amount of background material: https://www.beforetheflood.com/explore.

Future Food (2013), http://www.bullfrogfilms.com/catalog/ffs.html

With the world's population expected to rise to 9 billion people by 2050, this six-part series looks to Peru, Kenya, India, Nigeria, China, and the United States as it examines how we might continue to feed ourselves in the twenty-first century.

Home (2009)

This documentary by Yann Arthus-Bertrand and Luc Besson draws on aerial forage from fifty-four countries to depict the interconnections of the earth's problems and why they must be addressed. This film's debut was unique, as it was released and screened simultaneously in movie theaters, on TV, on DVD, and on the Internet.

How to Let Go of the World and Love All the Things Climate Can't Change (2016), http://www.bullfrogfilms.com/catalog/howto.html

This film travels to twelve countries on six continents to explore the realities and consequences of climate change.

An Inconvenient Truth (2006)

Former vice president Al Gore argues the case that we've reached a tipping point in climate change.

Let the Environment Guide Our Development (2013), http://www.ted.com/talks/johan_rockstrom_let_the_environment_guide_our_development

Johan Rockstrom is head of the Stockholm Resilience Centre (http://www.stockholmresilience.org), which focuses on cooperative approaches to sustainability. In this video, he talks about the special relationship people have with the earth and how it must be protected.

The Lorax (2011)

This animated feature is based on the book by Dr. Seuss (1972), which explores the impact of overconsumption, environmental degradation, and personal responsibility.

The State of the Climate—and What We Might Do about It (2014), https://www.ted.com/playlists/78/climate_change_oh_it_s_real

Economist Nicholas Stern puts forward a plan, which he delivered to the 2014 UN Climate Summit, for countries to work together to protect the environment.

3

Jump-Starting the Trip

The Role of Technology

A student in a dorm room, connecting one community at a time, and keeping at it until one day we connect the whole world.

—Facebook CEO Mark Zuckerberg, 2017[1]

Learning Objectives

After studying this chapter, you will be able to do the following:

- Explain what *flatness* means with respect to the relationship between the world's countries and peoples.

- Define *digitization* and the concepts of the *digital age* and the *information revolution*.

- Identify the key technological changes that have taken place in the modern era, and explain their significance.

- Define the *Industrial Revolution*, and explain the main changes that took place during its course.

- Explain the political, economic, and social implications of new technologies.

In his 2017 commencement address at Harvard University, Facebook CEO Mark Zuckerberg reflected on his work as an undergraduate to increase communication among Harvard students. What started as a closed and limited networking site eventually morphed into a cross-border phenomenon linking disparate people across the globe. Today, Facebook has a population of 2 billion—larger than any single country. The development of Facebook speaks directly to political commentator Thomas Friedman's suggestion that, contrary to Ferdinand Magellan's discovery nearly 500 years ago that the earth was round, the world is indeed flat. Friedman argues that modern technologies make economic and social relationships between people, businesses, and countries "flatter"—less hierarchical—and claims that they have opened up important new opportunities for advancement and development. The borders separating countries have become far more porous.[2]

Throughout history, it has been technology—from the invention of the wheel and the printing press to more modern modes of transportation and communication—that has increased the flow of people across the world's borders. Today, people around the world are more mobile than ever, and that mobility is clearly aided by technology. Cars and airplanes take us physically to the same places that smartphones and cyberspace allow us to visit virtually. As a result, technology transcends the boundaries that define our identity both at home and in the workplace—what we are able to do and how we communicate, travel, and learn.

These developments offer new ways for people to define themselves and relate to others. Through modern technologies, individuals are on the cutting edge of political change and social interaction. They have the ability to organize quickly to influence the political process. Groups that were once outsiders now affect policymaking. Social networks have launched national revolutions, and videos taken with mobile phones are often the best sources of information about what is going on in conflict situations. The technology that has allowed information to be converted to computer-ready formats—**digitization**—has fundamentally altered communication to provide more broad-based methods of delivery.

digitization the conversion of information to computer-ready format

Women sing along to patriotic songs while filming with cellphones on November 25, 2011, during a protest in Cairo's Tahrir Square to speak out against the Supreme Council of the Armed Forces (SCAF), which had governed Egypt since the February 2011 revolution. The protests ended after a week, with more than forty killed and thousands injured.

Monique Jaques/Corbis via Getty Images.

The events in the Middle East in 2011 that transformed the Egyptian, Tunisian, and Libyan governments and seriously challenged the Syrian government—the Arab Spring—are an excellent example of technology in action. Protestors organized massive gatherings through digital media, using social networks and mobile phone messaging. The rest of the world saw these incidents unfold using the same modes of participation, watching eyewitness videos of the crowds and the violence they frequently encountered. With this firsthand knowledge, empathy for the protestors grew. Today, that compassion develops from our view of refugees seeking safety from conflict and destruction. Those images might include the picture of a small Syrian boy that goes viral on the Internet as he is carried lifelessly from the water. Governments have come to recognize the potential of this information flow to threaten their authority and may react aggressively to control the narrative. This was the case in Cameroon in 2016, when the leadership sought to curtail social media by labeling it as a tool to disseminate false information and going so far as to declare it a form of terrorism.[3]

information revolution the rapid spread of and access to all forms of communication

digital age the development of digital technology in the twenty-first century characterized by the ability to transfer large amounts of information with ease and to access knowledge from virtually any location

The **information revolution** has enhanced our ability to communicate via multiple sources. We are truly living in a **digital age**. But is the world really flat, as Friedman would have us believe? The forces that define Friedman's argument include geographical border shifts—such as the tearing down of the Berlin Wall—as well as computer and software developments and alterations in commercial operations, trade, and worker productivity.[4] They include sharing information across borders through the Internet, outsourcing commercial operations to other countries for greater efficiency, and supply chain innovation to move products or services around the world quickly from production to the consumer. Technological innovation is the "steroid" that drives the "flatteners" at work today. It is a major force in transforming the world and interpersonal relationships. Yet, is technology really leveling the world?

Friedman's analysis is based on observations about the economic powerhouses of China and India. Not all countries have had the same opportunities and access to innovation. Another way to really understand the digital age is to recognize that the impact of technology is divided between those who have access and those who do not. Globally, there is a significant **digital divide**. For example, while it may seem as though we are all connected by the Internet, in fact, only about half of the world's population, 49.6 percent, is actually online.[5] Figure 3.1 illustrates Internet usage by geographic region in terms of the percentage of the population with access to the Internet. Accessibility varies widely—most notably deficient are Africa (only 27.7 percent of the continent's population has access), Asia (45.2 percent), and the Middle East (56.7 percent), compared to 88.1 percent for North America and 77.4 percent for Europe.[6] This is but one of many inequities that continue to dot the planet.

digital divide unequal access to the Internet that separates those who have it and those who do not

This chapter explores how technology has evolved and is driving many of the changes taking place in the world. It suggests how and why the underlying power of technological innovation should not be ignored. A brief account of the development of modern technology sets the stage for a discussion of how it is used to cross borders.

The Technological Frontier

Thousands of years ago, travel on foot limited people in their contacts and interactions to their immediate surroundings. Hundreds of years ago, advancements in maritime technology allowed people to travel greater distances, but they spent months or even years on the high seas to exchange goods and ideas.

The series of industrial and information innovations that allowed people to get news of new frontiers began in the mid-fifteenth century with Johannes Gutenberg's invention of the printing press. While information had previously been passed along verbally or written

FIGURE 3.1 ● World Internet Penetration Rates, by Geographic Region, 2017

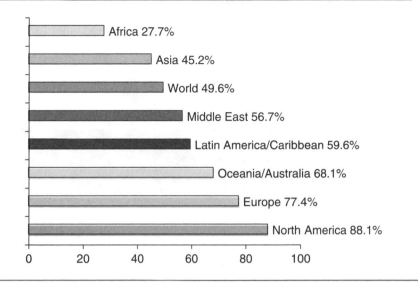

- Africa 27.7%
- Asia 45.2%
- World 49.6%
- Middle East 56.7%
- Latin America/Caribbean 59.6%
- Oceania/Australia 68.1%
- Europe 77.4%
- North America 88.1%

(x-axis: 0, 20, 40, 60, 80, 100)

Source: Data are from Internet World Stats, www.internetworldstats.com/stats.htm.

and copied by hand, the press allowed information to circulate more freely around the world. It gave more people the opportunity to become literate and allowed information to reach a wider audience. Across long distances, people could read the same words and develop common interests. And it moved very quickly! James Burke sheds light on this phenomenon, noting that "from the single Mainz press of 1457, it took only 23 years to establish presses in 110 towns: 50 in Italy, 30 in Germany, nine in France, eight in Spain, eight in Holland, four in England, and so on."[7]

Shortly thereafter, a transformation took place that introduced the machinery of the modern age. The **Industrial Revolution** brought about the transition from an economy based on the labor of humans and animals to one based on machines. Key inventions included spinning machines that converted wool and cotton into spools of yarn, steam engines and their application to trains and boats, and the mechanization

Industrial Revolution the eighteenth-century transformation from a human- and animal-based labor economy to one based on machines

Five hundred fifty years ago, the printing press (left) gave us the book as we have long known it—gatherings of printed pages set within a binding. E-book readers like the Kindle and the iPad were invented in the late 2000s, and now e-reader apps allow us to read on our smartphones (right).

iStock/© jpa1999.

iStock/mikkelwilliam.

of iron production.[8] The first steam engine was created in England and registered in 1698 by Thomas Savery. Thomas Newcomen would move it forward, and James Watt would improve the design to provide a model for the engine that would become a commercial success. So significant was Watt's contribution that a unit of power—the watt—was named after him. It is equal to 1/746 horsepower, or one volt times one amp.[9] If we look back to Thomas Savery's expectations as he wrote about the uses for his steam engine, we can understand how the measurement of horsepower evolved— that is, how many horses the use of this engine could replace.

IN THEIR OWN WORDS

THOMAS SAVERY

I have only this to urge, that water, in its fall from any determinate height, has simply a force answerable and equal to the force that raised it. So that an engine which will raise as much water as two horses working together at one time in such a work can do, and for which there must be constantly kept ten or twelve horses for doing the same. . . . I say, such an engine will do the work or labours of ten or twelve horses.[10]

Nicolas Perez/Wikipedia Commons.

Pictured here is a Watt double-acting steam engine, which sparked the Industrial Revolution and greatly expanded the horizons for trade across world borders. Steam engines are still utilized today, as steam turbine engines are used to produce much of the world's electrical power.

Trains would use the steam engine for transit, and the expansion of the railroads began. Critical to the Industrial Revolution, they facilitated the movement of goods and services across previously insurmountable distances. Raw materials could now be easily transported to manufacturing sites, thereby fostering the development of trade relationships. Eventually, large freight containers would be created that would move an unprecedented amount of resources and products around the globe, using existing rail networks, shipping, and cross-country roadways.

A second industrial revolution began in the latter part of the nineteenth century and brought electricity, the mechanization of production, and experiments with aviation. These advances underlie the great twentieth-century transformations. The advent of an affordable car that could carry people long distances on their own initiative and the creation of a consumer aviation market gave way to new modes of transportation. Initially available only to a wealthier clientele, air travel for the public has been in existence since the 1930s. Today, it has become financially accessible to the masses, both domestically and abroad. Between June 2015 and June 2016, the world's airlines flew 1.65 million scheduled flights into and out of the United States and carried 209.4 million passengers.[11] The number of automobiles operated globally has also grown, particularly in countries where sales were once limited. As China becomes the world's second-largest consumer market, it has become number one in sales of automobiles, purchasing 27.8 million cars in 2016, compared to the United States at 17.6 million.[12] Bullet trains are also popular in China, reaching speeds of more than 200 miles per hour. For example, the bullet train that runs between Beijing and Shanghai has cut travel time from ten hours to just over four hours.[13]

Technological innovation in transportation has even expanded to the point that space tourism has emerged as a new industry. While orbital space tourism opportunities remain limited and expensive, with only the Russian Space Agency providing transport thus far, its very existence marks an unprecedented level of technological sophistication. Guy Laliberte, founder of the Montreal-based Cirque du Soleil, paid $35 million for a twelve-day trip aboard a Russian Soyuz spacecraft in 2009.[14]

Virgin Atlantic mogul Sir Richard Branson is hoping to get into the business of space tourism with the creation of his company Virgin Galactic and its SpaceShip Two, which will provide transport for up to six passengers and two pilots.[15] This development suggests the expanding reach of globalization even beyond our own planet! Hollywood actor Ashton Kutcher was the 500th customer to reserve a $200,000 spot for space travel with Virgin Galactic, even though a 2014 test flight crash has delayed commercial service.[16] Despite the mishap, Virgin Galactic is moving forward, adding a second SpaceShip Two in 2016—the VSS (Virgin SpaceShip) *Unity*, named by world-renowned professor Steven Hawking—and is still signing up future astronauts for an increased fee of $250,000.[17]

Elon Musk, cofounder and CEO of Tesla Motors, has also gotten into the space travel business with his company SpaceX, which provides cargo service to the International Space Station. Musk predicts that his spacecraft will be able to carry people to Mars by 2025, beating NASA's projected timing of the 2030s.[18] Like Virgin Galactic, the company suffered a setback in September 2016 with the explosion of its Falcon 9 rocket that was to carry an Israeli-constructed satellite for Facebook into space to provide free Internet service to sub-Saharan Africa.[19]

Concurrent with the development of transportation innovation, the telegraph and telephone enabled instantaneous communication over long distances and fostered economic growth. Using the technology behind the telegraph, inventors created a "wireless" system for radio signals.[20] This system was initially protected by patents for military use in World War I, but the release of those patents after the war allowed for the mass availability of the radio, which brought information directly into people's homes. Access grew quickly, and it is estimated that 60 percent of American families bought radios between 1923 and 1930.[21] Telephone technology was also related to the telegraph, but progress was slow. By the 1930s, only 30 percent of US households had telephones. The percentage was even smaller in rural areas of the United States and lower still in other countries.[22]

Today, the number of landline phones in use has diminished significantly, as mobile phones have taken their place. By 2017, only 45.9 percent of Americans had a landline in their home, while 95 percent of US adults owned a mobile phone.[23] Globally, mobile phone subscriptions have more than tripled in the past ten years. By 2016, China had more than 1.3 billion subscribers, and India reached 1 billion. These figures translated to 92 phones per 100 people for China and 78 per 100 for India, compared to the numbers of sub-Saharan countries such as Niger (47), Uganda (50), and Malawi (35).[24] Africa and the Asia-Pacific region have seen the greatest expansion. Between 2005 and 2016, mobile cellular telephone subscriptions for Africa grew from 87 million to 772 million and went from 833 million to 3.8 billion subscriptions in Asia and the Pacific[25] (see Figure 3.2).

The development of **short message service (SMS)** technology that allows mobile phone users to text messages of up to 160 characters to one another has become the more pervasive new mode of communication, as texting is a part of daily life for millions of people around the globe. Today people rely on smartphones on a daily basis not only for communication but for taking and sharing photos, banking, online shopping, using maps, checking e-mails, and even word processing. Self-contained application programs, or apps, have added considerably to the user-friendliness of these devices and have revolutionized patterns of communication and information gathering. The top ten most popular apps in the world estimated by downloads in May 2016 are shown in Figure 3.3. It is interesting to note that, in addition to its more clearly branded apps, Facebook now owns both WhatsApp and Instagram.

short message service (SMS) technology that allows mobile phone users to text messages of up to 160 characters to one another

FIGURE 3.2 ● The Penetration of Communications Technology Worldwide, 2005–2016 (per 100 Inhabitants)

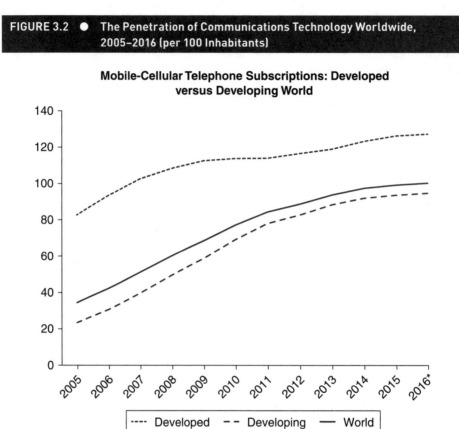

Mobile-Cellular Telephone Subscriptions: Developed versus Developing World

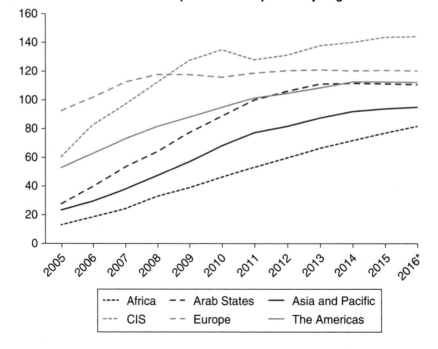

Mobile-Cellular Telephone Subscriptions: By Region

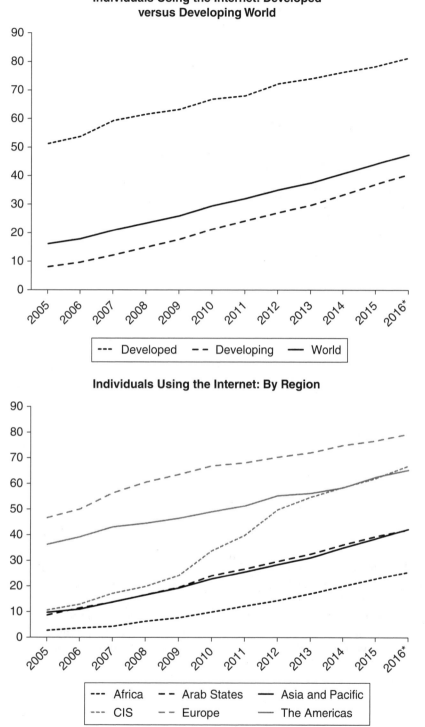

Individuals Using the Internet: Developed versus Developing World

Legend: --- Developed   – – Developing   — World

Individuals Using the Internet: By Region

Legend: --- Africa   – – Arab States   — Asia and Pacific
--- CIS   – – Europe   — The Americas

Source: ITU World Telecommunication/ICT Indicators database.

*Estimate.

Note: The developed/developing country classifications are based on the UN M49, and regions are based on the ITU regions; see http://www.itu.int/en/ITU-D/Statistics/Pages/definitions/regions.aspx.

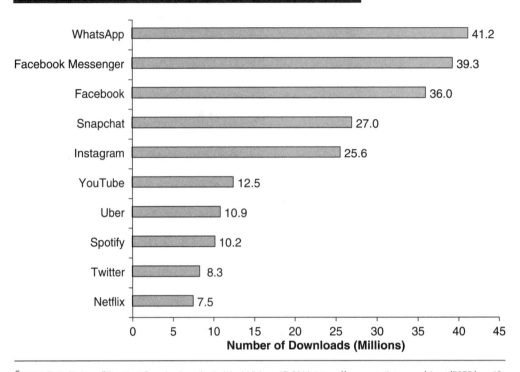

FIGURE 3.3 ● Top Ten Smartphone Apps in the World, 2016

App	Number of Downloads (Millions)
WhatsApp	41.2
Facebook Messenger	39.3
Facebook	36.0
Snapchat	27.0
Instagram	25.6
YouTube	12.5
Uber	10.9
Spotify	10.2
Twitter	8.3
Netflix	7.5

Source: Felix Richter, "The Most Popular Apps in the World," June 17, 2016, https://www.statista.com/chart/5055/top-10-apps-in-the-world.

Enter the Computer

The creation of the computer during World War II and subsequent expansion of that technology to business and home uses revolutionized access to information. The movement from computers that took up whole buildings to current desktops, laptops, and tablets happened in less than 50 years. Today, computer access to the world is held in your hand. Whether an Apple or Android aficionado, you have the ability to stay connected at all times and from anywhere in satellite service reach. The development of **cloud computing** removes the burden of running applications and programs from the device itself and places this task in a system of servers. It is a web-based service run by remote machines that provides extensive storage of information. What makes the cloud important is the ubiquity of smartphones, tablets, and laptops and the general access to information from virtually anywhere. An outgrowth of cloud computing is the development of **big data**. This refers to the increasing amounts and variety of data available today that can be used to analyze many different subject areas, including disease prevention, intelligence, security, and economic development.

The industry giants in this transformation have become household names—Bill Gates and Microsoft, and Steve Jobs and Apple. Separately and many times in competition with one another, these men and their companies transformed the computer industry into what it is today. Gates wrote the code that ran the first home computer (the IBM PC), which has evolved into the tenth generation of the Windows operating system. Steve Jobs saw things differently and led the Apple revolution as a way to connect people to their computers in new and innovative ways. Jobs wanted to apply the technology of computing to directly

cloud computing the delivery of web-based content via remote servers to multiple devices

big data the increasing amounts and variety of data available to analyze many different subject areas

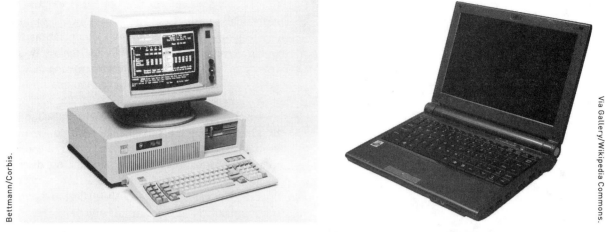

Bettmann/Corbis.

Via Gallery/Wikipedia Commons.

This 1984 IBM (International Business Machines Corporation) AT (advanced technology) computer was among the first personal computers (PCs)—effectively the "great-grandparent" of the computer you likely use or own. Today, laptops offer far more mobility, capacity, and computing power.

connect people to their machines. From the creation of the alternative operations systems that continue to pit PCs against its computers, Apple has been on the cutting edge of electronic breakthroughs, particularly as they apply to individual uses. These innovations have included the iMac computer, the iPod portable media player, the iPhone, and the iPad. These devices and the accompanying iTunes application allow people all over the world to share a market space. There they can purchase music and many other types of recordings, television shows, documentaries, and movies.

IN THEIR OWN WORDS
STEVE JOBS

Creativity is just connecting things. When you ask creative people how they did something, they feel a little guilty because they didn't really do it; they just saw something. It seemed obvious to them after a while. That's because they were able to connect experiences they've had and synthesize new things. And the reason they were able to do that was that they've had more experiences or they have thought more about their experiences than other people.

Unfortunately, that's too rare a commodity. A lot of people in our industry haven't had very diverse experiences. So they don't have enough dots to connect, and they end up with very linear solutions without a broad perspective on the problem. The broader one's understanding of the human experience, the better design we will have.[26]

The Role of Technology in Crossing Borders

The acceleration in information sharing, coupled with the extended movement of people and products, has contributed significantly to the opening of political, economic, social, and cultural borders. The development of relatively unrestricted means of communication is probably the single most significant contribution to the restructuring of the global arena.

A Masai warrior listens to music on an Apple iPod while surveying the landscape of Lewa Conservancy in Kenya.

Visions of America/UIG via Getty Images.

Global access to information 24/7 has empowered individuals, businesses, and governments to forge new opportunities and methods of operation that would have been unimaginable just ten or twenty years ago. As a result, people are crossing borders every day, sometimes without even looking up from their phones!

Advances in technology have also raised questions of privacy as surveillance techniques have been enhanced. Drone technology has advanced to allow information gathering at the most discrete levels, whether we like it or not. Planes can carry "dirt boxes" that can simultaneously collect data from thousands of cell phones in just one pass. The abilities of governments to utilize these sorts of technologies to monitor citizens and to abridge their rights have raised serious concerns.

At the same time, some have suggested that the very technologies that make it more difficult to mask activities actually result in greater accountability and transparency across the globe. Through the use of the expanding markets for commercial satellite imagery, for example, it becomes possible to access information and evidence despite elaborate efforts that might be in place to conceal it from others. American attempts to track North Korea's nuclear testing programs and China's land reclamation and infrastructure development projects in the South China Sea have been aided considerably by this satellite imaging. The growing use of drones and social media to both observe and record events as they are happening add to this transparency. These activities range from tracking political confrontations and military movements to coordinating disaster relief.[27] Taken together, these new forms of information gathering and modes of communication play a major role in crossing international divides and connecting the world's population in new and revolutionary ways.

Political Borders

Communications technology has become a critical source of political leverage, particularly for those who may have few other political resources. Citizens seeking change may take advantage of Internet access to orchestrate events designed to alter the status quo. In recent years, messaging, texting, and tweeting have been used extensively in places like Egypt, Venezuela, and even Iran to facilitate efforts to challenge those in power. Mobilizing support for these activities has been greatly enhanced by the use of social media to publicize the location of street demonstrations and to spread awareness of contentious or unpopular policies. The uploading of images or videos that capture happenings in real time can add to the dynamic of unsettled political circumstances. As suggested by Osama bin Laden's use of a flash drive to communicate with al-Qaida operatives and the utilization of cell phones to coordinate the 9/11 attacks, technology also contributes to the capacity to generate more extreme forms of political behavior. Today, that capability has been augmented by the growing sophistication of technologies and savvy of those who use them.

The Islamic State in Iraq and Syria (ISIS, also known as the Islamic State) is an important case in point. As ISIS has expanded its reach and clout, it has relied heavily on available technology to cross political borders in recruiting supporters and building social networks to advance its mission. It has gone to great lengths to craft its message to prospective fighters by producing videos and other graphics as part of an information offensive designed to appeal both visually and emotionally to its targeted audiences. Although these are modern-day equivalents of age-old propaganda techniques, they are particularly noteworthy for their capacity to reach significant numbers of people across great expanses with little more than an Internet connection. The results have been stunning, as ISIS has attracted recruits from around 100 countries and has dramatically increased the scope and range of its activities by inspiring "homegrown" sympathizers to engage in acts of terror in Europe, the United States, and beyond.[28]

Through its online presence and social media networking, ISIS has been able to fine-tune its outreach. In addition to maintaining a constant flow of material extolling its virtues and successes, it looks to "friend" contacts by building trust and establishing relationships to ultimately bring them into the fold. J. M. Berger notes that there are five steps to the process.[29] The first is discovery, whereby the potential recruits discover ISIS online or ISIS discovers them through their postings. The second step occurs as ISIS supporters create a micro-community around the prospective converts using social media contacts. They then move to the third step, isolation, where these individuals are urged to cut ties with their families, friends, and more mainstream religious communities. The fourth step brings the targets even further along as their contact with ISIS recruiters is moved to private or encrypted messaging platforms. In the fifth and final step, the recruits are encouraged to take action by traveling to join ISIS or carry out terrorist acts at home. Berger argues that in addition to constant surveillance and ongoing efforts to disrupt these interactions, the most critical juncture for those seeking to counter this activity occurs prior to the fourth step, when conversations are taken into private arenas.

This same technology that is used to foment political change can also be tapped by those in power with ample resources to deploy it—sometimes with profound repercussions. China has been particularly active in this regard. The country's battles with the global search engine Google have been highly publicized, as the government has long sought to restrict access to Internet sites and monitor usage. Google reversed its initial decision to self-censor and wound up losing significant market share to its Chinese competitor, Baidu. By 2015, Baidu had come to account for 92.1 percent of China's searches.[30]

China's efforts to control the message have also included an array of more proactive measures to package information and dispense it across social media to mobilize popular support. It is known to employ a considerable network of content creators and trolls to cast government policies in a favorable light while casting doubt on the motivations of critics and opponents. These efforts often focus on key foreign policy objectives, such as the unification of Taiwan, territorial claims in the South China Sea, and US military movements considered to be challenging or threatening to Chinese security interests.[31]

Russia's information warfare has also gained considerable notoriety. Russia continues to employ more mainstream methods to disseminate and report information, relying heavily on the government-supported Russia Today (RT) news service. It broadcasts around the world in multiple languages and has a significant YouTube presence. Beyond this activity, a legion of bloggers and commentators actively engage online on behalf of Russian policy interests. The efforts to provoke antigovernment sentiment in Ukraine to lay the groundwork for Russia's 2014 invasion of Crimea and to plant stories intended to influence the 2016 US presidential election are but two examples of these types of ongoing campaigns.[32]

For its part, the United States is also an active participant. In some cases, these actions are primarily defensive in nature. The link to a highly questionable story relating to

UNDERSTANDING CROSS-BORDER CONFLICT

HOW CAN INTERNATIONAL STUDIES HELP?

Cyber Espionage

In 2015, the United States and China signed an agreement intended to curtail their bilateral cyber espionage and to pursue efforts to promote international norms for state behavior in cyberspace. The accord was prompted by a considerable uptick in these types of activities that increased tensions and threatened to derail other forms of cooperation.

In 2014, the US Justice Department had filed criminal charges against five hackers in the Chinese military. The complaint accused them of using cyber spying to steal US trade secrets from six American firms in the nuclear power, metals, and solar products industries. Targeted companies included Westinghouse Electric, US Steel, SolarWorld, United Steelworkers Union, Allegheny Technologies Inc., and Alcoa World Alumina. Evidence suggested that the Chinese government not only condoned but supported the activities of the People's Liberation Army Unit 61398, based in a Shanghai suburb. The alleged hackers were young army officers who used military and intelligence resources to download industrial information, including strategic plans, from US businesses.

The Chinese government responded with accusations of its own, suggesting that the United States fabricated the evidence. It also cited data produced by the National Computer Network Emergency Response Technical Team Coordination Center of China (NCNERTTCC) suggesting that for just two months in 2014, 1.17 million host computers in China were directly controlled by the United States via the use of 2,077 Trojan horse networks or botnet servers and that the United States used 135 host computers to conduct 14,000 phishing operations and 57,000 backdoor attacks against Chinese websites.

While the 2015 agreement was a significant first step, its impact is not easy to determine. Though there is some indication that the number of attacks has slowed, others have suggested that electronic masking enhancements have made it more difficult to detect intrusions. In addition to an array of divergent political and economic interests, the differing histories and cultural perspectives of the United States and China regarding national security and intellectual property rights complicate efforts to move forward in addressing this critical issue.

Satellite image of PLA Unit 61398.

What is the role of crossing borders in resolving this conflict? How can the cross-disciplinary focus of international studies help?

Questions

- What are the political motives of China and the United States in pursuing cyber espionage?

- What are the economic implications for the parties involved?

- Can bilateral diplomatic initiatives effectively "tame" or restrict abuses of technology?

- Do social and cultural factors play a role in understanding the reasons for engaging in cyber espionage?

- Can international agreements to restrict cyber espionage make a difference?

Sources: US Department of Justice, "U.S. Charges Five Chinese Military Hackers for Cyber Espionage Against U.S. Corporations and a Labor Organization for Commercial Advantage," May 19, 2014, https://www.justice.gov/opa/pr/us-charges-five-chinese-military-hackers-cyber-espionage-against-us-corporations-and-labor; Shannon Tiezzi, "China's Response to the US Cyber Espionage Charges," *Diplomat*, May 21, 2014, http://thediplomat.com/2014/05/chinas-response-to-the-us-cyber-espionage-charges; Scott Warren Harold, "The U.S.-China Cyber Agreement: A Good First Step," RAND Corporation, August 1, 2016, https://www.rand.org/blog/2016/08/the-us-china-cyber-agreement-a-good-first-step.html.

Map data ©2014 AutoNavi, Google.

ISIS atrocities on the State Department's official Twitter account in 2015, for example, stemmed from the inability to effectively counter the group's online propaganda.[33] In other instances, there are purposeful initiatives to penetrate social media by planting information—both real and fabricated—or otherwise controlling the narrative of online discussion. The goal is to influence public perceptions and build support for policy. This so-called digital diplomacy has allegedly been a part of US strategy in its struggle against the Assad regime and ISIS in Syria, as well as in a host of other situations.[34]

There is certainly no monopoly on the types of states that are poised to resort to these types of measures, and there are numerous examples that may demonstrate this point. Turkey's powerful president, Recep Erdogan, enlists an army of some 6,000 social media operatives to undermine opposition to his government. While blocking access to virtually all social media, North Korea regularly penetrates South Korean cyberspace through postings to its more popular sites. In its effort to offset Russian infringements, Ukraine has constituted an "i-army" with an especially active Twitter account to put forward its position. Mindful of its challenge to sway world opinion, Israel's government manages some 350 official online channels across a range of social media to complement its more covert undertakings.[35] Sometimes these activities can have unintended and potentially dangerous consequences. In late 2016, Pakistan and Israel experienced some tense Twitter exchanges following the posting of a story on a fake news site suggesting that Israel would consider a nuclear attack on Pakistan if Pakistani troops moved into Syria. Israel's Defense Minister was compelled to intervene through a tweet verifying the fictitious nature of the report to defuse the escalating controversy.[36]

Beyond these infiltrations and manipulations, computer hacking by both public and private actors has grown to the point where it can seriously impact political outcomes. It has spawned a new and highly disruptive form of terrorism—**cyberterrorism**—whereby groups or individuals unlawfully attack and manipulate Internet information to further their personal or their group's interests.[37] These include hacking websites, gaining access to classified information, and compromising the activities of governments and businesses. The activities of WikiLeaks brought considerable attention to these practices.

cyberterrorism the unlawful attack and manipulation of Internet information to further personal or a group's interests

WikiLeaks was launched in 2007 by Julian Assange as a nonprofit organization that brings tightly held information to the general public.[38] Accepting secret information from anonymous sources, WikiLeaks has brought to light many classified documents that raise questions about governmental actions and policies. In 2011, it published numerous classified US government documents on the wars in Iraq and Afghanistan that included embarrassing cables among US embassies around the world. More recently, it leaked almost 20,000 e-mails from the US Democratic National Committee, as well as more than 30,000 e-mails from Hillary Clinton's private e-mail server while she was US Secretary of State. It also released e-mails from the ruling party of Turkey, as well as a classified report from the EU on possible military intervention against "refugee boats."[39]

Edward Snowden, a contract employee for the National Security Agency (NSA), gained considerable notoriety when he divulged thousands of top-secret documents that detailed a pattern of domestic surveillance.[40] Snowden argued that he acted in defense of the public by fostering an awareness of the types of monitoring that the US government was engaged in. He released the first documents from Hong Kong and was granted asylum in Russia, where he continued to speak out against American policy. A movie chronicling his activities, directed by Oliver Stone, was released in September 2016.

The disclosures of WikiLeaks notwithstanding, the ongoing efforts of governments to hack both allies and adversaries speak directly to the ways in which technology may be used to circumvent established political borders. Hacking entered into the 2016 US presidential election when it was revealed that Russia was behind confidential leaks of information from the Democratic National Committee and other party officials. The US Intelligence Community distributed a declassified report following the election that found that the Russian government sought to influence the outcome of the election in favor of Donald Trump through fake news reports and the release of potentially damaging personal e-mails from Hillary Clinton and her staff.[41] Drawing on information gathered by the Central Intelligence Agency (CIA), the Federal Bureau of Investigation (FBI), and the National Security Agency (NSA), the report concluded that the highest levels of the Russian government and President Vladimir Putin specifically approved a campaign to not only discredit candidate Clinton but also cast doubt on the US democratic process.

While looking to bury the controversy, the Trump administration found itself deeply enmeshed as new allegations regarding relationships between campaign officials, some of whom had taken on key government positions, and the Russians continued to surface. Within the first few months of taking office, the president fired his national security adviser, who had considerable ties to Russia, and the FBI director who was in charge of investigating the case. The US Congress launched a number of fact-finding hearings, and a special counsel with formidable and independent powers was appointed to probe deeply into the allegations of collusion. This stunning turn of events threatened to derail the new administration before it was even fully in place, and undermined its ability to move forward in advancing its political agenda.[42]

As it turns out, Russia's efforts in the United States were just part of a comprehensive and more longstanding effort to influence the outcomes of elections and events through hacking and the political manipulation of information. Cyberattacks in eastern and central Europe have been common. Over the past decade, Russia has acted to shut down Internet service in Estonia in response to the removal of a Soviet World War II memorial, attacked the central election commission websites in Ukraine and Bulgaria, and compromised the Warsaw Stock Exchange and other sites across Poland.[43] Russian hackers have also been accused of stealing data from German government computers and damaging the computer system of a French television station. In the aftermath of the 2016 US election, French and German officials were particularly wary of possible Russian interference in upcoming elections. The release of sensitive e-mails from Emmanuel Macron's campaign just days before the May 2017 French presidential election added to suspicions of Russian meddling.[44]

Russia is not alone in the drive to undermine cybersecurity. China is an active player as well. It has hacked the networks of embassies and other government offices of an array of countries to acquire information that might assist in the pursuit of its foreign policy objectives. Germany, India, South Korea, and Taiwan have been among its targets. China gained considerable attention in 2015, when it compromised the US Office of Personnel Management and stole some 22 million employee records. China's military has also been suspected of stealing data on vital US weapons programs.[45]

With more than two dozen states believed to be engaged in offensive cyber operations, the United States has not remained on the sidelines. It disrupted Iran's nuclear operations in 2010 by launching a lethal computer virus (most likely with support from Israel) and continues to engage vigorously in these sorts of activities. In 2017, for example, the United States appeared to have a hand in the failed test launching of at least one North Korean ballistic missile and was suspected of more pervasive involvement as part of its ongoing effort to counter North Korea's nuclear program.[46] Even as the dangers stemming from these cyber activities have become increasingly apparent, there is little reason to expect any curtailment, as they have emerged as critical tools in the pursuit of political security.

Economic Borders

In terms of economic borders, technology has truly transformed the nature of global transactions. From a personal perspective, we can buy goods from the far corners of the world without leaving our homes and have them delivered to us, sometimes even the same day. How does this happen? Technology has promoted the mobility of production processes, facilitating the movement of goods around the world. Remember the journey taken by a T-shirt introduced in Chapter 1? The cotton it was made from was grown in Texas; it then traveled to China, where the T-shirt was made. The shirt was sold in the United States at a retail outlet and ended up in an African market.

Through interfaces that include e-mail, instant messaging, and real-time face-to-face interaction through Skype, FaceTime, Adobe Connect, or GoToMeeting, people can web conference while sitting at home in their pajamas. Moreover, large transnational corporations can export advanced workflow software technology to different places around the globe to enhance their productivity by allowing teams to work on the same project around the clock. The project manager software giant SAP has made a name for itself in this regard, offering a service that "keeps projects rolling around the clock, around the globe."[47]

One company that has been at the cutting edge of these initiatives is Infosys, an international technology services firm that was founded in 1981 and is headquartered in Bangalore, India.[48] Infosys is important because, as a leading firm in a growing IT sector in India, it provides resources for industry worldwide, thereby supporting Friedman's ten flatteners (especially outsourcing). Friedman, in fact, came upon his realization that the world is flat after visiting Bangalore, India's information technology (IT) hub and the world's number one outsourcing location.[49] These connections speak to another of Friedman's flatteners—the idea that business practices are integrated, such that people can work together simultaneously and respond quickly to change from wherever they might be. Infosys provides a broad range of technological services that include banking, big data, cloud, distributive trade, micro-commerce, sourcing, procurement, and customer services.[50]

Beyond its role in transforming business information and communication practices, technology is affecting the pattern of commercial exchange itself. Face-to-face connections between buyers and sellers are giving way to online interactions. Worldwide, e-commerce is projected to rise from 7.4 percent of retail sales in 2015 to 14.6 percent in 2020. The largest online retailer, Amazon, had net revenues of more than $226 billion in 2016. While around 40 percent came from sales in the United States, Amazon has a global reach.[51] Even China has gotten into the act, with more than 200,000 businesses using Amazon to sell directly to consumers. Products are sent to Amazon fulfillment centers in the United States and can be easily integrated into its network. China's own e-shopping giant, Alibaba, has also made great waves, with online transactions sales totaling $248 billion.[52]

Internet technology has also transformed global financing—in both positive and negative ways. Billions of dollars are now transmitted electronically 24 hours a day, facilitating the flow of capital around the world. This has had some important impacts in terms of making capital available quickly to those who are in most need of it, in dire times of disaster, or simply through regular remittances to families back home from convenience stores all over the world, via services like MoneyGram, Western Union, or PayPal and its popular mobile payment service, Venmo. It has even created a new currency: bitcoin, an open-source technology that allows direct transactions without the involvement of banks or other facilitators. All transactions are handled electronically through mobile phones or computer.[53]

Created in 2009 by an individual or group believed to be using a pseudonym, bitcoin remains shrouded in some mystery. Bitcoins themselves are purchased on online exchanges and are stored in a "digital wallet" that serves as a virtual bank account that may be used to purchase goods or for savings. They are not insured, but neither are they regulated or easy to trace. This allows for a considerable degree of anonymity and has raised concerns about bitcoins' use in promoting illicit economic activity. Bitcoins are not tied to any single country, may be bought or sold through different currencies, and are simple to use in settling international payments. A small group of core developers oversee the system, and new coins may be minted by advanced users through a rather complex process.[54]

Bitcoin is not without its shortcomings. Its value has fluctuated widely, sometimes due to intense speculative activity or without discernable reason, leaving some users with significantly diminished assets. Periodic reports of hacking into exchanges, in one instance resulting in the loss of coins worth $65 million, have added to uncertainty.[55] A ransomware attack that infected some 300,000 computers worldwide in May 2017 brought further scrutiny when the hackers demanded payments in bitcoin to restore access to data.[56] They even offered assistance to some victims on how to set up and access bitcoin accounts! Despite these questions and drawbacks, more and more businesses are participating in the bitcoin network. Many are drawn by the ease of usage and the ability to avoid the fees that are charged to credit card transactions.

Whether through bitcoin or other mediums of exchange, electronic transfers of money have been quite useful to those seeking to limit their exposure. Human and drug traffickers, counterfeiters, money launderers, corrupt politicians, and terrorists can move money quickly online and have it withdrawn from ATMs around the world with a very scant recorded trail back to its origins. Governments frequently detect these deeds by following the money. The activities of Somali refugees and expatriates living in Kenya, for example, have come under scrutiny in this regard for suspected transfers of cash to al-Qaida through an allied organization operating in the area, al-Shabaab.[57] This group claimed responsibility for the Westgate Mall attack in Nairobi, Kenya, in September 2013 that killed sixty-seven people.[58] Alternative remittance systems (ARS), or *hawala*, an Arabic term that means "transfer," allow money to move electronically through gray areas without being identified by source.

How are these contacts made? There is a dark side to the web that allows secretive and often illegal exchanges to take place. This space provides an arena to advertise markets for products and services that extend beyond mainstream channels and creates a world for nefarious activity. How much should web exchanges be monitored? If there are illegal behaviors being touted on the Dark Web, why do governments seemingly look the other way? The following pro/con debate addresses these concerns and considers whether the free exchange of goods and services should be monitored more closely.

Advances in technology have had differing and sometimes contradictory effects. While they have made it easier for some to evade regulation or detection, they have also created opportunities for greater oversight and transparency. Even as big data serve commercial purposes by clearly identifying prevailing market conditions, this access to massive amounts of information can be instrumental in uncovering financial irregularities that may exist in either private or public sectors. The development of more sophisticated data management techniques, auditing procedures, and even mobile applications can be used to combat fraud and foster greater accountability. For example, the World Bank's Integrity app enhances scrutiny of its projects and provides a platform to report suspected abnormalities.[59]

It is interesting to note that the technology that has fostered the development of an interconnected financial system allows for actions to disrupt these flows or otherwise punish those engaged in activities deemed contrary to acceptable norms. In 2014, for example, President Barack Obama signed an executive order to freeze the US-based assets of more than twenty Russian officials involved with the military intervention in Ukraine. The threat of US sanctions against Chinese individuals allegedly complicit in a series of cybercrimes

PRO/CON

SHOULD GOVERNMENTS CURB ANONYMOUS MARKETS TO FIGHT CRIME?

Pro

Eric Jardine

Research Fellow, Centre for International Governance Innovation. Written for *CQ Researcher*, January 2016.

Governments absolutely must curb illegal anonymous markets to help fight crime. There now are anonymous markets for almost everything you can think of. Want an underage family member raped? You can arrange it in an anonymous Dark Web marketplace for around $36,000. Have someone murdered? The cost is between $45,000 and $900,000, depending on the victim's stature and how you want the murder to unfold.

Hiring a network of malware-infected computers from around the world to launch a denial-of-service (DoS) attack against a government, business or not-for-profit website will cost you around $150 for a week-long barrage. Hacking into someone's email or social media accounts runs about $220. For roughly $550, you can conduct hacks involving espionage or break into a secure website.

Oh, you also can buy guns and drugs on the Dark Web.

Anyone with a computer and an Internet connection can get onto the Dark Web and find anonymous markets like these. You could. I could. A young child could do it without the knowledge of his or her parents.

All you have to do is download a browser like Tor, go to a hidden wiki website and start clicking links until you find the service you're after. With cryptocurrencies like bitcoin, even the final transaction is anonymous. Nefarious goods and services can be purchased without the buyer ever having to leave home.

The problem with anonymous markets is twofold. First, the social costs of the things that can be purchased anonymously online are huge. The cost of DoS attacks runs upwards of $920 million per day. And, obviously, the individual and social costs of rape and murder are incalculable.

The other problem with these markets is that, more than at any other time in history, they decouple motive and ability. Before the Dark Web, you might have wanted to hack someone's website or hire a hitman, but you likely wouldn't have succeeded because you didn't know how. Now you can do those things—with ease.

Anonymity and free speech are important for democracy, but there is a line that is easily crossed in the Dark Web. The list of nefarious activities that are for sale in anonymous markets, combined with the huge social costs

Con

Jim Harper

Senior Fellow, Cato Institute. Written for *CQ Researcher*, January 2016.

An "anonymous market" is certainly an exotic-sounding beast. Some ill must be afoot when people make no exchange of personal information and use untraceable payment systems to buy and sell.

On the other hand, millions of ordinary Americans engage in commerce like this every day. Buyers whose identities are unknown to merchants, restaurateurs or kiosk operators purchase products and services in exchange for cash and courtesies alone.

Yes, some payment systems can be used to trace the actors, and some sales are captured on camera. But it's the exception, not the rule, to gather a stable, useful set of identifiers from daily commerce.

Should governments curb the anonymous markets that exist at fast food restaurants, newsstands and curio shops? Doing so would certainly help fight crime. Thousands of thefts, violent crimes and illegal drug transactions could be thwarted and prosecuted if every real-world commercial transaction required video or digital records of participants.

But such a requirement would defy the sacred principle in American criminal justice that a person is innocent until proven guilty. Americans should be free from surveillance absent suspicion of wrongdoing. Ordinary people participating in ordinary commerce are not obliged to make records of their activities for the benefit of later investigation. The "Dark Web" epithet hardly provides a rationale for a different rule for online transactions.

The Internet allows people to transact more quickly and efficiently and across greater distances than conventional communications. But until recently, such online transactions had to use centralized and fully traceable payment systems. We also have discovered that much of our online life is subject to comprehensive government surveillance.

Exotic name aside, anonymous online markets can recreate the offline status quo. While some early users of the "Dark Web" have employed it for illegal and sometimes nefarious purposes, a broader public will begin to use such tools to transact as they wish, free of prying corporate advertisers and aggressively attentive governments. The vast bulk of future private

(Continued)

(Continued)

and the disjunction of motive and ability, suggests only one potential response to the proposition: Governments must curb anonymous markets to help fight crime.

commerce will be unremarkable, except for the burgeoning economic growth it produces.

There are more than prudential reasons to resist branding anonymous commerce as dangerous. Efforts to stamp it out would suppress good people's use of privacy-protecting technologies while having only a marginal impact on the bad.

Source: Marcia Clemmitt, "The Dark Web: Does Identity-Masking Technology Increase Cybercrime?" *CQ Researcher* 26 (January 15, 2016): 49–72. Retrieved from http://library.cqpress.com.prox.lib.ncsu.edu.

Where Do You Stand?

1. Is the anonymity provided by the Dark Web critical to the preservation of democratic values?

2. Should governments intervene more directly in regulating anonymous markets to curb harmful or illegal activities?

aimed at the theft of intellectual property produced the 2015 agreement (referenced earlier) to work on establishing guidelines for future behavior. In 2016, the United States froze the American-based assets of North Korean leader Kim Jong-un for human rights abuses that included killings, torture, and forced labor.[60]

Social and Cultural Borders

Social and cultural borders are crossed every day as social media sites create communities of individuals who spontaneously can come together. As noted at the beginning of the chapter, Facebook, which reached 2 billion members in mid-2017, has become a truly transformative force as it has provided people across the world with the opportunity to connect seamlessly, even in the face of physical or political barriers that might preclude other forms of interaction. Facebook is not alone, as illustrated in Figure 3.4, which identifies the world's leading social networks.[61] The second most popular social network is YouTube, at 1.5 billion users, followed closely by WhatsApp (which enables its users to text one another anywhere in the world without a fee) and Facebook Messenger, at 1.2 billion users each, and the Chinese online communication platforms WeChat and QQ, connecting 938 and 861 million users, respectively.

Social media platforms can be significant in elections, as they create an identity among political supporters. In his election bid in 2008, Barack Obama was one of the first major political candidates to rely heavily on social media outlets to grow his message and gather potential voters. This carried through to the 2016 US presidential race between Donald Trump and Hillary Clinton, which saw many harsh words traded in the "Twittersphere." President Trump has since continued to rely on Twitter as a way to engage directly with his constituents. The opportunity to reach and potentially mobilize massive numbers of people instantaneously adds considerably to the allure. Social media sites are now vital tools for sitting or aspiring leaders and have made a difference in shaping outcomes ranging from the election of Rodrigo Duterte as president of the Philippines to the Brexit vote in England.[62]

FIGURE 3.4 ● Most Famous Social Network Sites Worldwide as of August 2017, Ranked by Number of Active Users (in Millions)

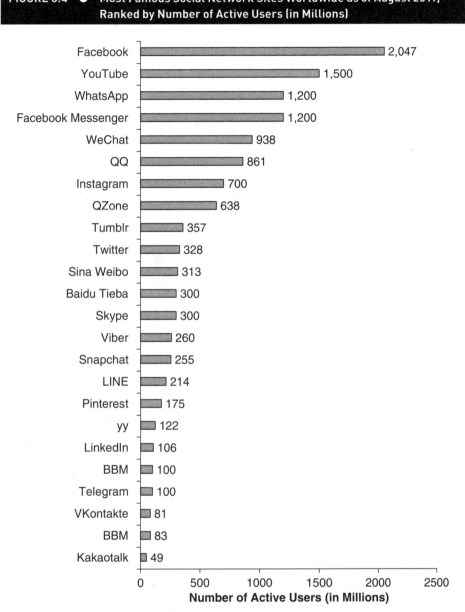

Site	Number of Active Users (in Millions)
Facebook	2,047
YouTube	1,500
WhatsApp	1,200
Facebook Messenger	1,200
WeChat	938
QQ	861
Instagram	700
QZone	638
Tumblr	357
Twitter	328
Sina Weibo	313
Baidu Tieba	300
Skype	300
Viber	260
Snapchat	255
LINE	214
Pinterest	175
yy	122
LinkedIn	106
BBM	100
Telegram	100
VKontakte	81
BBM	83
Kakaotalk	49

Source: "Most Famous Social Network Sites Worldwide as of August 2017, Ranked by Number of Active Users (in Millions)," *Statista*, August 2017, https://www.statista.com/statistics/272014/global-social-networks-ranked-by-number-of-users.

Critical to the growth of social media platforms has been **user-generated content (UGC)**. Sites such as YouTube connect people through both personal and informational videos. Users develop the content, and as a result, a home video can go viral in just a few hours as it is watched around the world. One of the first sites to offer shorter versions of shared videos was Vine, which offered six-second videos that looped. It created Vine stars as people watched their creations.[63] But Vine did not endure, even as the technology moved forward. Twitter, which owned Vine, discontinued the app in 2016. It has been replaced

user-generated content (UGC) social media content that originates through individual uploading of videos, blogs, pictures, tweets, or other types of expression

---

HOW YOU CAN CONNECT

You can "plug in" to developments shaping the world by . . .

• subscribing to a Twitter news feed to get real-time updates on breaking stories

• accessing your social media accounts to connect to those who may be directly involved in unfolding events

• generating your own content relating to particular programs or events you are attending

• surfing the web to acquire information that will further your awareness and understanding

---

with other video-sharing technologies, such as Facebook Live, which allows real-time streaming from its platform. Snapchat has also offered a new service with the introduction of its video-recording sunglasses, Spectacles, that can record ten-second video clips.[64]

These developments as they relate to cultural borders can be significant. On the one hand, they can offer ways to preserve traditional customs and values by documenting practices for future generations. Languages can be preserved and histories shared as groups seek to maintain their identities. Many groups have created webpages and Facebook sites to move this effort forward. For example, the indigenous people of New Zealand, the Maori, have a website (maori.com) that is devoted to promoting their culture, businesses, and tourism.

On the other hand, technological innovation and communication across borders can bring new styles of food, dress, music, and sports that become universal as opposed to specific to a state, nation, or people. World music, global hip-hop, and fashion trends that draw on artisanal skills from around the globe are examples of cultural identity changing in response to technological innovation that allows the selling of ideas, images, and goods readily across existing borders. The nonprofit organization TED (Technology, Entertainment, Design) supports a series of talks—TED Talks—that are short observations on "ideas worth spreading." They are currently translated into 114 languages by more than 27,000 volunteers, with a total of 113,164 translations and counting.[65] Talk about sharing ideas with the world!

New languages can even emerge as our connections grow. Language can adapt through interactions, such as the popularity of Spanglish—a cross between English and Spanish that is spoken in many parts of the Spanish- and English-speaking world today. Even texting and tweeting have created a new universal language of acronyms and emoticons such as LOL, TTYL, and :) that people around the world are using daily. You may even have your own Bitmoji, an individually tailored emoji that allows you to personalize your social media communications.

Advanced technology can also affect our ability to address significant social and humanitarian challenges that confront us. The emergence of "precision agriculture" in the fight against hunger is a case in point. The use of ultra-small nanoparticles to release pesticides and nanosensors to adjust moisture levels in the soil is a particularly promising innovation designed to increase crop yields while limiting environmental damage.[66] Nanotechnology is also seen as an increasingly important tool in developing new types of fuels that minimize carbon emissions and contribute to the fight against climate change.[67] Meanwhile, breakthroughs in the field of artificial intelligence and other technologies are opening up possibilities for improvements in health care, education, resource utilization, and other areas that would promote more inclusive and sustainable development.[68]

WHAT CAN YOU DO WITH INTERNATIONAL STUDIES?

Technology 24/7

John McGregor, International Studies Graduate Student and Soccer Blogger

New technology has completely changed the way I operate both inside and outside the classroom. My personal life and education are driven by these technological advances. It is the best way to keep in contact with friends and family now spread out all over the globe. In school, I use the Internet to conduct research and to communicate with my professors. While I still use the library for research, I usually identify the material I need online, even if I review or acquire it through the library. All my assignments are prepared on the computer, and are usually sent directly to my professors online. I have my computer or iPad with me for note-taking in all my classes.

Thanks to developments in new media, I obtain roughly 90 percent of my local, national, and international news from Twitter. It gives me the opportunity to follow an infinite number of journalists and news publications that deliver news and opinions constantly on a 24-hour cycle. The brevity of Twitter allows me to consume a large amount of news very quickly, while almost every post features a link that leads to a more in-depth story. The ability to tailor my news experience in a very personalized way allows me to pick sources that I know to be credible. As someone who is constantly on the go and relying on a mobile device, there is no more efficient way to stay informed.

I rely on my iPhone more than any piece of technology that I currently own. It plays a vital role in my daily routine, from supplying the alarm that wakes me to allowing me to check multiple e-mail accounts in seconds. It also lets me check Twitter to see what has been going in the world over the few hours I slept, all while downloading up-to-the minute weather reports that help me plan my day. It lets me stay in touch with friends through text messaging, video conferencing, and old-fashioned phone conversations. The iPhone certainly plays a vital role in my life, and its absence would greatly alter how I live on a day-to-day basis.

The biggest way in which technology has led me across international borders is through my love of soccer. The Internet and social media have allowed me not only to connect to fans all over the world, but to interact directly with the journalists and media sources dedicated to covering the sport. As someone who writes about soccer, it is an invaluable resource to be able to directly communicate with some of the best writers in the industry, who all have a significant presence on social media. This resource has increased both my knowledge of and love for the sport, while continuing to make me a better writer.

Personal photo by John McGregor.

Then again, sometimes all it takes is a single individual with a sense of purpose to make a profound difference. This was the case for Lara Setrakian, a former news correspondent who was moved by the ravages of the Syrian refugee crisis. With the support of the Doris Duke Charitable Foundation, she launched the Syria Deeply website in 2012 to heighten awareness of the tragedy by highlighting individual cases. She introduced her fourth single-issue website venture in 2016, a more expansive Refugees Deeply, which features original content posted by refugees themselves.[69]

A Final Thought on Technology Prior to the Journey

New technologies have changed how we live and interact with one another. Despite the technological divide, the spread of the Internet and satellite communications has brought the world together. The rapid way in which information can be shared globally gives states access to the same information and allows them to easily share their needs and concerns. When disaster strikes, the world can be there as people are called upon to text their donations for relief efforts.

Even some of the technology corporations that we have met here have come together to help people. Google.org, the philanthropy wing of Google, has given UNICEF a $1 million grant to respond to the Zika virus crisis and sent Google engineers to help map outbreaks and anticipate where new ones may occur.[70] In response to the refugee crisis, Google partnered with other organizations in the field to build an online information hub, develop translation cards, and install low-cost Wi-Fi in refugee camps.[71] Infosys has a philanthropic mission beyond IT through the Infosys Foundation, which promotes social responsibility and seeks to help the poorest of the poor in India through health care, education, and rural development.[72] The Bill and Melinda Gates Foundation has been a leader in social responsibility, most notably in the areas of global health and development. It is interesting to note the number of individuals with connections to the technology sector who rank among the leaders in American philanthropy (see Figure 3.5). And our friend Nathan, whom we met in Chapter 1, uses these new technologies to invest in people around the world from the comfort of his couch.

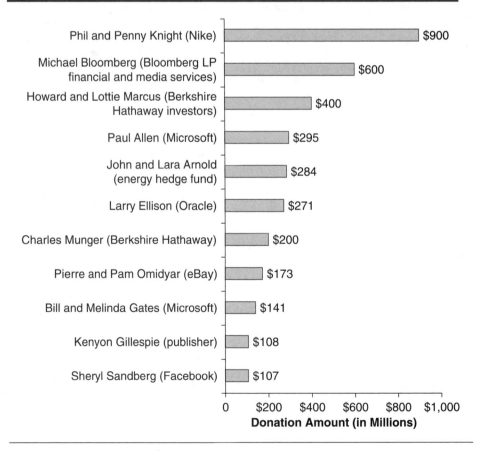

FIGURE 3.5 ● Leading Donors in the United States, 2016 (in Millions of Dollars)

Source: "The 2017 Philanthropy 50," *The Chronicle of Philanthropy*, Vol. 29, Issue 4, February 2017, pp. 8–21.

The extent to which we can use technology to promote greater cooperation will depend on our understanding of the divisions that exist and the challenges we face. The task is complicated by the borders that continue to separate us. The remainder of this book will provide you with a road map to traverse the globe across these political, economic, social, and cultural borders. Pack your bags—the course has been set—and let the journey begin!

Key Concepts

big data 58	digital divide 52	short message service (SMS) 55
cloud computing 58	digitization 51	user-generated content (UGC) 69
cyberterrorism 63	Industrial Revolution 53	
digital age 52	information revolution 52	

To Learn More

Books and Other Print Media

Aravind Adiga, *White Tiger* (New York: Free Press, 2008).

Aravind Adiga's debut novel, *White Tiger*, is about the letters from an Indian call center worker, Balram, to the Chinese prime minister in advance of an upcoming state visit. Balram wants the prime minister to know his story and how Indian society has been transformed by technological innovation.

Thomas L. Friedman, *The World Is Flat 3.0: A Brief History of the Twenty-first Century* (New York: Farrar, Strauss, and Giroux, 2007).

Thomas Friedman analyzes ten forces that have contributed to the deepening globalization of the world and have created new opportunities for China, India, and other emerging countries.

Walter Isaacson, *The Innovators: How a Group of Hackers, Geniuses and Geeks Created the Digital Revolution* (New York: Simon & Schuster, 2014).

Isaacson follows his work on Steve Jobs with a look at the innovators who created the digital revolution; he provides insights into how their minds work and what makes them so creative.

Walter Isaacson, *Steve Jobs* (New York: Simon & Schuster, 2011).

Walter Isaacson presents an intriguing biography of Steve Jobs, one of the most important pioneers in the computer industry, particularly in the development of devices such as the iPhone.

Thomas Rid, *Cyber War Will Not Take Place* (London: Oxford University Press, 2013).

This book explores the argument that cyber war is coming, suggesting that there is a real threat, but that it is less violent and more likely in the areas of espionage, sabotage, and subversion.

Clive Thompson, *Smarter Than You Think: How Technology Is Changing Our Minds for the Better* (New York: Penguin, 2013).

Clive Thompson challenges the fear of technology, profiling people who are using technology to change their lives and those of others in a positive way.

Daniel Trottier and Christian Fuchs (eds.), *Social Media, Politics and the State: Protests, Revolutions, Riots, Crime and Policing in the Age of Facebook, Twitter and YouTube* (New York: Routledge, 2015).

The essays in the volume explore the complex political role of social media platforms in different parts of the world as both facilitators of state power and as tools for those who seek to undermine that power.

Ashlee Vance, *Elon Musk: Tesla, SpaceX, and the Quest for a Fantastic Future.* (New York: Harper Collins, 2015).

This is a profile of Elon Musk, the well-known entrepreneur behind such innovations as SpaceX, Tesla, and SolarCity.

Paul Vigna and Michael J. Casey, *The Age of Cryptocurrency: How Bitcoin and the Blockchain Are Challenging the Global Economic Order* (New York: St. Martin's Press, 2016).

This book provides an intriguing look into the digital currency world of bitcoin. It suggests a growing role for digital currencies across the global economy, challenging more traditional modes of financial exchange.

Websites

CNN Tech, www.cnn.com/TECH/index.html

CNN offers updates on technology trends around the world today. Regular features, updated weekly, focus on the web, gadgets and gaming, mobile news, social media, and technology innovation.

Computer History Museum, www.computerhistory.org

This website is the home of the Computer History Museum, located in Mountain View, California, in Silicon Valley, where the information revolution began. It provides a history of the computer as well as the people who were the pioneers of the industry.

Facebook, www.facebook.com; LinkedIn, www.linkedin.com; Instagram, www.instagram.com; Snapchat, www.snapchat.com; and Twitter www.twitter.com

These are major social networking sites, at least some of which you have probably already joined!

Popular Science, www.popsci.com

Popular Science magazine has been documenting technology news since its inception in 1872. Today it offers insight into the latest technologies and their applications.

Wired, www.wired.com

This is the online version of the print magazine *Wired*, which covers cutting-edge technologies and frequently explores their social, cultural, political, and economic implications.

Videos

Actually, the World Isn't Flat (2012), http://www.ted.com/talks/pankaj_ghemawat_actually_the_world_isn_t_flat

Drawing on his book *World 3.0*, Pankaj Ghemawat addresses the role of hard data as it pertains to globalization and the "flattening" of the world through technology.

Burma VJ: Reporting from a Closed Country (2008)

This documentary about the 2007 protests against the military junta in Burma (Myanmar) centers around the role of video journalists and features footage shot on handheld cameras, some of which was smuggled out of the country.

Disconnect (2013)

This popular movie explores the conflict that can arise in the interface between real life and the digital age through three story lines.

The Fifth Estate (2013)

This movie tells the WikiLeaks story, with its founder Julian Assange portrayed by Benedict Cumberbatch.

Four Principles for the Open World (2012), www.ted.com/talks/don_tapscott_four_principles_for_the_open_world_1.html

Canadian businessman and author Don Tapscott discusses how the Internet is transforming the world into a more open and transparent society and touches on four principles to guide this process.

Her (2013)

This movie, starring Joaquin Phoenix, explores one man's relationship with an operating system that is designed to serve his every need, voiced by Scarlett Johansson.

I Lost My Job (2012)

This film addresses the growing phenomenon of technological unemployment, or when manual labor is displaced by new machines and computers, and its economic and social effects.

Internet Rising (2011), http://internetrising.net

This documentary explores the connections between technology and humans and addresses some of humanity's greatest questions, including our search for meaning and mindfulness.

Jobs (2013)

This movie tells Steve Jobs's story, with Ashton Kutcher starring in the lead role.

Snowden (2016)

Noted filmmaker Oliver Stone tells the story of Edward Snowden, a former contract worker with the National Security Agency (NSA) who revealed the agency's use of illegal surveillance techniques. He subsequently had to seek asylum in Russia to avoid prosecution for espionage.

The Social Network (2010)

A popular and award-winning movie, *The Social Network* tells the story of Mark Zuckerberg's rise from Harvard dropout to creator of the world's most powerful social network—Facebook.

4

Searching for Security

The Political World

Connectivity, not sovereignty, has become the organizing principle of the human species.

—Parag Khanna, geopolitical expert and best-selling author, 2016[1]

Learning Objectives

After studying this chapter, you will be able to do the following:

- Define the field of political science.

- Define the modern political system of states and explain its origins.

- Identify the main approaches to international politics and their central ideas.

- Explain the concept of balance of power.

- Describe the main events of the Cold War and explain their importance.

- Describe the main events of the post–Cold War era and explain their importance.

The search for security is driven by many factors, from the fear of war and terrorist attacks to the more personal need to lock our doors at night. Political entities have provided the structures to address these concerns, but they are no longer able to do it alone. The political borders that we have come to rely on may not be the best framework for responding to the demands of modern society—particularly when some of the forces that threaten our physical security do not stop at the border, such as communicable diseases, tainted waters, or politically inspired violence.

Globally acclaimed geostrategist Parag Khanna puts forth an interesting proposition as he questions the role of political borders in today's world. He believes that patterns of connectivity, which routinely transcend national boundaries, are far more critical to address the challenges that will affect our future security. He even goes so far as to suggest that, as the primary catalysts for this transnational connectivity, emerging megacities across the globe will continue to grow in terms of their importance and autonomy. It is political boundaries, however, that have had an enduring impact on the way in which the global arena operates. While there has been great talk in the era of globalization that nation-states are on the way out, to paraphrase Mark Twain, rumors of their death are greatly exaggerated.

The gathering of the twenty-nine member states of the North Atlantic Treaty Organization (NATO) for their 2016 summit in Warsaw tells us that the story remains largely the same. NATO's membership has continued to expand, and its mandate has extended to issues and conflicts beyond its historic reach, such as cyber and electronic warfare and the complexities of political turmoil in the Middle East. The underlying purpose of this military alliance, however, remains firmly in place—to protect the territorial integrity and security of its members.

The summit's official communique reiterates this core mission: "To protect and defend our indivisible security and our common values, the Alliance must and will continue fulfilling effectively all three core tasks set out in the Strategic Concept: collective defence, crisis management, and cooperative security. These tasks remain fully relevant, are complementary, and contribute to safeguarding the freedom and security of all Allies."[2] Advancing this agenda will not be easy. Protecting political borders continues to define the work of NATO and other regional and international bodies, but conflicts today are not simply confined by checkpoints, walls, or fences. The search for security has been a shaky one, marked by tensions and struggles within a global political order that has undergone significant transformations over time.

NATO security officials inspect the site of a powerful suicide attack in Kabul, Afghanistan, on May 31, 2017. At least 80 people were killed, and more than 350 were wounded after the explosion.

Haroon Sabawoon/Anadolu Agency/Getty Images.

Defining Political Borders:
The Origins of the Modern State System

The study of politics dates back to the writings of the earliest philosophers. Both Plato and his student Aristotle considered many of the fundamental questions that had to be addressed by groups of people as they sought to govern themselves and to provide for their safety in the fourth century BCE. Some of the earliest forms of governance, kingdoms and city-states, were determined by their leaders. How they related to one another was critical and based on an assessment of relative power.

The Athenian general and historian Thucydides is often considered one of the first proponents of power politics. He argues in *The History of the Peloponnesian War*, written in 431 BCE, that leaders who ignore the pursuit of power invite conflict.[3] His Melian dialogue is famous for elucidating this notion, as it captures the Athenians' view that the people of Melos, the Melians, could not remain neutral in the face of conflict. When the Melians refused to take up arms, the Athenians attacked without mercy.

Since these earliest days, states have been prone to violence. They have often resorted to war to settle conflicts where a more peaceful resolution is not readily apparent. Disputes over land and resources have been particularly common. These clashes can be traced, in part, to the importance of territorial control in determining the relative status and positioning of states and their capacity to protect their sovereign rights and interests. Hopes for revenge or reversing the outcome of previous struggles have also fanned the fires of hatred between peoples and added to the longevity of their conflicts. The artificial nature of many political borders has contributed further to this pattern. It has not been uncommon for rival ethnic, religious, or tribal groups to be thrown together politically within a designated space. Beyond the particular issues that may divide states from one another or undermine their ability to adhere internally, states exist within a broader political environment that affects their behaviors and activities.

imperial system a political organization in which one government is dominant over most of the world with which it has contact

feudal system a political organization in which loyalty and political obligations take precedence over political boundaries

anarchic system of states an organization of political units that are relatively cohesive but with no higher government above them

Joseph Nye identifies three forms of world politics that have emerged over time: an **imperial system**, a **feudal system**, and an **anarchic system of states**.[4] Imperial systems are characterized by the domination of a single power. Examples include the Roman Empire, Spain in the sixteenth century, France in the seventeenth century, and the British Empire in the nineteenth century (see Map 4.1). Other examples include ancient empires that were more regional in scope, such as those of the Aztecs, Incas, and Egyptians, who sought to control their contiguous environments.

A second way in which international political borders have been delineated is through feudal systems. Here, political loyalties were based on allegiance not to the land but to the landowner or local lord. In some cases, this obligation might have even been to a more distant ruler or religious leader. Such a system was particularly common after the collapse of the Roman Empire. As Nye suggests, these political ties did the following:

> They were determined to a large extent by what happened to one's superiors. If a ruler married, an area and its people might find their obligations rearranged as part of a wedding dowry. Townspeople born French might suddenly find themselves made Flemish or even English.[5]

The third form of political borders that Nye distinguishes is an anarchic system of states. This is a system composed of political units operating in an environment with no higher central authority. The city-states of Greece were organized in this way. The international political system we are familiar with today operates along these very same lines. The Treaty of Westphalia, which ended the Thirty Years' War (1618–1648) in Europe, is generally regarded as the origin of this system. This war was primarily a religious conflict that divided combatants along Protestant and Catholic lines. Its outcome would change the political landscape of the area.

MAP 4.1   ●   The Roman Empire: An Example of the Imperial System

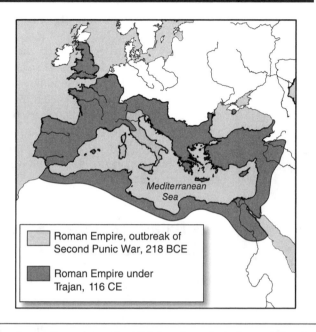

Mediterranean
Sea

Roman Empire, outbreak of
Second Punic War, 218 BCE

Roman Empire under
Trajan, 116 CE

Source: Henry R. Nau, *Perspectives on International Relations: Power, Institutions, and Ideas*, 3rd ed. (Washington, DC: CQ Press, 2012), 77.

The writings of Niccolo Machiavelli in the early 1500s captured the creation of the anarchic system of states quite well. Machiavelli was an official in Florence serving under the rule of Piero Soderini. When the Medici family ousted Soderini and came to power, Machiavelli was exiled to the countryside, where he would write his most famous work—*The Prince*. A man of the city relegated to farm life, Machiavelli sought to gain favor with the new rulers and get his job back. He put forward a series of recommendations and strategies for the leaders of the day, princes, to preserve their positions of power. His message was clear and reflected the conventional wisdom of the time—that the end justified the means and that all actions were acceptable in pursuing the desired goal. His advice to leaders was that it is better to be feared than loved. Machiavelli's assessment can be characterized as an early conceptualization of **realism**, a perspective that many believe best captures the essence of international politics since the days of ancient Greece. Realism argues that power is the most critical element in understanding the character of international relations. The state is the most powerful actor in the international system, and its pursuit of power drives its choices in relation to other states. The reliance on more traditional notions of power politics and alliances as a way to promote security agendas has persisted, even though significant changes to the international system have occurred.

The Westphalian accords in 1648 placed states at the center of a new European order. They defined states on the basis of territory and populations within their boundaries, the existence of a system of government, and the recognition of other governments. The system revolved largely around the notion of **sovereignty**, which provided states with the right to self-determination—to attend to their own affairs without the interference of others outside their borders. The signatories thought that this system would provide a solid basis for a relatively stable order. In practice, however, it was difficult to realize, as individual states and leaders had their own agendas.

realism a political philosophy that sees the struggle for power and the potential for conflict as a necessary evil in the pursuit of national interest

sovereignty the right of states to self-determination—to attend to their own affairs without being subjected to the unwanted interference of others

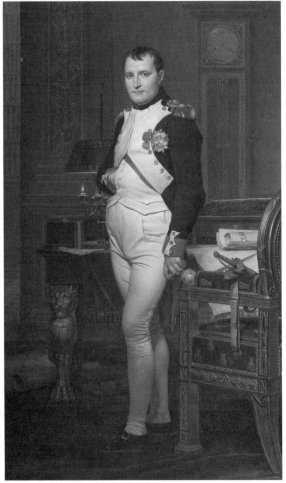

Wikipedia Commons.

A portrait of Napoleon by Jacques-Louis David.

nationalism a commitment to and support of the nation's interests

Napoleon is a good example of such a leader; he sought to extend France's reach as the nineteenth century began, posing a threat to the Westphalian system. He went too far in his quest for domination and was ultimately defeated by a coalition of Austria-Hungary, Britain, the Netherlands, Prussia, Russia, and Spain. The Napoleonic challenge revealed the fragile nature of this new order. It also illuminated the character of the system as it would evolve over the next 200 years. **Nationalism**—the commitment to and support of the nation's interests—emerged as a significant force. It brought diverse people together in pursuit of a common purpose, but also created rifts between them that provided the rationale for war.

The Balance of Power System: Its Failures and the Outbreak of War

Degrees of power would define the world order that emerged. Europe had come to dominate the international system, owing largely to the technological advances that had spurred the Industrial Revolution and the expansion of its colonial empires. Driven by the search for new riches and religious zeal, Spain and Portugal had been the first to expand outward, as they colonized the Americas prior to the mid-1700s. The British, Germans, Dutch, and French constituted the second wave, which lasted from about 1750 to 1870. Initially, these colonists went forth in pursuit of trade and markets. To continue growing, the industrial success that defined Germany and Great Britain at the beginning of the nineteenth century required raw materials and new markets. The less charted territories of Africa and Asia provided new ground. After 1870, economic imperatives drove the exploitation of colonies.

While political control in the first two waves of colonialism had not been an overriding objective, it gained prominence in the latter part of the nineteenth century as the means to assure cooperation. This was certainly the case with Great Britain's colonial empire, which encompassed large parts of the Indian subcontinent, Africa, and Southeast Asia. The French

IN THEIR OWN WORDS
NICCOLO MACHIAVELLI

If you have a choice, to be feared is much safer than to be loved. For it is a good general rule about men that they are ungrateful, fickle, liars and deceivers, fearful of danger, and greedy for gain. While you serve their welfare, they are all yours, offering their blood, their belongings, their lives, and their children's lives, as we noted previously—so long as the danger is remote.

But when the danger is close at hand, they turn against you. Then, any prince who has relied on their words and has made no other preparations will come to grief; because friendships that are bought at a price, and not with greatness and nobility of soul, may be paid for but they are not acquired, and they cannot be used in time of need.[6]

were actively engaged in colonial expansion in Africa and Southeast Asia. Italy, Germany, and Belgium also joined the scramble for territory during this period. Colonial expansion wreaked havoc on the African continent, as the European intruders uprooted indigenous groups and native cultures. The imperialist nations ignored African cultural identities in their pursuit of economic gain. Among the many legacies of colonialism are political borders that do not necessarily correspond to existing cultural borders. These colonial borders cut across land occupied by existing tribes, ethnic groups, and nations.

Preserving peace among the Europeans as they jockeyed for colonial empires required the maintenance of a fragile **balance of power**. Relying on transitory alliances to steady relationships, nation-states were able to prevent conflict while minimally cooperating with one another. Two major alliances emerged from these arrangements—the Triple Alliance formed by Italy, Germany, and Austria-Hungary in 1882, and the Triple Entente formed in 1907 by France, Great Britain, and Russia. These alliances solidified the political order but undermined the flexibility states needed to assure peace. Increasingly, states also wanted more power for themselves, and this desire outweighed their need to cooperate with others. No longer was it simply enough for one alliance to balance another.

balance of power a system of states that relies on shifting alliances to balance relationships and prevent conflict

The result was that the balance of power that had stabilized the international system began to erode. While the Austro-Hungarians sought to maintain their influence, particularly in the Balkans, other countries began chipping away at their power. The Germans were intent on expanding their power and prestige, sparking a naval arms race with Britain in the early part of the twentieth century. The French sought revenge for their 1871 defeat in the Franco-Prussian War, and Russia wanted a show of force to offset perceptions that it had lost its ability to exert influence in the international arena.[7] In all of these instances, cooperation as a means to peaceful relationships lost credibility. The final blow came on June 28, 1914, with the assassination of Archduke Franz Ferdinand, the heir to the Austro-Hungarian throne, by a Serbian nationalist. Within a month, the first full-scale world war had broken out.[8]

The discipline of **political science** emerged around this time, as scholars tried to be more systematic in their understanding of the forces that were driving state interests. Up until the late 1800s, political studies were closely tied to history and, to some extent, economics. The founding of the American Political Science Association in 1903 was a turning point in the development of the current field. The objective was to encourage research that would apply a more rigorous standard to understanding political behavior.

political science the systematic study of political behavior institutionalized at the turn of the twentieth century

Intellectually, new perspectives were gaining traction as well. While the power politics notion was validated by historical experience, there was growing support for a more benign view of the world. In contrast to realism and its emphasis on conflict, **liberalism** stemmed from the democratic tradition, emphasizing the potential for cooperation among states. This notion would greatly inform US president Woodrow Wilson, himself a political scientist with a PhD from Johns Hopkins University, as he contemplated the turmoil in Europe.

liberalism political philosophy from the democratic tradition that emphasizes the potential for cooperation among states

Wilson entered World War I cautiously and only after US interests were directly under attack. Guided by the liberal view that placed a high value on the extension of democracy and cooperation, Wilson did not believe that war was the best method to resolve conflict. He justified the US entry into the conflict by arguing it would be "the war to end all wars." He outlined his intentions in his "Fourteen Points" speech to Congress in 1917. In this address, Wilson argued for a new world order. He saw strong possibilities for the emergence of progressive leaders in the postwar era who would work together toward peace. This approach came to be known as **idealism**—some would even call it utopianism—and it represented a vision that would be difficult to attain. Idealism assumed that cooperation would triumph over conflict. Enlightened leaders would jointly establish a world order defined by group effort as opposed to individual interest. The "In Their Own Words" excerpt from President Wilson's speech delineates his vision for a new kind of cooperation.

idealism a political philosophy that emphasizes cooperation to establish a peaceful world order

IN THEIR OWN WORDS
WOODROW WILSON

It will be our wish and purpose that the processes of peace, when they are begun, shall be absolutely open and that they shall involve and permit henceforth no secret understandings of any kind. The day of conquest and aggrandizement is gone by and so is also the day of secret covenants entered into in the interest of particular governments and likely at some unlooked-for moment to upset the peace of the world. It is this happy fact, now clear to the view of every public man whose thoughts do not still linger in an age that is dead and gone, which makes it possible for every nation whose purposes are consistent with justice and the peace of the world to avow now or at any other time the objects it has in view.[9]

Central to Wilson's utopian idealism was the concept of collective security. Each state would reduce its military preparedness with the understanding that all would act together in the event of an attack against any one state. Education and cross-cultural understanding would be emphasized as a way of gaining trust. Peaceful coexistence and cooperation would be encouraged through an institutionalized international organization, the League of Nations.

Unfortunately, Wilson's plan came up short. The Treaty of Versailles that ended the war created the League of Nations, but an isolationist US Senate, wary of undertaking new international commitments, would not ratify it. The failure of the United States to join was quite a blow to its creator, President Wilson, and undermined the league's power from the start. Moreover, the notion of cooperation that framed the ideal world that Wilson envisioned was not realized. Wilson had hoped for a liberal order in which peace among states prevailed, reliant on the innate spirit of people to cooperate. International institutions would maintain that peace, and individual states would engage through those institutional mechanisms.

President Woodrow Wilson.

These assumptions proved naive, as the uneasy peace was jeopardized by the Russian Revolution, which overthrew the tsarist regime and marked the emergence of a communist Union of Soviet Socialist Republics (generally referred to as either the USSR or the Soviet Union) in the early 1920s. It bent further under the weight of global financial instability following the US stock market crash of 1929 and the aggressive military expansion of Germany and Japan. Tensions escalated on multiple fronts, threatening the sovereignty of many countries and the very existence of Jews and other groups. The peace shattered completely with the outbreak of World War II in 1939.

In the early days of World War II, the United States chose to operate on the sidelines. It eventually authorized the transfer of arms and other forms of military aid under the Lend-Lease Act, but entered the fray only directly following the Japanese attack on US forces and facilities at Pearl Harbor, Hawaii, in December 1941. The United States joined its European allies and its rival, the Soviet Union, to defeat a common German enemy as well as Japan and Italy. The war confronted the United States with a series of new security challenges that required significant changes in its previous isolationist philosophy and policy.

By the time the war was over, the positioning of states had changed dramatically. States that had previously dominated the anarchic system lay in financial, political, and physical ruin. The war had taken its toll. Atomic bombs dropped on Hiroshima and Nagasaki devastated Japan; Germany was divided into two countries, East Germany and West Germany; and many key European cities had been leveled by air strikes. The world needed new leadership in order to move beyond the wreckage. The United States had not suffered any physical destruction and emerged from the war as the world's only creditor country. A considerable segment of the US population believed that the future security of the country rested on its willingness and ability to play a major role in restructuring the pattern of international relations. Despite lingering opposition from isolationists who questioned the advisability of this strategy, the United States took on the challenge.

American tanks and troops at Checkpoint Charlie, a crossing point in the Berlin Wall between the American and Soviet sectors of the city at the junction of Friedrichstrasse, Zimmerstrasse, and Mauerstrasse, February 1961.

The United States assumed this responsibility somewhat reluctantly but did not take it lightly. The decision to return to a more insular posture after World War I had been a failure. The geopolitical strategies that had fueled the fires of many countries in their pursuit of power were now clear. The United States hoped to soften these inclinations with a cooperative spirit that might provide for a lasting peace. In short, it intended to move forward with a blend of realist and idealist approaches.

The creation of the United Nations (UN) in 1945 reflected this thinking. The victors of World War II crafted the organization to restore a sense of collective responsibility for maintaining the peace. Power politics was still important, however, necessitating the need to grant special privileges and authority to a Security Council of five designated Great Powers (China, France, the Soviet Union, the United Kingdom, and the United States) to assure their participation. Unlike the League of Nations, the UN attracted a wide range of eligible states to its ranks by limiting its mandate and its ability to take definitive action without the unanimous consent of its strongest members. This veto power of the "Big Five," as the permanent members of the Security Council came to be called, seriously undermined the body's overall effectiveness in the years ahead. The first ten years of the organization were marred by a rivalry between the United States and the Soviet Union that played out in the Security Council, preventing effective action.

During this time, realists honed their views of state relationships to reflect the divisions of the day. Political scientist Hans Morgenthau defined the political realism that characterized the emerging dynamics of the post–World War II period in his 1948 treatise, *Power among Nations: The Struggle for Power and Peace*. Morgenthau's views connected Machiavelli's and Thucydides's understandings of power and impulse with the modern world. The Great Powers' failure to create a cooperative international environment after World War II required a reevaluation of the motivations that guided state interaction.[10] Ultimately, individual states returned to the pursuit of power as a guiding principle.

The Cold War

Even as the United States was poised to assume leadership of the world, it was forced to confront the emerging power of its wartime ally, the Soviet Union. The Soviets had broad political aspirations and were unwilling to relinquish power to support the collective security interests of the rest of the world. Two relatively equal centers of power, the United States and the Soviet Union, became the dominant players in a **bipolar** world. As both sides recognized the need to avoid the potentially dire consequences of a heated or direct military confrontation, this period became known as the Cold War era. Each side expressed its animosity toward one another in low-intensity conflicts around the globe.

The Cold War was both an ideological struggle between economic and philosophical ideas (capitalism vs. communism) and a political competition where both sides sought to establish alliances that would extend their influence across the world. For its part, the United States pursued a strategy that came to be known as **containment**. Diplomat George Kennan explained it as a defensive strategy designed to limit Soviet efforts to extend their influence. The US leadership saw it as the best way to preserve a global balance of power. The Truman Doctrine, a policy put forth by US president Harry Truman to support Greece and Turkey economically and militarily against Soviet aggression, grew out of this idea and would be extended many times over.

The Soviet Union put forward its policies in a similar fashion as it expanded into Eastern Europe. Each side viewed the intentions of the other with considerable distrust and suspicion. The first major confrontation came in the crisis over a divided Berlin in 1948. Soviet leader Joseph Stalin sought to isolate the US zone of western Berlin through a blockade. The United States responded with a massive airlift in 1949, forcing the Soviets to lift their siege of the city.

Initially, the Cold War was mainly a European phenomenon, with the postwar division of Germany capturing the essence of the superpower rivalry. The Berlin Wall, built in 1961 to separate East Berlin from West Berlin, served as its most poignant symbol. The United States sought to both promote and protect the military security of its allies through NATO; the Soviets put forward an equivalent strategy by creating the Warsaw Treaty Organization (WTO), more commonly referred to as the Warsaw Pact.

In 1949, the establishment of a communist government in China under the leadership of Mao Zedong extended the struggle. With the support of the Soviet Union, China began to emerge as a power in its own right, as evidenced by its involvement in the Korean War in 1950. Under the auspices of the UN, the United States intervened in that conflict, ending a military and political stalemate. Meanwhile, the Russians and the Chinese soon found themselves embroiled in a rivalry of their own. They split by the early 1960s over ideological differences. To counter communist efforts across Asia, the United States moved to cement ties with Japan, its former enemy.

The basic intent of the two superpowers remained consistent throughout the Cold War era (1945–1989). Different phases periodically changed the way the game was played. The stakes were high as the specter of a mushroom-shaped cloud, embodying the risk of a nuclear confrontation, loomed. At times, Soviet efforts to consolidate and maintain power in relation to their East European partners took on a distinctively military character. In November 1956, Soviet forces invaded Hungary to counter what had become a spontaneous revolt against the Soviet-dominated government. Similarly, Soviet troops rolled into Czechoslovakia in August 1968 to bring the country back into line following the so-called Prague Spring, a period marked by the extension of political freedoms. Following the intervention, Communist Party leader Alexander Dubcek, who had initiated the reforms, abandoned the program.

The 1959 Cuban Revolution was especially critical, as it threatened the US political monopoly in the western hemisphere by extending Soviet influence to within ninety miles of American soil. Following a failed US effort to overthrow Cuban leader Fidel Castro through an invasion at the Bay of Pigs, the Soviet Union attempted to install nuclear missiles on the island. The United States learned of the undertaking prior to the completion of the project, setting up what was to become the defining moment of the Cold War. The 1962 Cuban Missile Crisis was the first (and only) direct superpower confrontation that threatened to involve the use of nuclear weapons. After a two-week standoff resulting from a US-imposed blockade of all traffic—air and naval—into the island, US president John F. Kennedy and Soviet premier Nikita Khrushchev resolved the situation diplomatically.

Going forward, each power tried to mold political events across the world. At times, this led to interventions with unpredictable outcomes. The US involvement in Vietnam in the 1960s is a good example. Driven to prevent the fall of pro-Western governments to communist insurgencies across Southeast Asia (by the so-called domino theory—if one fell, the next would follow), the United States fought a difficult and highly controversial war that lasted for more than a decade and failed to achieve its objectives. It also produced deep political divisions within the country while calling into question some of the basic tenets of foreign policy. When it was all over, the United States had lost considerable political and military prestige.

Not all states became parties to the Cold War, however, and many colonies endeavored during this period to assert their independence. Most notable was India, the jewel in the crown of the British Empire. While the movement had been growing in the interwar years, the divisiveness of World War II and the weakening of British influence globally that followed opened the door for India's formal declaration of independence in 1950. Pakistan followed in 1956. Given its newfound freedom, India quickly moved to declare itself "nonaligned" with either axis of power—the United States or the Soviet Union. Other states soon joined India, including Indonesia, Yugoslavia, Egypt, and Ghana. This group has endured and expresses its common interests in occasional nonaligned summits. Politically, the group functions today as a voting bloc in the UN, with around 120 members.

détente a policy designed in the late 1960s by US president Richard Nixon and Soviet premier Leonid Brezhnev to promote opportunities for US-Soviet cooperation, even while the broader rivalry persisted

As the costs of the Cold War mounted, both major powers sought to lessen their ongoing confrontations. By the late 1960s, veteran cold warriors US president Richard Nixon and Soviet premier Leonid Brezhnev had assumed leadership of their respective countries and had the political credentials to pursue a new approach. They designed a policy of **détente** that promoted opportunities for US-Soviet cooperation, even while the broader rivalry persisted. These efforts produced some worthwhile results, most notably in the area of arms control through the negotiation of two Strategic Arms Limitation Treaties (SALT I and SALT II). But the relaxation in tension was short lived. Détente could not get the two sides to agree on the basic principles of acceptable behavior—especially when it came to dealing with political unrest in Africa, Asia, Latin America, and the Middle East.

By the 1980s, the Cold War was heating up once again. Following a period of considerable Soviet meddling in other countries and limited response from a United States weary from its Vietnam experience, US president Ronald Reagan assumed a more aggressive strategy to turn the tide.

US president Ronald Reagan points at a map of the Soviet Union as he speaks to listeners about the need to control nuclear missiles.

Bettmann/Contributor via Getty Images.

The Reagan Doctrine signaled a renewed willingness to assert US interests where the Soviets had been active, such as Nicaragua and Afghanistan. Reagan also took steps to bolster US nuclear and conventional weapons capabilities. These policies were met with trepidation by both European allies and Latin American neighbors.

Meanwhile, the decades of global engagement had taken their toll on the Soviet Union. Difficulties in managing leadership succession, a stagnant economy, the prolonged war in Afghanistan, and growing political unrest in many of the Soviet republics themselves contributed to the eventual demise of the communist regime. Across much of Central and Eastern Europe, prodemocracy movements ultimately led to the toppling of many governments that the Soviets had installed and supported. Just as the Berlin Wall had come to epitomize the Cold War, its fall in 1989 marked the end of this era. By 1991, the Soviet Union itself ceased to exist. The bipolar structure rapidly gave way to a more multipolar one with new centers of power.

As the lone remaining superpower, the United States appeared poised to preside over what President George H. W. Bush declared to be a "new world order" that would require less in the way of active manipulation and management of the global arena. It did not take long for that optimism to fade. Despite its many dangers, the US-Soviet rivalry of the Cold War had provided a degree of predictability and stability to international relations. Neither side anticipated the challenges to international security that the demise of their rivalry would create.

The Post–Cold War World

Early Uncertainties

The world that emerged after the Cold War saw significant changes to the international order. The demise of the Soviet Union and the many new countries that emerged in its aftermath resulted in a new distribution of power. The former communist state of Yugoslavia, for example, became engulfed in a civil war. It broke apart as Slovenia, Croatia, and later Bosnia and Herzegovina asserted their rights to sovereignty (see Map 4.2). While the dominant Serbians were able to accept the new states of Croatia and Slovenia, they were not willing to let Bosnia and Herzegovina go as easily, and a protracted battle ensued. It was not only within the former Soviet bloc that the equation was shifting.

MAP 4.2 ● Yugoslavia: Before and After 1991

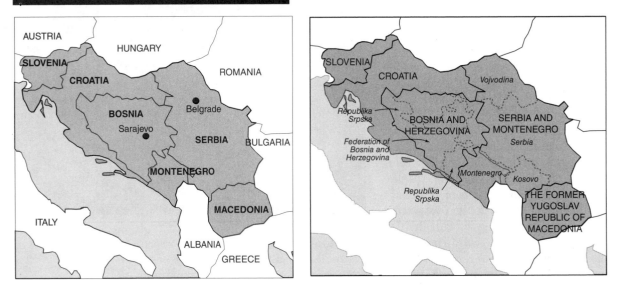

Source: Bruce Bueno de Mesquita, *Principles of International Politics*, 3rd ed. (Washington, DC: CQ Press, 2005), 123.

Political instability escalated in the Middle East, erupting in the outbreak of all-out military conflict in 1991—the so-called Gulf War. Iraqi president Saddam Hussein, hoping to acquire control over additional territory and oil, invaded neighboring Kuwait. Despite warnings from the United States, Hussein anticipated little, if any, response. He guessed wrong, and Iraqi troops were forced into a hasty retreat as President George H. W. Bush authorized a massive US invasion with support from an impressive coalition of governments worldwide.

The Gulf War was significant for a number of reasons. First, it forced states to reconsider the ways in which regional balances could be preserved without the counter positioning of opposing superpowers. Second, US efforts to gain the approval of the UN and countries with a stake in the outcome suggested the potential for multilateral management of future crises. The international coalition that formed in response to the Iraqi invasion of Kuwait was unprecedented. Finally, the decision of the United States to leave Hussein in power rather than risk protracted involvement indicated a reluctance to extend commitments beyond those to address direct threats to American interests.

Scott Peterson/Liaison.

A United Nations soldier stands over a group of Somali people on June 6, 1993, in Mogadishu, Somalia.

The African continent was also unsettled, as conflicts unfolded in the countries of Somalia and Rwanda. By 1992, Somalia's ongoing civil conflict left no one effectively in charge, as small groups of warlords fought for control of the country. The majority of the citizens were starving to death after a failed crop season. The United States spearheaded a coalition of forces that intervened for humanitarian and peacekeeping purposes. Given the coalition troops' limited mandate, which did not allow engaging in military action, they found themselves in a compromised position. As a result, they suffered some significant casualties that included the dragging of a dead US soldier through the streets of Mogadishu. The movie *Black Hawk Down* (2001) captured the intensity of the conflict.

Rwanda posed an even more difficult challenge, as feuding ethnic groups took their animosities to the extreme in a bloodbath in 1994. Hutu extremists sought restitution against the Tutsis for past wrongs in a killing rampage that lasted more than 100 days. International attention to the tragedy was limited, as the Somali experience weighed heavily in the decision of others to avoid Rwanda altogether. Widespread atrocities resulted in the slaughter of an estimated 800,000 civilians and the outflow of large numbers of refugees to neighboring countries.

These types of ethnic and religious-based conflict would continue to undermine the peace across a wide range of countries and prove difficult to resolve. South Sudan offers a particularly poignant example. After the country gained its hard-fought independence from Sudan in 2011, a power struggle between the president (from the Dinka tribe) and his political rival (from the Nuer tribe) morphed into full-scale combat in late 2013 marked by purposeful ethnic targeting. As the battle intensified and the death toll mounted, the UN worked hard to craft a settlement. Persistent hatreds made it impossible to fully implement an August 2015 agreement, and the conflict raged on. Despite mounting casualties and the growing threat of genocide, peace was elusive, and the difficulty in securing commitments for a regional protection force to augment the existing UN peacekeeping mission called the very future of the state into question.[11]

Crossroads

Beyond these realignments and dislocations, the most significant event that would define the post–Cold War world occurred during the morning of September 11, 2001. On that day (commonly referred to as 9/11), hijacked airplanes crashed into the twin towers of New York's World Trade Center and into the Pentagon in Arlington, Virginia. A fourth hijacked plane, targeting Washington, DC, was brought down by passengers in a crash landing in Pennsylvania. No one survived. In total, almost 3,000 people were killed in the various assaults. These attacks, orchestrated by Osama bin Laden and his Islamic al-Qaida network, revealed the dangerous undercurrents jeopardizing the world's political stability. The United States and an array of partners responded forcefully, with President George W. Bush declaring a global war on terror that started with an invasion of Afghanistan in early October 2001.

The war in Afghanistan pitted the United States against a government controlled by the Taliban, an Islamic fundamentalist group with close ties to al-Qaida—the organization that claimed responsibility for the 9/11 attacks. The Taliban were ousted early on, but the political restructuring process proved difficult and unwieldy. The NATO-led international security force, composed largely of US military personnel, found it difficult to bring order to the country or to fully guarantee the future of the Afghan government against a continuing insurgency led by Taliban and al-Qaida forces. The conflict dragged on, jeopardizing the plan to turn over the bulk of responsibility for security to Afghan forces by mid-2013 and to remove NATO combat forces by 2014.[12]

While not seen as having the capability to recapture power, the Taliban retained sufficient clout to prolong hostilities, and the Afghan government continued to be plagued by inefficiency and corruption. President Hamid Karzai, an often difficult partner, was succeeded by Ashraf Ghani in 2014. The United States proceeded with a revised timetable that still called for drawing down military engagement by the end of 2014 and for the withdrawal of all troops in 2016.[13]

US expectations regarding the future capabilities of Afghan security forces were overly optimistic. Following the exit of the bulk of NATO forces, the Taliban launched a series of military initiatives and succeeded in reacquiring control over pockets of territory. US airstrikes continued, and 8,400 American troops remained on the ground at the end of 2016. While certainly far below previous levels (reaching approximately 100,000 in 2010), this failure was a significant disappointment for the outgoing Obama administration, which had pledged to bring involvement to an end. The future remains uncertain, as it often has throughout the history of Afghanistan, with the Taliban demonstrating fierce determination to counter externally led efforts to impose domestic order.[14]

Fear that a former adversary, Saddam Hussein, had access to weapons of mass destruction extended the war on terror into Iraq, as the United States invaded in 2003. There was insufficient evidence from the outset to document the existence of these weapons, undermining the credibility of the intervention. Critics charged that the US initiative was designed to settle an old score with Hussein for his earlier invasion of Kuwait and his alleged role in a plot to assassinate president George W. Bush's father. A long, protracted conflict would begin that ultimately resulted in not only the overthrow of Hussein but also his trial and subsequent death sentence. Efforts to forge a political balance among Iraq's competing groups (Shia Muslims, Sunni Muslims, and Kurds) were met with stiff resistance, and the war continued. In 2011, a deal was struck that paved the way for the removal of US combat forces and for moving forward with the complex task of rebuilding the country.

The drama did not end there. Sectarian violence continued to plague the country, resulting in around 8,000 civilian deaths in 2013. The Shia government of Nouri al-Maliki was unable to gain full control, and animosities persisted. The reconstituted Iraqi army, which had been dismantled following the ousting of Hussein, remained

PRO/CON

ARE US GROUND TROOPS NEEDED TO DEFEAT THE ISLAMIC STATE?

Pro

James Jay Carafano

Vice President, Foreign and Defense Policy Studies, Heritage Foundation. Written for *CQ Researcher*, March 2016.

The United States should be prepared to send ground troops back to fight in Iraq and help keep the peace. The Middle East is too important to risk the region spiraling into war and chaos.

The Middle East matters. More than just a big gas pump, it is pretty much at the crossroads of global affairs. International routes of sea and air trade, finance and human migration crisscross the region. As a global power with international interests to protect, Washington cannot afford to ignore what is happening in the Middle East.

Most concerning is the rise of the Islamic State, or ISIS. Despite recent reversals, it still controls nation-size territory in Iraq and Syria, issues its own currency and commands a small army.

The capacity of a terrorist group to act as a state carries grave dangers. The ISIS "brand" as a rising caliphate animates Islamist extremists across the globe. As long as ISIS survives and thrives, it will inspire more terrorist attacks worldwide.

The terrorist state itself could become a global platform for transnational terrorism, just as Afghanistan was until the post–Sept. 11, 2001, invasion by the United States and other Western nations. In some respects, ISIS already has assumed that role. What makes the possibility of terrorists mixing in with legitimate refugees heading to Europe so dangerous is that, once they make it there, they can fall in with existing terror networks.

Danger flows in the opposite direction, too. Nations such as Australia have found that once their radicalized citizens make it to the battlefields of Iraq, they reach back to try to set up terror networks in their homelands.

Beyond the transnational threat, a massive Sunni terrorist state in the center of the Middle East significantly raises the potential for regional war.

The United States thus has every reason to end ISIS' territorial control in Iraq. But what will it take? The Obama administration believes a light touch—supporting the Iraqi military, aerial bombing and selected special operations—will suffice. That plan has not worked yet.

Con

Daniel L. Davis

Retired Lieutenant Colonel, US Army; Winner, 2012 Ridenhour Truth-Telling Prize. Written for *CQ Researcher*, March 2016.

It seems intuitive to some people: "The battle against the Islamic State, or ISIS, using only airpower has been inconclusive, so if we want to defeat them, as unpalatable as it may be, we're going to have to send in ground troops to finish them off."

A number of counterintuitive facts, however, render that conclusion wrong. Deploying ground combat forces will not defeat ISIS, nor will it safeguard American security. Sending ground troops almost certainly will worsen the situation.

It is true that two years of airstrikes against ISIS targets in Syria and Iraq have proven inconclusive. But our failure to take out ISIS isn't because we've deployed insufficient combat force. We haven't succeeded because we've relied on the wrong instrument. Military power does have a role, but it should be secondary to diplomacy. A national effort relying primarily on diplomacy has a chance to achieve U.S. objectives, whereas a military-first approach does not.

For ISIS to even exist, much less succeed, it must have an effective logistics system. No militant organization can fight unless it has steady deliveries of food, water, clothing, ammunition, weapons, spare parts and fuel for vehicles and generators, plus effective battlefield health care and a constant supply of replacement troops. Render that logistics system inoperative and ISIS dies in the field.

ISIS is landlocked everywhere it controls territory. It can sustain itself only if it has the secret support—either passive or active—of the states surrounding it: Iran, Turkey, Jordan, Saudi Arabia or others. The United States should use its robust intelligence capability to identify all the sources from which ISIS receives its massive logistics, then employ its diplomatic might to pressure those groups or states to cease such support. The military would be used to enforce interdiction efforts.

The 2004 battle of Fallujah against Iraqi insurgents graphically demonstrated that U.S. ground troops can destroy an enemy house by house but also can devastate

(Continued)

(Continued)

Certainly, by the end of President Obama's term, we'll know if it has a chance. The key is Mosul. If the Iraqis can't take that city back, they can't break the back of ISIS. If ISIS retains Mosul, the only realistic option for rooting them out is to reintroduce substantial U.S. combat forces.

civil infrastructure and embitter the population. After achieving an unequivocal military victory on the ground, Fallujah was then lost to ISIS almost without a fight. So the battle was a tactical victory but a strategic defeat. If we don't want to repeat the mistake on a much larger scale, we must subordinate the use of the military and unleash our full diplomatic force.

Source: Reed Karaim, "Defeating the Islamic State," *CQ Researcher* 26 (April 1, 2016): 289–312. Retrieved from http://library.cqpress.com.

Where Do You Stand?

1. Does the strategic importance of the Middle East warrant the presence of US combat troops?
2. Will US ground forces tip the balance in the war against ISIS?
3. Is diplomacy more effective than military force in countering the influence of ISIS?

relatively weak and ineffectual as it attempted to operate without US backup. The situation took a dramatic turn in June 2014 when a major offensive launched by an al-Qaida offshoot—the Islamic State in Iraq and Syria (ISIS)—destabilized the country. The strength and effectiveness of the group reflected both the weakness of the Iraqi government and the inability to contain the effects of events elsewhere in the region at the border's edge. ISIS took full advantage of its successes in attracting recruits and funding as it waged war against Syria's Assad regime, and its incursion across the Iraqi border was part of its broader strategy. It aimed to establish an Islamic state incorporating major Sunni population centers across northeastern Syria and northern Iraq without regard for preexisting state boundaries. The offensive also brought ISIS into conflict with the Kurds—Sunni Muslims with their own language and culture living mainly across parts of Iraq, Iran, Turkey, and Syria—who had long sought the establishment of their own independent state of Kurdistan (see Chapter 5 for additional discussion).[15] What role should the United States play in curtailing the activities of ISIS? The "Pro/Con" feature explores whether ground troops should be deployed to make a difference.

As the insurgency spread across Iraq, ISIS gained control over a number of key cities and showed little restraint in dealing with its opponents. Haider al-Abadi, Iraq's Shia prime minister, fared somewhat better than his predecessor in mobilizing opposition to ISIS but found it difficult to hold back the group's territorial advances. The growing threat prompted the United States to reluctantly enter the fray once again. Although the United States was determined to avoid a significant direct presence, US military backing for the effort against ISIS widened through the launching of airstrikes and the deployment of troops in advisory and combat support roles. By early 2017, US military forces numbered approximately 5,000. Despite rising casualties and the loss of considerable territories previously under its domain, ISIS continues to prove a formidable adversary, and Iraq remains unsettled.[16]

In some respects, the continuing odyssey in Iraq reflects the challenges of imposing order in a world marked by significant conflict that often spills across religious, ethnic, or territorial lines. It also suggests the difficulties of reconciling these differences during periods of political transition and readjustment. This proved to be the case with the events that unfolded across North Africa and the Middle East in 2011 during what became known as the Arab Spring.

A seemingly isolated decision of a street merchant in Tunisia to burn himself to death to protest treatment by police set off protests across the country calling for the resignation of its authoritarian leader. Prodemocracy demonstrations quickly spread to other countries across the area. By the time it was over, a number of longstanding rulers were gone. Perhaps most noteworthy was the forced resignation of Hosni Mubarak, the president of Egypt since 1981, and the killing of Muammar al-Qadhafi, who ruled Libya for forty-two years.

The Arab Spring, which was seen at the time as a historic opportunity for people to reclaim control over their political lives, did not produce uniform results. In Syria, for example, the regime of Bashar al-Assad strongly resisted efforts to unseat it, and a protracted and bloody civil war ensued. The struggle was complex, falling along sectarian lines and extending beyond the country's borders. Sunni Muslims comprised the majority of Syria's population, while Assad came from the Alawite Muslim minority—a Shia sect—that had attained political dominance during the previous regime headed by his father. Assad also enjoyed strong support from Lebanon's Hezbollah, among others, which sent forces to Syria to fight on behalf of the government. Syria's opposition included an array of groups, including many loyal to al-Qaida and fiercely anti-American.

Assad went to great lengths to hold on, even resorting to the use of chemical weapons (CW) against civilian populations. While on the verge of military intervention in 2013 on humanitarian grounds, the United States ultimately decided to forgo this option. It also had difficulty constructing an effective policy in support of an acceptable alternative to Assad. The situation was complicated further by the territorial advances of ISIS and the growing role of other Sunni jihadists in opposition to the regime.

The situation took a significant turn in September 2015, when Russia's military intervened directly in support of the teetering Assad government. Through airstrikes and other forms of combat support, Russia succeeded in fortifying Assad's position by targeting not only ISIS, but other key rebel forces as well. Syria's army recaptured critical territory, and decisive military action by the Russian air force and pro-government militias in Syria's largest city, Aleppo, in late 2016 prompted the opening of indirect peace talks shortly thereafter sponsored by Russia, Iran, and Turkey. With Russia poised to become the pivotal power broker and the United States largely marginalized, both countries looked to common ground to establish a framework for future coop-

Anas Al Damashqy/Anadolu Agency/Getty Images.

Two Syrian children walk through the debris along wrecked buildings after the Assad regime's missile attack on civilian residential areas in the opposition-controlled Tishreen neighborhood of Damascus, Syria, on February 22, 2017.

eration to bring an end to this deadly conflict. Another chemical weapon attack allegedly authorized by Assad in April 2017, followed by a retaliatory strike by the United States utilizing powerful cruise missiles, suggested the difficulty of the task ahead. As the war has dragged on, the human toll has mounted. An estimated 400,000 Syrians have lost their lives, more than 6 million people have been displaced internally, and nearly 5 million have taken refuge in neighboring countries and beyond.[17]

The unfolding story in Egypt also exemplifies the difficulty of bringing the democratic aspirations of the Arab Spring to fruition. The transition was rocky as competing groups vied for power. Taking advantage of its tightly organized political network, the Muslim Brotherhood swept to victory in Egypt's first post-rebellion election. The Muslim Brotherhood, with its anti-Western stance and intention of moving the country toward more traditional Islamic law, had been forced to operate deeply underground for decades. Egypt's secular opposition, which had been so prominent in the protests that toppled Mubarak, was too diffuse to mount an effective campaign. The victorious Muslim Brotherhood candidate, Mohamed Morsi, moved swiftly to push through a new constitution to consolidate power and implement his political and social agendas. He also began to alter the country's foreign policy on a number of key fronts, thereby affecting the region's tenuous balance and raising concerns among US policymakers.

Egypt's military grew increasingly disillusioned and, in 2013, deposed Morsi, dismantled the Muslim Brotherhood's leadership, and once again banned the organization from the political arena. In 2014, an election heavily choreographed by the military provided little choice and brought its leader, Abdel Fattah el-Sisi, to power. While the ascendance of the military restored stability, it also meant that Egypt returned to conditions strikingly similar to those evident during the Mubarak years. The government has moved steadily to consolidate its power and to curb all opposition, while strengthening its strategic cooperation with the United States. Efforts by Islamists to challenge the regime have resulted in periodic attacks that threaten the security of the Sinai Peninsula that borders Israel, however, and economic uncertainties have continued to fuel political discontent.[18]

In addition to the shifting political winds blowing through the Middle East, there were numerous other unfolding events that exemplified the multiple forces driving changes across the world. The 2016 peace accord ending the fifty-two-year civil war in Colombia between the government and the Revolutionary Armed Forces of Colombia (commonly known as FARC) suggested opportunities for reconciliation. The bloody conflict—which took well over 200,000 lives and left an additional 25,000 missing—extended beyond the struggle for political power and involved drug lords seeking to control the country's lucrative illicit trade. By the early 2000s, Colombia supplied around 90 percent of the world's cocaine, while FARC had its hand in an estimated 60 percent of Colombian cocaine exported to the United States.[19]

The peace did not come easily. After four years of contentious negotiations hosted by Cuba, the final deal included provisions for disarming remaining rebels, punishing those convicted of serious war crimes, and the progressive civil and political reintegration of FARC members. Many Colombians expressed concerns over what they saw as the overly lenient treatment of the rebels, and voters narrowly rejected the agreement in a national referendum. The Colombian Congress unanimously approved subsequent revisions, and the amended treaty (which did not require voter approval) was put in place. For his efforts, Colombian president Juan Manuel Santos was awarded the 2016 Nobel Peace Prize.[20]

The more fluid security environment of the post–Cold War period also made it possible to consider moving beyond longstanding interstate differences. Perhaps most notable was the breakthrough in US-Cuban relations in late 2014. As noted in the "Turning Point" feature, the restoration of diplomatic relations ended decades of hostility and presented opportunities to extend commercial and cultural ties. It also ended one of the more outmoded bilateral relationships in the world that was based on geopolitical principles of the previous Cold War era. Even so, it took new leadership on both sides and required the delicate external mediation of Pope Francis to move the process forward. While the endurance of the accord is still questionable, given the change in the US presidential administration in 2017, there are many potential benefits as the two countries proceed to chart their new course.

TURNING POINT

DECEMBER 17, 2014

The United States and Cuba

Cuba has long been a popular destination for non-American travelers; however, once American travel restrictions eased during the Obama administration, tourism to Cuba greatly expanded.

What?

On December 17, 2014, US president Barack Obama and Cuban president Raul Castro concluded a historic agreement that went a long way toward ending more than fifty years of hostility rooted in the politics of the Cold War. The accord called for the full restoration of diplomatic relations (which had been severed in 1961) and the introduction of several important steps designed to bolster economic ties between the two countries.

Why?

The hostility defining the relationship since the 1959 Cuban revolution no longer serves the interests of either country. The Cuban economy has struggled since the demise of the Soviet Union in the early 1990s robbed the country of its primary supporter and benefactor. The US economic embargo of Cuba (referred to by the Cubans as the blockade) appears to have run its course. Despite strong political support for the policy in the United States throughout its existence, it has hurt American businesses and investors who have lost out on opportunities to participate in the Cuban market.

How?

While the shift may be driven by economic considerations, there have also been changes in political conditions. Raul Castro assumed formal power in late 2008, succeeding his brother Fidel, who had ruled Cuba since the revolution. Faced with an array of serious economic challenges, he began to implement a series of reforms to consolidate his own position and to jump-start the economy by allowing for some private enterprise. Obama was committed to an improvement of overall relations throughout most of his presidency. His parallel effort to close the prison holding suspected terrorists at the US naval base in Guantánamo Bay, Cuba, complicated matters. As Cuban and American negotiators struggled to agree on final details, a personal appeal by Pope Francis to the two leaders played a key role in sealing the deal.

Will It Make a Difference over Time?

The announcement of the accord produced a flurry of activity. The reopening of embassies marked the resumption of full diplomatic ties, and a series of measures related to banking and travel opened new avenues for commercial and cultural exchange. Obama's visit to Cuba in March 2016 was the first by a sitting US president since 1928, and direct airline service between the two countries began in August 2016. There are still a host of obstacles that will affect the chances of extending the relationship. Two events in November 2016 have proven to be particularly impactful—the election of Donald Trump, a strong critic of the initiative, and the death of Fidel Castro. To make the diplomatic relationship stand the test of time, the United States will need to consider ending (or, at the very least, significantly moderating) the embargo. In June 2017, President Trump announced the rollback of some market-opening measures previously negotiated. As expected, Cuba responded angrily, and the reconstituted bilateral relationship was significantly strained. Moving forward, the United States will need to consider how it might develop an approach that can effectively address its often conflicting commercial and political interests. For its part, the new generation of Cuban leaders coming to power will need to determine whether it is willing to engage further with the United States by steering a course that embraces and builds on the domestic economic and political openings already in place.

What Do You Think?

Is this truly a turning point in the relationship? Do the changes already in place serve the mutual interests of both parties? Will the opening endure? The following resource can help you get started in framing your view:

Danielle Renwick, Brianna Lee, and James McBride, "U.S.-Cuba Relations," *CFR Backgrounders*, Council on Foreign Relations, September 7, 2016. http://www.cfr.org/cuba/us-cuba-relations/p11113.

Meanwhile, the efforts of some other states to assert themselves and to wield their influence have threatened the stability of the international order. The nuclear ambitions of North Korea and Iran, discussed in greater detail in Chapter 5, have proved to be particularly problematic. Both countries chose to proceed with their programs despite intensive multilateral efforts to derail them. North Korea has provided an important challenge, as it has not hidden its military intentions. Although in many respects a failed state incapable of sufficiently feeding or otherwise sustaining its own people, North Korea has launched a nuclear weapons development program and has moved forward aggressively with the effort. Diplomatic attempts to persuade North Korea to suspend these activities have not succeeded, and the country's volatile and unpredictable leader, Kim Jong-un, has proceeded with the testing of warheads and missiles. The potential for conflict remains considerable, particularly in light of the continuing tensions between North and South Korea dating back to the war of the early 1950s.[21]

Iran has posed an even greater immediate threat to the peace. The country's considerable political agenda has included the desire to extend its political clout across the Persian Gulf, facilitate the spread of fundamentalist Islamic ideology, destroy Israel, and develop a nuclear capability. While Iran claimed that its nuclear aspirations were confined to peaceful purposes only, the United States was not convinced and moved to impose economic sanctions, such as limiting purchases of oil and freezing access to Iranian assets held in American banks.[22] Following years of difficult and often hostile negotiations, a 2015 agreement called for Iran to significantly limit nuclear activity and submit to external oversight in return for relief from the sanctions that were impacting the country's economy.[23] Serious questions remain as to the effectiveness and likely endurance of the pact, especially in light of the renewed tensions between Iran and the United States that surfaced in early 2017. Beyond specific disagreements over interpretations of certain provisions of the deal and measures of compliance, Iran's broader geostrategic ambitions and alliances stand in stark contrast to those of the United States.

A New Cold War?

As aspiring powers have sought to acquire greater leverage over the direction of the world, more established ones have attempted to hold on to their influence. The United States has maintained a central global role, although it has struggled to control the course of events and is reluctant to commit to the open-ended use of military force. Russia has made it clear that it does not intend to recede into the background and works to parlay its considerable military strength and wealth generated by ample oil and gas reserves to extend its political and military reach. Vladimir Putin, the country's dominant political figure, has taken firm control in directing the effort. After completing the constitutionally mandated limit of two terms as Russia's president (2000–2008), Putin stepped down but was then reelected for a new term in 2012. He had engineered a constitutional change to extend presidential terms to six years and looked forward to realize his goal of returning Russia to international prominence.

Putin's game plan became readily apparent. Coming on the heels of the 2014 Winter Olympics in Sochi, choreographed to showcase the country's renewed vigor and capabilities, the Russian military crossed over the border with Ukraine to occupy Crimea. The subsequent annexation of the peninsula, which had historic ties to Russia and was home to ethnic Russians enthusiastically welcoming the change, marked a significant shift in the region's political equation. Putin's actions did not come as a particular surprise. Relations with Ukraine had deteriorated following the ousting of the country's pro-Russian president and the new leadership's efforts to strengthen ties with the European Union (EU) and the United States.

Russia's initiative signaled its intention to act unilaterally to support its vital strategic interests (among other things, Russia's Black Sea fleet was based in the Crimean port of

UNDERSTANDING CROSS-BORDER CONFLICT
HOW CAN INTERNATIONAL STUDIES HELP?

Crisis in Ukraine

In 2014, antigovernment protesters in Ukraine ousted their president, Viktor Yanukovych, after he announced that Ukraine would reverse course and extend its ties to its neighbor to the east, Russia. In response to the upheaval, Russian forces crossed into the Crimean Peninsula, an administrative division within Ukraine (see Map 4.3). In relatively quick succession, pro-Russian separatists seized parts of eastern Ukraine, the country elected a new president (Petro Poroshenko, a confectionary entrepreneur known as the "chocolate king"), and Russia moved troops and military equipment into eastern Ukraine, where a referendum orchestrated by separatists endorsed Russia's actions and its annexation of Crimea. The United States and others resoundingly criticized Russian activities and imposed considerable sanctions as part of their effort to get Russia to relent.

But why should a crisis in Ukraine elicit such a Russian response in the first place? Ukraine declared independence from Soviet Russia in 1991, and elected its first president at the end of that year. Although Ukraine was universally recognized as a sovereign state, Russian president Vladimir Putin sought to reassert control. One key reason was Crimea's strategic location. The Crimean coastal city of Sevastopol had been the historic base for Russia's Black Sea fleet and had remained so after Ukraine gained independence through a leasing agreement. The economic connections were also quite extensive. Gas pipelines from Russia to Europe crossed Ukraine, while Ukraine was heavily dependent on Russia for its oil supply. In addition, the eastern part of the country was populated largely by ethnic Russians who sought to reunite with Russia.

While the immediacy of the crisis passed, the controversy has persisted, and efforts to resolve it have gained little traction. Nearly 10,000 deaths have been reported, and an estimated million residents in the affected areas have been displaced. A 2015 peace plan remains far from implementation, Poroshenko has made little headway in dealing with the country's political and economic challenges, and Russia's position remains intact. Despite some movement in early 2017 to break the impasse, the future has remained uncertain.

Sources: Alan Yuhas, "Ukraine Crisis: An Essential Guide to Everything That's Happened So Far," *Guardian*, April 13, 2014, http://www.theguardian

MAP 4.3 ● Ukraine, Russia, and the Crimean Peninsula

Source: CIA World Factbook (https://www.cia.gov/library/publications/the-world-factbook/geos/up.html).

.com/world/2014/apr/11/ukraine-russia-crimea-sanctions-us-eu-guide-explainer; Nikolas Gvosdev and Noel Konagai, "What Lies Ahead for Ukraine?" *Council on Foreign Relations*, May 4, 2016, http://www.cfr.org/ukraine/lies-ahead-ukraine/p37832.

What is the role of crossing borders in resolving this conflict? How can the cross-disciplinary focus of international studies help?

Questions

- What is the role of geography in this unfolding drama? Why do national borders matter here?
- What are the political motives and stakes for the countries involved?
- What are the economic implications for Ukraine and Russia?
- What role do social and cultural factors play in adding to the complexity of the crisis?
- Can the international community offer any solution?

Sevastopol), even at the expense of other political and economic considerations. Already strained, Putin's relationship with US president Obama soured further. Russia did not back down, despite the imposition of US economic sanctions. The situation in eastern Ukraine remained unsettled, with pro-Russian activists seeking to gain additional control. The threat of further Russian military intervention remained a distinct possibility.[24]

The rift between Russia and the United States continued to deepen, fueled by the growing strains between the countries' two leaders. This had a familiar tone and seemed to suggest that, in some respects, the world might be turning back to the previous era of great power conflict. As noted previously, Russian intervention in the Syrian civil war thwarted US efforts to alter Syria's government and further complicated the strategy to defeat ISIS. Russia's increasing military spending and preparedness, closer ties with China, and support of authoritarian regimes around the world added to the tensions. The rancor persisted to the very last days of the Obama administration, when Russian diplomats were expelled from the United States as retaliation for the alleged intrusion in the situation in Syria.

In yet another curious twist, however, the relationship appeared to be on the verge of a new course following the 2016 US presidential election. Allegations of Russian cyberattacks to influence the outcome of the election in favor of Trump and questions relating to connections between key Russian figures and Trump advisers lingered, but there were initial signs that presidents Trump and Putin would move forward to repair relations across a number of fronts. The US decision to impose sanctions on Russia in response to growing evidence of its electoral interference, Russia's expulsion of American diplomats to protest this action, and the divergent paths of the countries' foreign policies in Syria and elsewhere make this a difficult task.[25]

If Russia symbolizes the attempt to recapture past glory, China's emergence as a formidable global power represents the changing dynamics of the global political landscape. As the world's second largest economy, China forged an ambitious array of initiatives as it sought to advance its policy interests. It significantly enhanced its military capabilities, built a lucrative weapons export industry, actively supported economic development projects in Africa and Latin America, and nurtured ties across the Asia-Pacific and beyond. Although emphasizing the primacy of its regional pursuits, China's global reach and influence was becoming increasingly apparent. Even as it looked to avoid volatile confrontations that could jeopardize its commercial concerns, China did not hesitate to assert its geostrategic interests by challenging Vietnam and the Philippines and laying claim to the island chains in the vital South China Sea. It bristled at periodic US criticisms of its human rights and trade policies and made it clear that it would do things its own way and would not accept unsolicited external intrusions.

China's foreign policy took a bit of a turn when Xi Jinping assumed leadership of the country in 2013. It continued to look at ways of building bridges to the United States through cooperative efforts in dealing with such challenges as North Korea and climate change. At the same time, Xi was more assertive in strengthening China's military posture and in pressing its territorial claims. This led to growing tensions with some of its neighbors and the United States, which viewed China's efforts to lay claim to islands in the South China Sea as a power grab intended to expand its geopolitical and military dominance. In addition, Chinese initiatives to extend the country's economic clout across Asia and the Western Pacific, through such projects as the Asian Infrastructure Investment Bank and the Silk Road Economic Belt, challenged US influence.[26]

Meanwhile, China grew closer to Russia in the aftermath of the annexation of Crimea. The international sanctions imposed on Russia served as a key catalyst, prompting the countries to enhance their bilateral Strategic Partnership as an affirmation of their rights to defend core interests against perceived threats. The 2014 agreement contained numerous provisions designed to extend economic and financial ties and to more closely align their broader political objectives. The strong interpersonal relationship between Xi and Putin solidified the arrangement.[27]

The growing bond between Russia and China presents a challenge to the United States, even as it conjures up memories of the kind of big power rivalries that characterized the Cold War era. Some observers go so far as to suggest that the United States might consider a return to the triangular diplomacy of that period to offset Sino-Russian initiatives. Popularized by Henry Kissinger, the architect of US foreign policy from 1969 to 1977, the strategy would call for acting on identifiable mutual interests with each country to build a stronger relationship than they have with one another. The underlying structure of today's global geostrategic environment is vastly different from that of the Cold War, so such an approach does not seem particularly warranted. The United States has a considerable stake in effectively managing each of these relationships, however, and will be hard pressed to develop the appropriate mix of policy tools needed. In addition to addressing the aforementioned tests relating to Russia, the Trump administration faces considerable challenges as it navigates the commercial and security issues critical to maintaining productive ties with China.[28]

HOW YOU CAN CONNECT

You can engage politically by . . .

- joining a political party or political advocacy group
- voting in an election or referendum, if this option is available to you
- volunteering or working on behalf of a political candidate, political official, or political cause
- participating in a political protest

How do we make sense of the rapid pace of events and the realignments across the world, even just within the past few years? Some political scientists have introduced a new way of thinking about the international order, **constructivism**, which emphasizes the role of ideas in defining interests. Constructivists argue that the underlying forces frequently driving decisions are based on artificially constructed perceptions and the historical and emotional baggage attached to them—what international relations scholar Nicholas Onuf has called "a world of our making."[29] Feminist views of international relations have emerged from this perspective, giving rise to feminist critiques of the masculine images of world order. Noted feminist scholar Ann Tickner, for example, employs a gendered approach to challenge the way we interpret global issues and behaviors.[30] Even as we embrace alternative explanations and methodological tools to enhance our understanding, more traditional notions of power politics and alliances still have their place in helping us unravel the intricacies of our political world.

constructivism a view of the global order that sees the state and the rules that govern it as an artificial construct

Conclusion: The Quest for Security

Political borders, such as those separating rival powers and major military blocs, have constituted the principal fault lines of international politics throughout our history. World War I, World War II, and the Cold War between the United States and the Soviet Union provide recent examples. For some, traditional political boundaries have lost their significance, as struggles today often fall along ethnic, racial, religious, linguistic, caste, or class lines. This erosion of the building blocks of the political world represents a growing analytical problem as well. It is not easy to fully account for the multiple factors driving relationships in our changing international system.

The conflicts that have emerged in this new political environment pose some unique challenges. While there are scant indications of a return to the politics of the Cold War, we are living in a more complex, multilayered security system that is difficult to manage and control. As technology has brought the world closer together, it has also made it more difficult to limit the spillover from situations that threaten the peace. The failure to reduce ongoing animosities or to address lingering frustrations has added to the chaos. Liberalism suggests that the more people cross political borders, the more their interactions provide opportunities for a more peaceful planet. However, realists would remind us that there are numerous conflicts across the globe at any given time that are driven by outright power considerations. Constructivists argue that we must rethink our traditional ways of conceptualizing the world to better understand one another.

As we noted at the outset of this chapter, states remain the most powerful actors in the global arena. However, their ability to address problems that are increasingly global in nature has been affected by the multiple pressures impinging on their political borders. In addition to perpetuating interstate rivalries that undermine the peace, these forces have empowered nonstate actors that have sought greater leverage to press their agendas across existing boundaries. The need to accommodate these realities will be explored in Chapter 5 as we consider a few of the more formidable security dilemmas we are confronting today—the Israel/Palestine conflict, weapons of mass destruction, and international terrorism.

Key Concepts

anarchic system of states 78	détente 85	nationalism 80
balance of power 81	feudal system 78	political science 81
bipolar 84	idealism 81	realism 79
constructivism 97	imperial system 78	sovereignty 79
containment 84	liberalism 81	

To Learn More

Books and Other Print Media

Amitav Acharya, *The End of American World Order* (Cambridge, UK: Polity Press, 2014).

Amitav Acharya argues that Western hegemony and the postwar liberal world have come to an end and likens the emerging system to a multiplex theater offering a range of configurations under a single roof.

Cynthia Enloe, *Bananas, Beaches and Bases: Making Feminist Sense of International Politics*, 2nd ed. (Berkeley: University of California Press, 2014).

Cynthia Enloe lays the foundation for a feminist perspective on international relations, illustrated by many updated examples of power relations between genders and other groups.

Parag Khanna, *Connectography: Mapping the Future of Global Civilization* (New York: Random House, 2016).

This is the latest installment of Parag Khanna's ongoing look into the megatrends serving to elevate the role of connectivity while diminishing the salience of national borders in shaping the future of the twenty-first century.

Joshua Kurlantzick, *Democracy in Retreat: The Revolt of the Middle Class and the Worldwide Decline of Representative Government* (New Haven, CT: Yale University Press, 2013).

In spite of various efforts in the Middle East and elsewhere to move toward the democratization of the political order, Joshua Kurlantzick takes a pessimistic view of these initiatives and notes an actual strengthening of antidemocratic forces.

Niccolo Machiavelli, *The Prince*, 2nd ed. (New York: W. W. Norton, 1992).

Niccolo Machiavelli's prescriptions for how a prince should behave provide an excellent view of not only the political machinations of his day but also the practical realities of governing.

Kishore Mahbubani, *The Great Convergence: Asia, the West, and the Logic of One World* (Philadelphia: PublicAffairs, Perseus Books Group, 2013).

This intriguing discussion suggests that globalization has resulted in an increasing convergence of attitudes and values between Asia and the West that should preclude intense conflict if both sides (particularly the West) can accommodate their policies to a changing world order.

Michael Mandelbaum, *Mission Failure: America and the World in the Post–Cold War Era* (New York: Oxford University Press, 2016).

Michael Mandelbaum offers a far-ranging critique of American foreign policy in the post–Cold War period, highlighting some of the more significant failures to project or defend US interests around the world.

Hans Morgenthau, *Politics among Nations: The Struggle for Power and Peace* (New York: Knopf, 1948).

Hans Morgenthau's assessment of the emerging post–World War II world remains a classic for understanding the way in which power politics and political realism have guided international relations.

Joseph S. Nye, Jr., *Is the American Century Over?* (Cambridge, UK: Polity Press, 2015).

This is a brief yet informative discussion of America's changing place in the world by one of the leading foreign policy analysts.

David B. Ottaway, *The Arab World Upended: Revolution and Its Aftermath in Tunisia and Egypt* (Boulder, CO: Lynne Rienner, 2017).

David Ottaway looks at the forces giving rise to the 2011 Arab Spring and examines the very different sets of outcomes in two of the states at the center of the drama.

Alexander Wendt, *Social Theory of International Politics* (Cambridge, UK: Cambridge University Press, 1999).

Alexander Wendt offers a cultural theory of international politics that forms the basis of constructivism.

Websites

Carnegie Endowment for International Peace, www.carnegieendowment.org

The Carnegie Endowment for International Peace is a global think tank that produces reports on the issues that affect the search for peace.

Foreign Affairs, www.foreignaffairs.com

Foreign Affairs is a US journal published by the Council on Foreign Relations that aims to promote discussion on US foreign policy and global affairs.

Foreign Policy, www.foreignpolicy.com

Foreign Policy is a US journal owned by the *Washington Post* that covers issues of global politics and economics and publishes the Top 100 Global Thinkers and Failed States Index annually.

International Relations Theory, www.irtheory.com

The International Relations Theory website gives an overview of the various theories that inform the way in which international relations scholars view the world.

World Politics Review, www.worldpoliticsreview.com

World Politics Review is a web-based news organization that offers news and opinions on many topics, including global politics, economics, culture, security, and environmental issues.

Videos

Black Hawk Down (2001)

This popular movie, based on real events, tells the story of the Battle of Mogadishu, in which an elite group of US soldiers sought to capture the Somali leader and found themselves engaged in a fierce battle for their lives.

Cold War (1998)

This twenty-four segment series, presented by CNN, offers a comprehensive look inside the Cold War and the key events that shaped it.

Frontline

The PBS documentary news program features episodes on a range of current issues, many of them global in nature. See http://www.pbs.org/wgbh/pages/frontline for the programs that are in the *Frontline* library and available for online viewing.

Hijacking the Arab Spring? The Rise of the Islamists (2012), http://www.films.com/ecTitleDetail.aspx?TitleID=28179

This film looks at Islamic groups and organizations seeking to acquire power across the Middle East and North Africa following the 2011 uprisings.

The Hurt Locker (2008)

This Academy Award–winning movie, based on true events, follows the story of a sergeant in charge of a bomb disposal team in Iraq.

Putin's Way (2015), http://films.com/ecTitleDetail.aspx?TitleID=115980&r=S

This is an informative biographical sketch of Russian leader Vladimir Putin that provides insight into his style and perspective.

TED: Global Power Shifts (2013), https://www.ted.com/playlists/73/the_global_power_shift

This includes a compilation of videos covering a range of issues that speak to some of the ways in which power has shifted in today's world.

Wag the Dog (1997)

This amusing yet thought-provoking film, starring Robert De Niro and Dustin Hoffman, has withstood the test of time with its depiction of a producer hired to construct a war to cover up a political scandal.

Where to Invade Next (2015), http://wheretoinvadenext.com

Satirist and political activist Michael Moore visits countries in Europe and Africa to uncover things that the United States might learn from them.

5

Challenges to Security

We are in a new and dangerous nuclear era with outdated nuclear policies and an increasing risk of nuclear use. In this new era of nine nuclear armed nations, reliance on nuclear weapons for security is becoming increasingly hazardous and decreasingly effective, as a deterrent to prevent war.

—Sam Nunn, former US senator and cofounder of the Nuclear Threat Initiative, 2016[1]

Learning Objectives

After studying this chapter, you will be able to do the following:

- Understand the dynamics of the Israeli-Palestinian conflict.

- Explain the concepts of deterrence and mutual assured destruction (MAD).

- Identify the main areas of concern with respect to weapons of mass destruction.

- Understand the concept of terrorism and the motives of some of the key actors engaged in these activities.

The combination of nuclear weapons and terrorist activities places the world today at significant risk. Former US senator Sam Nunn and media mogul Ted Turner founded the Nuclear Threat Initiative organization in 2001 to prevent the use of nuclear, biological, and chemical weapons (CW) and strengthen global security. They believe that these weapons pose the greatest threat to peace in the world today. In fact, conflict is always present due to the nature of nation-states, the people who live in them, and the way in which these people define their interests. The potential for destruction has never been greater, given the unstable political climates in many areas of the world. As a result, the most fundamental global political challenges relate to matters of war and peace and the arsenal of weapons readily available to both states and nonstates alike.

Since its earliest days, the nation-state system has been prone to violence. Nationalism has been a contributing factor. State leaders have often used symbols of pride and purpose to mobilize support and to justify actions, particularly in response to perceived threats or injustices. Nationalism has served as an important tool of governments to defend, protect, or advance state interests. It has also been used to promote and rationalize aggressive or belligerent behaviors.

Unfortunately, states have often resorted to war to settle conflicts, even before they may have exhausted all possibilities for a more peaceful resolution. Disputes over land and resources are particularly common. Such conflict can be traced, in part, to the importance of ownership and control in determining the relative status and positioning of states, as well as their capacity to protect their sovereign rights and interests. The long history of many territorial conflicts in the Balkans, the Middle East, and elsewhere adds to their endurance. Hopes for revenge or reversing outcomes of previous encounters often fan the fires of hatred between peoples and make it difficult to find common ground for peaceful coexistence.

The artificial nature of many boundaries and borders has contributed further to this pattern. It is not uncommon for rival ethnic, religious, or tribal groups to be thrown together politically within a designated space. Such delineations have proven especially troublesome in the developing world, where the end of colonialism led to the creation

A giant column of dark smoke rises more than 20,000 feet into the air after the second atomic bomb ever used in warfare explodes over the Japanese port and town of Nagasaki, on August 9, 1945. Dropped by the US Army Air Force's B-29 plane *Bockscar*, the bomb killed more than 70,000 people instantly, with tens of thousands dying later from effects of the radioactive fallout. This photo was made three minutes after the atom bomb struck Nagasaki. Almost seventy years later, nuclear weapons, as well as biological and chemical weapons (CW), remain among the biggest challenges to world security.

National Archives.

of new states—which sat on top of and often crossed over much older nations—without much consideration for historical differences and grievances. The results are predictable. Civil wars erupt, and governments fall apart easily. Rwanda, Somalia, Yugoslavia, Iraq, Syria, and many other places have suffered catastrophic human tolls. When a particular group is separated and seeks to come together to claim its sovereign rights that other powers do not recognize—such as the Kurds in Iraq, Iran, and Turkey—matters are further complicated. The ongoing conflicts in much of the Middle East illuminate these challenges.

Conflict in the Middle East: Israel and Palestine

While protests across the Middle East in the spring of 2011 altered the political landscape and set the stage for new fissures through the region, the longstanding tension between Israel and Palestine continues to lie at the heart of much of the instability in the area. The conflict goes back to biblical times and incorporates a number of the issues that have caused disputes among other people elsewhere—land, resources, religion, and the desire for revenge. Its more immediate roots can be traced to the early twentieth century, when Britain became the latest in a long succession of great powers to control the area.

After World War I and the defeat of the Turkish Ottoman Empire, the British administered Palestine—the territory that today comprises Israel and Jordan. They put forward their vision for the future in the 1917 **Balfour Declaration**, which called for the eventual creation of a Jewish national home in Palestine while still preserving the rights of non-Jewish communities.[2] Britain presided over Palestine through a mandate of the League of Nations but had a difficult time maintaining order. It increasingly resorted to force to counter the activities of both Arab and Jewish militias looking to advance their respective political power and to undermine the British occupation. Meanwhile, the demographic balance of Palestine changed considerably in the 1930s with the arrival of thousands of European Jews escaping the scourge of the Holocaust, which would subsequently claim more than 6 million victims.

The effort to implement the spirit of the Balfour plan proceeded in 1947, with the decision by the United Nations (UN) to endorse the partition or division of Palestine into independent Jewish and Arab states, with Jerusalem designated an international city. In 1948, the state of Israel was established—welcomed by Jews as the miracle of independence and regarded by Arabs as *al-nakba*, the catastrophe. Setting a pattern that was to characterize much of the future between these rivals, a war ensued that engulfed many countries across the region. When the fighting stopped, the situation on the ground was quite different from what had been envisioned by the UN. Israel survived, but the country was smaller geographically. The city of Jerusalem was divided, and Jordan gained control of additional territory on the West Bank of the Jordan River that was home to significant numbers of Palestinian Arabs.

Other wars would occur as the years progressed, but the one in 1967 would have the most profound implications for Israeli-Palestinian relations (see Map 5.1). The Six-Day War, as it came to be called, established Israel's sovereignty over all of Jerusalem and the West Bank territories. Israel also gained control over Gaza, a narrow strip of land off the Mediterranean coast that had belonged to Egypt, as well as some other strategic terrain (the Sinai Desert, also acquired from Egypt, and the Golan Heights from Syria).

While enhancing Israel's physical security, its possession of these lands added to the animosities and political stalemate. Diplomatic efforts failed to secure a deal that would involve the exchange of land in return for peace guarantees. Palestinians did not acknowledge the legitimacy of the state of Israel, and Israel did not accept the right of Palestinians to have their own state in the occupied territories. The precarious coexistence of the two sides was often marked by significant outbursts of violence.

Balfour Declaration the 1917 British plan calling for the eventual creation of a Jewish national home in Palestine

MAP 5.1 ● Israel: A Map of Disputed Areas

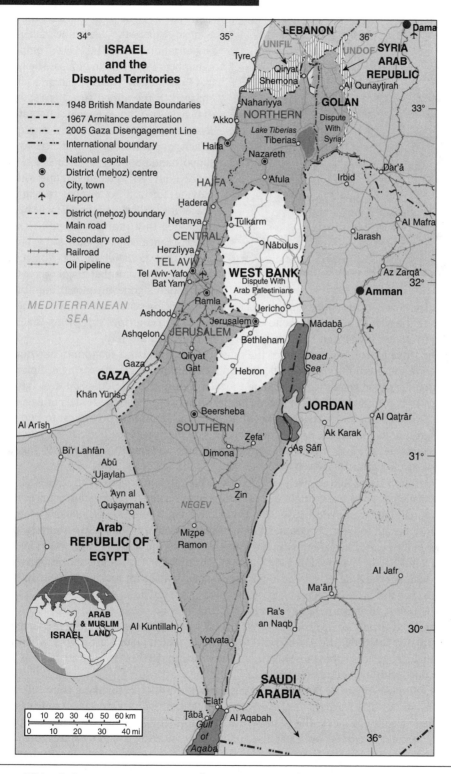

AP Photo/Doug Mills.

Taken on September 13, 1993, this photo captures the historic handshake between PLO leader Yasser Arafat (right) and Israeli prime minister Yitzhak Rabin (left), with US president Bill Clinton looking on, which took place at the White House in Washington, DC.

Camp David Accords the 1979 peace agreement between Egypt and Israel

intifada the Palestinian uprising against Israel

Oslo Accords the 1993 Israeli-Palestinian agreement that was designed to set the stage for a comprehensive and permanent peace

With no government of their own, many Palestinians turned to a political movement born in the 1960s to lead the fight against Israel—the Palestine Liberation Organization (PLO). The PLO encompassed a number of Palestinian groups. The largest was Fatah, led by Yasser Arafat and actively engaged in the armed struggle. Fatah and Arafat gained considerable international recognition and notoriety for their airplane hijackings and other violent acts to gain support and publicity for their cause.

Without an agreeable framework for moving forward to resolve the impasse peacefully, Palestinians and Israelis became embroiled in a protracted conflict, which was complicated even further by broader issues that destabilized the region as a whole. In 1973, another major war erupted, which had significant global implications due to its effect on oil supplies and prices. Arab oil-producing states that held a considerable share of the world's available oil chose to suspend sales to countries supporting Israel. The price of oil skyrocketed, and the world economy contracted severely.

The United States was mindful of the substantial political and economic consequences of continuing turmoil in the Middle East and became proactive in seeking a diplomatic solution. US involvement would become a regular feature of the Middle East saga as it continued to unfold. In 1978, US president Jimmy Carter convinced the leaders of Egypt and Israel, Anwar Sadat and Menachem Begin, to join him for an intensive effort to find common ground to address the underlying conflict. The meetings took place at the official US presidential retreat in Camp David, Maryland, and the agreements signed in 1979 became known as the **Camp David Accords**.[3]

The Camp David Accords were a major breakthrough. Egypt became the first Arab state to formally recognize Israel's right to exist, while Israel agreed to return substantial portions of Egyptian land captured in 1967. The United States also pledged considerable economic and military aid to Egypt, beginning a long relationship that would help sustain the peace between Egypt and Israel. Resolving the issues relating to the status of Palestinians living in Gaza (and elsewhere) proved illusory, however. Anwar Sadat, the leading spokesman for the Arab world at the time, was branded a traitor by many Arabs for making peace with Israel. In 1981, he was assassinated in Egypt while reviewing a military parade.

The failure to make headway on the Palestinian issue escalated tensions. Palestinian resistance to Israel's occupation of the West Bank and Gaza intensified, resulting in a more coordinated **intifada** (the Arabic word for *uprising*), which would last from 1987 to 1993 and included terrorist attacks inside Israel. The situation deteriorated considerably as Israel responded with increasing military force.

The human, financial, and political costs of the conflict were taking their toll. With the assistance of an experienced Norwegian diplomat, Palestinian and Israeli negotiators met secretly to tackle the impasse under the watchful eye of the United States. In 1993, PLO chairman Yasser Arafat and Israeli prime minister Yitzhak Rabin came to the White House to sign the **Oslo Accords**. The agreement provided for the withdrawal of Israel from parts of the occupied territories and the creation of a transitional Palestinian governing authority. It also called on both sides to begin working on a comprehensive and permanent agreement. Arafat accepted Israel's right to exist in peace, while Rabin recognized the PLO as the legitimate representative of the Palestinian people.[4] The handshake between these long-term rivals suggested better days to come. It was followed by the signing of a formal treaty between Jordan and Israel in October 1994. Throughout the history of this conflict, however, agreeing on the details was always problematic. Negotiations stalled, enthusiasm for a conclusive deal waned, and Yitzhak Rabin was assassinated in 1995 by an Israeli citizen opposed to relinquishing any land to the Palestinians.

Attempting to salvage the deal as he approached the end of his presidency, Bill Clinton summoned Arafat and Israeli prime minister Ehud Barak to Camp David in July 2000. Optimism quickly faded, as both Arafat and Barak balked while Clinton escorted them to the initial meetings. Neither one wanted to be the first to enter the building or to appear too willing to make concessions to achieve an agreement. By many accounts, Barak offered territorial concessions well beyond any that had been on the table previously or that were likely to garner majority support back home. It did not matter, as the talks adjourned after approximately two weeks without a deal in place.[5] Shortly thereafter, a second intifada erupted.

With violence continuing to escalate, UN secretary-general Kofi Annan brought together representatives from the United States, the European Union (EU), and Russia to find a way out of the deadlock. The group, which came to be known as the Quartet, produced a **Road Map for Peace** in 2003 that established a framework for a two-state approach to the Israeli-Palestinian conflict with very explicit goals and a timeline to reach them. The road map directly addressed the core issues that framed the conflict and endorsed the principle of a two-state solution. This was the first time the United States publicly supported full Palestinian sovereignty.[6]

Road Map for Peace the 2003 plan that established the framework for a two-state solution to the Israeli-Palestinian conflict

Arab opposition to the US invasion of Iraq in 2003 disrupted the Israeli-Palestinian peace process. Arafat became less inclined to negotiate. Israel responded more forcefully to the violence in the territories but became increasingly frustrated with its inability to gain control over the situation. Arafat's death in 2004 and Israel's military withdrawal from Gaza in 2005, however, seemed to set the stage for a breakthrough.

Internal Palestinian politics made it difficult to capitalize on this opportunity. Mahmoud Abbas, the head of Fatah, was elected president of the administrative body governing the Palestinian territories, the Palestinian Authority. But he had little luck in moving discussions with Israel forward. His popularity among Palestinians quickly faded, even as he held on to power in the West Bank. When Palestinians went to the polls in Gaza in 2006, they voted overwhelmingly for Hamas, an organization opposed to any negotiations and committed to the destruction of Israel. A violent struggle broke out, and Hamas drove the Fatah forces loyal to Abbas out of Gaza. Palestinian leadership was now divided, making the prospects for peace with Israel more remote.

Meanwhile, matters became even more complicated when war broke out between Israel and Lebanon in 2006. The Israeli military was pitted against Hezbollah, an Islamic party

THOMAS COEX/AFP/Getty Images.

The Old City of Jerusalem, with Islam's holy site the Dome of the Rock mosque (top right) seen from the West Bank town of Abu Dis, separated by Israel's barrier.

supported by Syria and Iran. To the surprise of many, Hezbollah forces proved formidable on the battlefield and revealed Israel's vulnerability through their missile attacks on a number of Israeli cities. Palestinians welcomed this turn of events, and the resistance gained momentum. Hezbollah proceeded to expand its political leverage inside Lebanon and, together with its political allies, garnered enough electoral support in 2011 to gain control of the Lebanese government. This development added to the uncertainties of the region.

After decades of violence, the Israeli-Palestinian conflict continues to defy resolution. In 2008, a violent confrontation between Israel and Hamas in Gaza further eroded the possibility for a negotiated settlement. Since then, efforts to bridge stubborn and core differences have brought additional frustration and tension, and the key protagonists continue to operate at cross-purposes. In a move designed to force Israel's hand, President Abbas pushed for full UN recognition of Palestinian statehood. Although coming up somewhat short, he did succeed in upgrading its "permanent observer" designation to "non–member state" status in 2012. This recognition was largely a symbolic victory. But it provided Palestinians with the opportunity to join UN agencies, including the International Criminal Court (ICC), where they could advocate more directly for their cause.

The further deterioration of Israeli-Palestinian relations prompted yet another attempt by the United States to turn the tide. In 2013, US secretary of state John Kerry launched an intensive round of negotiations reminiscent of the 1970s when then-secretary Henry Kissinger laid the groundwork for the eventual peace between Israel and Egypt. This time, the obstacles proved insurmountable. After months of wrangling, the effort to create a framework to consider solutions to outstanding issues collapsed in April 2014, and the prospects for a permanent peace predicated on the two-state model dimmed.[7] Deadly clashes between Israel and Hamas soon followed and included the launching of thousands of Palestinian rockets into Israel and an intensive Israeli ground assault into Gaza.

In some respects, this latest outbreak resembled previous skirmishes with its considerable human toll, physical destruction, and unwillingness of either side to yield political ground. After seven full weeks of violent exchanges, Israel and Hamas agreed to a ceasefire, but subsequent efforts by the United States and others to get Palestinians and Israelis back to the negotiation table bore little fruit. Israel's prime minister, Benjamin Netanyahu, averse to moving forward without sizeable Palestinian concessions, fortified his position with a strong electoral victory in 2015. Shortly thereafter, a new wave of street violence in Israel—marked by Palestinians' stabbing attacks on Israelis—disrupted the calm.

The continuing hostilities are taking their toll. The distrust and outright hatreds that fuel the struggle are intensifying, and the chances of returning to a formula incorporating a two-state solution are diminishing. In its place emerges a future that will most likely include recurrent outbreaks of violence and a further hardening of attitudes and positions. Israel looks to fortify its security by expanding Jewish settlements on land that might be part of a future Palestinian state and by building an expansive security wall to stave off terrorist attacks. Palestinians, for their part, press their case for independent political legitimacy in the UN and other international organizations while declining to repudiate the use of violence to weaken Israel militarily and diplomatically.

While the particular circumstances have changed over the years, the core issues have not. The Israeli-Palestinian conflict is about the right to sovereignty and security. It is a dispute over land and political boundaries that involves access to water and other basic resources. It is also about access to holy religious sites. Perhaps most important, the conflict represents a history of two peoples locked in a profound and enduring struggle to control their own destinies. As such, it is a microcosm of the types of conflicts that have played a critical role in shaping our political world, and it represents an ongoing challenge with little hope for resolution in the immediate future. And if this was not complicated enough, it is a struggle that is highly sensitive to spillover from events and developments elsewhere in the region and beyond—such as Iran's quest for nuclear power, the civil war in Syria, and the rise of Islamic insurgencies—that are not easily contained by the political borders of today's world.

Weapons of Mass Destruction

Critical to our understanding of the instability in the world today are **weapons of mass destruction**, which may be nuclear, chemical, or biological. These weapons present unique challenges, given their devastating capacity to wreak havoc and inflict harm. Some have suggested that this awareness has served as an important restraint over time, given the enormity of moral responsibility that would fall squarely on the shoulders of those who would sanction or facilitate use of these weapons. These taboos have weighed on international efforts to ban their presence or to, at the very least, make their deployment less likely.[8] But is this sufficient?

weapons of mass destruction nuclear, chemical, and biological weapons

Even as we have moved beyond the constant nuclear threat that darkened the Cold War era, progress in curtailing the development and spread of deadly weapons has been limited. Many governments and groups still seek to secure the most advanced weapons available, while some strategic thinkers (particularly those with a realist perspective) argue that it is precisely the potential threat of the weapons' use that serves to maintain the peace. Avoiding the unthinkable may rest largely on the ability of the international community to effectively apply the lessons of the past.

From the earliest days of the nuclear age, governments have recognized the need to restrict the global weapons infrastructure. The array of agreements and treaties is impressive—at least on paper. A few of these are particularly noteworthy. In 1968, the members of the nuclear club designed the Non-Proliferation Treaty (NPT) to limit the production of such weapons, while the 1972 Anti–Ballistic Missile Treaty (ABM) sought to ban the development of defensive systems that might encourage the first use of nuclear weapons. The nuclear powers also moved forward with the Limited (1963) and then more Comprehensive (1996) Test Ban treaties to discourage further research and development activities. In the early 1970s, the Soviet Union and the United States began discussions that lasted more than two decades to restrict the number and types of weapons composing their respective strategic arsenals. The result was a series of Strategic Arms Limitations Treaties (SALT I and II) and the Strategic Arms Reduction Treaty (START). The 1987 Intermediate Range Nuclear Forces (INF) accord, moreover, ended the deployment of US and Soviet medium-range missiles across Europe.

This picture, taken on July 4, 2017, and released by North Korea's official Korean Central News Agency (KCNA) on July 5, 2017, shows North Korean leader Kim Jong-un (center) celebrating the successful test-fire of the intercontinental ballistic missile Hwasong-14 at an undisclosed location.

STR/AFP/Getty Images.

In 2010, the United States and Russia sealed the first major nuclear weapons treaty in nearly two decades, agreeing to slash their strategic warhead arsenals. Diplomats modeled the treaty, which was dubbed New START and took effect in January 2011, on the original START agreement that had expired in 2009. It required both the Americans and the Russians to reduce the stockpiles of their most dangerous weapons and to meet the specified targets by February 2018. Nuclear warheads were limited to 1,550 per country (30 percent lower than before), and the number of deployed and nondeployed strategic

WHAT CAN YOU DO WITH INTERNATIONAL STUDIES?

Implementing United Nations Resolutions on Women, Peace, and Security (WPS)

By Lori Perkovich, MS Graduate, New York University, Global Affairs

Completing a bachelor's degree in international studies and political science at UNC Charlotte created a solid foundation for pursuing a graduate degree in global affairs. While completing my MS at New York University's Center for Global Affairs, I joined the Global Network of Women Peacebuilders (GNWP) in 2014. GNWP encompasses more than 90 member organizations worldwide. Its mission is to enhance the capacity of women's organizations and civil society organizations to use legal mechanisms to protect women's rights and ensure their leadership and participation in decision making, peacebuilding, conflict prevention, conflict resolution, and reconstruction. Specifically, GNWP facilitates effective implementation of United Nations resolutions UNSCR 1325 and 1820 and the supporting Women, Peace, and Security (WPS) resolutions at the national and local levels.

My position at GNWP started as an internship and turned into a consultancy where I have worked for more than two years. I have had the opportunity to implement programs, facilitate workshops, speak on panels, conduct research, and participate in advocacy for ongoing peace processes in seven countries in Africa, including the Democratic Republic of the Congo (DRC), Ethiopia, Kenya, Liberia, Rwanda, South Africa, and South Sudan. Furthermore, I have worked with young women and girls to improve literacy rates and ensure that they understand their rights according to international law.

I spend much of my time with two of our programs, Localization and the Girl Ambassadors for Peace. Localization constitutes a bottom-up approach to the implementation of the WPS resolutions and National Action Plans (NAPs), with local authorities and communities taking ownership of the implementation. The Girl Ambassadors program provides literacy, peacebuilding and leadership development for literate young women and girls. The Girl Ambassadors then go out to teach illiterate girls and to promote their understanding of gender concepts and the relevant United Nations resolutions. Theater is used to raise awareness of WPS issues in rural communities in DRC and South Sudan.

Advocacy occurs in various ways. For instance, we worked behind the scenes with UN representatives, the Intergovernmental Authority on Development (IGAD)

Photo courtesy of Lori Perkovich.

negotiators, and civil society to lobby for the hiring of a gender advisor for the South Sudan peace process, as well as requesting an increase in women's participation in the process. Now that the peace agreement has been signed, our focus has shifted to ensuring implementation and monitoring the peace agreement. This includes facilitating meetings between civil society and supportive member states of the UN in New York. The organization also arranges meetings and town halls convening civil society and representatives of IGAD, the Joint Monitoring and Evaluation Commission (JMEC), and local governments in South Sudan to discuss implementation. The civil society survey conducted in 2015 was another significant undertaking. It generated responses from 317 civil society organizations in 71 countries, one of which was DRC, where I facilitated one of the corresponding focus groups. The data collected helped develop recommendations made in the Global Study on UNSCR 1325, an independent study commissioned by the UN secretary-general on women, peace, and security.

As a nontraditional student who had more than fifteen years of experience in communication before going to college to complete her degree, my first recommendation is this: Leave your comfort zone and do not necessarily allow your past to dictate what you do next. Explore and take calculated risks to achieve your goals—they lead to new experiences that will benefit you. My second piece of advice: Do not underestimate the importance of networking. In the past two years, I have established and now maintain strong cooperative relationships with representatives of civil society, NGOs, UN entities, UN member states, and African Union members because of my contributions at GNWP and my time spent building connections. These relationships may be the key to a successful future.

long-range delivery vehicles was capped at 800. The terms also included verification pro-visions that provided for eighteen onsite inspections per year. The treaty's duration was set at ten years, with an allowable five-year extension. While the pact established "hard" numerical limits, its overall impact was limited by the absence of constraints on efforts to modernize weapons systems within the established parameters.[9]

Beyond the nuclear threat is the danger posed by chemical weapons (CW), biological weapons (BW), and other weapons of mass destruction. As far back as 1925, the Geneva Protocol banned gas and bacteriological weapons, which had devastating effects in World War I. The 1972 Biological Weapons Convention (BWC) and the 1993 Chemical Weapons Convention (CWC) included widespread participation from countries all over the world. These agreements prohibited possession of these dangerous agents while committing all signatories without existing capacity to give up their rights to future development. This did not stop the Syrian government from manufacturing or using CW against its own citizens in 2013, resulting in the deaths of more than 1,400 people— including more than 400 children. Even after Syria was prodded into joining the CWC to avoid a military confrontation with the United States, the government and some rebels engaged in the country's ongoing civil war continued to avail themselves of this option. Chlorine, a choking agent that was not banned by the treaty due to its various legal uses, was the instrument of choice in more than 150 instances, with civilians being the most frequent targets.[10]

As it turned out, many of these efforts to curtail the deadliest of weapons had limited impacts. Without assurance of effective verification or compliance, it proved difficult to move very far along the road to disarmament. The nuclear states understood the serious-ness of the threat but not sufficiently to prevent an unnerving arms race fueled by tensions between the superpowers. The early 1980s were particularly delicate, as the United States launched a Strategic Defense Initiative (SDI) to offset growing Soviet strength. The US mili-tary designed this so-called Star Wars program with the latest technologies, and President Ronald Reagan touted it as a plan that would render nuclear weapons obsolete. Star Wars raised serious questions about the violation of prior agreements relating to the creation of defense-weapons systems and the demilitarization of outer space. While some people credited SDI with getting the Soviets back to the negotiating table, others decried its role in encouraging forays into new areas of weapons development.

Reagan was following the logic of **deterrence**, which involved crafting a credible means to dissuade others from initiating the use of nuclear weapons. For much of the Cold War, experts credited the concept with preventing nuclear war. Precluding a first strike required the development of an effective retaliatory, or second-strike, capability. As a result, during the Cold War, the Soviet Union and the United States felt constantly compelled to one-up each other's new weapons programs with the deployment of air-, land-, and sea-based systems. This very costly and dangerous arms race extended through much of the period. Despite sporadic efforts to curtail these activities, the absence of foolproof monitoring pro-cedures gave way to new waves of development.

deterrence the inhibition of a first strike nuclear attack by an effective retaliatory or second-strike capability

Although the thinking behind deterrence was fairly straightforward, different views on how to best actualize the strategy complicated its implementation. In the 1970s and 1980s, for example, the United States flirted with conflicting approaches. One proposal called for the construction of multiple installations over vast distances of American soil to include "dummy" silos devoid of armed missiles. This nuclear shell game was intended to under-mine Soviet confidence in their targeting decisions.

Critics called for an opposite method that concentrated the placement of missiles with-out much regard for concealing their whereabouts. They argued that if the weapons were densely packed in heavily fortified silos within a few miles of one another, the heat and debris resulting from the impact of the first incoming missile would undermine the capacity of additional incoming missiles to destroy the other silos—thereby preserving the capacity to retaliate. Based on very different assumptions and expectations, these approaches reflected

David Pollack/Corbis via Getty Images.

A poster from 1951 distributed by the Federal Civil Defense Administration encouraging citizens to participate in civil defense.

mutual assured destruction (MAD) the logic of nuclear deterrence that assumes that the certainty of a nuclear retaliation would prevent governments from launching such an attack in the first place

the inherent logic of deterrence—that is, to project the certainty of retaliation that will inflict massive and unacceptable levels of damage and would prevent governments from launching such an attack in the first place. Pundits aptly labeled this strategy **mutual assured destruction (MAD)**.

The United States remains the only country to have used nuclear weapons, with its bombing of the Japanese cities of Hiroshima and Nagasaki in 1945 during World War II. The rivals' restraint during the Cold War was impressive, because neither the Soviet Union nor the United States relinquished their nuclear options. Some experts have suggested that it was precisely the possibility of mutual destruction that moved the two superpowers to avoid direct confrontation, even when relations were at their lowest points. The lessons of the 1962 Cuban Missile Crisis, when the two countries came perilously close to a nuclear exchange, influenced this thinking. Deterrence has always been an imprecise notion. It assumes rational decision making, the capacity to determine an effective retaliatory capability, and knowledge of when enough retaliatory weapons are in place so that deterrence has been achieved. Deterrence further presupposes that nuclear weapons are reserved as a last resort. However, the risks of miscalculation and misperception during times of tension and crisis call this strategy into question.

Even with these concerns, the record suggests that deterrence has worked, and the effort to control nuclear and other weapons of mass destruction through treaties and other international agreements has made a difference to this point. But the weapons game has changed considerably since the days of the Cold War. The superpowers guaranteed that they would defend their allies. Without that guarantee, states that previously had no need for nuclear weapons are now crowding the playing field. In addition, new countries have moved into the nuclear club—most notably India and Pakistan—and many others are eagerly seeking entry.

As noted in Chapter 4, the initiatives of North Korea and Iran have been most pronounced (see Figure 5.1). North Korea has maintained an active weapons agenda for many years. It withdrew from the NPT in 2003, has conducted significant tests of explosive devices, and is generally considered capable of enriching uranium and producing weapons-grade plutonium. The on-again, off-again Six Party Talks (with China, Japan, Russia, South Korea, and the United States) have produced few results, and the regime continues to move forward aggressively with its program.

North Korea deploys short- and medium-range ballistic missiles and has successfully launched long-range rockets. It has developed a warhead small enough to fit on a missile, a step that is a potential game changer in terms of the direct threat this poses to the United States. In addition, the country has long maintained a stockpile of biological agents and possesses an estimated 2,500 to 5,000 metric tons of chemical weapons.[11] The rhetoric of

FIGURE 5.1 ● North Korea's and Iran's Nuclear Weapons Capabilities

Iran's nuclear facilities

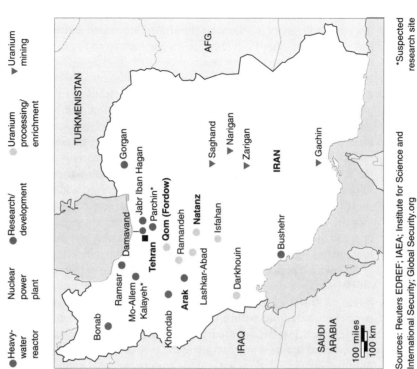

North Korea's nuclear facilities

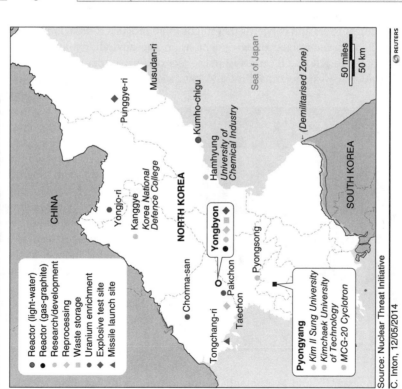

North Korea's young and unpredictable leader, Kim Jong-un, has added to concern. While it may be tempting to dismiss Kim's bravado, given the country's desperate economic needs and weak political standing, he has demonstrated his intention to proceed with his activities and a willingness to threaten the United States and America's allies across the region. Even China, his closest ally, has grown both weary and wary of Kim's recklessness and is looking to moderate his behavior.

Meanwhile, the dramas surrounding Iran's nuclear ambitions have both regional and global implications. Iran's government has held steadfast to its declared right to nuclear power while maintaining that it is interested in using it only for peaceful purposes. The international community has responded with skepticism, and Iran has been hit with a battery of economic sanctions under the authority of a succession of UN Security Council resolutions. After years of unproductive efforts to reach even modest accommodation, the P5+1 (named to reflect the Security Council's permanent members, China, France, Russia, the United Kingdom, and the United States, in addition to Germany) secured a short-term deal in late 2013. Iran agreed to freeze key components of its program for six months in return for relief from some sanctions. These confidence-building measures brought the parties back to the negotiation table and bought additional time to secure a more permanent accord.

Following a period of exhaustive and often conflictual discussions, a broad agreement—officially known as the Joint Comprehensive Plan of Action, or JCPOA—was reached in July 2015. It was a formidable achievement, given its many sticking points and significant opposition to it from within both Iran and the United States. The arrangement aims to curb Iran's nuclear development program for ten to fifteen years by capping its stockpile of low-enriched uranium and removing the core of its plutonium reactor in exchange for the lifting of sanctions. It does not end the enmity or considerable distrust framing the bilateral relationship. But it does offer an open line of communication, albeit a rather tenuous one, to address issues and concerns that might undo progress to this point.

There is widespread disagreement as to the advisability and impacts of the deal. Supporters argue that it came just in the nick of time, as Iran was within months of achieving nuclear weapons capability. By acknowledging Iran's right to a nuclear program, it gave the country an opportunity to save face and enabled negotiators to avoid a potentially dangerous confrontation. The elimination of sanctions provided a boost to Iran's economy, which had declined precipitously, and opened channels for investment and other business activities with the West. While not necessarily eliminating Iran's long-term weapons aspirations, the deal is seen as a breakthrough that might induce further cooperation across a range of issues—nuclear and non-nuclear alike.[12]

Critics have not been swayed by these arguments and have focused largely on the fact that the arrangements put in place did not serve to dismantle Iran's nuclear infrastructure. They see the agreement as merely a temporary fix and as a potential source of nuclear proliferation, as Iran's rivals seek to keep pace to counter its considerable ambitions and interests. Uncertainties relating to the effectiveness of monitoring and enforcement have also raised concerns. By most accounts,

An attendee holds a sign opposed to the Iran nuclear deal during a Tea Party Patriots rally on Capitol Hill in Washington, D.C.

Andrew Harrer/Bloomberg via Getty Images.

Iran retains the capability to move forward over time with the production of weapons-grade materials, the building of warheads, and the deployment of short, intermediate, and potentially long-range delivery vehicles.[13]

It is too early to evaluate the extent to which this pact has achieved its broad objectives. Iran appears to have honored most of its commitments, and it has benefited considerably from sanctions relief, which has unfrozen assets in foreign banks and has led to an uptick in commercial activity. The International Atomic Energy Agency (IAEA) has maintained its access to monitor compliance, although some have suggested that the Iranians continue to hone their weapons capabilities at facilities that are off-limits to inspectors. The United States and its partners have held firm to their belief that encouraging Iran's cooperation is the best path to avoiding a future showdown. The Trump administration is highly skeptical, however, and has assumed a harder line in its dealings with Iran as it assesses the future utility of the agreement.[14]

North Korea's and Iran's explorations of their nuclear options are probably the tip of the iceberg, as many governments and groups see nuclear weapons as the path toward increased political leverage and latitude (see Table 5.1). Their efforts pose a serious challenge to the effective application of the idea of deterrence, which developed at a time when prospects for deployment remained within the exclusive preserve of the world's superpowers.

The characteristics and political agendas of the new players pose another challenge to deterrence. Authoritarian and unpredictable leaders are especially enamored with the nuclear route, as are countries with either longstanding or particularly intense rivalries at their doorsteps. Nuclear development feeds on itself by providing inducements to governments or groups with unfinished business. As in the case of India and Pakistan, the results can be unsettling. Prime Minister Zulfikar Ali Bhutto, who committed Pakistan to developing nuclear weapons in 1972, declared that Pakistanis would have nuclear weapons, even if they had to "eat grass."[15]

Advances in technology have raised questions about the ability to maintain an effective deterrent, as it is now far easier than it was during the Cold War to acquire some nuclear capability. Component parts have become far more portable and difficult to track, as they can be easily transported around the world. Furthermore, the rapid growth of the Internet and the increasing sophistication of electronic information transmission systems have significantly enhanced production and assembly capabilities—with respect to both weapons and delivery systems.

The availability of multiple means of acquiring these weapons has also undermined our security. While conventional arms traders have long worked these routes, these

TABLE 5.1 ● Members of the Nuclear Club, 2016

Nuclear Weapon States	Nuclear Weapon Possessors**	States of Proliferation Concern
China	India	Iran
France	Israel	North Korea
Russia*	Pakistan	Syria
United Kingdom		
United States		

Source: Arms Control Association, 2016, www.armscontrol.org/factsheets/Nuclearweaponswhohaswhat.

*Also controls weapons from the Soviet era located in Belarus, Kazakhstan, and Ukraine.

**Known to possess nuclear weapons but are not part of the NPT.

TABLE 5.2 ● Biological and Chemical Weapons Capabilities				
	Biological Weapons (BW) Capabilities		Chemical Weapons (CW) Capabilities	
Country	State Declaration	Allegations	State Declaration	Allegations
Albania	None	None	Mustard gas and other chemical agents were declared and destroyed in 2007 and 2012	None
China	Denies having an active BW program	The United States claims China has an extensive BW program and multiple delivery systems, but a recent report did not address compliance	Denies having an active CW program	The United States has alleged that China maintains a CW program; a recent report cited no concerns
Cuba	Denies having an active BW program	The United States claims Cuba has had a limited BW program; a 2017 report cites no concerns over compliance with the Biological Weapons Convention (BWC)	None	None
Egypt	Some reports in 1972 of a BW program; currently claims to be opposed to production and stockpiling of BW	Egypt may not have eliminated stockpiles; a 2017 report does not mention any problems relating to compliance with BWC	No significant declaration of CW	Used CW against Yemen previously; not a signatory to the Chemical Weapons Convention (CWC)
India	Claims to be in compliance with BWC	No allegations; India has robust delivery systems capabilities	Chemical agents were declared and destroyed in 2009	No allegations; India retains the capability to make chemicals that can be used in CW production
Iran	Has denounced BW	Intelligence sources claim Iran has the capability to make limited quantities of BW but do not have conclusive evidence of this	Has denounced CW	Intelligence sources claim Iran has the capability to make CW, but are unable to ascertain whether Iran is violating CWC obligations
Iraq	None since 2003; admitted to testing and stockpiling BW in the 1990s but has since destroyed them	2010 report indicated that Iraq is not violating BWC	None significant since 2009; possessed extensive CW systems previously and used them	Program was mostly dismantled in the 1990s, but unknown quantities remain; plans to fully dismantle are incomplete
Israel	Has not joined BWC	Possibly had a BW program in the past, but there is no conclusive evidence currently; the country has a robust pharmaceutical and biotech industry	Has not ratified CWC	Possibly had a CW program in the past, but there is no conclusive evidence currently; the country has a robust chemical industry

Country	Biological Weapons (BW) Capabilities		Chemical Weapons (CW) Capabilities	
	State Declaration	Allegations	State Declaration	Allegations
Libya	Has eliminated its BW program	2010 report indicated Libya is in compliance with BWC	Declared in 2003 that its CW program would be eliminated; stockpile was destroyed in 2016	None
North Korea	Has not declared BW systems	2010 report indicated that North Korea may consider BW use	Has not declared CW systems	Widely believed to have an extensive stockpile and no plan to destroy it
Russia	Declared having extensive stockpiles and a BW program in 1992; current possessions unknown	2010 report indicated dual-use research, although not inconsistent with BWC; 2017 report questions Russia's compliance with BWC obligations	Declared the world's largest CW stockpile and has commenced destruction; completion is estimated by 2020	The United States continues to express reservations about Russian compliance
South Korea	None	None	Declared stockpile and completed destruction in 2008	None
Sudan	None	None	Declared small stockpile in 1999	Sudan may have used CW in past; no recent allegations
Syria	Syria has "hinted" at BW capabilities	2010 report indicated Syria continues activities banned by BWC	Declared CW stockpile and facilities after using CW against rebels in Syria	Syria has an extensive CW program
Taiwan	None	None	Declared having small quantities of CW for research	None
United States	Declared and destroyed BW stockpiles by 1973	Russia claims the United States is undertaking BW research	Declared large CW stockpile; destruction is underway, to be completed by 2023	Russia claims inspection of US facilities may be blocked by legislation; says the United States did not report moving CW from Iraq to the United States between 2003 and 2008

Source: Arms Control Association, "Chemical and Biological Weapons Status at a Glance," last updated June 2017, http://www.armscontrol.org/factsheets/cbwprolif.

channels are now also flowing with nonconventional weapons and technology. The breakup of the Soviet Union in the early 1990s brought many of these items to traders. Their quest for personal financial gain, quite apart from political considerations, inspired the sale or transfer of weapons systems housed across a number of former Soviet republics. The suspected sale of sensitive information by individuals in such disparate places as the United States, Iraq, and Pakistan speaks further to the complexities of controlling the proliferation problem. Today's global arms bazaar is a vibrant one, with both organized and ad-hoc private exchanges adding to an already active market fueled by government military assistance and sales programs.

Finally, nonstate actors are increasingly involved in this drama. CW and BW pose a particular risk, given the stockpiles available and accessible (see Table 5.2). Many disgruntled groups and terrorist organizations across the world have explicitly stated their intentions in this regard. Incidents involving the suspected or actual use of these devices have brought panic to Tokyo subways, the London transportation system, and the US Postal Service. These episodes may provide a crucial glimpse into the future.

Terrorism

terrorism the threat or use of violence to change an existing political order

While conflicts in the Middle East and the development and spread of exceedingly destructive weapons systems have undercut global stability, it is **terrorism** that most directly shakes our sense of personal security. It is increasingly difficult to escape its potential reach. We have become accustomed to reminders as we make our way through airports or train stations around the world. Places of worship, hotels, restaurants, landmarks, and even college campuses and other open spaces are fair game. The chances of being victimized are slim, but there is really no escape from confronting the dangers of this phenomenon.

In 2016, for example, the US Department of State cited 11,072 acts of terror resulting in more than 25,000 deaths and 33,800 injuries. Attacks took place in 104 countries, with more than half occurring in just five (Iraq, Afghanistan, Pakistan, India, and the Philippines).[16] Despite the increasing number of serious incidents and growing recognition of the magnitude of the threat, there has not been a coherent and coordinated global response. Part of the problem has to do with language and perspective. Who is a terrorist, and what constitutes a terrorist organization? How would you categorize an al-Qaida fighter in Iraq, a Tamil Tiger in Sri Lanka, a PKK (Kurdistan Workers' Party) operative in Turkey, or a Basque separatist in Spain? The answers may vary depending on your point of view.

One way to address this dilemma might be to focus on the tactics that are employed. Generally speaking, terrorism involves the threat or use of violence to instill fear and create uncertainty; this definition rests on broad intents and purposes. A terrorist attack is a premeditated political act that is often directed at civilian targets and designed to change an existing political order. Most groups utilizing these methods, however, strongly resist this labeling. Instead, they justify their activities in terms of a struggle for high or lofty ideals. It is often said that one person's terrorist is another's freedom fighter.

Anyone who reads or watches the news commonly associates terrorism with nongovernmental groups and networks. However, governments are directly and indirectly complicit in some of these activities. In its annual report, the US Department of State identifies those governments it categorizes as state sponsors of terrorism.[17] These countries cannot receive US aid in the form of arms, are restricted with respect to the items with military and civilian applications they may purchase from the United States, and are eligible only for very limited types of US aid. The 2016 list included Iran, Sudan, and Syria—countries long at odds with the United States and disdainful of its designations and policies. It is interesting to note that Cuba, a fixture on this list for many years, was removed in 2015 as part of the diplomatic rapprochement between the two countries. Those appearing on the list defiantly dismiss its validity, citing the United States itself as the chief perpetrator of terrorist activity.

Terrorism is by no means a new phenomenon. The word itself originated during the French Revolution and the Jacobin Reign of Terror from 1792 to 1794. Individual terrorist acts can be traced at least as far back as ancient Greek and Roman times, and group terrorism became more common during the Middle Ages.[18] At times, terrorism has changed the course of history on a large scale, as when the 1914 assassination of Austrian archduke Franz Ferdinand by a Serb extremist sparked the outbreak of World War I.

Governments and the media tend to focus considerable attention today on religious, especially Islamic, fundamentalists who may seek violent means to resist outside influences and to promote traditional values and customs. Terrorism is not restricted, however, to a particular ideology or political perspective. It may be born out of frustration and adopted by groups or individuals with unresolved grievances. Terrorism is a calculated political tool that may compensate for otherwise limited resources or leverage. Some terrorists ally with groups that do not share their political agendas but may have other common interests. In Colombia, for example, **narcoterrorism** blended the political ideology of the FARC (Colombian Revolutionary Action Front) with the financial interests of local drug lords. This relationship served to prolong a civil conflict, which lasted for more than fifty years and resulted in the deaths of more than 200,000 people until it finally ended through a negotiated peace in 2016.[19]

Terrorism appears in many shapes and forms. Its perpetrators use terrorist acts for a wide range of purposes. Terrorism victims may be individuals, as in the kidnapping or execution of journalists, employees of transnational corporations (TNCs), or political figures. They may be groups, such as passengers on hijacked airplanes or workers and visitors in embassies or other buildings of political or symbolic importance. Innocent bystanders may be caught up in bombings of hotels and restaurants in areas catering to tourists and other foreign nationals or attacks on public transportation systems.

While the specific methods and objectives of terrorist groups may differ considerably, they share a number of common purposes. First and foremost, they want attention. Their actions may seem random, but this is generally not the case. The inability to predict when or where they will occur spreads fear and uncertainty. The more extreme or violent the event, the better the publicity will be.

Such exposure may serve a number of needs. Gaining sympathy for the cause is often a key motive, although particularly deadly attacks can have the opposite effect of galvanizing opposition. The cycle may include equally violent acts of retaliation, offering additional opportunities to build momentum for future actions. Terrorist actions themselves are useful recruiting devices. The ability to execute an attack—even if the result is less than completely successful—enhances the legitimacy and credibility of the initiating group. The martyrdom of suicide bombers is compelling to people who feel alienated or hopeless or seek some financial remuneration for their families. For many years, Palestinian families received compensation from Libya and other groups for the sacrifices of their relatives. The deaths of activists add to the sense of outrage among supporters and often attract replacements.

Since the 9/11 attacks on the United States, many governments have joined in a concerted effort to uncover and destroy terrorist networks operating across much of the world. The global war on terror has become intense and lethal. The United States has assumed leadership and has used all means deemed necessary in pursuing this agenda. It has also attempted to enlist the support of allies and other countries particularly vulnerable to attack.

The US government has realigned and redesigned its intelligence and security operations to enhance **counterterrorism** capabilities. The controversial 2001 **USA PATRIOT Act** provided for the expansion of government surveillance and expanded the government's law enforcement powers in dealing with terrorism. The creation of the Department

Getty Images.

This is an undated file photo of al-Qaida leader Osama bin Laden in Afghanistan. While bin Laden is now dead (he was killed in a US raid on his compound in Pakistan in 2011), other terrorist leaders and groups persist.

narcoterrorism the alliance of drug traffickers and antigovernment revolutionaries, often used in reference to political violence in Colombia

counterterrorism political and military measures designed to prevent acts of terror

USA PATRIOT Act the controversial 2001 law that expanded the government's law enforcement powers in dealing with terrorism

of Homeland Security and the post of director of national intelligence represented the largest increase in the US federal bureaucracy since the creation of the Central Intelligence Agency, National Security Council, and Department of Defense through the National Security Act of 1947. Meanwhile, efforts to better secure US borders and to draft new legislation governing immigration became a lightning rod during the 2016 presidential election and are a high priority for those who believe that the country remains vulnerable to infiltration.

The global effort to contain terrorism has produced mixed results and faces a difficult future. First, the covert and secretive nature of terrorist groups makes them difficult to track and expose. Whenever possible, terrorist leaders operate under the cover of rugged terrain that is familiar to them, and often enjoy the protection of compliant or supportive local populations. Such legitimacy enables them to stay "underground" for long periods of time, surfacing only when absolutely necessary. The elusive Osama bin Laden successfully adhered to this strategy for nearly a decade while maintaining refuge in the region bordering Afghanistan and Pakistan.

Second, a ready reservoir of potential terrorists and an ample supply of leaders are waiting to serve their causes. The United States claimed many victories during the early years of its war on terror launched by the George W. Bush administration. Evidence suggested that the campaign had indeed impacted the leadership ranks of al-Qaida and other terrorist networks. In 2004, for example, the Associated Press (AP) news service identified a dozen young leaders of groups associated with the al-Qaida network in the Middle East, North Africa, South Asia, and Europe.[20] By mid-2006, almost half had been killed or forced into hiding to avoid detection.[21] But it was difficult to gauge the longer-term effects of these developments.

The media heralded the June 2006 killing of Abu Musab al-Zarqawi, the leader of al-Qaida in Iraq, as a potential turning point in that war. He had become the symbol of the insurgency and had been behind many of its most violent episodes. His death came only days after the highly publicized arrest of Islamic activists suspected of plotting assassinations of officials and the bombing of landmarks and government buildings in Canada. Al-Zarqawi was replaced quickly, however, and the war in Iraq dragged on for many additional years. Al-Qaida persevered, and its unifying figure, bin Laden, eluded his pursuers until the US commando attack on his compound in Pakistan resulted in his death in 2011.

The elimination of bin Laden did not destroy the movement. Subsequent US efforts to weaken the central organization under the direction of Ayman al-Zawahiri, bin Laden's successor in Pakistan, did have an effect. However, the organization proved resilient, and a number of its more active and powerful affiliates actually thrived within a more decentralized structure and gained greater latitude in planning and financing their operations. This more autonomous arrangement also made it more difficult to counter them.

The Al-Qaida Arabian Peninsula, commonly referred to as AQAP and based in Yemen, is a case in point. Taking advantage of Yemen's longstanding economic challenges and political fragility, AQAP has built a strong network of supporters and fighters and assumed a particularly aggressive posture in carrying out its missions. The United States, recognizing the growing threat to its interests, has responded forcefully by launching a series of drone attacks targeting AQAP's leadership and bases. Many of these strikes have accomplished their tactical objectives, but AQAP remains a considerable force with support across a number of states. Ironically, Saudi Arabia's 2015 military intervention in Yemen's civil war, backed by the United States, has strengthened AQAP's position. It is believed to control around $100 million of the country's assets, has considerable leverage within the critical oil sector, and rules over important pockets of territory. It has also demonstrated its capabilities beyond the region on occasion. In 2015, for example, it launched a dramatic attack on the Paris offices of the satirical newspaper *Charlie Hebdo*.[22]

Al-Qaida in the Islamic Maghreb (AQIM) has attained similar prominence through its work. This affiliate operates in the Sahara and Sahel (in the region known as the Maghreb in premodern times), which includes Algeria, Morocco, Tunisia, Libya, and Mauritania. Originating in Algeria in the 1990s as the Armed Islamic Group, the organization aligned with al-Qaida in 2006. This merger led to a significant uptick in its activities, including its involvement in the attacks on the US diplomatic compound in Benghazi, Libya, in 2012 and the hostage crisis at an Algerian gas facility in 2013, designed to undermine Western influence and install fundamentalist Islamic regimes across the region. It has also worked with other insurgency groups and has proven its resiliency through a series of kidnappings, bombings, and other missions.[23]

While AQIM maintains its focus on Algeria, it has extended the range of its operations through West Africa. Mali has been a particularly popular target since France's intervention in 2013, and the group has been aided in its efforts to gain a foothold there by the lawlessness, government inefficiencies, and harsh treatment of local inhabitants by security forces seeking to impose order. In 2016, al-Qaida was linked to more than 100 incidents in West Africa and, in addition to its ongoing campaign in Mali, AQIM was credited with organizing attacks on foreigners in Burkina Faso, Ivory Coast, and elsewhere.[24]

Third, many of these groups have become quite capable in their use of media and advanced forms of electronic communication. They have capitalized on the development of 24/7 news coverage by CNN, among other news services, as well as people's access to news from any source in the world. Elaborate news networks have emerged in many parts of the world and provide opportunities for extended coverage. The Qatar-based **Al Jazeera** network, for example, has become very influential, with its reports highlighting the conditions that give rise to terrorists and mold their missions. Al Jazeera also emerged as the vehicle of choice for bin Laden to transmit tapes designed to convey his public thoughts and messages. In March 2008, he issued a statement condemning European involvement in Afghanistan and denouncing the pope as a responsible party for the publication of political cartoons in Denmark that al-Qaida saw as disparaging the prophet Muhammad.

Al Jazeera the broadcast network based in Qatar

Access to the Internet has contributed further to raising the profiles of terrorist groups. Not only do sophisticated terrorist websites and social networking sites provide basic information, publicize activities, and recruit new members; they also serve as a means for communicating plans for upcoming missions and even chronicling events as they unfold. Meanwhile, an increase in cyberterrorism disrupts and penetrates the security of targeted government and corporate websites. The control of information is key in the struggle against terrorism, making cyberspace an important battleground.

Fourth, the global effort to counter terrorism suffers from the ability of terrorists to intimidate or even blackmail states that are within their sights. The case of Saudi Arabia is illuminating. For decades, Saudi Arabia and the United States have maintained a close strategic and financial relationship. The threat to the Saudi monarchy posed by Iraq in 1991 was an important consideration prompting the United States to launch Operation Desert Storm. Protecting the royal family and the security of Saudi oil fields remain key US objectives in the Persian Gulf. However, Saudi Arabia was also home to bin Laden and to most individuals implicated in the 9/11 attacks. It remains an active and fertile recruiting ground for terrorists. The Saudi government's reluctance to crack down on this situation has stemmed, in part, from the fear of increased domestic targeting. More important, some of these terrorist groups have received support from sympathetic Saudi officials, even as they have launched attacks within the country with the intent of destabilizing the government. This Saudi ambivalence speaks directly to the difficulty of devising effective counterterrorism measures on a broader scale.

Finally, terrorist groups have an ever-growing number of options with respect to establishing bases for their operations. Despite increased surveillance and periodic detection,

An Islamic State fighter waving a flag while standing on a captured government fighter jet in Raqqa, Syria, in 2015.

terrorist cells take advantage of porous borders across much of the world and often function with few constraints in the very countries they seek to target. They find hospitable and welcoming environments elsewhere as conflicts evolve and supportive leaders emerge.

Perhaps most noteworthy here is the story of ISIS. As noted in Chapter 4, the group gained notoriety in 2014 when it became enmeshed in the deepening struggles in Iraq and Syria. Up to that point, it had gone through a number of iterations since its formation in 2003. It aligned with al-Qaida, but subsequently took a different path as it pursued its own strategic course. Unlike al-Qaida, which was focused primarily on confronting the United States and its allies, ISIS looked to move more immediately and aggressively in acquiring territory and establishing an Islamic state or caliphate on behalf of Sunni Muslims that would reflect traditional values. The vision is for a singular state comprising the eastern Mediterranean region, formerly known as the Levant—hence, the inclination of some, including the US government during the Obama presidency, to refer to the organization as the Islamic State of Iraq and the Levant, or ISIL. Adding to some confusion over its proper name is the fact that others prefer to use Daesh, its Arabic language acronym. In June 2014, the group announced the birth of the caliphate and proclaimed itself the Islamic State (IS) in recognition of its achievements.[25]

For ISIS, there was much to celebrate and the promise of even greater triumphs. Aided by the deepening chaos in Iraq and Syria, ISIS moved forward with a number of decisive victories and came to control some 35,000 square miles of land across the two countries, with the northern Syrian city of Raqqa as its de facto capital. It also undertook some daring missions, including attacks on civilians in Paris and Brussels, that demonstrated its expanded reach and capacity to inflict considerable harm. From mid-2014 to mid-2016, it was responsible for more than 140 attacks in 29 countries (beyond Iraq and Syria) that claimed more than 2,000 lives.[26] It relished the attention and worked to instill fear by engaging in some particularly horrific acts, such as the beheadings of captives, the destruction of antiquities in the Syrian city of Palmyra, and the targeting of Yazidis and other communities deemed a threat to the realization of its religious prophesy. Its leader, Abu Bakr al-Baghdadi, remained defiant as he directed the campaign.

ISIS became adept at its use of social media for recruitment purposes and attracted tens of thousands of fighters, many from Western countries, to its cause. It also amassed an estimated $2 billion war chest from the sale of oil, ransom payments, extorted taxes, and trafficking in people and antiquities. This impressive rise elicited a response from the United States, which initiated 17,000 airstrikes, a series of targeted assassinations, and other measures to halt these advances. By late 2016, it was estimated that around 43 percent of the land within the caliphate had been lost and 75 percent of ISIS fighters had been killed.[27] Russia's military incursion into Syria to support the Assad regime's effort to regain full control of the country also contributed to undermining ISIS.

Despite these reversals, ISIS is not likely to disappear anytime soon. It continues to exploit the sectarian hatreds and political instability that dot the region and maintains the capacity to attract sympathizers willing to strike indiscriminately. In the United States, victims have included local health-care workers in San Bernardino, California; nightclub

FIGURE 5.2 ● The Fight against the Islamic State

Fight against Islamic State

Recent air strikes and Islamic State control zones as of Aug. 19

● Primary airbase   ✛ Emergency airbase   ✴ US-led coalition air strikes on July 7 - Aug. 21 *

IS control status

■ **Attack zone** Where IS participated in or perpetrated attacks

■ **Control zone** Where IS has defensible control

■ **Support zone** Where IS moves freely and attacks are often staged

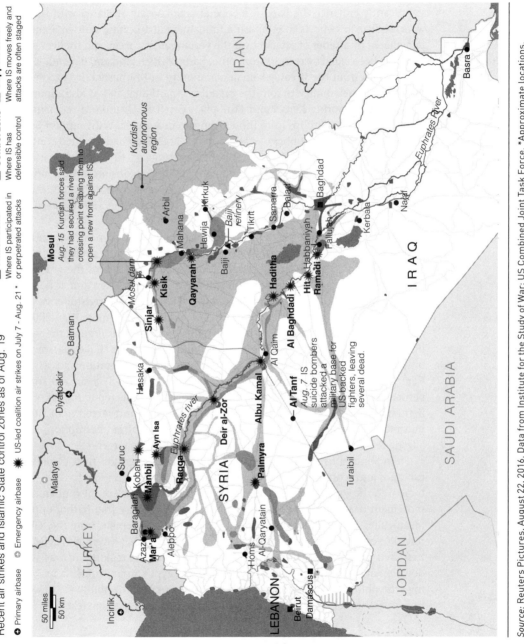

Source: Reuters Pictures, August 22, 2016. Data from Institute for the Study of War; US Combined Joint Task Force. *Approximate locations.

123

patrons in Orlando, Florida; and students on the campus of Ohio State University. Europe also remains within reach, as suggested by bombings in Istanbul and the massacre of bystanders celebrating France's National Day in Nice. Through its network of branches spread across the Middle East and North Africa, it continues to actively engage in Egypt, Saudi Arabia, Libya, and beyond (see Figure 5.2).

Somalia's al-Shabab organization has also taken full advantage of such opportunities to significantly enhance the base of its operations. Loosely affiliated with the al-Qaida network, al-Shabab's efforts to establish a fundamentalist Islamic state in Somalia have been punctuated by a series of attacks over the years against a weak and ineffectual government and have been aided by recruits from other parts of the region and beyond. A growing number of youth from the sizeable Somali community in Minnesota, for example, have made their way to the country to join the organization. Al-Shabab has also mounted successful strikes in neighboring Kenya and Ethiopia, as well as Uganda in retaliation against the presence of military troops from those countries in Somalia. With support from local clans and financing from a number of state sponsors, al-Shabab had acquired control over much of southern and central Somalia. While it has struggled to hold on to its territory with the strengthening of the central government and the expansion of US counter-insurgency efforts, it still remains a formidable force capable of launching deadly missions against authorities and civilians alike. It was responsible for more than 350 attacks in Somalia alone from 2010 to 2016.[28]

Boko Haram, operating across northern Nigeria, has also benefited from unsettled local conditions and gained considerable recognition for its brazen assaults. Looking to forge an Islamic state in a country split between Muslims and Christians, the group (whose name in Arabic translates into "Western education is a sin") has taken aim at both political and religious targets. Its attacks on schools and abductions of young students, many of them female, have been especially contentious. The kidnapping of more than 200 schoolgirls in April 2014 sparked outrage from human rights organizations around the world but highlighted the difficulty of preventing these types of activities. Boko Haram has also demonstrated its intent to broaden its reach by conducting operations across the borders of Cameroon, Chad, and Niger. It has engaged directly with ISIS since a strategic alliance between the groups was cemented in 2015, and added to its reputation as one of the deadliest terrorist forces through its use of child operatives and targeting of sites designed to maximize casualties. With its vast territory, institutionalized corruption, and oil wealth, Nigeria represents a particularly attractive and vulnerable target.[29]

From Somalia to Nigeria to Yemen to Syria, terrorist groups have capitalized on political chaos and economic misfortune to establish and maintain safe havens. In Afghanistan, moreover, the government has been unable to break the back of the fundamentalist Taliban movement or to gain full control over parts of the country that harbor opposition forces. Meanwhile, as these networks spread, it is difficult to remain immune. China has been forced to counter the efforts of the East Turkestan Islamic Movement (ETIM), while Russia has faced a stubborn insurgency in the North Caucasus region and was stunned by the downing of one of its passenger jets flying over Egypt's Sinai Peninsula in 2015. The growing accessibility of lethal nonconventional weapons and the ability of these organizations to penetrate borders far from home suggest their widening global reach.[30]

What Can Be Done?

In many respects, today's international system is limited in terms of its ability to handle conflicts. While the more powerful states closely monitor events that affect their vital interests and are willing to intervene—politically, diplomatically, and militarily—to protect those interests, they increasingly do not have the capacity to act unilaterally. The United States continues to serve as one of the most powerful actors, but a number of other states wield sufficient influence to thwart US efforts to place its overarching imprint on various regions and their conflicts.

The Israeli-Palestinian conflict exemplifies the challenge of calming tensions that destabilize the global political arena. The United States and other powers both in and outside the region have used varying techniques over the years to bring about a solution, ranging from promises of financial and military assistance to threats of diplomatic and economic sanctions. External mediation has proven useful at times, particularly in terms of defusing crises. But the conflict remains today what it has been throughout history—a struggle for security and the ability to control one's own destiny. Continuing efforts by the United States and other influential parties are necessary to keep the peace process alive. A resolution of this enduring conflict will be possible only when the protagonists themselves come to realize that their goals can be attained solely through a lasting and comprehensive peace.

International agreements offer another way to foster cooperation, especially in the area of nuclear weapons. Progress on the Comprehensive Nuclear Test Ban provides hope but also suggests limits to what can be accomplished. The Comprehensive Nuclear Test-Ban Treaty was negotiated through the UN General Assembly in the mid-1990s. By 2016, 183 states had signed the treaty, and 166 had ratified it.[31] It cannot enter into force, however, until forty-four nuclear-capable states endorse it, and only thirty-six have done so to date. The United States signed the treaty in 1996, but the US Senate has been unwilling to approve it. China, Iran, and Israel have also not seen fit to move forward with authorization. India, North Korea, and Pakistan—three countries whose inclusion is indispensable to the effectiveness of this treaty—have chosen not to support it.

The struggle against terrorism has yielded some important but limited success. Terrorism remains a useful tool for those frustrated by the inability to find a full airing of their grievances. It is also particularly alluring for those who are lacking in conventional military strength. A growing body of literature suggests that if more countries embrace a democratic form of government, guided by the rule of law and expanding participation in the political process, there will be less inclination to resort to terror or other forms of conflict to advance particular political interests.

The spread of democracy may not be enough, however, to bring about a world markedly more peaceful than the one we know today. While democracies may not fight one another, they are frequently involved in disputes with authoritarian regimes.[32] Moreover, the process of trying to achieve democracy can be an important source of conflict itself. The attempted transitions to democracy in the Middle East following the Arab Spring of 2011 actually fueled tensions, as different groups that had long been denied access to power sought to use elections to impose their own perspectives and agendas.

It is not simply the division of the world by political borders that produces the challenges of war, weapons of mass destruction, and terrorism. Economic interests and disparities in wealth have also contributed to their development. The ability to transform political relationships is frequently influenced by these considerations. Chapter 6 examines the economic borders of the world and the fault lines that will affect our future.

Key Concepts

To Learn More

Books and Other Print Media

Yonah Alexander, *The Islamic State: Combating the Caliphate Without Borders* (Lanham, MD: Lexington Books, 2016).

This book is a useful reference for understanding the appeal and successes of ISIS and offers insight into countering its efforts.

Yossi Alpher, *No End of Conflict: Rethinking Israel-Palestine* (Lanham, MD: Rowman & Littlefield, 2016).

Yossi Alpher offers a sobering assessment of the evolution of the conflict as it has affected Israel's political environment, suggesting little chance for a comprehensive peace. Rather, he argues for efforts to soften the worst impacts of the situation in moving forward.

Martha Crenshaw and Gary LaFree, *Countering Terrorism: No Simple Solutions* (Washington, DC: Brookings Institution Press, 2017).

These two analysts highlight the difficulties in developing effective policies to counter today's terrorist networks.

Alexandre Debs and Nuno P. Monteiro, *Nuclear Politics: The Strategic Causes of Proliferation* (New York: Cambridge University Press, 2017).

Part of the Cambridge Studies in International Relations series, this book examines the factors contributing to the willingness of certain states to pursue nuclear development policies in response to security concerns.

James L. Gelvin, *The Israel-Palestine Conflict: One Hundred Years of War*, 3rd ed. (New York: Cambridge University Press, 2014).

This comprehensive review establishes historical and geopolitical contexts for viewing the Israeli-Palestinian conflict. The updated edition looks at the effects of the 2011 Arab uprisings across the Middle East and Palestinian efforts to secure UN recognition.

Joseph S. Nye Jr. and David A. Welch, *Understanding Global Conflict and Cooperation: An Introduction to Theory and History*, 9th ed. (Upper Saddle River, NJ: Prentice Hall, 2012).

This is a definitive work on the role of conflict in shaping international politics.

Steven Pifer and Michael E. O'Hanlon, *The Opportunity: Next Steps in Reducing Nuclear Arms* (Washington, DC: The Brookings Institution, 2012).

This book, written from a US national security perspective, looks at the continuing challenge of addressing all aspects of nuclear weapons policy. It offers a set of policy guidelines and recommendations for confronting this still overwhelming global threat.

Todd S. Secher and Matthew Fuhrmann, *Nuclear Weapons and Coercive Diplomacy* (New York: Cambridge University Press, 2017).

This book examines the use of nuclear weapons in the conduct of foreign policy, arguing that these weapons are far more impactful in advancing deterrence and self-defense than they are for coercive purposes.

Mark Silinsky, *Jihad and the West: Black Flag Over Babylon* (Bloomington: Indiana University Press, 2016).

Mark Silinsky, a defense analyst, traces the meteoric rise of ISIS on the world stage and its appeal to potential fighters.

Websites

Center for the Study of Weapons of Mass Destruction, http://wmdcenter.ndu.edu

The center is part of the National Defense University and offers a wide range of studies and information relating to weapons of mass destruction.

International Atomic Energy Agency (IAEA), www.iaea .org

The IAEA is an intergovernmental organization (IGO) within the UN system that is the focal point for nuclear cooperation.

Israel-Palestine: Creative Regional Initiatives (IPCRI), www.ipcri.org

Based in Jerusalem, IPCRI is a joint Israeli-Palestinian public policy organization seeking to develop practical solutions to the conflict.

Middle East Institute, www.mei.edu

The Middle East Institute is a Washington, DC, think tank that promotes research and discussion of Middle East issues.

United Nations Office for Disarmament Affairs (UNODA), www.un.org/disarmament

Established in 1998 as a department of the UN Secretariat, UNODA promotes disarmament and the nonproliferation of weapons.

Washington Institute for Near East Policy, www.washington institute.org

The Washington Institute for Near East Policy is an educational foundation, or think tank, that conducts scholarly research and policy analysis relating to the Middle East.

Videos

"American Terrorist" (2015), http://www.pbs.org/video/2365470951

This PBS *Frontline* documentary follows an American terrorist recruited by Pakistan, David Headley, and chronicles the failure of electronic surveillance to prevent his role in planning the deadly attack on Mumbai in 2008.

"Command and Control" (2017)

This somber episode of the PBS *American Experience* series is based on the book by Eric Schlosser, which assesses the dangers of the world's nuclear arsenals.

Eye in the Sky (2015)

This thought-provoking, full-length thriller stars famed actress Helen Mirren as a military commander confronting the ethical dilemmas of using drones in the fight against terror.

Fighting in the Fifth Dimension (2012), www.aljazeera.com/programmes/aljazeeraworld/2011/10/2011101916939402528.html

From Al Jazeera World, this documentary explores what is called the "fifth dimension of warfare," or cyberwar, a phenomenon made possible by technological innovations.

Iran's Nuclear Deal (2016)

This BBC program offers an inside look into the negotiations leading to the historic 2015 agreement.

ISIS, Birth of a Terrorist State (2015), http://films.com/ecTitleDetail.aspx?TitleID=94597&r=S

This documentary traces the rise of ISIS and explores its significance and impact.

Middle East: Challenges in Defining an Israeli-Palestinian Border (2012), www.nytimes.com/interactive/2011/09/05/world/middleeast/challenges-in-defining-an-israeli-palestinian-border.html

This is an excellent resource produced by the *New York Times* and accessible online that explains the key issues and challenges involved in reconciling Israeli-Palestinian differences. It is divided into five segments and includes a series of short clips that address the complexities of the conflict. Separate "Individual Voices" clips feature people impacted directly.

My Land: Seeing Both Sides of the Israeli-Palestinian Conflict (2011), http://www.films.com/ecTitleDetail.aspx?TitleID=28184

This account by a filmmaker born to a Moroccan Muslim father and Tunisian Jewish mother addresses the challenges faced by Israelis and Palestinians in moving beyond the divergent perspectives that contribute to the perpetuation of the conflict.

One Day of War (2005)

While a bit dated, this program was produced by the BBC and offers great insight into the nature and range of conflict across the world by covering sixteen separate wars over the same twenty-four-hour period.

"The World Doesn't Need More Nuclear Weapons" (2016), https://www.ted.com/talks/erika_gregory_the_world_doesn_t_need_more_nuclear_weapons

In this TED talk, activist Erika Gregory argues for more intensive efforts to proceed with global disarmament in light of existing stockpiles and the uncertainties of controlling their potential use.

6

Seeking Prosperity
The Global Economy

For Americans enjoying peace and prosperity, it has been all too easy to ignore the turmoil elsewhere. How can capitalism be in trouble when the Dow Jones Industrial average is higher than Sir Edmund Hillary? Americans look at other nations and see progress, even if it is slow and uneven. Can't you eat a Big Mac in Moscow, rent a video in Shanghai, and reach the Internet in Caracas?

—Economist Hernando de Soto, 2000[1]

Learning Objectives

After studying this chapter, you will be able to do the following:

- Define *capitalism* and identify its major features.

- Describe the historical development of the modern economic system, and explain the key concepts of *liberalism*, *mercantilism*, *comparative advantage*, and *hegemon*.

- Understand the Bretton Woods System and identify its major features.

- Understand the post–Bretton Woods economic system, and explain the role of neoliberalism within it.

- Define *dependency theory* and explain its role.

- Identify the group of postcommunist countries developing most rapidly and describe the factors contributing to their growth.

- Identify the key economic actors today and describe how economic trends are affecting their status.

The words of noted Peruvian economist Hernando de Soto at the turn of this century remain relevant today. The global economy affects the food we eat, the clothes we wear, the products we use, the cars we drive, the technology at our fingertips, the jobs we work, and the material wealth we can expect to attain. As de Soto suggests, it also generates very different sets of interests and perceptions regarding its successes and failures. States struggle to bring greater order to their financial markets, and companies weigh the merits of operating in unfamiliar locations. Meanwhile, countless individuals cope with the uncertainty of a transforming job market or are in search of their next meal.

As globalization has brought disparate parts of the world closer together, it has also compounded the difficulties of managing economic relationships. Since the early 1990s, a more privatized and deregulated global economy has developed that transcends state boundaries. The global market system has become highly integrated and interdependent. Private transnational commercial enterprises, whose activities often render political boundaries obsolete, have progressively expanded. Economic disasters that start in one locale can quickly reverberate to other parts of the globe. As states promote and defend their interests, they may be inclined to act in ways that disrupt the flow of financial resources or commercial exchanges. Their willingness to empower regional or global organizations with the authority to impose uniform standards or behaviors is also limited.

A significant shift in the relative positioning of a number of pivotal players across the system adds to the uncertainty. The United States, the dominant force throughout much of the twentieth century, is struggling to maintain its global economic leadership. Meanwhile, China has emerged as one of the world's leading economies as it has expanded its stake in the United States and elsewhere through investments and debt financing. Poorer countries and those that have recently emerged from decades of isolating themselves from global

Though economic borders have grown increasingly porous, in places like Dharavi, one of the world's largest slums, in Mumbai, India (foreground), the gulf separating its inhabitants from the people living and working in the glittering high-rise buildings in the background is vast. This chapter explores the ways in which the growth of global capitalism has both separated and joined world citizens.

Satish Bate/Hindustan Times via Getty Images.

capitalism a system of economic organization based on private property and free markets

capitalism face their share of challenges. Whereas some proponents view globalization as a way to catch up economically and offer people a way out of persistent poverty, detractors caution that they will continue to remain susceptible to forces beyond their control and be forced to adopt policies that undermine the prospects for sustainable development. The uneven performance of the global economy makes it difficult to assess these arguments.

At the start of the twenty-first century, it appeared as though the opening of markets would bring a number of beneficial results. Global output rose, owing largely to a significant expansion in the volume of trade and capital investment following a brief financial crisis in the late 1990s. Emerging and developing economies fared particularly well, outpacing more advanced countries in terms of their overall growth and export activity. This ride ended abruptly in 2007 and 2008, as reckless lending practices led to the collapse of the US housing market. Given the interconnectedness of global financial networks, the damage spread quickly. Markets contracted, and the world became mired in a deep recession that unraveled much of the progress of the previous decade.

Government bailouts and austerity measures, while far from popular, helped in navigating through the debacle. But the damage was considerable, thereby shattering confidence in a system of unrestricted free markets, even as signs of recovery appeared. The prolonged and tenuous pace of that recovery is a continuing source of concern. From 2011 to 2016, annual global growth has averaged just over 3 percent. Advanced economies remain weak (averaging around 1.5 percent annual growth), while emerging and developing economies have been forced to realign priorities in response to lagging global demand and shifting commodity prices. Political pressures to adopt more inward-looking policies to protect local interests, coupled with a spike in terror and discord over the resettlement of refugees from the Middle East and beyond, have contributed further to uncertainties.[2]

As we move forward, questions remain as to the world economy's underlying character and direction. Is it poised to work toward the elimination of disparities between the rich and the poor? Can it avoid disruptions of trade stemming from the efforts of countries to protect domestic industries threatened by global completion? Is it capable of strengthening institutions that might foster better management of crises that arise? Can it provide the financial stability required to promote sustained and sustainable growth? It is difficult to predict the direction of things to come.

This chapter looks inside the global economy and some of the key issues affecting its operation. It begins with a historical overview of global economic development and the emergence of contrasting economic ideas. It then proceeds to review some of the critical events that have shaped the transformation of the system into what it is today.

Defining Economic Borders: A Very Short History

Historians trace the origins of the modern capitalist world economy to the sixteenth century, with the rise of European expansionism and the development of **mercantilism**—a policy approach that emphasized the expansion of exports and the protection of domestic markets as the means to extend wealth and power. This, in turn, led to the emergence of economic **liberalism**, the principle that markets are the best path toward improvements in quality of life. As the Arab-Muslim empire declined and the Ottoman Turks defeated Constantinople, Europeans began to expand the scope of their political, military, and financial influence. Portugal and Spain were particularly adept in their explorations of Africa and the Americas. They were soon eclipsed by Dutch, British, and French explorers, who benefited from the support of their respective monarchies and the active involvement of their growing merchant classes in developing new markets. Merchants were instrumental in shaping a new economic order that moved beyond feudal relationships to one in which capital fueled broader commercial ties.

mercantilism the economic approach that promotes the aggressive pursuit of exports and the simultaneous protection of domestic markets to acquire and expand wealth and power

liberalism the economic approach, commonly traced to the writings of Adam Smith, that emphasizes the role of the free market in promoting economic growth and prosperity

The establishment of joint stock enterprises owned by their contributing investors marked the emergence of private corporate actors in building overseas trading networks. The Dutch East India Company was the first trading company of its kind created to facilitate the spice trade. Founded in 1602, it developed into the largest European trading company by 1620.[3] With the advent of the modern state in 1648 as a result of the Peace of Westphalia, trade in manufactured goods became a key factor in accumulating national wealth and power. Intense competition prompted states to aggressively pursue export outlets while restricting the access of foreigners to home markets. These mercantilist policies extended both the breadth and depth of their influence, but they invited retaliation and threatened to disrupt the flow of commercial activity. As both a trade strategy and a more general way of thinking about the forces driving the world economy, mercantilism emphasizes intense competition for limited resources and vigilance in protecting national interests, regardless of international consequences. This approach has remained popular to this day, particularly during periods of economic contraction, when competition is most intense.

By the late 1700s, Britain was becoming a dominant force. As the birthplace and center of the Industrial Revolution, it had the resources and capability to extend its commercial reach. The development of new technologies provided the incentive to seek additional materials and new markets. Britain's overwhelming political and military power produced a vast colonial empire that contributed greatly to its dominance during this period. Although other European nations sought to limit competition by restricting imports of British goods, Britain's exports continued to rise. The British Parliament's 1846 repeal of its Corn Laws, designed to protect national agriculture through tariffs and other measures, signaled an important move to freer trade and was met with similar initiatives by a number of Britain's European partners.

IN THEIR OWN WORDS
ADAM SMITH

Every individual necessarily labours to render the annual revenue of the society as great as he can. He generally, indeed, neither intends to promote the public interest, nor knows how much he is promoting it. By preferring the support of domestic to that of foreign industry, he intends only his own security; and by directing that industry in such a manner as its produce may be of the greatest value, he intends only his own gain, and he is in this, as in many other cases, led by an invisible hand to promote an end which was no part of his intention. Nor is it always the worse for the society that it was no part of it. By pursuing his own interest he frequently promotes that of the society more effectually than when he really intends to promote it. I have never known much good done by those who affected to trade for the public good.[4]

During this period, the drive for expansion and growth encouraged the adoption of progressive policies based on the principles of economic liberalism. Eighteenth-century thinkers such as Adam Smith and David Ricardo advocated free and open markets as the best means to enhance the lives of people across the world. Adam Smith was a Scottish political economist and philosopher considered by many to be the father of modern economics. While acknowledging the market's often chaotic and uneven nature, his 1776 work, *The Wealth of Nations*, put forward the case for allowing its "invisible hand" to ensure the spread of its benefits.

Like Smith, the British political economist David Ricardo opposed protectionist trade policies. He argued that free trade would extend the availability of goods and services and

Depositors gather outside the shuttered doors of American Union Bank in New York City, 1931, during the Great Depression.

comparative advantage the idea that countries should produce and export goods that they can produce at a lower cost than others and import items that others produce at lower cost

promote efficiency by encouraging countries to specialize in producing and exporting goods for which they had a **comparative advantage**. Liberal thinkers recommended importing a product when the relative cost of domestic production exceeded that of buying it elsewhere, taking into account the lost revenues resulting from the decreased production of other items. In short, these theorists saw an open economic system as the best option for producing the greatest good for the largest number of people. These ideas were not accepted by those who did not have the political or economic capabilities to compete effectively in the marketplace.

While British colonialism was indispensable to the expansion and integration of the global economy, it also contributed to growing inequities in the levels of economic prosperity between the colonizers and the colonized. In addition to maintaining open markets and the free movement of goods across oceans, Britain gained considerable advantage by serving as the world's financial center and presiding over an international monetary system based on gold and supported by its national currency (the pound). Its colonial activities and role in opening China and Japan to trade also helped bring disparate places into a unified system that was structured to advance the interests of its more powerful members. The costs and burdens of that leadership, however, eventually took their toll.

By the latter part of the nineteenth century, Britain was losing is preeminent position. Industrial development was spreading rapidly across Europe and beyond. Japan was emerging as a major industrial power, due to strong government guidance and its large business conglomerates, and it launched a series of military adventures to extend its imperial reach. The United States, for its part, was extending its overseas activities and interests beyond the Americas and would eventually emerge as a global power. Across Europe, economic rivalries intensified as political tensions led to the appearance of two competing alliances that were destined to collide. These conflicts resulted in the outbreak of war in 1914.

World War I was an important turning point. Beyond the financial and commercial disruptions, the war marked the beginning of the end of European colonial empires and Britain's dominant role in the world's financial and commercial systems. Heavy European war debts and German reparations requirements significantly slowed the pace of economic recovery. Meanwhile, the United States was enjoying a period of economic expansion marked by the growth of manufacturing and consumption. The values of many companies increased, fueled in part by speculative stock purchases with borrowed money. As the economy slowed and stock prices began to decline, the system began to unravel. The collapse of the US stock market in 1929 had immediate and profound international ramifications.

By this time, the United States had become a major economic player. The Great Depression following the stock market crash extended well beyond America's borders. To protect US markets and limit exposure to outside forces, Congress increased import duties through the Smoot-Hawley Tariff Act in 1930. Competing nations organized trade blocs in response, further fracturing preexisting relationships. One after another, countries began defaulting on their loans as they were unable to sustain economic activity. Meanwhile, declining markets in the leading industrial countries resulted in a significant drop in demand for raw materials and primary exports from the developing world.

The growing economic malaise was transforming economic and political life in these areas. In Latin America, a wave of military takeovers empowered repressive regimes that promoted economic nationalism. In Africa, organized resistance to colonial rule was mounting. Populist movements were also gaining momentum across Asia and the Middle East to challenge struggling colonial powers.

With the British unable and the United States unwilling to take the lead, global economic conditions deteriorated. A weakened British pound undermined the stability of the world's monetary system, while trade barriers limited commercial interactions. The 1931 collapse of the German economy dealt a devastating blow. It fueled the rise of Adolf Hitler and his drive to restore German prosperity and pride through aggressive military and political expansion. Japan charted a similar course as it moved into China and other neighboring territories to establish the Greater East Asia Co-prosperity Sphere. Before long, much of the world was drawn into another encompassing and protracted conflict—World War II.

In part, the absence of leadership or direction had led to this disarray. Throughout its history, the modern world economy has often operated under the wings of a **hegemon**, or dominant power. The hegemon invests many of its resources to keep the system operating in an orderly and predictable fashion. As Yale historian Paul Kennedy has argued, however, hegemons tend to overestimate their capabilities in manipulating economic and political structures to preserve their advantage.[5] The relative decline of these great powers ushers in periods of uncertainty marked by the absence of effective management. Eventually a new hegemon arises, and the cycle begins again. The events that led up to World War II followed from the progressive decline of British hegemony.

hegemon the dominant power in the global economy

The Bretton Woods System

As World War II was drawing to a close, the United States emerged as the world's leading economy. The physical and financial devastation of Europe stood in contrast to conditions in the United States, which spearheaded the drive to recovery. In 1944, Allied officials met in the New Hampshire resort town of Bretton Woods to discuss postwar reconstruction. They ultimately agreed on a broad set of arrangements for what would become known as the Bretton Woods system, which would guide the operation of the world economy from the end of World War II to the early 1970s. Based on liberal economic principles, the Bretton Woods system relied heavily on the ability of the United States to shoulder much of the initial burden. Although weary from war, the United States could not turn its back to the emerging political and military challenge of the Soviet Union. To gain its allies' support, the United States tolerated their efforts to protect their fragile economies from unfettered competition and agreed to move slowly in fashioning a more open trading system. All sides understood that once economic recovery had gained momentum, the responsibilities for managing and sustaining an open world economy would be shared.

With this in mind, the United States proceeded on multiple fronts. The 1947 Marshall Plan, named for Secretary of State George Marshall, was especially noteworthy. It provided substantial funds to assist European recovery from the war and to promote the resumption of commercial activity. The United States contributed approximately $13 billion in aid to sixteen countries, and by 1951, industrial production in these countries was 37 percent higher than in 1947, and exports had risen at an annual rate of more than 20 percent.[6] The Soviet Union refused to participate in the program, seeing it as a mechanism to further American influence and interests. As it turned out, the Marshall Plan was an important catalyst in rebuilding the economies of countries that proved critical to US efforts to contain Soviet political and military aspirations.

The Bretton Woods system revolved around a well-defined set of goals and institutions. The International Monetary Fund (IMF) was established in 1944 to oversee the world's

US Secretary of the Treasury Henry Morgenthau Jr. speaks at the conference that established the International Monetary Fund.

reciprocity the idea that countries would respond to actions taken by their trade partners to reduce trade barriers with similar reductions of their own

nondiscrimination the idea that countries would extend preferential trade status to all their trade partners

most-favored nation (MFN) a means to promote trade equality by guaranteeing that if one country is given better trade terms by another, all other partners must receive the same benefit

financial system and function as its central bank, offering technical assistance and training and acquiring capital from member states to stabilize currency values. It also provided short-term loans for countries facing immediate needs and particularly difficult economic circumstances. The US dollar was the backbone of the emerging financial order and came to be considered "as good as gold." This term reflected confidence in the long-term strength of the dollar, whose value was set and backed by this precious commodity with enduring value.

The International Bank for Reconstruction and Development (IBRD), more commonly known as the World Bank, was another key Bretton Woods institution. The World Bank was designed initially to further accelerate recovery from the war by lending funds for longer-term economic development projects. Finally, the Bretton Woods architects formed the General Agreement on Tariffs and Trade (GATT) to promote greater cooperation in opening markets by reducing tariffs. The GATT agreements were predicated on two basic principles to guide policies—**reciprocity** in the dismantling of trade barriers and **nondiscrimination** in the treatment of imported goods. The idea was to get countries to progressively eliminate preferences and protectionism by extending **most-favored nation (MFN)** status to all of their trading partners.

With these mechanisms in place, the post–World War II global economy began to take shape. It relied extensively on the United States for direction and leadership. The Bretton Woods system stimulated economic recovery and growth, especially in Western Europe and Japan, where the United States had a large stake in assuring sustained economic progress. The success of Bretton Woods and the enhanced political and economic capabilities of American allies provided additional leverage in the struggle with the Soviet Union.

The effectiveness of the United States in managing these affairs actually eroded its dominant position. On the political and strategic front, the need to counter Soviet activities required commitments and actions that were both costly and, at times, rather risky. Excessive US spending to meet its growing financial obligations also began to take its toll. By the late 1960s, confidence in the dollar had fallen, and many countries feared an impending adjustment that would lower its value to address the mounting deficit. These developments prompted US president Richard Nixon to prohibit withdrawals of gold from the United States in exchange for dollars. He took this step—known as the "closing of the gold window"—to prevent a further outflow of gold, which would undermine the value of the dollar. This decision marked a fundamental shift in policy and reflected increasing US frustration with its closest partners.

Tensions had mounted as the world became a more dangerous place. The Cold War heated up considerably during the 1960s, but America's allies did not universally share its view of the Soviet threat. A number of them began to question US actions, particularly as they related to the impacts of weapons development and deepening involvement in Vietnam. For its part, the United States grew resentful of this lack of support and unwillingness to assume an additional share of the burden. Furthermore, US efforts to convince the European Economic Community (EEC) and Japan to open their markets wider to US products went largely unheeded. This was not surprising, as these countries had benefited considerably over the years from their relatively free access to the US market without having to reciprocate fully. The broad consensus that had propelled the Bretton Woods system was unraveling.

At the same time, political changes in other parts of the world were affecting the foundation of the global economy. The end of colonialism led to the creation of new countries across Africa and Asia with limited capabilities and considerable needs. The transition to independence was frequently violent and destructive, adding further to the tasks at hand. Expectations were high and in stark contrast to the harsh realities of everyday life. Insufficient support from international agencies and more developed countries raised serious questions about the future path to development.

In response, less developed countries (LDCs) from Africa, Asia, and Latin America joined forces in the United Nations (UN) to establish the Group of 77 (G77), named for the number of states that participated. This body was designed to air collective concerns and to engage industrial countries in continuing discussions on the need for economic restructuring on a global scale. These countries are often referred to today as the Global South, to reflect the fact that most of them are located in the world's Southern Hemisphere (see Map 6.1).

The G77 critique saw the inequities of the Bretton Woods system as part of the historical evolution of a global capitalist economy that empowered and enriched a few core countries at the expense of a far greater number of peripheral ones. The unequal economic relationships between the core and the periphery, they argued, extended beyond the formal bonds of colonialism and perpetuated the gap in levels of economic development. Influenced by Marxist thought, sociologist Immanuel Wallerstein had been the first to propose this theory, which he called "modern world systems."[7]

Political economist Andre Gunder Frank, among others, further examined the constraints of this system, focusing on the structures of dependence that continued to disadvantage the countries on the periphery.[8] He noted that LDCs were mostly relegated to the exchange of raw materials or food products, which were generally cheaper and frequently subject to considerable price fluctuations, for more expensive manufactured goods. International investment and finance sectors, dominated by large and mostly American companies and banks, dictated the terms of their engagements with LDCs in need of their capital. In the late 1960s, **dependency theory** provided an intellectual framework for many G77 members who no longer saw the value of incremental change. Citing the

dependency theory the view that the development of countries in the Global South is limited by the unfavorable terms utilized to integrate them into the global capitalist economy

MAP 6.1 ● Group of 77 (G77) Countries

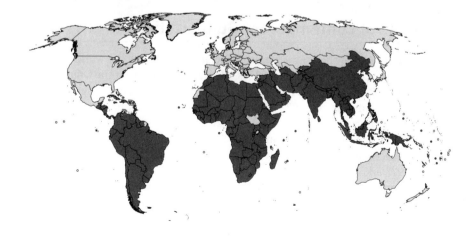

Note: The G77/Global South countries are shaded in a darker blue.

inability to break the cycle of poverty within established frameworks, in the 1970s they called for the creation of a New International Economic Order (NIEO), a reform program designed to comprehensively restructure global economic relationships. In his 1969 book *Latin America: Underdevelopment or Revolution*, Frank explains the basic underpinnings of dependency theory.

The NIEO was a comprehensive package designed to bolster LDCs' economic performance and capacity. It included plans to provide preferred access to global markets, enhance and stabilize the prices of food and raw materials, offer financial and technical assistance at more favorable terms, encourage local input in devising development projects, and monitor the business practices of large transnational corporations (TNCs). Most developed countries were not willing to make sweeping concessions or respond under pressure. Noting their continued confidence in the liberal principles of free and open exchange, they moved forward with their existing economic agendas. Despite its widespread support across the developing world, the NIEO program had minimal impact at the time. Some critics of globalization today harken back to some of its underlying concerns, however, especially as they relate to the pressures faced by developing countries to adjust their policies to those of more powerful economic actors.[9]

IN THEIR OWN WORDS
ANDRE GUNDER FRANK

It is generally held that economic development occurs in a succession of capitalist stages and that today's underdeveloped countries are still in a stage of history, sometimes depicted as an original stage, through which the now developed countries passed long ago. It is also widely believed that the contemporary underdevelopment of a country can be understood as the product or reflection solely of its own economic, political, social, and cultural characteristics or structure. Yet historical research demonstrates that contemporary underdevelopment is in large part the historical product of past and continuing economic and other relations between the satellite underdeveloped and the now developed metropolitan countries. Furthermore, these relations are an essential part of the structure and development of the capitalist system on a world scale as a whole.[10]

Beyond Bretton Woods: The Roots of Contemporary Globalization

Any hope of resolving these differences cooperatively faded as the world economy came under enormous pressure during the 1970s. Most Arab members of the Organization of the Petroleum Exporting Countries (OPEC) imposed an embargo on oil shipments to countries supporting Israel during the 1973 Middle East war. OPEC was founded in 1960, and its original members were Iran, Iraq, Kuwait, Saudi Arabia, and Venezuela. By 1973, OPEC had expanded, and its members controlled 55.7 percent of the world's crude oil production. Their decision to restrict supply resulted in an unprecedented quadrupling of prices between 1973 and 1974.[11]

With so much of the world dependent on the availability of inexpensive oil, the effects of this unanticipated crisis were widespread. Economic output contracted as money became tight and prices soared. Many companies were forced to cut back their operations and workforces. In the United States alone, the economy fell 6 percent between 1973 and 1975, and unemployment surged to 9 percent.[12] The world was slipping into recession. The OPEC countries emerged as the major sources of financing at this time, depositing the sizable earnings from oil sales in international banks. These banks, in turn, lent these **petrodollars** (US dollars acquired through the sale of petroleum) to countries so that they could purchase the oil they needed to keep their economies afloat.

petrodollars US dollars earned through the sale of petroleum

These conditions made it difficult to sustain global economic activity, even as efforts proceeded. The Tokyo Round, the latest in a succession of negotiations sponsored by GATT to combat trade protectionism, began in 1973. Previous accords had focused on reducing or eliminating tariffs across a broad range of products. As a result, countries resorted to other measures to limit access to their markets. The Tokyo Round developed new codes of conduct covering these nontariff barriers (NTBs), such as subsidies to domestic producers, government purchasing practices favoring national firms, and excessive customs duties designed to undermine the competitiveness of imported goods. These agreements proved difficult to monitor and enforce, however, and provided only modest relief in offsetting the mercantilist trading practices that gained footing during these uncertain times.

The gradual easing of oil prices offered some hope. Economic uncertainty posed a unique dilemma for oil producers because of their considerable loans and investments. By 1974, OPEC members had sent about one-third of their $60 billion surplus revenue to the United States, investing mainly in Treasury bills and other short-term holdings.[13] The 1979 war between Iran and Iraq, two of the largest oil producers, once again forced many countries to borrow heavily to secure necessary imports. Fearful of massive defaults on outstanding loans, large international banks extended payment schedules and offered additional financing. Some of these institutions incurred significant costs for their uncharacteristically risky behavior, but this patchwork prevented a global economic meltdown.

By the mid-1980s, signs of recovery were emerging. However, the global economy was a far cry from that envisioned at Bretton Woods. Transnational connections between states and other actors were expanding, contributing to the emergence of a system of "complex interdependence."[14] While the incentives for cooperation were significant, managing relationships was a daunting task. This was evident in the international monetary system, where the fixed exchange rate system of Bretton Woods gave way under the pressure of widely shifting currency values. Currencies would now fluctuate or float on an ongoing basis so that their worth would more accurately reflect daily ebbs and flows in economic conditions. Money markets had become far more fluid and speculative, with private financial institutions, TNCs, and even individuals buying and selling currencies on a regular basis.

Getty Images.

Oil fields like the one shown here are part of a global industry that today produces many billions of barrels of oil annually. The production and sale of oil and gas spurs development worldwide but also leads to economic and political instability.

The global economy had also become intensely competitive. Many American companies in particular had seen their positions erode over the previous decade and now were forced to cut costs and aggressively pursue new markets to keep pace with European and Japanese businesses. LDCs also began to figure prominently in the marketplace. A number of "newly industrializing countries," or NICs, such as Taiwan, Singapore, and South Korea (known today as "emerging markets"), became more significant players by providing reduced labor costs or other financial enticements to companies from developed countries.

Keeping markets open remained a challenge. The demands of what economist Lester Thurow labeled "head-to-head" competition made it difficult to offset the inclinations of many countries to protect their respective interests.[15] In 1986, GATT inaugurated a new set of multilateral discussions—the Uruguay Round—to continue efforts to combat trade restraints. The United States pressed hard to incorporate an initiative to liberalize the fast-growing services sector (e.g., accounting, financial, insurance, legal), where it looked to ensure access to a broad range of markets. This did not sit well with other aspiring providers, however, who pushed to maintain protections that might enable them to emerge as viable competitors. Overall, this round of talks was highly contentious and would take nearly a decade to complete.

The most significant breakthrough was the creation of the World Trade Organization (WTO). Established in 1995, the WTO supplanted GATT as the body responsible for preserving open markets. It provided officials with enhanced capabilities to settle disputes and to enforce established rules. Both the mandate and the membership of the WTO expanded over the years, but the organization struggles to this day as countries continue to ignore existing mandates to gain competitive advantage.

Meanwhile, Japan and the United States endured strains in their critical relationship. Linked closely through trade and investment, the United States guaranteed Japan's military security as part of the arrangement at the close of World War II. Japan's meteoric rise as a global economic power was due, in large part, to its proactive business practices. With limited natural resources, Japan pursued a mercantilist development strategy. This approach put the country at direct odds with the United States and other partners, who complained about currency manipulations and pricing practices designed to preserve low-cost advantages for Japanese products.

Japan's large industrial groups or *keiretsu*, such as Mitsubishi, had proven effective in penetrating the US market with high-quality products. Japan also expanded its direct presence in the United States by establishing production facilities, purchasing prominent companies, and acquiring prime real estate in major cities. By 1990, about 1,350 Japanese-owned manufacturers employed approximately 290,000 workers in the United States.[16] Meanwhile, Japan continued to offer preferential treatment to its domestic companies. The widening and persistent trade gap, which was running between $40 and $50 billion at the time, was a particular source of friction.[17] The two countries' extensive interconnectedness compelled them to address their more serious grievances through ongoing negotiations, such as the 1990 Structural Impediments Initiative (SII), to avoid a potentially disastrous all-out trade war.

Concurrently, Western Europe embarked on a path to further economic and political integration. In 1957, Italy, France, Belgium, Luxembourg, the Netherlands, and West Germany created the European Economic Community (known as the EEC, or Common Market) to promote closer ties and policy coordination among its members. Over time, the organization extended its membership and its mandate. It was renamed the European Community (EC) in 1967 to reflect a commitment to broader cooperation and gained new momentum with the addition of the United Kingdom, Denmark, and Ireland in 1973. Membership grew to twelve members with the entry of Greece in 1981 and Portugal and Spain in 1986.[18]

This development brought new challenges. Adding countries with weaker economies strained EC resources. Members also argued over the taxes required to finance subsidies to farmers under the Common Agricultural Policy (CAP). Great Britain was particularly vexed by what it saw as a disproportionate share of the cost it was expected to bear in funding this program. Nevertheless, a broad sense of common interest prevailed. Through the leadership of Jacques Delors, the president of the European Commission, a plan was launched to move toward a fully integrated market and jointly managed monetary system.

The United States, Japan, and Europe were locked in an increasingly competitive struggle as they moved to recover from the disruptions of the 1970s. US president Ronald Reagan and British prime minister Margaret Thatcher took the lead in pushing for balanced budgets, a more limited government role in the economy, and policies that encouraged private sector initiatives. This renewed support for traditional liberal economic principles came to be known as **neoliberalism**. They put forward these ideas as a formula for domestic economic restructuring and to promote a more open global economy.

neoliberalism the economic principles that promote free market capitalism and reflect the ideals of contemporary globalization

Neoliberal practices prompted considerable controversy, especially across the developing world. Freer trade undermined the ability of weaker countries to compete effectively, and large transnational companies gained considerable leverage by overwhelming smaller local firms with their substantial capital and superior technological capabilities. LDCs faced increasing demands for domestic reform along neoliberal lines, while the global economy offered little opportunity for them to advance.

In addition, the IMF **conditionality** policy frustrated many prospective borrowers. To qualify for IMF loans, countries were obliged to adopt more "responsible" policies that often limited spending for social welfare programs or projects to support the most vulnerable segments of their populations. Applicants generally had little choice but to accept these terms to secure necessary financing. These experiences reinforced broader resentments relating to perceived inequities embedded within the system and the continued ability of its wealthier and more powerful members to dictate terms of involvement.

conditionality the requirements imposed on prospective borrowers by the IMF or other lending institutions that emphasize economic growth over welfare considerations

The world economy was becoming increasingly difficult to navigate, as countries sought to balance their domestic needs and international obligations. A consensus was emerging, at least among the more advantaged participants, around the need to work toward further integration of the market system through a set of fairly well-defined principles. However, international institutions remained weak, less developed countries remained highly skeptical, and a number of bilateral and multilateral disputes emerged that threatened this fragile arrangement.

A series of extraordinary and mostly unanticipated events outside the global capitalist orbit helped define its direction. The decades of the Cold War had severely weakened the economies of the Soviet Union and its satellite countries across Eastern Europe. In the late 1980s, mounting resistance led to the fall of Soviet-backed regimes in such places as Albania, Czechoslovakia, Poland, Romania, Yugoslavia, and East Germany. The dismantling of the Berlin Wall symbolized the end of the Cold War era. The Soviet Union itself did not survive. These developments offered both monumental challenges and opportunities, unleashing a set of forces that shaped the global economy as we have come to know it today.

Emerging Economic Centers

The experiences of the world's emerging market economies provide a good snapshot of how today's system operates. The more dynamic of these are the BRICS, an acronym referring to Brazil, Russia, India, China, and South Africa. By 2015, these countries accounted for approximately 53 percent of the world's population, 23 percent of global GDP, and 19 percent of total exports.[19] Their steady growth and expanding economic clout prior to the 2008–2009 financial crisis suggested a global economy on the cusp of a significant reordering. Their more recent struggles, however, have dampened those expectations.

While external markets have recovered incrementally from the financial shocks, the BRICS have lost some of their earlier resiliency. As a group, they tend to lag behind in transparency and institutional accountability and have had difficulties in sustaining productivity. The decline in foreign finance capital has also taken its toll. In 2015, the global investment bank Goldman Sachs closed its BRICS fund after it had declined 88 percent from its peak in 2010. Individual countries also endure their own dramas. In Brazil and South Africa, for example, ongoing political scandals and uncertainties have made it more difficult to tackle economic challenges stemming from declining commodity prices and increasing debt.[20] A closer look at the experiences of Russia, China, and India offers some additional insight into the journey of this group of countries.

Russia's early efforts to enter the global capitalist orbit were uneven. The introduction of political and economic reforms did not bring about an expected improvement in overall living standards. Instead, a relatively small group of investors with access to government officials gained considerable wealth and influence. These new elites, commonly referred to as the *oligarchs*, took advantage of their position to challenge the government's control over economic policy until their activity was eventually curtailed by Russian president Vladimir Putin (2000–2008 and 2012–present).

Russia's economy expanded considerably under Putin initially, owing largely to its flourishing energy industry and rising prices for oil and natural gas on world markets. Rates of economic growth remained healthy and steady—expanding an average 7.1 percent between 2004 and 2008. Russia's recovery from the global financial crisis was also impressive, posting gains of 4.5 percent in 2010 and 4.3 percent in 2011. Although still plagued by a fair share of corruption and inefficiency, Russia's economy was in relatively good shape when Putin reacquired the presidency in 2012. Its modest growth over the next couple of years reflected the overall sluggishness of the global economy. More recent declines (–3.7 percent in 2015 and –0.8 percent in 2016) stem from the considerable drop in oil and natural gas prices and the impact of US and European economic sanctions following Russia's contentious takeover of Crimea.[21] Its more assertive global political posture, which often puts it at odds with the United States, is likely to affect future economic policies and relationships.

China's emergence as one of the world's leading economies has been steadier, with an average annual growth rate that generally exceeded 10 percent for close to a decade and a gross domestic product (GDP) that has risen to more than $11 trillion. But even China has suffered the aftereffects of the global recession, as its rate of growth fell below 8 percent in 2012 and 2013 and has continued to decelerate (to 7.3 percent in 2014, 6.9 percent in 2015, and 6.6 percent in 2016). In addition to slackening demand for its exports, increasing emphasis on restructuring and enhancing the country's domestic consumer markets has shifted production and spending priorities.[22] Even so, China's growth and development remain the envy of many, and it still seems poised to surpass Japan and perhaps even the United States as the world's largest economy before the end of the twenty-first century.

China is deeply enmeshed within the global economy and linked to the United States through expanding trade and the financing of US debt. At the same time, its ruling Communist Party has resisted US pressure to enact human rights reforms and continues to challenge US policy and influence on a number of diplomatic fronts across the world. China applies its own unique vision in the pursuit of its broad economic and political agenda. This development dates back to the 1970s, when its leader, Deng Xiaoping, introduced market principles to redesign the country's socialist economy. This model of "socialism with Chinese characteristics" has endured. It is reflected in the special administrative regions in Macao and Hong Kong, where there are different sets of rules and regulations to facilitate the coexistence of socialist and capitalist principles. Encouraged by the government, developers have made the island of Macao the world's casino capital, exceeding Las Vegas in revenues from its gambling operations. A leading global financial center, Hong Kong is an important economic asset to China and critical to its future economic planning.

China's success may be traced, in part, to its advantages as a producer of lower-cost goods and its vast market potential. International companies have flocked to the country to capitalize on its huge and inexpensive workforce. For its part, China has welcomed foreign investment to fuel its ambitious modernization agenda. In 2016, foreign direct investment (FDI) was $126 billion, a slight decline from its record $126.3 billion in 2015. While the rate of growth has varied over the past few years, China ranks among the leading destinations for foreign investment across the world.[23]

China has amassed additional wealth by parlaying its role as a leading manufacturing center into an aggressive export strategy. Despite an overall slowdown, China's foreign trade in 2016 was around $3.7 trillion, resulting in a healthy $509.9 billion surplus. Its lopsided relationship with the United States—which led to a surplus of $347 billion in traded goods in 2016—remains a particularly sore point between the two countries. The United States has accused China of keeping its currency (the yuan) undervalued to enhance the pricing advantages of Chinese products. China has denied this claim, suggesting instead that US firms need to become more efficient to compete effectively in Chinese markets.[24] In return for the capital and technology secured through outside investment, China provides consumers elsewhere with an array of inexpensive goods. Meanwhile, China's more than 1.3 billion people are especially attractive to retailers. Chinese consumers may shop at Walmart after dropping by McDonald's or KFC, whose menus have been tweaked to reflect local tastes. The economic indicators in Table 6.1 reflect China's performance and some of its more recent struggles.

STR/AFP/Getty Images.

New cars are seen in a parking lot of the Brilliance factory in Shenyang, in China's northeast Liaoning province on July 17, 2017.

In many ways, China's expanding presence speaks to the fundamental transformation of the global economy. Despite the continuing dominance of its Communist Party and differences with the West on many strategic issues, China has embraced core capitalist economic precepts and has become both a critical partner and formidable competitor. As an outlet for investment and a source of finance, China has considerable latitude to pursue its own economic and political interests, even when they diverge from those of its key partner-competitors. China's use of prison and child labor and its alleged manipulation of its currency are especially contentious. The significant stake these global partner-competitors have in each other's economies, however, provides an important incentive to negotiate solutions to political and economic disputes.

India's emergence as an important player in the twenty-first century also reflects shifting roles across the global economy. With its longstanding democracy and strong educational system, India has attracted foreign businesses and investors seeking to engage the country's economic and human resources. Although it is one of the world's most populous countries, many of its more than 1 billion people endure conditions of extreme poverty, even as a vibrant English-speaking middle class has developed. Continuing religious tensions between Hindus and Muslims, along with other differences that surface in India's multiethnic society, periodically result in bombings and other acts of violence. Modern office parks house some of the world's most sophisticated software firms in areas surrounded by shantytowns that lack any modern conveniences. Although it is a country of paradoxes, India has become one of the world's most dynamic economies and has secured an important niche in the rapidly developing information technology (IT) sector.

India has had considerable success in the global marketplace. Its top IT companies are among the world's leaders, while six of its cities continue to rank among the top eight outsourcing destinations. Tata Consultancy Services (TCS) has more than 350,000 employees

TABLE 6.1 ● Measuring China's Growth*	2012	2013	2014	2015	2016
Gross domestic product (GDP)	8,750.3	9,635.2	10,557.6	11,181.6	11,391.6
Real GDP growth	7.9%	7.8%	7.3%	6.9%	6.6%
Foreign exchange reserves	3,311.6	3,821.3	3,843.0	3,330.4	3,010.5
Exports	2,048.9	2,210.0	2,342.7	2,276.5	2,097.4
Percentage change	**7.9%**	**7.9%**	**6.0%**	**−2.8%**	**−7.9%**
Imports	1,817.8	1,950.3	1,960.2	1,682.0	1,587.5
Percentage change	**4.3%**	**7.3%**	**0.5%**	**−14.2%**	**−5.6%**
World trade balance	231.1	259.7	382.5	594.5	509.9
With United States (goods)	315.1	318.7	344.9	367.2	347.0
Inward foreign direct investment used (FDI)	111.7	117.6	119.6	126.3	126.0
Percentage change	**−3.7%**	**5.3%**	**1.7%**	**5.6%**	**−0.2%**

Sources: Trade and FDI: Ministry of Commerce, People's Republic of China, http://english.mofcom.gov.cn/article/statistic and http://www.tradingeconomics.com/china/foreign-direct-investment for 2016 FDI; GDP: International Monetary Fund, World Economic Outlook Database, October 2016, https://www.imf.org/external/pubs/ft/weo/2016/02/weodata/index .aspx; US Trade: United States Census Bureau, https://www.census.gov/foreign-trade/balance/c5700.html; Reserves: Stastista, The Statistics Portal, https://www.statista.com/statistics/278206/foreign-exchange-reserves-of-china.

*Numbers shown are in billions of US dollars.

worldwide and is the largest IT services firm in Asia, and Infosys Technologies, with close to 200,000 workers and revenues exceeding $9.7 billion, ranks among the leading IT service providers globally. Tata Motors has continued on a path to become an important global player in the industry. It purchased Jaguar and Land Rover from Ford for $2.3 billion in early 2008 and has worked to bring automobile ownership within the reach of millions of Indian families through its Nano model for approximately $2,500. This effort has not been an easy one, however, as the Nano has lagged in sales due to a series of production and quality control issues.[25]

Meanwhile, wealthy Indian entrepreneurs are being courted by foreign firms eager to secure contracts for services previously performed in house. Anyone in the English-speaking world in need of assistance with a malfunctioning computer or booking reservations for an upcoming airline flight has a good chance of connecting to a call center in India. These facilities are staffed by young, highly educated Indian workers pursuing modern lifestyles that stand in stark contrast to traditional Indian values.

India's engagement with the global economy has raised questions regarding its impact. Soaring economic growth has done little to lessen the gap between India's modern and traditional sectors. The draw of the country's relatively inexpensive, technologically savvy workforce has proven unsettling in other parts of the world. Companies based in the United States and other high-wage countries have transferred millions of white-collar jobs to India. It is far more profitable for them to **outsource** particular jobs to other companies and **offshore** complete business operations to other locales. An estimated

outsource, or offshore often used interchangeably, these terms refer to the displacement of work activity; outsourcing involves the transfer of certain specific functions performed within a company to an outside provider, and offshoring entails the relocation of an entire business operation to another country

3 million people are employed in the business processing out-sourcing (BPO) sector across India. In 2015 alone, moreover, nearly 2.4 million US jobs were transferred to workers in India and other low-wage countries.[26]

Within a global economy that has sputtered over recent years, countries across the developing world have held their own. At the height of the global financial crisis in 2009, for example, advanced countries contracted 3.4 percent, while developing countries actually grew 2.4 percent. This pattern has continued. While the global economy has recovered modestly (with 3.4 percent growth in 2014, 3.2 percent in 2015, and 3.1 percent in 2016), developing countries have expanded at a higher rate (4.6 percent in 2014, 4 percent in 2015, and 4.2 percent in 2016). This level is below the pace of preceding years. It exceeds the performance of more developed economies, however, which continue to struggle with high levels of debt, unemployment, government austerity measures, and a host of other economic difficulties (see Map 6.2).[27]

These figures contribute to the notion that the world economy has turned "upside down," as developing countries account for more capital investment, trade, and consumption of resources.[28] In 1999, the Group of Seven industrial countries (popularly known as the G7 and including Canada, France, Germany, Italy, Japan, the United Kingdom, and the United States) accounted for about 50 percent of world output; by 2016, its share had declined to around 31 percent. The IMF expects this figure to fall to under 29 percent by 2020, as countries such as China, India, Brazil, and Mexico—among others—continue to expand their economies.[29]

While it may be tempting to conclude that there has been a leveling of the global economic playing field, there are considerable disparities. The more dynamic economies in the Global South contribute significantly to the overall picture, but many others have continued to lag seriously behind due to economic or political challenges. In East Africa, for example, severe drought has devastated crops in Eritrea, Ethiopia, and elsewhere, resulting in widespread famine. In Somalia, the ability to deal with this situation has been compromised further by a protracted civil war and a dysfunctional government. The unsettled nature of the global economy as a whole has hit developing countries hard. Uncertain employment and income prospects hamper both public and private efforts to improve living conditions. While the overall rate has declined, there are still more than 767 million people, comprising more than 10 percent of the world's population, living in extreme poverty (on less than $1.90 per day), with half of them under the age of eighteen. Sub-Saharan Africa is most seriously impacted, with more people living under these conditions than all other regions combined.[30]

The difficulty of maintaining steady worldwide demand for commodities contributes heavily to the challenges across the Global South. Lower prices limit the funds available to reduce poverty and promote more sustainable development. These economies also remain dependent on continuing public and private capital flows from developed countries facing their own sets of financial constraints. As a result, enthusiasm for globalization has waned, and populist leaders promising to reassert national control over resources and economic policy, such as Venezuela's Nicolas Maduro and South Africa's Jacob Zuma, have gained traction. Support for these leaders stems from a desire for more leverage over the terms of participation in the global economy but does not necessarily signal a desire to retreat entirely from that engagement.

IndiaPictures/UIG via Getty Images.

Employees at a busy call center in Bangalore, India, provide customer support for callers worldwide. These jobs provide new opportunities for a rising Indian middle class but raise criticism in other countries that jobs are being outsourced.

MAP 6.2 ● Real Gross Domestic Product Growth, 2016

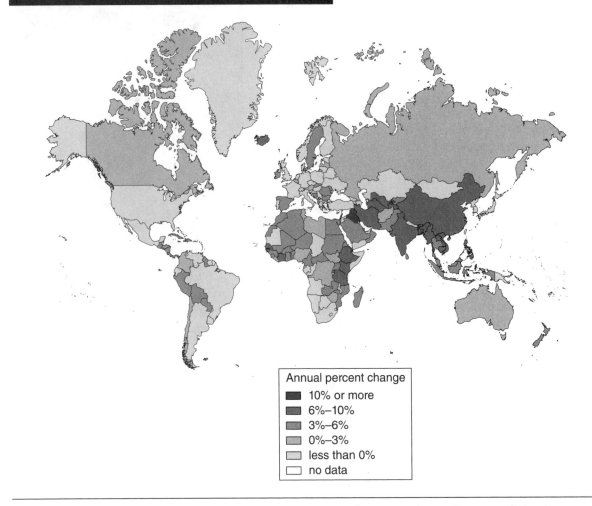

Annual percent change
- 10% or more
- 6%–10%
- 3%–6%
- 0%–3%
- less than 0%
- no data

Source: International Monetary Fund, IMA Data Mapper, "Real GDP Growth," http://www.imf.org/external/datamapper/index.php.

UNDERSTANDING CROSS-BORDER CONFLICT

HOW CAN INTERNATIONAL STUDIES HELP?

Tragedy in Bangladesh

On April 23, 2013, the multistory Rana Plaza building in an industrial suburb of Dhaka, the capital of Bangladesh, collapsed (see Map 6.3). More than 1,100 people were killed, and another 2,500 escaped the wreckage, many with significant injuries. This was the deadliest in a series of disasters that continue to affect garment factories in the country.

Bangladesh has more than 5,000 of these factories, emerging as one of the world's leading clothing exporters, second only to China. The textile industry employs about 4 million people and is critical to the country's economic health, accounting for 17 percent of GDP and more than 75 percent of total exports. The Rana Plaza building itself contained five separate garment shops under contract with some twenty-nine global brands, including such trendy retailers as Canada's Joe Fresh, the United Kingdom's Primark, and Italy's Benetton. With its substandard construction, cracks developed, and an inspection conducted the day prior to the collapse deemed the structure unsafe. Factory supervisors discounted the findings and ordered workers back into the building the next morning. Tragedy struck when the large and heavy power generators previously placed on the upper floors to compensate for regular power failures were turned on.

This disaster highlighted the circumstances faced by workers (overwhelmingly female), who have come to occupy critical roles in industries deeply impacted by the demands and pressures of globalization. In addition to receiving low compensation (the minimum monthly wage is $68, compared to $280 in China), they often endure harsh and unsafe working conditions as employers locate production facilities in the Global South to minimize costs in a highly competitive global market where consumers expect quality and inexpensive goods. In this instance, the toll was considerable. While a $40 million fund under the auspices of the International Labour Organization (ILO) was established to compensate victims and their families, only about half of the brands associated with the building contributed. Bangladesh enacted a series of new oversight measures, but the lack of sufficient numbers of inspectors and the resistance of influential factory owners to adopt enhanced regulation have limited the measures' impact, and few factories have earned safety certifications.

What is the role of crossing borders in addressing this issue? How can the cross-disciplinary focus of international studies help?

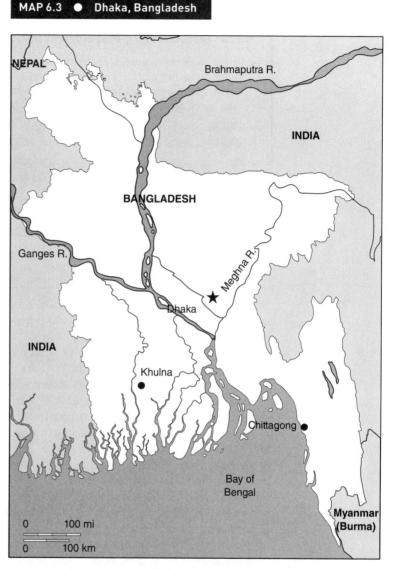

MAP 6.3 ● Dhaka, Bangladesh

- What role do social and cultural factors play in contributing to these types of conditions?

- Can the international community offer any solution?

Questions

- What is the role of geography in this situation?

- What are the political motivations of the countries and companies involved?

- What are the economic implications for Bangladesh and the global garment industry?

Sources: Sajjad Hussein, "Six Months After Bangladeshi Factory Collapse, Workers Remain in Peril," *CNN*, October 24, 2013, http://www.cnn.com/2013/10/24/opinion/bangladesh-garment-workers; Bruce Kennedy, "The Bangladesh Factory Collapse One Year Later," *CBS News*, April 23, 2014, http://www.cbsnews.com/news/the-bangladesh-factory-collapse-one-year-later; "Protestors in Bangladesh Demand Justice on Rana Plaza Anniversary," *DW*, April 24, 2016, http://www.dw.com/en/protesters-in-bangladesh-demand-justice-on-rana-plaza-anniversary/a-19211006.

HOW YOU CAN CONNECT

You can encounter the global economy in your own backyard by . . .

- identifying international companies in close proximity to your community and researching their activities and impacts; you might also seek information on companies that may have outsourced considerable numbers of jobs or even moved their entire operation abroad

- experiencing the service of a call center operating in another country firsthand by seeking assistance via phone or online for an electronic device

- visiting a local business that is run by someone from a local international community or caters to a segment of that international community

- Talking with students or professors at your college or university who come from other countries to learn about their journeys to where they are today

Key Players in Transition

Uncertainties affect people across the global economy. The realignment of some of the more pivotal players in the post–World War II period has added to this dynamic. Countries that played a major role in fueling growth during the latter half of the twentieth century are now attempting to retain their vibrancy in the face of increasing competition and demands from others for a broader distribution of resources.

Japan, which enjoyed extraordinary economic performance in the 1970s and 1980s, has floundered in a prolonged recession that calls into question its basic economic orientation and strategy. Japan built its expansion on a fragile foundation of overvalued land and stock market prices. The collapse of that financial bubble in the early 1990s sent Japan's economy into a persistent tailspin.

To make matters worse, Japan's political environment, which has had its share of instability, discourages significant restructuring. The governing *iron triangle* of politicians, bureaucrats, and big business that oversaw the economic boom continues to dominate the system even as it has been pressured to modify its approach to reestablish the country's global competitiveness. In the early 2000s, Japan enacted reforms that included privatizing inefficient government agencies, forcing banks to write off bad loans, and limiting any tax increases in an effort to increase corporate and individual spending. These were critical to the resumption of economic growth. A succession of political and financial scandals, resulting in the election of six prime ministers over seven years, precluded much progress. Shinzo Abe, who had served previously and was elected again in 2012, has reestablished political stability but has had a difficult time restoring Japan's economic luster.

From every indication, Japan's return to economic vibrancy will be a slow process. In recent years, growth has been modest at best, despite government efforts to stimulate production and employment. While actually retracting slightly in 2014, the economy grew at a rate of less than 1 percent in both 2015 and 2016.[31] The extensive damage and lingering disruption from the massive earthquake and tsunami in March 2011 have contributed to this weakness. Significant increases in government spending to jump-start the economy have, thus far, failed to appreciably expand activity. Wages continue to lag behind, and the anticipated growth in exports resulting from efforts to lower their costs abroad has yet to materialize. Japan's debt has accelerated, adding further to the struggle.

Even such enduring symbols of Japan's global economic prowess as Honda, Sony, and Mitsubishi have had their share of hard times. Meanwhile, Toyota, long known for its quality control and assurance, continues to cope with the fallout from periodic product recalls stemming from shoddy production practices and ineffective managerial oversight and responsibility. To counter slumping sales and preserve their competitive posture, many Japanese companies have had to rethink such traditional business practices as lifetime employment guarantees, strategic partnerships with non-Japanese companies, and the off-shoring of production facilities. For example, in 2016, in order to comply with US legislation that mandated the use of domestic components, 80 percent of the parts that went into the Accords manufactured by Honda came from the United States or Canada.[32] As a result of this legislation, Honda and other manufacturers have established American affiliates of many of their suppliers.

Europe, for its part, has attempted to move forward through a broad-based integration strategy. The 1992 Treaty of Maastricht resulted in a set of agreements to promote deeper cooperation. In recognition of this effort, the EC was renamed the European Union (EU). The building of this association of twenty-seven countries proceeded through the creation of a single European market and a jointly managed monetary system. Through delicate maneuverings and compromises, the countries worked together to strengthen the EU governing institutions. However, breakthroughs did not come easily and have been difficult to sustain.

In 1999, the EU took a landmark step with the introduction of a single currency, the euro. Initially, eleven of the fifteen EU members at the time adopted it, and Greece followed shortly thereafter. (Denmark, Sweden, and the United Kingdom continued to use national currencies.) Participants are required to meet targets relating to inflation, interest rates, and debt. They are also subjected to rules and policies of the European Central Bank, a body that limits the sovereign authority of individual governments and seeks to ensure that the euro works to broaden EU trade and investment goals. There are currently eighteen states in the eurozone. These are members of the EU that use the euro as their official currency and have moved toward even greater economic coordination and political management.

Support for an enhanced EU mandate is, in part, a response to the challenges that many EU members (and aspiring ones) face in coping with new economic realities. Broader integration promotes the levels of cooperation and efficiency required to compete effectively in global markets, although it is sometimes difficult to reconcile divergent interests and perspectives. The debt crisis that engulfed a number of European economies in 2010 and 2011 dampened enthusiasm for this strategy considerably.

Some of the more stable and established members of the EU, such as Germany and France, have found it increasingly difficult to bail out members facing severe capital shortages, such as Greece and Italy, while continuing to attend to traditional entitlements and social welfare policies at home. The flood of refugees entering the continent has magnified the financial challenge and resulted in controversy as to whether they should be welcomed at all. The relatively weaker economies that do not curtail their expenditures have placed considerable strain on the euro and undermined its value. Surging government debts resulted initially, in large measure, from spending to stimulate recovery from the global recession. More recently, they have stemmed from efforts to address lingering economic weaknesses and heightened political pressures to confront them. EU countries continue to face severe challenges, as they cope with limited growth (1.6 percent in 2014, 2.3 percent in 2015, and 1.9 percent in 2016), financial uncertainty that threatens the stability of the euro, and an unemployment rate hovering around 10 percent.[33]

These economic difficulties have also taken their toll politically. The 2014 elections to the European parliament resulted in victories for parties skeptical of deeper integration in a number of key countries. In 2016, the unanticipated decision of voters to approve Britain's withdrawal from the EU—Brexit—was a startling blow that cast doubt on the very future of the EU itself. Additional information on the circumstances leading up to the referendum and some of its potential implications can be found in the "Turning Point" feature in Chapter 10. As suggested in the debate in this chapter's "Pro/Con" box, much will depend on the outcome of deliberations between the British and the EU and the ultimate terms for withdrawal that are negotiated.

The United States remains the world's largest economy, although its growth has been sluggish over recent years as it grapples with the continuing effects of the global financial meltdown of 2008–2009. Housing and employment markets have strengthened, but the overall pace of the recovery has been slower than many had anticipated (2.4 percent in 2014, 2.6 percent in 2015, and 1.9 percent in 2016).[34] Until recently, the United States advanced free market principles in both regional and global forums, to realize the opportunities generally accruing through these policies. These include the expansion of markets for US exports, the creation of jobs to support these activities, and the availability of cheaper products to consumers. Nevertheless, many have come to question this approach, pointing to the loss of US manufacturing jobs as factories relocate to lower-wage countries such as Mexico, the Dominican Republic, Indonesia, and China. Other sectors have also suffered, as advances in IT and telecommunications make it easier for companies to turn to India and other countries for cheap labor. Highly trained and relatively inexpensive workforces in these places are now engaged in a wide array of increasingly complex tasks previously performed in the United States. These concerns gained traction over the course of the 2016 elections and contributed to the popularity of the Trump message.

current account the equivalent of a country's checkbook, reflecting the combined balances on trade in goods, services, income, and net transfers

The cost of maintaining America's economy is also a source of contention, particularly as it impacts increasing budget deficits and debt. The US **current account** deficit, which reflects a net outflow of money from the country, was estimated to be $469.4 billion in 2016.[35] Although moderating significantly over recent years, the country is still saddled with an annual government budget deficit of around $616 billion (down from $1.1 trillion in 2012). With an outstanding national debt of close to $20 trillion, it is difficult for the United States to sustain itself financially.[36] Once the world's leading creditor country, the United States now faces a more vulnerable economic future as it has to rely on China and other foreign sources of financing. By 2016, foreigners owned approximately $6.3 trillion of the US national debt held publicly, with $1.2 trillion held by China.[37]

The ebbs and flows of the global economy—and the uncertainties facing many countries as they chart their course—are reflected in the volatility of oil prices. Oil continues to drive much economic activity across the world, and its availability at a reasonable cost is critical to stable markets. This is not easy to guarantee. To begin with, demand for oil fluctuates widely. Figure 6.1 suggests, moreover, that the members of OPEC account for an overwhelming 81.2 percent of proven reserves and are in a position to control production decisions. In the United States and numerous other consumer countries, enthusiasm for conservation or the pursuit of alternative energy sources as a substitute for oil waned after the crises of the 1970s and generally resurface only during periods of rising prices.[38]

The thirst for oil in China, India, and other emerging economies has rapidly expanded with industrial development. Although tempered a bit by the global recession of 2008–2009, the demand for oil increased as the recovery proceeded and remained strong into 2014. At that point, the economic slowdown in China and other countries that had accounted for this surge began to impact supply significantly. The precipitous drop in prices that followed is noted in Figure 6.2. As evident in Figure 6.3, moreover, prices remained quite low throughout 2016.[39]

PRO/CON

IS BRITISH WITHDRAWAL FROM THE EUROPEAN UNION INEVITABLE?

Pro

Camino Mortera-Martinez

Research Fellow and Brussels Representative, Centre for European Reform. Written for *CQ Researcher*, December 2016.

A complete withdrawal (known as a "hard Brexit") seems highly likely. But the possibility remains of a "soft Brexit"—a less acrimonious divorce that benefits both parties. After all, Switzerland, Norway and Iceland, which are not EU members, are part of the European Union's internal market and Schengen's borderless area.

But a soft Brexit depends on whether the British government and the EU can come to some accommodation on several key issues, including Britain's openness to allowing EU workers into the country.

The problem, as it often is, is politics. The British government insists on having its cake and eating it, too. British Prime Minister Theresa May, who took over in July, shortly after Britons voted in favor of Brexit, is in political trouble: As a former Home secretary, she knows what is at stake for her country (and the EU) if a hard Brexit happens. She also campaigned to remain in the EU, so she now finds herself having to unsay what she said.

May is not delusional. She knows that, whatever deal she may get, it will be less advantageous than the one she has now, unless she bows to unpalatable conditions such as Britain making budgetary contributions to the EU and accepting generous terms for EU migrants. But by acknowledging this, she risks alienating her backbenchers.

As a prime minister whose main task is to take Britain out of the EU, that is a luxury she cannot afford. As a result, May remains vague and contradictory at times. And she sometimes lets her ministers run wild.

The alarming tone of October's Conservative Party conference, where ministers floated ideas, such as requiring companies to declare the number of foreign workers they employ or deporting European doctors en masse, has convinced Brussels that even a soft Brexit is impossible.

Neither Brussels nor London has been very good at talking to each other recently. Brexit is partially the result of this lack of communication. A soft Brexit can still happen, but it would require Brussels to pick up the phone when London is calling.

Con

Donald Tusk

President, European Council. Excerpted from October 13, 2016, speech to European Policy Centre.

Our task will be to protect the interests of the European Union as a whole and the interests of each of the 27 member states, [and] to stick unconditionally to the treaty rules and fundamental values.

By this I mean the conditions for access to the single market with all four freedoms [the free movement of goods, capital, services and people]. There will be no compromises in this regard.

When it comes to the essence of Brexit, it was largely defined in the U.K. during the referendum campaign. We all remember the promises, which cumulated in the demand to "take back control."

Namely the "liberation" from European jurisdiction, a "no" to the freedom of movement or further contributions to the EU budget. This approach has definitive consequences, both for the position of the U.K. government and for . . . negotiations. Regardless of magic spells, this means a de facto will to radically loosen relations with the EU, something that goes by the name of "hard Brexit."

This scenario will in the first instance be painful for Britons. In fact, the words uttered by one of the leading campaigners for Brexit and proponents of the "cake philosophy" was pure illusion: that one can have the EU cake and eat it too. To all who believe in it, I propose a simple experiment. Buy a cake, eat it and see if it is still there on the plate.

The brutal truth is that Brexit will be a loss for all of us. There will be no cakes on the table. For anyone. There will be only salt and vinegar. If you ask me if there is any alternative to this bad scenario, I would like to tell you that yes, there is. And I think it is useless to speculate about a "soft Brexit" because of all the reasons I've mentioned. These would be purely theoretical speculations. In my opinion, the only real alternative to a hard Brexit is "no Brexit."

Even if today hardly anyone believes in such a possibility. We will conduct the negotiations in good faith, defend the interests of the EU 27, minimise the costs and seek the best possible deal for all. But as I have said before, I am afraid that no such outcome exists that will benefit either side.

(Continued)

(Continued)

The British government should also accept that there will be no single market without free movement of people across borders. If it does, it may seek an association agreement similar to that of Norway, which would benefit both parties. For the time being, however, this seems unlikely.

Of course, it is and can only be for the United Kingdom to assess the outcome of the negotiations and determine if Brexit is really in its interests.

Source: Corine Hegland, "European Union's Future," *CQ Researcher* 26 (December 16, 2016): 1037–1060. Retrieved from http://library .cqpress.com.

Where Do You Stand?

1. Does the vote in favor of Brexit serve the best interests of Britain at this time?

2. How realistic is the likelihood of *a soft* Brexit?

FIGURE 6.1 ● Organization of the Petroleum Exporting Countries Members: Proven Crude Oil Reserves, 2015 (Billions of Barrels)

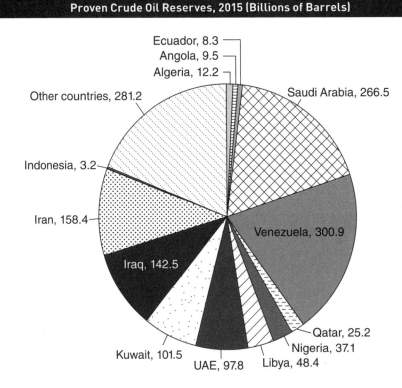

OPEC share: 81.2 percent*

Source: OPEC, *Annual Statistical Bulletin,* 2016 edition, www.opec.org.

*This represents 81.2 percent of the world's proven oil reserves.

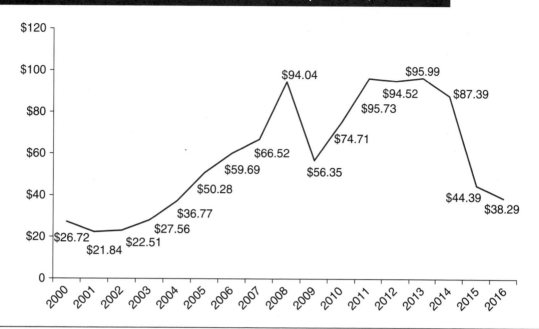

FIGURE 6.2 ● Average World Crude Oil Prices (US Dollars per Barrel), 2000–2016*

Source: US Energy Information Administration, US Department of Energy, *Monthly Energy Review*, March 2017, https://www.eia.gov/totalenergy/data/monthly/pdf/mer.pdf.

*Domestic first purchase price, annual average.

While depressed oil prices are welcomed by consumers, they are a source of concern for investors who see them as a signal of broader economic malaise. At the same time, it is important to understand the many forces that influence these rates and the variability

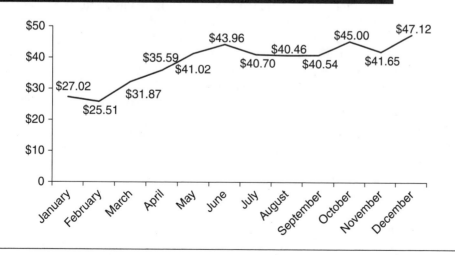

FIGURE 6.3 ● World Crude Oil Prices (US Dollars per Barrel), 2016*

Source: Energy Information Administration, US Department of Energy: *Monthly Energy Review*, March 2017, www.eia.gov/totalenergy/data/monthly/pdf/mer.pdf.

*Prices as of the last week of each month.

of the market. Because oil is purchased around the world with US dollars, any significant fluctuations in the value of the currency affect prices directly. The heightened involvement of speculators must also be considered. These speculators often sign contracts for future deliveries at the current price, particularly if they are anticipating potential increases. Their purchases are often considerable, thereby impacting available supply and prevailing prices.

Political instability in the Middle East and other major supply areas also remains a factor. In Saudi Arabia and other oil-producing countries in the Persian Gulf, internal opposition threatens the future of longstanding monarchies. Ongoing political tensions in Iraq, Iran, Nigeria, and Venezuela add to these uncertainties and threaten to interrupt production or otherwise disrupt the flow of oil to its intended destinations. With supplies so vulnerable to shifting political winds, oil markets remain unpredictable and may be subject to unanticipated hikes. Rising prices may offer windfall profits to oil companies and producer countries; however, they disrupt economic activity and create severe hardships for dependent consumers.

Conclusion: The Evolution of the World Economy

The world economy is constantly changing. On the one hand, the spread of globalization has benefited people previously outside the mainstream, who have become deeply engaged and productive participants. In China and other emerging economies, for example, eager governments and bold entrepreneurs have parlayed local advantages into impressive growth and development. A good case in point is Chen Ou, one of a growing number of young Chinese innovators seeking to capitalize on the country's growing market opportunities. He received his MBA at Stanford University and founded an online gaming platform while still in school. He then started jumei.com, a cosmetics e-commerce venture with 4 million registered users that features products from Calvin Klein, Estee Lauder, and other leading brands.[40]

At the same time, the extension of the free market has destabilized the lives of many others who continue to operate on the periphery without sufficient tools to compete. This has certainly been true for Ping, a young woman from Vietnam whose encounter with the outside world brought her into the web of human trafficking—a growing segment of today's global economy that involves recruiting and transporting persons through force or coercion. This sector generates around $150 billion in profits annually and impacts almost 21 million people.[41] Although promised a job in another Vietnamese city at the age of twelve, she found herself transported to China, where she was sold into prostitution. Confined to working in a brothel for more than a year under harsh supervision, she was finally rescued and returned home. She is now training for a career in hairdressing, but still suffers from physical and emotional symptoms stemming from her ordeal.[42]

This contrast between Ou and Ping epitomizes the complex and often contradictory nature of today's global economy. It affects the fates and fortunes of countries and their people in very different ways. The challenge is magnified by the shifting boundaries of economic activity and the absence of broad consensus on the policies that are most useful and desirable in tackling issues that are pivotal to the economic well-being of people (e.g., stabilizing financial markets, managing debt, and alleviating poverty).

As the world's economies have been brought closer together, new entrepreneurship opportunities have materialized to address outstanding problems. A particularly creative approach is that of Piece & Co., a for-profit enterprise that has established new forms of collaboration in the global marketplace. The company connects major brands such as Nike, J. Crew, and Nordstrom with female artisans in developing countries who craft an array of fashionable products. In addition to providing sustainable employment outlets for these women, the partner companies benefit by selling high-quality and desirable items.

Under the leadership of its founder, Kathleen Wright, Piece & Co. has brought more than 5,000 artisans into its global network.[43]

Important questions remain as to the future resiliency of the world economy and the extent to which it will be poised to meet the basic and sometimes divergent needs of its varied participants. Trade, investment, and finance are three critical areas that will require considerable attention. Chapter 7 looks at the challenges of addressing these issues.

Key Concepts

capitalism   130
comparative advantage   132
conditionality   139
current account   148
dependency theory   135

hegemon   133
liberalism   130
mercantilism   130
most-favored nation (MFN)   134
neoliberalism   139

nondiscrimination   134
outsource, or offshore   142
petrodollars   137
reciprocity   134

To Learn More

Books and Other Print Media

Jeffrey A. Frieden, *Global Capitalism: Its Fall and Rise in the Twentieth Century* (New York: W. W. Norton, 2006).

This book is a good review of the earlier wave of globalization in the early twentieth century and how it collapsed with the outbreak of World War I in 1914. It is very helpful in understanding contemporary globalization and the idea that it is necessarily inevitable and irreversible.

Paul Kennedy, *The Rise and Fall of the Great Powers* (New York: Random House, 1987).

Paul Kennedy's classic and comprehensive history of the development of the global economy focuses on how great powers arise and eventually lose their preeminent status.

Michael Mandelbaum, *The Road to Global Prosperity* (New York: Simon & Schuster, 2014).

While acknowledging the concerns stemming from the fallout from the financial meltdown in 2008, this book puts forth an optimistic view of the future of globalization and its capacity for spreading wealth across the world.

Paul Mason, *Postcapitalism: A Guide to our Future* (New York: Farrar, Strauss and Giroux, 2016).

Paul Mason looks at some of the more profound changes, especially those relating to information technology, that are changing the underlying foundation of capitalism. While noting that these forces are a source of considerable tension and dislocation, he argues that they may offer the opportunity to establish a more sustainable and just economic order.

Thomas Piketty, *Capital in the Twenty-First Century* (Boston: Belknap Press, 2014).

This widely discussed and rather controversial book analyzes data from twenty countries and argues that the inequalities of wealth generated by contemporary capitalism threaten democratic values.

Joseph P. Quinlan, *The Last Economic Superpower: The Retreat of Globalization, The End of American Dominance, and What We Can Do about It* (New York: McGraw-Hill, 2011).

This book is an intriguing look at the reconfiguring of the global economy following the 2008 financial crisis, with special emphasis on the rise of China and other emerging market economies.

Ruchir Sharma, *The Rise and Fall of Nations: Forces of Change in the Post-Crisis World* (New York: W. W. Norton & Company, 2016).

Ruchir Sharma stipulates ten rules that he believes are the keys to success and failure in the world economy and proceeds to identify the likely winners and losers.

Michael Taillard, *101 Things Everyone Needs to Know about the Global Economy: The Guide to Understanding International Finance, World Markets, and How They Can Affect Your Financial Future* (Avon, MA: Adams Media, 2013).

As advertised, this book features brief definitions and descriptions of 101 commonly referenced concepts, terms, and phenomena.

Steven R. Weisman, *The Great Tradeoff: Confronting Moral Conflicts in the Era of Globalization* (Washington, DC: Peterson Institute for International Economics, 2016).

Steven Weisman looks at some of the moral and ethical concerns regarding globalization that surfaced during the financial crisis of 2008–2009 in a discussion that has considerable relevance in assessing the controversies over the direction of today's global economy.

Websites

Europa (the European Union [EU]), http://europa.eu

This official website of the EU contains a wealth of information on the organization and its member states.

Group of 77 (G77), www.g77.org

This organization represents the interests of developing countries within the UN and beyond.

International Labour Organization (ILO), www.ilo.org

The official website for this UN specialized agency contains information about the ILO, along with publications, research, labor standards, and a statistical database.

Organisation for Economic Co-operation and Development (OECD), www.oecd.org

This organization's website houses its storehouse of data and statistics and provides access to publications and reports.

Organization of the Petroleum Exporting Countries (OPEC), www.opec.org

OPEC is an intergovernmental organization (IGO) representing the major oil-producing states, primarily those in the Middle East. The official website hosts information about the organization, including data, publications, and other media.

US-China Business Council (USCBC), www.uschina.org

The USCBC is a private, nonprofit organization of US companies that do business with China.

Videos

Capitalism: A Love Story (2009), http://documentary-movie.com/capitalism-a-love-story

This film by humorist and social critic Michael Moore offers a highly critical look into the dynamics of modern capitalism, focusing on the corporate dominance of everyday life. Both highly acclaimed and heavily criticized (depending on one's political perspective), the film is quite useful in generating discussion and debate.

Capitalizing Happiness (2016), http://topdocumentary films.com/capitalizing-happiness

This film profiles Brazilian entrepreneur Ricardo Semler and his efforts in guiding one of the country's most profitable companies. It raises important issues about the nature of capitalism and the connection between workplace satisfaction and productivity.

Commanding Heights: The Battle for the World Economy (2003)

A three-part series tracing the transformation of the global economy from the beginning of the twentieth century to the 1990s, this is an excellent source for understanding the conflicting views on the relationship between governments and markets. The contrasting ideas of economists John Maynard Keynes and Friedrich von Hayek are noted throughout as a means for understanding current disagreements over economic policy. There is also a comprehensive website with many special features hosted by PBS.

Fashion Victims (2013)

This Australian documentary looks at the tragic collapse of the Rana Plaza building in Bangladesh.

Globalization at the Crossroads (2013), https://www.you tube.com/watch?v=Gnh5MIiG4gQ

This informative and enlightening program features economist Hernando de Soto, who examines the importance of extending property rights to the world's poor to enable them to access the potential benefits of globalization.

The Globalization Trilogy (2011)

This collection of three videos explores different levels of today's global production and consumption chain.

It includes *Store Wars: When Wal-Mart Comes to Town* (2001), which examines US consumerist culture; *China Blue* (2005), which uncovers labor conditions in Chinese sweatshops; and *Bitter Seeds* (2011), which focuses on farmers in India growing cotton for export to China's garment factories.

"Keynesianism: It's All About Spending" (2010) and "Fight of the Century" (2011), https://www.youtube.com/watch?v=d0nERTFo-Sk;https://www.youtube.com/watch?v=GTQnarzmTOc

These are lighthearted and entertaining yet informative music videos produced by EconStories that indicate how the ideas of Hayek and Keynes informed the debates over how to respond to the 2008–2009 financial crisis.

"New Thoughts on Capital in the Twenty-First Century" (2014), https://www.ted.com/talks/thomas_piketty_new_thoughts_on_capital_in_the_twenty_first_century

This TED Talk by Thomas Piketty offers a good introduction to and synopsis of his landmark study listed previously in the suggested print resources, which addresses economic inequality.

1-800-India (2006)

This film examines the human and cultural impact, especially on women, of the emergence of India as a leader for outsourced white-collar jobs.

7

Challenges to Prosperity

We must rebalance this unjust economy.

—Winnie Byanyima, Executive Director, Oxfam International, 2017[1]

Learning Objectives

After studying this chapter, you will be able to do the following:

- Identify the key arguments framing the debate over free and fair trade.

- Identify the different types and sources of global investments and recognize the controversies over the growing role of transnational corporations.

- Understand the major characteristics of the global financial system and how the activities of public institutions and private lenders influence development.

- Explain how recent events have influenced perceptions and ideas regarding the value of globalization in advancing the prosperity of countries across the world.

The World Economic Forum (WEF) is an independent nonprofit foundation that brings together political, financial, civil society, and corporate leaders to promote networking and to address an array of global issues. It convened in Davos, Switzerland, in January 2017 for its forty-seventh annual meeting, under the general theme of "Responsive and Responsible Leadership," to discuss the need for strengthening collaboration in addressing the key challenges facing the global economy in the coming years. This chapter's opening quote from the executive director of the London-based Oxfam International, Winnie Byanyima, was taken from one of the WEF sessions; as Byanyima observes, widening inequality across the world is a critical problem that threatens our future. This has been an evolving position for the WEF, but the magnitude of the problem makes it difficult to ignore. Income disparities continue to widen. The richest 1 percent have come to own more than all the rest of us, while eight men have accumulated more wealth than the 3.6 million people who comprise the bottom half of the world's population.[2] (See Map 7.1.) Long considered a representative of more entrenched political and business interests and a strong advocate for extending globalization, the WEF has expanded its support base and invited celebrities such as actor Leonardo DiCaprio, rock legend Bono, and rapper will.i.am to its annual meetings to raise awareness of and funding for debt relief, AIDS research, and other humanitarian causes.

For some critics of the WEF and its underlying approach, this has not been enough. They have organized their own gathering, the World Social Forum, which offers individuals and representatives of groups and organizations that are part of the antiglobalization movement an opportunity to voice their concerns. The World Social Forum has been meeting since 2001 (either annually or biennially), seeking to advance alternative models of economic and social development. Attendees see themselves as politically and economically disadvantaged and likely to fall further behind within a free market system. Meeting in Montreal in August 2016 under the banner "Another World is Necessary," they reiterated their position that the global capitalist system is inherently unfair by design, and that only a significant overhaul will provide for a more equal distribution of wealth.[3]

Much of their skepticism stems from the neoliberal "rules of the game" that are administered largely by governments and businesses with the greatest leverage within

A worker guides sacks of coffee beans along a conveyor belt at the Molenbergnatie NV coffee and cocoa handling terminal at the Port of Antwerp in Belgium. The global trade in commodities like coffee is a sign of potential increases in prosperity worldwide, yet the world's citizens do not share the rewards equally.

Jasper Juinen/Bloomberg via Getty Images.

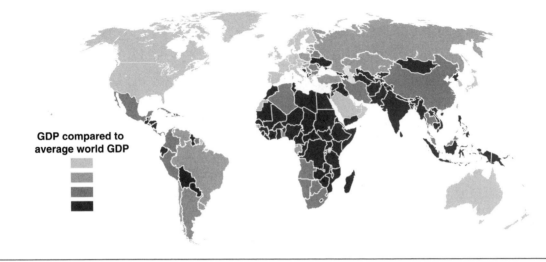

MAP 7.1 ● Global Inequality Compared to Average World GDP

GDP compared to
average world GDP

Note: Countries in lighter shades have gross domestic products (GDPs) above the average world GDP. Countries in the darker shades have GDPs that are below the average world GDP with the darkest shade indicating the lowest GDPs.

the global economy. Economist Joseph Stiglitz, who has written widely on the challenges and limitations of globalization, believes that these rules undermine the sovereignty of developing countries by restricting their ability to control decisions affecting their well-being.[4] Despite their broader access to world markets, many of the countries of the Global South remain highly critical of the system. They want to see the world's economic powerhouses more directly address such challenges as pervasive poverty, trade fairness, transnational corporate behavior, unregulated capital flows, and debt relief.

Even as these pleas for greater inclusiveness have gained wider airing, another front in the debate over globalization has opened in recent years. Centered mainly in advanced industrial countries, it has been driven by resistance to the adjustments required to operate in an open market system. The outsourcing of jobs and the relocation of production facilities to lower-wage countries in the Global South has powered much of the opposition. Alleged manipulations of trade rules and currency values to enhance competiveness have also been a considerable source of concern. The response has been a call for a more nationalistic approach, which, among other things, would include the imposition of tariffs and other measures to manage and even constrain global markets. The British vote to leave the EU and the election of US president Donald Trump in 2016 suggested the growing significance of this opposition.

The widening and deepening debate over globalization and its impacts suggests a somewhat unpredictable future. Very different perspectives fuel the disagreements that play out when international agencies such as the World Trade Organization (WTO) meet to consider ways to address complaints about the trade policies of certain members or when leaders gather to develop plans to maintain the flow of global credit. Supporters of globalization point to the likely benefits of preserving open markets, which spread capital and other resources to areas in need. Opponents focus on the costs to workers and the disadvantaged without the requisite skills or wherewithal to operate in this environment. They complain that the imposition of globalization's neoliberal principles and policies does not account sufficiently for unique local needs or circumstances.

Decisions made today about trade, investment, and finance will shape the future of the world economy. The willingness of governments to address their differences prior to taking retaliatory action will determine the character and structure of international trade. Where Korea's Hyundai Motor Company or some other transnational company locates its next assembly plant will impact employment prospects across its production and distribution network. The lending practices of Germany's Deutsche Bank and other leading financial institutions will affect the stability and potential expansion of global capital markets. In the sections that follow, we take a look at these issues that affect our sense of economic security and welfare.

Free versus Fair Trade

The volume of trade has expanded considerably since the end of World War II. The progressive reduction of tariffs and other barriers that countries use to protect their domestic markets has facilitated a broader exchange of goods and services. Total trade in 2000, for example, was twenty-two times the level in 1950.[5] Advances in technology have contributed to this growth. Massive container ships now carry more cargo than ever before, thereby reducing the unit cost of transportation. The capacity of the largest ships has continued to rise, more than doubling since 2000.[6] Ports have worked to dredge their waters and enhance their facilities to accommodate these mega-vessels. The completion of the Panama Canal project in 2016, referenced in the "Turning Point" feature, was heralded as a significant breakthrough in further expanding the flow of goods across the world.

There are incentives to keep trade lines open. Exports are an important source of income and employment, while imports offer opportunities to enhance quality of life by providing consumers with a broader array of products. For the world's poorer countries, in particular, trade is a means to engage with the global economy and to gain access to critical items such as food and medicines that might not be available otherwise. At the same time, economic and political considerations can often affect the ability to maintain unrestricted markets.

While the United States, Germany, and other advanced industrial economies continue to rank among the most active traders, the structure of the world trade system is changing. Emerging market economies are playing an increasingly larger role. China has become the largest exporter, accounting for 13.2 percent of the world's total value in 2016. This dominance has been largely due to China's ability to produce low-cost goods and an economic development policy that has emphasized the importance of maximizing the country's export potential. Although sputtering somewhat in recent years, other emerging markets such as Mexico, India, and Brazil have also come to acquire respectable shares of the market. These same countries are also significant importers, further reflecting their growing presence on the global economic stage. Russia's recent slide may be attributed to its heavy reliance on energy-related trade and the decline in oil and gas prices (see Table 7.1).

A wider group of countries have the opportunity to participate fully in today's trading system. Long before the recent wave of antiglobalization sentiment began to spread across the Global North, however, many countries in the Global South decried what they saw as an inherent unfairness in the trade system that left them marginalized and pressed for preferential treatment to level the playing field and to improve their competitiveness. These concerns have been raised at meetings of the WTO and other trade forums and have limited efforts to build broader policy consensus.

The trade system itself is heavily influenced by the ups and downs of the global economy (see Table 7.2). After rising steadily for a number of years, for example, trade contracted sharply (by about 23 percent) as the effects of the financial meltdown in 2008–2009 spread across the world. This was the steepest decline in more than seventy years. While it rebounded by about 20 percent in 2010, growth has been uneven in subsequent years

TURNING POINT
JUNE 26, 2016

The New Panama Canal

Part of the newly constructed Panama Canal expansion project runs to the left of the Miraflores locks along the canal on April 7, 2016, in Panama City, Panama.

Joe Raedle/Getty Images.

What?

On June 26, 2016, the new Panama Canal opened with the passage of a Chinese cargo ship through its extended locks. Originally scheduled for completion in 2014 to coincide with the centennial anniversary of the original canal, the $5.4 billion expansion project doubles the canal's capacity and now permits ships holding 13,000 containers (nearly three times the previous maximum size allowable) to make their way through the waterway linking the Pacific and Atlantic oceans.

Why?

The decision to move forward with the project in 2007 was prompted by the progressive expansion of international trade, especially that involving China, and advances in shipbuilding that facilitated the production of supercargo ships capable of accommodating ever-increasing loads. Initially opened in 1914, the Panama Canal was too narrow to service these new vessels. Shippers were forced to utilize more costly and inconvenient routes, while the canal was losing considerable potential business. With around 90 percent of all trade by sea, only 5 percent was passing through the canal. Goods from China and other Asian countries intended for the East Coast of the United States, for example, were often unloaded at Long Beach, California, or other West Coast ports and then transported by rail or truck to their destinations.

How?

The project was complex and involved the building of three new locks that required significant dredging and excavation.

It also called for the adoption of new navigation procedures that would place additional burdens on tugboat operators responsible for guiding the ships through the canal. The effort was plagued by controversy and doubts from the outset. The awarding of the building contract to a Spanish-led consortium, which included a Panamanian company owned by the family of the canal administrator at the time, raised questions about the integrity of the process. As work proceeded, many issues arose relating to the quality of materials utilized in construction, cost overruns, water levels in Gatun Lake, and whether the new locks could be navigated safely. Some have argued that the new locks, while 1,400 feet long and 160 feet wide, do not provide a sufficient margin of error for successful navigation. Despite these concerns and a number of technical glitches along the way, construction proceeded, and the project was completed. It is estimated that by 2021, the canal will bring in $2.1 billion annually in additional revenue.

Will It Make a Difference over Time?

While the new canal opened amidst considerable fanfare, some questions remain as to its enduring effects and benefits. The continuing availability of sufficient water in Gatun Lake and the actual design of the new locks themselves are somewhat problematic. During the first month of operation, there were three incidents that resulted in damage to ships that were unable to successfully navigate through the waterway. In the short term, the impact will be less than anticipated initially. The slow pace of economic recovery from the Great Recession worldwide and the softening of the Chinese economy in particular have negatively affected the volume of international trade. Over the longer term, however, many believe that this ambitious project will pay considerable dividends in terms of jobs, efficiencies, and overall economic security. Perhaps most important, it is seen as an important means to reduce maritime shipping costs and to foster the further development of Atlantic-Pacific commercial exchange.

What Do You Think?

Is this truly a turning point that will enhance the value and utility of the canal? Will the canal meet expectations in terms of usage and its projected benefits? To help you get started in framing your views, you might want to take a look at the following resource:

Walt Bogdanich, Jacqueline Williams, and Ana Graciela Mendez, "The New Panama Canal: A Risky Bet," *The New York Times*, June 22, 2016, http://www.nytimes.com/interactive/2016/06/22/world/americas/panama-canal.html?_r=0.

TABLE 7.1 ● Merchandise Trade 2016: Select Exporters and Importers

	Exports			Imports		
	Value*	Percentage Share	Rank	Value*	Percentage Share	Rank
China	2,098	13.2	1	1,587	9.8	2
United States	1,455	9.1	2	2,251	13.9	1
Germany	1,340	8.4	3	1,055	6.5	3
Japan	645	4.0	4	607	3.7	5
France	501	3.1	7	573	3.5	6
Republic of Korea	495	3.1	8	406	2.5	10
Mexico	374	2.3	13	398	2.5	12
Russia	282	1.8	17	191	1.2	24
India	264	1.7	20	359	2.2	14
Brazil	185	1.2	25	143	0.9	28

Source: World Trade Organization Secretariat, Press Release, April 12 2017.

*In billions of US dollars.

due to the irregular pace of economic recovery. China's economic slowdown and volatile global financial markets have proven especially challenging, prompting a considerable 13 percent drop in the dollar value of world trade in 2015 and an overall sluggishness that persisted into 2016. While projected to recover modestly in upcoming years, in line with

TABLE 7.2 ● Merchandise Trade 2016 (in Billions of US Dollars)

	Exports				Imports			
	Value	2014	2015	2016	Value	2014	2015	2016
World	15,464	0.3	−13.5	−3.3	15,799	0.6	−12.5	−3.2
North America	2,219	3.1	−8.0	−3.2	3,067	3.4	−4.5	−2.9
Europe	5,942	0.5	−12.5	−0.3	5,920	1.2	−13.2	0.2
Latin America	511	−7.0	−21.1	−5.6	533	−4.0	−16.4	−14.5
CIS*	419	−5.8	−31.9	−16.2	333	−11.7	−32.4	−2.6
Africa	346	−7.6	−29.6	−11.5	501	0.4	−13.8	−9.5
Middle East	766	−4.3	−34.4	−9.5	665	2.1	−7.7	−7.2
Asia	5,262	2.6	−7.9	−3.7	4,781	0.1	−14.5	−4.7

(Annual Percentage Change columns: 2014, 2015, 2016)

Source: World Trade Organization Secretariat, Press Release, April 12, 2017.

*Commonwealth of Independent States (Russia and former Soviet republics: Armenia, Azerbaijan, Belarus, Georgia, Kazakhstan, Kyrgyz Republic, Moldova, Tajikistan, Turkmenistan, Ukraine, and Uzbekistan).

an expanding global economy, that prediction itself is uncertain. The antiglobalization sentiment sweeping across the United States, Britain, and elsewhere has dimmed support for open markets and could unleash a wave of protectionist legislation that would disrupt cross-border flows of goods and services.[7]

Maintaining stable and cooperative trade relationships in the face of these challenges can be problematic. Countries often find it difficult to withstand the temptation to seek any possible advantage in their dealings with others, especially if they are under pressure at home to focus more exclusively on building domestic capacity and creating more jobs. This can lead to the use of policy tools that may be questionable in terms of their legality. The WTO has handled more than 500 complaints through its dispute settlement process since 1995. These cases have covered an array of subjects, ranging from Antigua's claim that the United States had unlawfully closed its market to Antiguan remote gambling services, to Japan's concerns over China's use of quotas and questionable licensing requirements to restrict exports of rare earth metals critical to the development of new technologies, to charges leveled by Brazil relating to Thailand's sugar subsidies. The WTO has had a mixed record in terms of reconciling differences and defusing tensions that arise from these conflicts.[8]

Beyond these particular disputes is the broader philosophical debate with respect to the utility of alternative approaches to trade, and particularly the advisability of free versus fair trade policies. As one of the centerpieces of the post–World War II global economy and contemporary globalization, free trade emphasizes the need to eliminate both institutionalized and informal barriers to maximize the exchange of goods and services. Supporters argue that open markets provide for efficiencies that moderate prices, stimulate economic growth, and offer the "greatest good for the greatest number" across the globe. As noted in Chapter 6, it has been difficult to maintain the system. Even as government officials frequently endorse free trade in principle, their actual commitment in practice does not always follow.

Trade policies can be quite contentious and highly sensitive to political pressures and maneuverings, especially when world economic output is contracting and jobs are at risk. Citizens expect governments to protect their interests, particularly if they see themselves as threatened by competition. For many, free trade is seen as the primary source of their vulnerability. They advocate instead for policies that reflect principles of fair trade as the means to advance their interests. This might include the imposition of barriers to restrain imports or support for domestic producers to enhance their competitive edge. The case for fair trade is a complicated one involving a diversity of perspectives and agendas. For some, the banner of fair trade is put forward as a means to address the interests of those disadvantaged by an open market system. More recently, this concern has gained considerable traction across the Global North and has focused largely on workers who have been displaced by companies that have relocated operations to places offering labor or other cost advantages. A common justification for imposing tariffs or other measures to encourage domestic production is the need to bring back jobs and to shield workers from the uncertainties of global competition.

Certified fair trade coffee with an eco-friendly product label.

For others, the pursuit of fair trade emphasizes the circumstances faced by many small farmers—especially in the Global South—as they operate within global supply networks. All too often, it is argued, these growers are victimized by the ups and downs of commodity markets—losing out when prices are low and being too far down in a chain that is dominated by transnational agribusinesses and distributors to benefit when prices rise. This has led to the emergence of a worldwide, consumer-driven movement designed to bring about changes in the arrangement.

Many of us come into contact with this as we shop, even if we are not necessarily aware of it, with the fair-trade labeling that appears on certain products. Coffee may be the most familiar, as we often find that option—albeit at a somewhat higher cost—on the menus of the coffeehouses we frequent. This certification denotes a guaranteed price paid to indigenous growers, regardless of prevailing market conditions. While touted as an important breakthrough in bringing equity issues to the fore of the trade agenda, there are questions as to its effectiveness in addressing the challenge. Some have suggested that even as farmers may be protected against dramatic drops in the market, they do not secure their rightful share of benefits when higher prices prevail.[9]

The multiplicity of interests affected by trade policy makes it difficult to strike an acceptable balance. This was evident when the WTO kicked off the **Doha Round**, its first multilateral negotiations of the twenty-first century, in Qatar in 2001. The Doha Round sought to build on previous efforts to reduce obstacles to trade, while advancing a "development agenda" focusing largely on the needs and concerns of poorer countries. Serious discord plagued the meetings almost from the outset. In 2006, negotiations broke off over questions relating to the willingness of countries to make concessions to further this goal. Some of the more significant differences that surfaced reflected the mix of approaches utilized by states at any given time, regardless of their "official" policy.

Doha Round the most recent international trade negotiations conducted under the auspices of the WTO

Both before and since the suspension of the Doha talks, **protectionism** in agriculture has been a particularly delicate issue. The countries of the Global South have pushed hard for the timely elimination of American, European, and Japanese subsidies. At the same time, they have argued the need to retain their right to preserve their own subsidies to offset competitive disadvantages and to gain preferential access to lucrative markets in the Global North. The response of the developed countries has been measured. In their efforts to placate powerful farming interests at home, they have called instead for a gradual and reciprocal process that corresponds more closely to WTO principles and accounts for the politically sensitive nature of these matters.

protectionism government policies that restrict imports in an effort to shield local businesses from global competition

These countries also debate a number of other matters that affect their competitive posture. **Intellectual property rights (IPRs)**—the patent, copyright, and trademark protections extended to individuals and organizations whose original ideas have led to the design of particular products or other types of creative works—have been especially contentious. The developers of intellectual property (disproportionally located in more advanced countries) argue in favor of retaining these exclusive rights to encourage further innovation. Those who are critical of these IPR protections point to their role in limiting the diffusion of knowledge to the Global South. This is particularly problematic with respect to extending access to critical medicines at affordable cost in the poorest countries.[10]

intellectual property rights (IPRs) patents, copyrights, and trademarks extended to individuals and organizations to protect their ownership of products or other creative works generated through their original ideas

While the disagreement over IPRs continues, counterfeiters and copyists commonly infringe on these protections. They may circumvent the rules by selling pirated software on a Beijing corner, a knockoff pocketbook on a New York street, a pair of "designer" jeans in Moscow, an "exclusive" watch in a back alley in Cairo, or an airplane replacement part from a bogus yet well-designed and legitimate-looking website. Markets for these types of goods are robust, as prices are a fraction of what they would be if purchasing the authentic item. Counterfeit merchandise now accounts for an estimated $461 billion or 2.5 percent of total world trade. China, Hong Kong, and other developing countries have benefited handsomely from these practices and are resistant to greater enforcement of protections for the owners of intellectual property.[11]

The breakdown of the Doha Round illustrates the unwillingness of many countries to open themselves fully to the global market. It also suggests their continuing reluctance to extend the regulatory and enforcement capabilities of the WTO. Such ambivalence has contributed to the emergence of an alternate strategy to advance and protect national interests—regional trade pacts. Some recommend this approach as an initial building block for developing trust and establishing guidelines that would ultimately lead to broader global cooperation. Others argue that the elimination of barriers and expansion of transactions within these regional compacts is a more manageable track that might reduce dependence on other markets that are more difficult to control.

The European Union (EU) has led the way in promoting regional integration. The development of a single market has been intended to maximize trade among members by promoting the free movement of goods within the bloc. Regional free trade arrangements have gained considerable popularity elsewhere. Across Asia, for example, the Association of Southeast Asian Nations (ASEAN) and the Asia-Pacific Economic Cooperation (APEC) body have worked to enhance trade and investment linkages in the region. China has also entered the fray through agreements with ASEAN and other initiatives such as the ASEAN-China Free Trade Area (ACFTA) that tie it closer to other countries across the area.

Similar measures have taken root in the Americas. Since the 1990s, governments have used regional compacts to build export-oriented development strategies and to meet heightened global competition. Argentina, Brazil, Paraguay, and Uruguay came together in 1991 to form the Common Market of the South, or Mercosur. The historically dominant role of the United States has complicated efforts to accommodate interests across the region and to allay fears of undue American intrusiveness.

North American Free Trade Agreement (NAFTA) an arrangement designed to expand cross-border trade and investment signed by Canada, Mexico, and the United States in 1994

In 1994, the United States, Canada, and Mexico signed the **North American Free Trade Agreement (NAFTA)**, which extended market access and broadened commercial ties among the three partners. Opposition arose in many quarters. In the United States, workers feared a significant transfer of jobs across the Mexican border. A staunch NAFTA critic, US businessman and third-party presidential candidate Ross Perot injected this issue into the 1992 presidential election. Although Perot captured only a small fraction of the vote, he galvanized concerns about the potential impact of NAFTA on US employment and trade prospects. American environmental and labor rights groups also weighed in, arguing for stricter workplace standards. Ultimately, there were separate protocols attached to the agreement to guard against potential environmental and labor abuses. In Mexico and other parts of Latin America, NAFTA once again raised the specter of overarching US control.

The controversies surrounding NAFTA have continued to this day. Much of the debate centers on its purported impact on employment. Donald Trump mounted a blistering attack during the 2016 US presidential campaign, noting his intention to undo the treaty. It is difficult to reach any definitive conclusions with regard to it overall effects, however, as different studies have produced widely varying results. Although NAFTA has been credited with creating millions of export-related jobs in the United States, some critics have argued that the displacement of domestic production has cut millions of others. Those losses have been highly concentrated in the manufacturing sector, particularly the US automobile industry. Similarly, Mexico has lost an estimated 1.3 million farm jobs by lowering tariffs that had been used previously to compete with heavily subsidized US agribusinesses. The anticipated improvements in the quality of life for Mexican workers have not materialized for the most part, thereby prompting increasing numbers to seek refuge in the United States. There is also evidence to suggest that the rules to protect the environment and to govern working conditions in the manufacturing and assembly plants near the United States–Mexico border have had limited effectiveness.

Since NAFTA has been in place, trade and investment flows across the region have expanded considerably. From 1993 to 2015, for example, trade among the partners nearly quadrupled—from $294 billion to roughly $1.1 trillion. The value of Mexican exports to the United States increased 637 percent, from $40 billion to more than $294 billion per year, while US exports to Mexico rose 455 percent. This resulted in a dramatic shift in the relationship, as a $1.1 billion US trade surplus turned into a $63.2 billion deficit.

Debris lies on the floor of the administration building of the abandoned Packard auto assembly plant in Detroit, Michigan, on Tuesday, April 21, 2015. Arte Express Detroit LLC chief executive officer Fernando Palazuelo bought the Packard plant in 2013 and is working to restore the site in hopes of bringing jobs and commerce to the neighborhood.

Meanwhile, Canada emerged as the leading market for American agricultural products, with total imports from the United States increasing around 166 percent (from $100.4 billion to $266.8 billion annually) over the life of the treaty. Overall, NAFTA constitutes the world's largest free trade area, linking some 450 million people producing $20.8 trillion in goods and services. Its impact, while significant, has not proven as consequential as either its supporters or opponents have suggested (see Figure 7.1).[12]

Other efforts to deepen economic integration across the Americas have produced their own controversies. Perhaps most instructive was the opposition to the Free Trade Area of the Americas (FTAA). Intended to link the markets of thirty-four countries in 2005, the effort stalled as negotiators could not reconcile differing perspectives as to how the FTAA would affect job growth, labor rights, and the survival of small farmers and local businesses.[13] There has been no subsequent effort to reopen formal discussions. Instead, governments have proceeded to negotiate agreements with individual trade partners in the region to expand their commercial dealings.

According to the WTO, opening national markets to international trade "will encourage and contribute to sustainable development, raise people's welfare, reduce poverty, and foster peace and stability."[14] The rhetoric of free trade continues to fuel regional and international negotiations, but countries that may be among the most vocal supporters of freer markets often engage in protectionist policies to further their national interests. Despite their longstanding commitment to open trade, for example, the United States and Canada continue to extend preferential treatment to domestic companies when awarding contracts for defense-related projects and have employed restrictions in energy and other sectors to promote local business.[15]

The sluggish recovery from the 2008–2009 global financial crisis has further dampened support for free trade, even at the bilateral level, across many parts of the world. In the United States, groups representing workers and domestic producers lobbied hard, yet unsuccessfully, to derail a pact with South Korea due to concerns over higher trade deficits, lost jobs, and the continuation of aggressive Korean trade practices.[16] In Malaysia, activists protested the country's proposed agreement with the United States, arguing that it would further undermine the competitiveness of local businesses and would imperil Malaysian farmers unable to keep pace with their stronger US counterparts who flood the Malaysian market with cheap rice (a staple of the local diet).[17] These sorts of misgivings are clearly evident in two of the more noteworthy cross-regional trade deals under recent consideration—the Trans-Pacific Partnership (TPP) and the Transatlantic Trade and Investment Partnership (T-TIP).

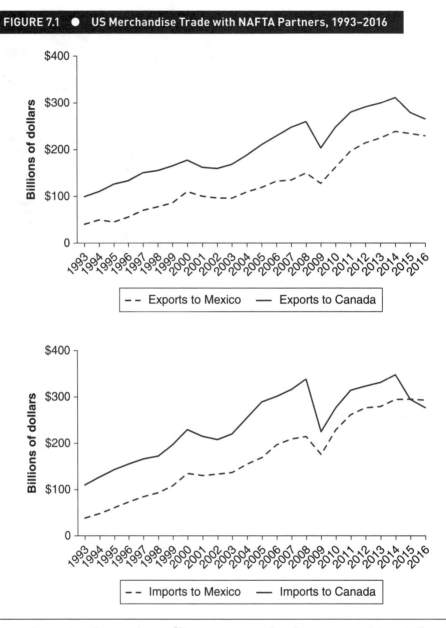

FIGURE 7.1 ● US Merchandise Trade with NAFTA Partners, 1993–2016

Source: Congressional Research Service, "The North American Free Trade Agreement," Appendix Table A-1, February 22, 2017, https://fas.org/sgp/crs/row/R42965.pdf.

The TPP, under discussion for more than a decade, was envisioned to include twelve countries with 800 million people that account for around 40 percent of the world's gross domestic product (GDP) and close to one-third of total trade. It also would have covered about 40 percent of US trade. It excluded China and was put forward, in part, to counter China's trade initiatives across the region and beyond. The treaty incorporated a comprehensive package of proposals intended to open markets and to promote cross-border exchange. In addition to affecting some 18,000 existing tariffs, it had provisions to guard the rights of workers and to extend intellectual property protections that would especially benefit pharmaceutical and software developers. Heralded as a model that might frame future accords, the TPP also contained a highly controversial proviso that would have allowed countries and companies to contest domestic laws or regulations of members that were seen as impeding market access.

The debate over the TPP crystallizes the broader free trade–fair trade divide. Supporters point to its potential to enhance exports and expand skilled employment opportunities. Opposition has come from a number of quarters. There are those who believe it goes too far in exposing member states to the uncertainties of the market and limiting their sovereign authority. Others decry its role in promoting big business, displacing manufacturing jobs, and undermining the rights of workers. Passage was a high priority of the Obama administration, but the TPP was resoundingly criticized by Donald Trump, who announced shortly after assuming the presidency that the United States would not participate. This kills the treaty for the time being, as it had required approval of a minimum of six countries that account for 85 percent of the group's economic output and would be of only marginal utility without American participation.[18]

Activists hold a rally to protest the Trans-Pacific Partnership (TPP) in front of the White House on February 3, 2016, in Washington, DC.

Olivier Douliery/Getty Images.

The T-TIP faces a similarly uncertain future. While estimated to boost the economies of the Europe Union and the United States and to vastly expand their already considerable commercial and investment ties, the proposed pact has encountered stiff resistance from both sides. Once again, jobs are at the center of debate, with some sectors standing to benefit from market-opening measures and others potentially jeopardized. Agriculture has been particularly contentious, given the traditionally generous subsidies on both sides of the Atlantic and the EU's strict regulation of genetically modified products that would be called into question. Like the TPP, provisions to extend arbitration rights and dispute settlement instruments have been seen by some as unwarranted intrusions and biased in favor of investors and large corporations. In addition to lingering differences between EU and US negotiators on many of the treaty's details, overall enthusiasm has significantly waned since the 2016 US election and Britain's EU exit vote.[19]

When Ford and General Motors decide to relocate auto assembly plants to save on production costs, Americans lose job opportunities, while Mexican workers acquire them. When hospitals and physicians in Europe or Japan seek use of the latest technology to assist in diagnosing patient illnesses, they may turn to Trivitron Healthcare in India, where highly trained technicians are able to perform the task at a relatively reasonable cost. When China assembles and exports inexpensive cell phones and other electronic items, consumers in the importing countries benefit. The basic challenge facing today's trade system is to accommodate the needs of countries to address their national interests while securing their commitment to an approach that does not unduly threaten the flow of goods and services across the world. As the passionate and high-stakes debates over free and fair trade suggest, this is no easy task, and it will require a delicate balancing of policies and perspectives.

Transnational Investment: Blessing or Curse?

Cross-border investment is another key ingredient fueling the development of the global economy. Between 1991 and 2000, trade among industrial countries expanded an impressive 63 percent. But capital flows topped that, growing by a whopping 300 percent.[20]

Women workers box pairs of Reeboks at the Kong Tai shoe factory, which makes sneakers under contract with Reebok, in the special economic zone of Shenzhen, China.

portfolio investment the purchase of stocks, bonds, or other financial assets that does not result in direct management or control over an enterprise

direct investment the acquisition of corporate assets through the purchase of property, a plant, or equipment

transnational corporations (TNCs) companies that operate on a global scale with integrated operations across regions and countries

Advances in transportation and telecommunications have made it easier for companies to manage operations abroad. The emergence of new market-oriented economies and the liberalization of financial markets have also contributed to this expansion.

Foreign investment generally comes in two forms. **Portfolio investment** includes the purchase of stocks or bonds. This type of investment tends to be mobile and sensitive to shifts in financial conditions that affect profitability and might prompt a transfer to another, more lucrative locale. Countries that rely on this money must pay particular attention to maintaining interest rates that offer an acceptable rate of return and other incentives that assure an attractive investment climate. The United States is no exception, as it has grown increasingly dependent on investment from China and other countries to cover its burgeoning deficits. If a government cannot bring its spending under control, it must borrow from foreign nations in ever-increasing amounts.[21]

Direct investment occurs when a foreign entity acquires a stake in an enterprise through the purchase of property, a plant, or equipment. This makes direct investment more visible than portfolio investment. Much direct investment originates with the world's largest **transnational corporations (TNCs)**, which operate on a global scale with integrated operations across any number of regions and countries. Some TNCs have more assets than many countries. In 2016, for example, revenues for Walmart (United States) exceeded the GDP of all but twenty-three countries; oil and gas multinational Royal Dutch Shell (Netherlands) had revenues that were higher than Chile's GDP; Toyota's (Japan) revenues topped the GDP of Greece; while Singapore's GDP was less than the revenues of China's largest electric utility company, State Grid.

Private corporate networks and alliances may be more central to the future world economy than more traditional interactions among nation-states. The top 500 global companies have $27.6 trillion in revenues, employ 67 million people, and represent 33 countries. Of the world's 50 largest economic entities, eight (16 percent) are TNCs. However, this figure does not provide the complete picture. While 22 of these companies (29 percent) rank among the world's top 75 economic units, 45 (45 percent) of them are on the list of the 100 largest.[22] Five of the ten largest are petroleum and energy-related companies. The list in Table 7.3 gives you a feel for the countries and TNCs driving much of today's economic activity.

TABLE 7.3 ● Country and Transnational Corporation Revenues, 2016		
Rank	Country or Corporation	Gross Domestic Product or Revenue (in Billions of US Dollars)
1	United States	18,561.9
2	China	11,391.6
3	Japan	4,730.3

Forrest Anderson/The LIFE Images Collection/Getty Images.

Rank	Country or Corporation	Gross Domestic Product or Revenue (in Billions of US Dollars)
4	Germany	3,494.9
5	United Kingdom	2,649.9
6	France	2,488.3
7	India	2,251.0
8	Italy	1,852.5
9	Brazil	1,769.6
10	Canada	1,532.3
11	Republic of Korea	1,404.4
12	Russia	1,267.8
13	Australia	1,256.6
14	Spain	1,252.2
15	Mexico	1,063.6
16	Indonesia	941.0
17	Netherlands	769.9
18	Turkey	735.7
19	Switzerland	662.5
20	Saudi Arabia	637.8
21	Argentina	541.7
22	Taiwan	519.1
23	Sweden	517.4
24*	Walmart (US)	482.1
25	Belgium	470.2
26	Poland	467.4
27	Nigeria	415.1
28	Iran	412.3
29	Thailand	390.6
30	Austria	387.3
31	Norway	376.3
32	United Arab Emirates	375.0
33	Egypt	346.6

(Continued)

TABLE 7.3 ● (Continued)

Rank	Country or Corporation	Gross Domestic Product or Revenue (in Billions of US Dollars)
34	Venezuela	333.7
35*	State Grid (China)	329.6
36	Hong Kong	316.1
37	Israel	311.7
38	Philippines	311.7
39	Ireland	307.9
40	Malaysia	302.7
41	Denmark	302.6
42*	China National Petroleum (China)	299.2
43	Singapore	296.6
44*	Sinopec (China)	294.3
45	Pakistan	284.5
46	South Africa	280.4
47	Colombia	274.1
48*	Royal Dutch Shell (Netherlands)	272.1
49*	Exxon Mobil (US)	246.2
50	Finland	239.2
51*	Volkswagen (Germany)	236.6
52*	Toyota (Japan)	236.5
53	Chile	234.9
54*	Apple (US)	233.7
55	Bangladesh	226.8
56*	BP (Britain)	225.9
57*	Berkshire Hathaway (US)	210.8
58	Portugal	205.9
59	Vietnam	200.5
60	Greece	195.9
61	Czech Republic	193.5
62*	McKesson (US)	192.4
63	Romania	186.5

Rank	Country or Corporation	Gross Domestic Product or Revenue (in Billions of US Dollars)
64	Peru	180.3
65	New Zealand	179.4
66*	Samsung Electronics (Korea, Republic)	177.4
67*	Glencore (Switzerland)	170.4
68	Algeria	168.3
69*	Industrial & Commercial Bank of China (China)	167.2
70*	Daimler (Germany)	165.8
71*	United Health Group (US)	157.1
72	Qatar	156.6
73	Iraq	156.3
74*	CVS Health (US)	153.2
75*	EXOR Group (Italy)	152.5

Sources: "Global 500 2016," http://beta.fortune.com/global500/list/; IMF, World Economic Outlook Database, October 2016, https://www.imf.org/external/pubs/ft/weo/2016/02/weodata/index.aspx.

*Transnational corporation.

In many respects, TNCs lie at the heart of the globalization debate. Supporters tout their role in expanding production and trade. They generate employment and integrate developing countries into the global economy by infusing capital, supplying jobs, and transferring modern technology. TNC investment helps countries build infrastructure and enhance their capacity for economic growth.

The emergence of TNCs headquartered in developing countries, moreover, suggests some movement toward the progressive leveling of the global economy. In 2016, a total of 156 (31 percent) of the leading 500 firms were located in emerging or developing countries (see Figure 7.2 for the total numbers). China alone accounted for 103 (66 percent) of the companies in this group.[23] South Korea's Samsung (electronics), Brazil's JBS (food production), and China's SAIC (motor vehicles) reflect this new wave in what used to be an exclusively Western phenomenon. China is marketing distinctively Chinese-branded products worldwide. Lenovo, the world's largest personal computer (PC) maker, took its brand beyond China with a line of low-priced machines following its purchase of the IBM corporation's PC business in 2005.[24] Concluding that PC companies could not flourish or even survive by simply producing computers, Lenovo moved forward by entering the expanding tablet and smartphone markets. In 2012, the company launched its first smart TV as part of its strategy of offering a full range of Internet consumer devices. It is now a $45 billion company with customers in 160 countries.[25]

China's auto industry has also been on the move. One of its leading automakers, Geely, purchased Sweden's Volvo Cars for $1.8 billion from Ford Motor Company in 2010. Ford had sold its Jaguar and Land Rover brands to India's Tata Motors for $1.7 billion in 2008. Capitalizing on its Volvo connection, Geely is looking to its China Euro Vehicle

FIGURE 7.2 ● Number of Global 500 Companies, 2016

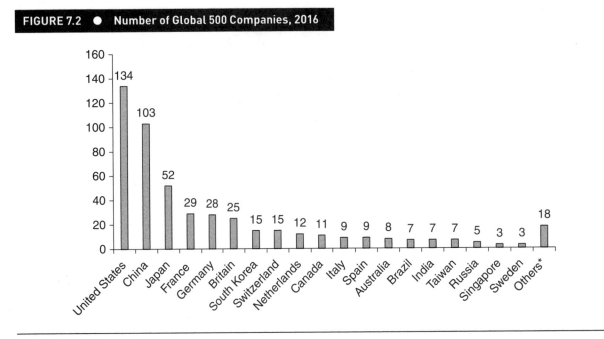

Source: "Global 500 2016," http://beta.fortune.com/global500/list.

*Countries with one or two companies.

Technology development hub in Sweden to develop a platform for small car models for the US and European market. Great Wall Motors, another Chinese firm, opened an assembly plant in Bulgaria in 2012 and now has a network of fourteen dealerships across the country. It is building a large-scale facility in Russia, scheduled to open in 2018, and plans to eventually sell a wide range of models across Europe. Sales of Chinese autos around the world are expected to increase as companies continue to enhance the quality and appeal of these vehicles.[26]

These success stories notwithstanding, critics of TNCs are far more suspicious of their motives and wary of their clout. They argue that, rather than actively seeking or competing for TNCs' investment by offering overly generous tax breaks and other financial incentives, countries—particularly those in the Global South—should avoid this "race to the bottom" and rely more heavily on expanding their domestic capabilities. As noted earlier, working conditions in some of their factories and plants have prompted charges that these facilities are modern-day sweatshops, where employees are subjected to unsafe and unhealthy environments. Clothing giant H&M, for example, has been the subject of criticism for continuing safety issues and depressed wages across its factory network in South Asia. It has pledged to improve these sites by 2018.[27] Nike altered its production of athletic footwear after similar revelations regarding conditions in its plants in Indonesia, Mexico, and elsewhere. In response to a campaign launched by the United Students against Sweatshops, a grassroots organization lobbying on behalf of worker rights, some universities have ended relationships with suppliers of licensed apparel found to tolerate labor abuses in their production facilities.[28] Even Apple, a company admired for its innovation and marketing prowess, was pressured into making significant improvements to its operations following numerous investigative reports relating to safety and other workplace conditions at its plant in China.[29]

Complaints against TNCs have also surfaced with respect to a host of other issues, ranging from their undermining of environmental protection efforts to their alleged role in perpetuating extreme income disparities and poverty across the Global South. In early 2006, Internet giants Google, Yahoo, and Microsoft faced strong criticism from human rights activists around the world for their role in helping China's government curb political opposition. The companies were restricting Internet searches to sites acceptable to the government and providing it with personal tracking data.

The challenge for Internet providers in China is considerable. China seeks access to the most advanced technology (AT) and uses that technology to pursue its core political interests. Google has had its share of controversy stemming from its efforts to satisfy the Chinese government in order to maintain its business. It endured cyberattacks allegedly aimed at stealing technology and Gmail account information of suspected Chinese human rights activists and chose to compromise on some of its basic principles as a result. Despite these efforts, the relationship was severed in 2010, and China moved forward with domestic providers. In 2016, however, Google signaled interest in a potential return, and the Chinese government permitted access to Google's search engine for one hour in late March. This brief opening notwithstanding, the censorship issues that led to the breakup remain in place. China asserts its right to "cyber sovereignty" and has enacted cybersecurity laws designed to control governance of the Internet within its borders. Some difficult decisions lie ahead for Google if it proceeds with efforts to regain its Chinese presence.[30]

Unlike China, with its considerable leverage and economic clout, many other host countries find it difficult to curtail the autonomy of these investing companies or to regulate their impacts. But it is not impossible. In South Africa, for example, foreign companies such as Anglo American and BHP Billiton in mining and Coca-Cola and Nestle in food and beverages have worked cooperatively with government authorities to promote adherence to strict environmental standards. The active engagement of nongovernmental organizations (NGOs) and local agencies to monitor compliance has been instrumental in the success of this arrangement.[31] Conditions are not always so favorable, however, to reining in the activities of TNCs. In the Niger Delta of Nigeria, millions of barrels of oil have spilled over the years. This has contaminated swamps, rivers, and farmlands and has seriously affected the health of people in the region. Shell, ExxonMobil, and other oil companies operating in the area do little to alter their practices, for the most part, and continue to conduct their businesses with little regard for the environmental or health effects of their activities. In this particular case, moreover, the Nigerian government has not gone very far in holding these companies accountable.[32]

Broader efforts by the United Nations (UN) and other international bodies to address the activities of TNCs have met with mixed results. One of the more ambitious was the Multilateral Agreement on Investment (MAI), launched in 1995 under the auspices of the Organisation for Economic Co-operation and Development (OECD). While the OECD now includes a fairly diverse group of advanced and emerging market economies, it was composed almost exclusively of more advanced countries at the time. The MAI negotiations sought to develop a treaty, open to both OECD members and nonmembers alike, that assured foreign investors fair and uniform treatment while granting host countries greater authority to mandate responsible behavior within their borders. Discussions broke off in 1998, however, with opponents charging that the proposed accord was weighted heavily in favor of the TNCs.[33] In 2000, the UN concluded a global compact addressing child labor, environmental protection, and other matters relating to corporate behavior. However, the agreement was voluntary and opposed by Greenpeace and other environmental advocacy groups seeking binding and enforceable codes of conduct.

As markets become more interconnected, regulating TNCs is more problematic. The formation of cross-border business alliances and joint ventures complicates matters. The automobile industry is a case in point. Although some partnerships—such as General Motors/Toyota and Daimler/Chrysler—did not survive the 2008 economic downturn, others continue. While Ford (United States) sold its major stake in both Mazda (Japan) and Aston Martin

(United Kingdom), it retains a share in both companies. Meanwhile, Aston Martin was acquired by an international consortium that included two investment firms based in Kuwait. Fiat (Italy) has controlling financial interest in Chrysler (United States) and is looking to a potential merger with another major manufacturer, and General Motors (United States) has a partnership in place with China's SAIC Motor Corporation. The alliance forged between France's Renault and Japan's Nissan also has ties to Germany's Daimler and Russia's leading carmaker, AvtoVAZ. With an eye toward developing new market opportunities, Volkswagen has invested in Israeli rideshare startup Gett, which operates in sixty cities across the world, while Toyota has concluded a strategic arrangement that makes its fleet available to Uber.[34]

The story does not stop there. Countries that seek to promote their own companies or patriotic consumers who want to buy domestic products may find it difficult to execute those plans. Five of the top eight "most American" car models in 2016—as measured under the terms of the American Automobile Labeling Act and containing a minimum of 75 percent US or Canadian parts—came from Japanese automakers Toyota and Honda (see Table 7.4). In addition, numerous models produced by US-based companies do not qualify

---

TABLE 7.4 ● Buying an American Automobile?

Thinking about a new car or truck anytime soon? There are many things to consider. How much will it cost, and is it affordable? How fuel efficient is it? Is it reliable? Is the styling suitable? Does it have desired options?

Some Americans feel that it is important to support the national economy by purchasing an American vehicle. Indeed, a few decades ago, it was not all that uncommon to hear the slogan repeated on commercials and advertisements that "what's good for General Motors is good for America." But the globalization of the auto industry makes it increasingly difficult to identify the makes and models that might fit this mold. What are your feelings about buying domestic?

American-Made Vehicles, 2016

Rank	Make/Model	Percentage of Domestic Parts	Percentage of Vehicle Value Benefiting the United States*	Assembly
1	Buick Enclave	80	90	Michigan
2	Chevrolet Traverse	80	90	Michigan
3	GMC Acadia	80	90	Michigan
4	Honda Accord	80	81	Ohio
5	Honda Pilot	75	78.5	Alabama
6	Honda Odyssey	75	78.5	Alabama
7	Toyota Sienna	75	78.5	Indiana
8	Toyota Camry	75	78.5	Kentucky or Indiana

Sources: Kelsey Mays, "The 2016 Cars.com American-Made Index," June 28, 2016, https://www.cars.com/articles/the-2016-carscom-american-made-index-1420684865874; Kogod School of Business, "2016 Kogod Made in America Auto Index," http://kogodbusiness.com/reports/auto-index; Steven Peters, "50 Most American Cars," June 30, 2016, http://247wallst.com/special-report/2016/06/30/most-american-cars.

*Figures include where the vehicle is produced and assembled and the country of origin for research and development.

as "domestic," because they are assembled abroad with limited American-made parts. The next time you are sitting at a traffic light, think about the Honda Accord idling next to your Volkswagen assembled in Mexico. Chances are that it was put together by American workers in Ohio with at least some of its parts made in China by Honda's Japanese suppliers.[35]

Even as TNCs may offer countries opportunities to enhance their economic growth, these firms remain the targets of critics who question their considerable economic and political influence. While a case can be made for measures to curtail their autonomy, TNCs require sufficient inducements to encourage their further investment and production. Many host governments are reluctant to intrude on their activities or to pursue some recourse when they fail to adhere to acceptable business practices. An established set of multilateral rules regulating TNC behavior would go a long way toward relieving some of these tensions. TNCs are not likely to submit to any significant restraints, so, as in the case of trade policy, finding the right balance will be a challenge.

Finance and Aid: Promoting or Hindering Development?

Today's financial system is noted for its unpredictability. Within a few months in 2016, for example, markets swung excessively in response to events—both anticipated and not—that would have profound effects on global political and economic conditions. In March, China confirmed expectations when it announced that it had lowered its economic growth target. In July, following a heated campaign, Britain unexpectedly voted to leave the European Union. Then, in November, the United States sent shockwaves by electing Donald Trump as president—defying most polls and the predictions of political pundits. In each instance, it was uncertainty that drove the markets and rattled global investors. In a world defined by its instability and interconnectedness, maintaining order and confidence in the financial system is difficult.

Financial markets are truly global, difficult to regulate, and marked by extraordinary transfers on a daily basis. It is estimated that around $5 trillion changes hands each day in foreign currency transactions.[36] The security of these markets is critical to the efforts of countries to manage their accounts, retain access to capital and investment, preserve the values of their currencies, and remain competitive in international trade.

The International Monetary Fund (IMF) continues to play an important role in steadying markets. With 189 members, the IMF works to promote cooperation on monetary policy and to stabilize currency exchange rates. Its primary activity is to assist countries attempting to balance their accounts and meet their outstanding obligations. It does so through an extensive network of lending programs supported by more than $325 billion raised through member payments (known as quotas). The IMF has made a special effort to extend aid under favorable terms to low-income countries, and between 2009 and 2014, it increased this type of lending to $11 billion. In 2015, it launched a number of initiatives to support some of the poorest and most vulnerable countries.[37]

Despite these seemingly good works, the IMF has been buffeted by blistering criticism. Antiglobalization protestors usually target its general meetings, like those of the WTO, and

Ratib Al Safadi/Anadolu Agency/Getty Images.

A child hides under a cardboard box from the sun while holding a water bottle supplied to families by the Lebanese Red Cross (LRC) staff at the Qob Elias refugee camp in Lebanon.

view the IMF as an extension of its largest and most influential member, the United States. They charge it with advancing US policies and prescriptions through what has become known as the **Washington Consensus**, a set of economic policy reforms imposed on prospective borrowers by the IMF and other Washington, DC–based financial institutions as a condition for receiving funds. The IMF's Structural Adjustment Programs (SAPs) emphasize measures to advance free market principles and often include steps to liberalize trade and finance, privatize state enterprises, and reduce government spending. The IMF defends these policies as essential to promoting efficiency and breaking the cycle of indebtedness.

Critics charge that these policies add to the vulnerabilities of recipient countries, exaggerate inequalities, and place disproportionate burdens on their poorest inhabitants. In Mozambique, for example, the IMF mandated the ending of government subsidies for urban transport and other basic services in return for its 2008 support. Subsequent price increases sparked considerable protests that were put down forcefully by the government. In 2009, the IMF required Jamaica to eliminate tax exemptions on basic foodstuffs such as bread, vegetables, and fish meal as a precondition for its $1.2 billion loan. While suggesting that it is now looking to streamline and relax its conditions, the IMF can still impose stiff terms. A $1 billion loan to Bangladesh in 2013, for example, came with the proviso that prices for electricity and petroleum would rise and taxes would increase for such basic food staples as rice, lentils, and cooking oil. A study by the European Network on Debt and Development has concluded that the number of conditions attached to IMF loans is actually increasing.[38]

The World Bank is another key node in the global financial network. Its lending activities are more project oriented than those of the IMF and may include assistance to build roads as well as communications, energy, and other infrastructure to improve a country's prospects for long-term development. In fiscal 2016, the World Bank had commitments to more than 1,600 projects totaling $61.2 billion. This included $16.2 billion in interest-free loans and grants to the world's poorest countries under the auspices of the organization's International Development Association. Although substantial, this overall figure reflects the lingering effects of the global recession and is still below the $72.2 billion in World Bank contributions in 2010.[39] While the World Bank is particularly interested in promoting grassroots and private sector initiatives, it also encourages governmental reform to strengthen public policy. To supplement the funding supplied by its members, the World Bank raises money through private financial markets to support its work.

Originally, the World Bank followed a top-down approach and applied many of the same structural adjustment principles used by the IMF to almost all its funded projects. More recently, the Bank has encouraged broader input into the framing of its initiatives to ensure that its activities are more consistent with local needs and conditions. Its Country Partnership Framework (CPF) aims to zero in on circumstances relating to extreme poverty and shared prosperity. In Bangladesh, for example, the Bank's proposed CPF for fiscal 2016–2020 is designed to create a plan that is aligned with the country's national goals.

Washington Consensus
the set of economic policy reforms imposed by the IMF and other Washington, DC–based financial institutions on potential borrowers

AP Photo/Wilfredo Lee.

Demonstrators protesting the IMF carry signs as they march from the White House to the IMF building. The protesters were calling for the World Bank and the IMF to accelerate their debt reduction efforts for the world's poorest countries.

It is a multipronged approach that incorporates three focal points—growth and competitiveness, social inclusion, and climate and environmental management. With its emphasis on building infrastructure and reducing poverty through employment and education, it seeks to involve and generate the support of local stakeholders.[40]

Since 2000, the World Bank has also been heavily involved in promoting the UN's efforts to improve education, health, and material well-being in poorer countries. It incorporated specific targets and performance indicators to frame its activities in meeting the 2015 Millennium Development Goals (MDGs) and is now working to advance the Sustainable Development Goals (SDGs) initiative through its Global Partnership for Social Accountability, which includes close to 50 governments and more than 250 civil society and private sector members.[41]

Regional bodies such as the African Development Bank, the Asian Development Bank, and the Inter-American Development Bank have contributed to these efforts. Despite having more limited resources than the World Bank, they often focus on supporting projects likely to make the greatest difference to individual lives. The African Development Bank's desalinization venture in Senegal is a case in point. This initiative is aimed at increasing the amount of cultivable soil by recapturing salinized land from the sea to promote greater food self-sufficiency. Similarly, the Bank's Lake Turkana wind power project in Kenya looks to enhance power-generating capacity and provide clean and affordable energy to greater numbers of inhabitants across the country.[42]

The activities of these public international and regional lending institutions notwithstanding, developments in private financial markets will increasingly influence the future security of the world's financial order (and the fate of its poorer countries). The events of 2008 and 2009 spoke directly to this emerging trend. Problems in the US mortgage market spread quickly, revealing some fundamental weaknesses in the global financial system, which was operating, in part, beyond effective control. The progressive deregulation of financial markets over previous years had encouraged banks to create new instruments that enabled them to engage in highly profitable and excessively risky lending practices. One of these instruments was **securitization**, the pooling of various loans (including those with considerable risk) into **securities** and selling them to other institutions.[43]

Even as financial institutions looked to spread the risk, they could not avoid the consequences. Lenders drastically curtailed their activities and scrambled to protect their assets. For many, it was too late. Some of the world's largest investment banks (e.g., Bear Stearns, Lehman Brothers), which played a vital role in financing the global economy, collapsed, and major institutions around the globe found themselves perilously close to failing as well. Ultimately, a number of governments spent considerable sums of money to rescue imperiled banks and companies, thereby adding to their **sovereign debt**.[44] While there was much debate over the advisability of these bailouts, they did contribute to the survival of the world's financial system—albeit in a more fragile state. Important issues remained as to how governments might restore the confidence of prospective investors while avoiding excessive spending and deficits that would undermine the sustainability of the process.[45]

Nobel laureate economist Paul Krugman has noted that these developments bore striking similarity to the Asian financial crisis of the late 1990s, when the collapse of Thailand's currency (the baht) set in motion a chain of events that threatened the economic security of numerous countries in the region and well beyond. Up to that point, Thailand had been a magnet for investment because of its relatively secure and expanding economy. Problems began after a series of bad loans by local banks and excessive government spending resulted in the use of $33 billion of the country's reserve assets. Jittery foreign investors withdrew some $9 billion, and, without this backing, the baht lost approximately half its value. Many Thai citizens found their dreams of wealth turn literally overnight into the

securitization the pooling of various loans (including those with considerable risk) into securities and selling them to other institutions

securities bond or stock certificates

sovereign debt a government's outstanding financial liabilities and obligations

nightmare of bankruptcy. Panic spread quickly across the region to Indonesia, Malaysia, and South Korea, as investors removed more than $100 billion. Before long, the drama extended to disparate places such as Brazil and Russia, as investors searched in vain for opportunities to limit their financial risk.[46]

These events underscore the challenges of today's financial system and the vulnerabilities of countries reliant on the flow of private capital to stimulate and sustain their development. With an emphasis on mobility and maximum return on investments, global finance is a fast-paced and volatile game. As noted earlier, trillions of dollars exchange hands electronically on any given day in a relatively seamless fashion. Professional money traders, investors, lenders, and borrowers determine the flow of funds that affect the health of the global economy and its constituent parts. While sound financial management calls for prudent and reasoned behavior, it also places a premium on risk taking and speculative activity. The expansion and deregulation of financial markets has contributed significantly to the potential for growth by providing countries with additional funding options and opportunities. But this money may disappear as quickly as it materializes if investors lose confidence or interest—for either real or imagined reasons.

Financial markets have been under considerable pressure as the global economy has struggled to recover its vibrancy. In 2016, net private capital flows to emerging markets totaled $640 billion. This figure was considerably above the $263 billion in 2015, but still far below previous levels. Between 2000 and 2015, these flows declined $1.1 trillion as investors sought to minimize their risks and reacted to the diminished growth projections. While flows are expected to continue their modest rise in 2017, estimated at $770 billion, they remain highly sensitive to broader market conditions as well as particular events or circumstances that may arise (see Figure 7.3). The loss of enthusiasm for globalization, as evidenced

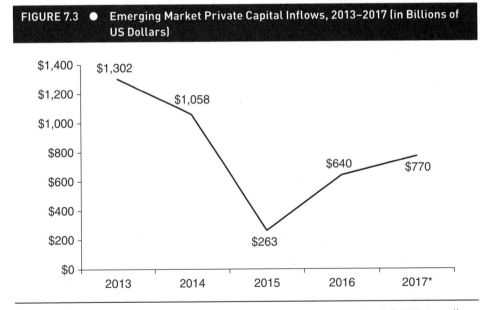

FIGURE 7.3 ● Emerging Market Private Capital Inflows, 2013–2017 (in Billions of US Dollars)

Source: Institute of International Finance," Capital Flows to Emerging Markets," April 7, 2016, https://www.iif.com/publication/capital-flows-emerging-markets-report/april-2016-capital-flows-emerging-markets; "Capital Flows to Emerging Markets," November 2, 2016, https://www.iif.com/publication/capital-flows-emerging-markets-report/november-2016-capital-flows-emerging-markets.

*Projected.

by the British vote to leave the EU and the election of Donald Trump in the United States, could significantly impact future levels.[47] Subject to short-term ebbs and flows, these private markets account for an increasing share of capital flows across the global economy and add to its uncertain future.

WHAT CAN YOU DO WITH INTERNATIONAL STUDIES?

International Economics and Development

By Puneet Gupta, International Studies Graduate Student, New Delhi, India

For me, all economic issues like trade, investment, and finance are important, not only professionally but also personally. Professionally, developing countries like my home, India, depend a lot on donor funding from abroad. If there are trade imbalances that induce the government of either the home country or the foreign country to change its trade policies, both the countries will be impacted not only in terms of trade but also in terms of capital flows.

On a personal front, investment and finances are very important in my life. As someone has said: "If you want to save your money, then save the taxes, and the money will automatically be saved." If you invest rightly and save the maximum possible tax you can, you can create a fortune for yourself in a very short duration of time. One very good example of this can be a tax-saving systematic investment plan. These small strategies benefit not only the person but also the government, as the economy gets a continuous supply of the household savings in terms of investment and assistance in keeping its growth up. I have found that I unintentionally tend to compare the demand and supply of anything I am talking about or even while thinking, but this is primarily because that's the kind of orientation I have.

I believe international finance and trade play a very important role in addressing the development challenges like poverty, especially in a developing country like India. Globalization has been the biggest contributory factor. With world economies being so interconnected and dependent on each other, even a person sneezing in one part of the world can impact another entirely different part of the world! International finance becomes all the more complex with the interconnected development issues like poverty, malnutrition, lack of sanitation, gender inequality, and environmental degradation.

Recently, I came across a case study of Aravind Eye Care, an Indian specialized eye-care institution

Personal photo by Puneet Gupta.

focusing on protecting people's eyesight with the help of cataract surgeries. It has a very nice business model of catering to the people at the bottom of the pyramid while also generating profits at the same time. It charges market price from the rich people and cross-subsidizes poor people. International trade and support has been an important factor in the company's success. The intraocular lenses (the costliest thing in cataract surgery) that the institution used previously had to be imported, but Aravind has set up a manufacturing unit in India itself, which has reduced its cost dramatically. It has been able to do so through technology transfer from the United States. This would not have been possible without the technology support and the interconnectedness of the global economy.

What Can Be Done?

The global economy is dynamic and unpredictable. It is difficult to manage the complex relationships of its participants, especially as they have become more interconnected through trade, investment, and financial networks. Keeping trade lines open while accommodating a diversity of national interests is essential. Some form of collective management would be useful, particularly in terms of addressing issues of fairness that have surfaced in both developed and developing countries.

The fragile state of the world's financial markets continues to cause concern. Since the mid-1990s, the system has confronted a series of crises brought on by risky and, at times, irresponsible behavior. Governments often find it difficult to cut back on expenditures to address excessive debt as they respond to the demands of their citizens for services and an acceptable quality of life. Meanwhile, banks across the world resist governmental intrusions and continue to execute complex and sometimes questionable transactions. As the United States and others moved toward greater oversight of financial institutions in the aftermath of the crisis in 2008—reversing a pattern of progressive deregulation—some economists questioned the potential impact of these measures on the willingness and ability of prospective investors to fortify capital markets.[48] These restrictions have eased, and investors continue to pursue opportunities offering potentially lucrative returns. As suggested by recent trends, however, they do remain highly sensitive to short-term shifts in conditions and resistant to efforts to curtail their autonomy.

As the global economy moves through the twenty-first century, more effective multilateral leadership could help manage the dramas that lie ahead. The **Group of Twenty (G20)** Finance Ministers and Central Bank Governors, representing leading industrial and emerging market countries that account for around 85 percent of global output, has assumed a more prominent role. Established in 1999, the G20 looks to build support for common approaches in meeting the world's financial challenges.[49] At its 2016 summit in China, for example, its members reiterated support for policies designed to further spread the benefits of globalization and to promote sustainable development. The G20 functions primarily as a forum for discussion at this point, however, with no mandate to enforce compliance with its agenda.[50]

Group of Twenty (G20) the G20 Finance Ministers and Central Bank Governors, representing leading industrial and emerging market countries

Even as we have seen increasing sentiment for putting national interests first when devising policy options, it is the *global* economy that will determine future job and income prospects across the world. A national economy's ability to succeed will depend largely on an understanding of the system's rigors and demands. For most countries (and their people), the challenge will be to extend and upgrade the skills needed to secure a creative and competitive edge. Given the pace of technological change and development, this will be an ongoing process. Considerable flexibility will also be required to take advantage of the opportunities and to counter the threats that arise in this borderless and integrated economic environment.

Key Concepts

direct investment 168
Doha Round 163
Group of Twenty (G20) 180
intellectual property rights
  (IPRs) 163

North American Free Trade
  Agreement (NAFTA) 164
portfolio investment 168
protectionism 163
securities 177

securitization 177
sovereign debt 177
transnational corporations
  (TNCs) 168
Washington Consensus 176

To Learn More

Books and Other Print Media

Dean Baker, *Rigged: How Globalization and the Rules of the Modern Economy Were Structured to Make the Rich Richer* (Washington, DC: Center for Economic and Policy Research, 2016).

This provocative book suggests that key economic policies have been purposefully developed to advantage those at the top rungs of the economic ladder and have contributed to growing inequality.

Jennifer Clark, *Mondo Agnelli: Fiat, Chrysler and the Power of a Dynasty* (Hoboken, NJ: John Wiley & Sons, 2012).

A fascinating glimpse into the realm of global business, this case study of Italian automaker Fiat (founded by the Agnelli family) traces its development and how it acquired control of a bankrupt Chrysler in 2009.

Michal J. Enright, *Developing China: The Remarkable Impact of Foreign Direct Investment* (New York: Routledge, 2017).

This book assesses the importance of foreign direct investment in China's development and analyzes the country's complex policies regulating that activity. It includes case studies of some major foreign companies doing business in China and looks at investments across a number of Chinese cities.

Susan George, *Shadow Sovereigns: How Global Corporations Are Seizing Power* (Cambridge, UK: Polity Press, 2015).

This highly critical review decries the expanding influence of the world's largest transnational corporations over policies within states and across the global economy.

John Hilary, *The Poverty of Capitalism: Economic Meltdown and the Struggle for What Comes Next* (London, UK: Pluto Press, 2013).

Focusing on the levels of inequality and the environmental degradation across the world today, this book offers a critical view of neoliberal capitalism and suggests an alternative to this model as a means for addressing these critical challenges.

Douglas A. Irwin, *Free Trade under Fire* (Princeton, NJ: Princeton University Press, 2015).

This book looks at some of the more significant controversies surrounding free trade and its impact on competitiveness, jobs, and income inequality.

Daniel Jaffee, *Brewing Justice: Fair Trade Coffee, Sustainability, and Survival* (Oakland: University of California Press, 2014).

This is an in-depth study of coffee farmers in Mexico engaged in the fair trade market. It explores the impacts of their participation on their everyday lives and contrasts their experiences with those of farmers from the same region who are involved in the conventional market system.

Mi Park, *The IMF and the WTO: How Does Geopolitics Influence Global Finance and International Trade?* (Vancouver, BC, Canada: Coal Harbour Publishing Ltd., 2017).

This study analyzes the current state of global economic governance, with particular reference to the efforts of the IMF and WTO. It also explores some alternative institutions that have emerged in response to changing international conditions.

Jeffrey D. Sachs, *The End of Poverty: Economic Possibilities for Our Time* (New York: Penguin, 2005).

Economist Jeffrey Sachs lays the groundwork for how we should respond to global poverty in this seminal and influential work.

Ruchir Sharma, *Breakout Nations: In Pursuit of the Next Economic Miracles* (New York: W. W. Norton & Company, 2012).

Ruchir Sharma explores the shifting balance of global economic power and suggests more—and perhaps surprising—changes to come. Unconvinced of the staying power of some of the more recent emerging market economies, he traces the conditions and circumstances likely to produce the next wave of "breakout nations."

Joseph E. Stiglitz, *Making Globalization Work* (New York: W. W. Norton & Company, 2007).

This book offers a comprehensive discussion of the ways in which globalization has transformed trade, investment, and finance. Focusing on the ways in which globalization has contributed to greater disparities in wealth and opportunity across the world, Joseph Stiglitz recommends a wide range of reforms to address these issues.

Ndongo Sylla, *The Fair Trade Scandal: Marketing Poverty to Benefit the Rich* (Athens: Ohio University Press, 2014).

This critical review of the fair trade movement suggests that, contrary to stated claims, the process does not often work to appreciably benefit poorer producers at the bottom of the commodity chain.

Websites

CorpWatch, www.corpwatch.org

CorpWatch is part of the global movement that promotes environmental, social, and human rights and offers information on the activities of corporations and governments around the world that affect those rights.

Fairtrade International, www.fairtrade.net

Fairtrade International is an organization working on behalf of farmers and workers operating within the global fair trade system.

G20, www.g20.org

The Group of 20 includes nineteen countries and the European Union, which collectively account for more than 80 percent of global economic output. The body serves as a forum for cooperation on critical economic and financial matters.

International Monetary Fund (IMF), www.imf.org

The IMF was established in 1944. It oversees the world's financial system, provides loans to countries facing immediate and particularly difficult economic circumstances, and offers technical assistance and training.

World Bank, www.worldbank.org

The International Bank for Reconstruction and Development (IBRD), more commonly referred to as the World Bank, was established in 1944 to provide loans and grants for projects that reduce poverty and promote sustainable, long-term economic development.

World Economic Forum (WEF), www.weforum.org

The World Economic Forum is the independent nonprofit foundation that hosts an annual meeting in Davos, Switzerland, attended by political, financial, and corporate leaders to promote interpersonal networking and to address an array of global issues.

World Social Forum, https://fsm2016.org/en

The World Social Forum is the annual meeting attended by individuals and representatives of groups and organizations that are part of the antiglobalization movement and that seek to advance alternative models of economic and social development.

World Trade Organization (WTO), www.wto.org

The WTO is an international organization established in 1995 to develop and oversee the rules that guide global trade.

Videos

*Bananas!** (2009)

This documentary focuses on the conflict between Nicaraguan banana plantation workers and the Dole Food Company over alleged cases of sterility caused by a banned pesticide.

"Capitalism Will Eat Democracy—Unless We Speak Up" (2016), https://www.ted.com/talks/yanis_varoufakis_capitalism_will_eat_democracy_unless_we_speak_up

This TED Talk by former Greek minister of finance Yanis Varoufakis offers a critique of the global financial system and the role of unaccountable financiers and corporations within it.

Cappuccino Trail: The Global Economy in a Cup (2004)

This documentary addresses issues of equity and profit in international trade by following the trail of two coffee beans grown in Peru—one that takes the route of the open market and another that becomes part of a gourmet coffee introduced by a British company committed to paying fair prices to farmers. It is a good introduction to understanding some of the concerns driving the fair trade movement.

Comrade Kamprad: IKEA Goes to Russia (2005)

This film is an entertaining and informative account of the efforts of Ingvar Kamprad—the founder of the Swedish retailer IKEA—to establish his business in Russia. The program follows Kamprad on a trip to Russia, where he confronts a series of logistical and political challenges (including the demands of a local official to be compensated for his support in navigating bureaucratic hurdles).

Global Car: Who Really Builds the American Automobile? (2009)

Focused around the production of a Dodge Ram pickup truck, the program highlights the truly global nature of a process that incorporates the use of hundreds of manufactured parts circulating across forty countries.

Money, Power and Wall Street (2013), http://www.pbs.org/wgbh/frontline/film/money-power-wall-street

This four-part series from PBS's *Frontline* program offers an investigative look into the global financial meltdown of 2008–2009 and its aftermath. It weaves a complicated web of how the crisis unfolded and the many considerations that had to be taken into account as policies were developed to prevent the collapse of the global finance system.

Poverty, Inc. (2014), http://www.povertyinc.org

This is a sobering critique of the network of public and private aid organizations and agencies addressing issues of poverty across the developing world.

Power of the Poor (2009), https://www.youtube.com/watch?v=rxd55k2w6tM

This is another powerful video from Peruvian economist Hernando de Soto that focuses on the marginalization of the poor across the world and ways they might gain greater leverage in satisfying their needs within the framework of capitalism.

Sweet Poison (2013)

This documentary offers a critical analysis of the "aid industry" and some of the significant limitations of international assistance programs across the developing world.

The World According to H&M (2014), https://www.youtube.com/watch?v=1icriGcEK24

This is a very critical look inside the global business operations of Swedish clothing retailer H&M.

8

Protecting Identity

The People of the World

We tried to be polite about our eating, but there were many new foods
on the Mays's table, and we could not know what was a danger and what
was not.

—Dave Eggers, quoting Lost Boy Valentino Achak Deng in *What Is the What*, 2006[1]

Learning Objectives

After studying this chapter, you will be able to do the following:

- Define the concept of culture.

- Explain how Enlightenment views shaped the concepts of culture and identity.

- Explain how social forces divide people into various groupings and shape views of identity.

- Identify and compare the different academic fields that study culture and identity.

- Explain how globalization can serve as a driver for cultural integration and polarization, as well as homogenization and hybridization.

In traveling to different places, we frequently encounter objects, foods, and social practices that are new to us. Unfamiliar US sights and smells were overwhelming to Valentino Achak Deng when he first arrived in the United States from Sudan. One of the "lost boys" who fled their native homeland in the midst of civil war, Valentino had spent many years as a refugee in Ethiopia and Kenya before seeking asylum in the United States. Many foods that Americans commonly eat, such as fresh fruit, vegetables, and cow's milk, were so different that they made him sick. But such physical discomfort was only part of what he suffered as he tried to adjust to a new culture.

The other sickness Valentino felt was from a jarring shift away from Sudanese social and cultural expectations. This reaction is commonly referred to as **culture shock**, a psychological and sometimes physical response to the challenges of traveling to or living in another country or different culture. Culture shock can occur when you are in a new realm where customs, practices, eating, and living arrangements are different. Culture shock occurs when people are removed from their comfort zone. While some people are fascinated by differences, others are overpowered by them and can even be repulsed, and still others experience all these emotions at the same time. Food was not the only thing Valentino found challenging as he entered his new life in the United States. He physically suffered from headaches and had to deal with new things he had never seen. For example, when Valentino and his fellow Sudanese roommate first moved into an apartment in Atlanta, they did not know that they could turn off the air conditioner, and in Dave Eggers's fictionalized memoir based on Valentino's experience, they "slept with all of [their] clothes on, covered in blankets and towels, every linen [they] owned."[2]

Valentino was excited to begin his life in the United States. It was a dream come true, but initially it was overwhelming. He would go on to establish the Valentino Achak Deng Foundation (www.vadfoundation.org), which today is helping the people of South Sudan, in the wake of continuing tragic ethnic conflict. Valentino's experience reminds us that it is very hard to know what life is *really* like in a country or region until you directly experience it. It is very easy, however, to have the illusion of knowing what it will be like—from

culture shock a physical and psychological response to cultural differences when traveling away from home

Muslim children break their Ramadan fast after sunset by eating halal Mexican tacos from a food truck, during a campaign called "Taco Trucks at Every Mosque" at the Islamic Center in Santa Ana, California.

MARK RALSTON/AFP/Getty Images.

seeing images furnished by popular media, from reading, or perhaps from having met a few people from that place. Reconciling the differences between what you expect and how things really are can be very challenging.

Simply recognizing another culture is not the same as living in it. Every culture has distinct characteristics. Some differences are obvious, such as language, religion, and political organization. Others can be so subtle that they are unsettling to foreign visitors, such as how to greet someone (the Japanese bow, for instance) or when dinner is served (very late in Spain). Even if you speak the same language, reality can be very different from your expectations. The popular British actress Emma Watson, who played Hermione Granger in the Harry Potter films, notes the culture shock she experienced when enrolling at Brown University: "I don't know anything about American history or presidents. I don't know what tailgating is! I've never been to an Olive Garden!"[3] While visitors may be vaguely aware of such cultural differences, making adjustments is a complex process. They can feel uncomfortable and off balance for quite some time. Adaptation comes in waves, which continue upon reentry to your home country, as illustrated in the culture shock curve of a foreign student's emotions in a new host country (see Figure 8.1).

People's actions are a result of their social and cultural surroundings—where they live, where they went to school, their parents' beliefs, their ethnicity, their race, their religion, and their gender. These variables not only color how individuals experience their own cultural identity but can also affect how they relate to other cultures. It is these unique sociocultural variables that influence human behavior.[4] However, we cannot always see them for ourselves. It is often only when these defining characteristics are challenged that we can gain clarity on who we are and our similarities and differences. When people believe that others are trying to change their basic identity, they may move beyond uneasy feelings to a backlash against those who are challenging them. The tightening of religious beliefs along fundamentalist lines, the ethnic conflict that emerges, and even the failure of states that have not respected differences in the first place are all examples of these types of responses.

FIGURE 8.1 ● The _W_ Curve

SHOWN HERE is what is called the _W_ curve, which represents the ups and downs of cultural adjustment, from the time of leaving home to that of returning.

The "W" Curve

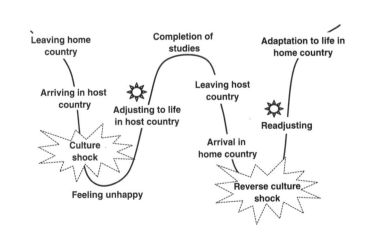

Source: https://i.pinimg.com/736x/c7/71/2b/c7712b8bb8000e99fb606e7f03e5169e—culture-shock-cultural-diversity .jpg.

Social divisions constitute another border that determines how people perceive themselves and their relationship to others. In addition to characteristics such as language, religion, and ethnicity, people also define themselves on the basis of their social standing—distinguished by birthright, relative power, and wealth. How much money people have, the value of their homes, or their status in the community can further delineate their identity.

Together, cultural and social borders significantly influence identity and the steps people will take to preserve it. They are what define us—our common practices. How we respond to differences can disorient us. Ethnicity, race, gender, and religion further delineate our identity. All these characteristics create the cultural framework in which we place ourselves. Reflecting these distinctions, the United Nations Educational, Scientific and Cultural Organization (UNESCO), a specialized agency of the United Nations (UN) devoted to the fostering of peace through intercultural dialogue, defines **culture** as follows: "the set of distinctive spiritual, material, intellectual and emotional features of society or a social group . . . that encompasses, in addition to art and literature, lifestyles, ways of living together, value systems, traditions and beliefs."[5] We can build on this definition to understand who we are and our relationship to others.

> **culture** "the set of distinctive spiritual, material, intellectual and emotional features of society or a social group . . . that encompasses, in addition to art and literature, lifestyles, ways of living together, value systems, traditions and beliefs," as defined by UNESCO

Cultural and Social Borders: Understanding Identity

Historically, people gathered into distinct groups based on common practices and the need for survival. The naturally occurring geographic boundaries that brought people together were the primary markers of identity. The basic needs for water, food, and shelter unified them. Means of communication, religion, and societal practices further solidified their relationships. Tradition or physical strength determined leadership within the group. For each unit, a sense of identity also emerged from its shared experiences and indigenous traits.

As particular groups of people began to encounter other groups—the "other" became a defining factor in distinguishing their identity. Trade routes developed, and accounts of early long-distance journeys reflected how people saw themselves as different or superior. Cultural anthropologist Ida Magli notes that the first published "anthropological" description of Native Americans as a result of these early journeys appeared in 1512.[6] These observations relied both on the physical characteristics of the peoples they encountered and on these people's clothing, weapons, and customs. Englishman John White would bring these images to life with his watercolor drawings of the Algonquian Indians he encountered when he sailed with an early expedition to Virginia in 1585. His images offered Europe some of its first visual representations of this new land and its inhabitants.

Many students of culture argue that the emergence of the modern state system crossed many naturally occurring borders and became a primary source of conflict among peoples, beginning in the 1600s. Anthropologist Manning Nash goes so far as to suggest that the nation-state is responsible for "the rise and definition of social entities that are currently called ethnic groups."[7] While cultural diversity and political differences existed prior to the emergence of the state system, the system's development and the diversity of people within state borders facilitated the differentiation of ethnicity. In many cases, this led to ethnic conflict. The delineation of borders in the African subcontinent provides an excellent example.

As illustrated in Map 8.1, more than 300 distinct cultures can be drawn on the same piece of land where only fifty-four states exist. Colonial powers frequently drew these political borders to enhance their own political and economic interests. By splitting indigenous groups across these newly created borders, colonizers were able to divide and conquer. At the same time, previously independent indigenous groups were forced into closer contact with others, increasing the potential for conflict.

MAP 8.1 ● A Map of Cultures in Africa

Source: "AfricaMap," *WorldMap*, accessed August 21, 2017, https://worldmap.harvard.edu/africamap.

The Age of Enlightenment

While the delineation of political borders often had negative effects on different civilizations, an understanding of the concept of culture evolved concurrently with the creation of nation-states. As trade routes expanded and settled into patterns of interaction, people began to consider their identity. The emergence of this system of states and the self-inspection the Enlightenment inspired from the mid-1600s to the 1800s helped formulate the concept. European and US intellectuals advocated a society based on personal choice, guided by reason. Scholars of the day, called the *philosophes* (Enlightenment thinkers), included British (David Hume and John Locke), French (Francois-Marie Arouet de Voltaire and Jean-Jacques Rousseau), German (Immanuel Kant), and even some early US (Benjamin Franklin, Thomas Jefferson, and Thomas Paine) authors. Their general argument sought to move away from a worldview dominated by religion and suggested a more scientific approach to understanding the realities of the day.

Cultural anthropologist Adam Kuper identifies three schools of thought that emerged during this time to understand culture generally and justify the territorial expansion that was taking place—the enlightened view of the French, the romantic or counter-Enlightenment vision of the Germans, and the traditional outlook held by the English.[8] The Enlightenment formed the French view of culture as a progressive, cumulative, and distinctly human achievement. Everyone could evolve to be civilized as the French defined it: having a cosmopolitan understanding of the world. As such, territorial expansion would provide opportunity to those they encountered by giving them the option to embrace "civilization."

In contrast, the German perspective held that cultures were distinguished by natural and spiritual sources. This viewpoint was greatly influenced by the Reformation of the Christian church, which sought a more direct relationship between the people and religion. The splintering of the church led to a major political realignment in Europe. The promotion of a more egalitarian understanding of Christianity held that people should not be required to aspire to others' notions of "civilization," instead preserving the authenticity of their culture. The English relied on a classical view of the world, focusing on history, described by English poet Matthew Arnold as "the best that has been known and said."[9] Their world was steeped in traditions that offered a way to live. Like the French, the British believed that their practices were superior and should have been adopted by everyone they encountered. The colonial empire they built during this time flowed from these views, and many of the practices they promoted endure today.

This illustration, a watercolor by Englishman John White, dates back to 1585 and depicts an Algonquian Indian fire ceremony. White's images shaped European conceptions of native American groups.

For example, while no longer expansionist in their political objectives, British traditions continue not only in the United Kingdom but throughout many of the countries that consider themselves part of the Commonwealth. An association of fifty-two states that grew out of the British Empire (see Table 8.1), the Commonwealth was formally established in 1931 to promote "democracy, freedom, peace, the rule of law and opportunity for all."[10] Decades after the end of colonialism, this diverse group still recognizes the head of the Commonwealth as Her Majesty, Queen Elizabeth II of England. The elaborate practices surrounding the marriage of Prince William and Princess Kate in 2011 are another example of how this adherence to custom and ritualized behavior has been perpetuated. The royal titles attached to their young children, Prince George and Princess Charlotte, further these traditions.

Enlightenment views evolved in conjunction with a changing economic reality. The search for riches, new markets, natural resources, and slaves fueled exploration. Through this process, cultural understanding was refined but incomplete. Identity was understood, for the most part, relative to others. As the Enlightenment gave way to the Industrial Revolution, social divisions became more complex with the emergence of new classes of workers and entrepreneurs. Social status became an additional factor in the definition of identity.

Social Borders

There always have been social divisions, whether defined by birth or privilege of wealth. In some societies, this class structure is quite rigid, such that those who are of the "highest" classes are born into it. The inheritance lines of the monarchies in Morocco and Saudi Arabia are two examples. Frequently, financial riches come with this hereditary stature. The **caste system** found in South Asia is another instance of birthright determining social identity. It has deep roots in the Hindu religion but has migrated to other cultures over time as a form

caste system a division of society based on birth that originally developed from the Hindu religion

TABLE 8.1 ● Commonwealth Member Countries

Antigua and Barbuda	Kenya	Singapore
Australia	Kiribati	Solomon Islands
The Bahamas	Lesotho	South Africa
Bangladesh	Malawi	Sri Lanka
Barbados	Malaysia	St. Kitts and Nevis
Belize	Malta	Saint Lucia
Botswana	Mauritius	St. Vincent and the Grenadines
Brunei Darussalam	Mozambique	Swaziland
Cameroon	Namibia	Tonga
Canada	Nauru	Trinidad and Tobago
Cyprus	New Zealand	Tuvalu
Dominica	Nigeria	Uganda
Fiji	Pakistan	United Kingdom
Ghana	Papua New Guinea	United Republic of Tanzania
Grenada	Rwanda	Vanuatu
Guyana	Samoa	Zambia
India	Seychelles	
Jamaica	Sierra Leone	

of social stratification. There is little room to change your fate in life when it is dictated by birth. For example, caste distinctions in remote areas of Nepal perpetuate ancient practices, where women are married as children and sent to live in outbuildings during menstruation to prevent bringing "bad luck" to their families and animals.[11] Members of lower castes are required to wash their dishes before using them to share a meal with people from another caste, and even then, their dishes may be used only after "purifier" has been sprinkled on them.

Caste differences can also lead to violence. The rape and hanging of two young girls, ages twelve and fourteen, in Uttar Pradesh, India, horrified the nation and the world in 2014. The father of one of the girls, who was from the Dalit caste, accused members of the dominant caste in the area, the Yadavs, of conspiracy to carry out this heinous crime. In 2016, four Dalit men accused of killing a sacred cow were publicly beaten in the Indian state of Gujarat, the home base of Indian prime minister Narenda Modi. In fact, they were simply disposing of a dead cow killed by a lion, a century's old job inherited and determined by their social status.[12] A video of the beating went viral, raising awareness of the continuing injustice of the caste system, where Dalits, often referred to as "untouchables," are considered to be the lowest caste. They face widespread discrimination and only limited protection from the legal system. (See Figure 8.2.)

Where you are born can dictate your opportunities as well. In China, this distinction is applied to rural and urban birthrights. People born in rural areas have very limited opportunities, even if they move to an urban area. China has a registration system—*hukou*—that is based on one's parents' birthplace.[13] City dwellers are entitled to public education if they have inherited an urban registration. The vast numbers of rural migrants now moving

FIGURE 8.2 ● India's Caste System

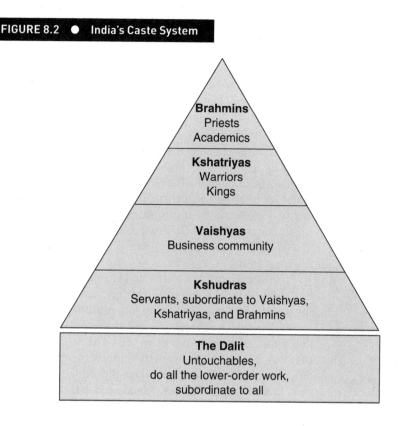

Brahmins
Priests
Academics

Kshatriyas
Warriors
Kings

Vaishyas
Business community

Kshudras
Servants, subordinate to Vaishyas,
Kshatriyas, and Brahmins

The Dalit
Untouchables,
do all the lower-order work,
subordinate to all

to urban areas in China, however, retain their rural registration, and the only education they can get for their children must be obtained privately and is frequently substandard. As a result, children are often left with relatives in their home villages—an estimated 60 million in 2016, one-fifth of all children in China.[14] The government has taken some steps to lessen the problem in cities with populations under 5 million, but it remains significant in the sixteen largest cities in China, where most rural migrants have moved.[15] Leslie Chang chronicles the story of many of the women and men who come from rural areas to China's bustling cities for work in her book *Factory Girls*. These mostly young women find themselves creating a new cultural identity, as they are no longer from the rural area but do not really qualify for the privileges of urban residency.

Social identity can also be defined by the job that you perform, a concept that found new meaning with the creation of a worker class and a wealthy class of factory owners during industrialization. The wealthy group wielded political power, while the lower or working classes were those who toiled in the factories, confined to poorly paying jobs with little hope for advancement. The promise of industrialization, however, was that it would bring about a redistribution of wealth that would allow individuals to move from one social status to another.

The reality did not live up to expectations, as the underlying social stratifications were perpetuated. The writings of German-born philosophers Karl Marx and Friedrich Engels sought to explain why the workers in society would not benefit from the economic developments that were occurring during industrialization. In their classic work *Manifesto of the Communist Party*, first published in 1848, they took a historical perspective to argue that industrialization was developing in a fundamentally unequal way and created further social borders within societies.

On March 4, 1990, in Bucharest, two Romanian workers dismantle a statue of Russian Bolshevik revolutionary leader Vladimir Ilyich Lenin to signify the demise of the communist regime.

ANDRE DURAND/AFP/Getty Images.

Class divisions that had separated people by birth now hinged on new wealth and the jobs people performed. The **bourgeoisie**, the owners of the means of production, had little respect for the **proletariat**, the workers, except for the extent to which the workers would enhance their wealth. Marx and Engels believed that the only way to address these inequities was a restructuring of the social order. They sought the creation of a new social movement—**communism**—that would champion the communal values of the worker class. It was up to those who embraced this perspective, the communists, to unite and overthrow the oppressive bourgeoisie. Moreover, they believed that the inequities of wealth would lead to a spontaneous uprising among the workers. Marx and Engels concluded their *Communist Manifesto* with an exhortation to the world's workers to rise up in a revolution against the bourgeoisie.

The problem was that Marx's and Engels's expectations that the workers would spontaneously unite did not happen, and the subsequent struggle to bring communism to bear required another approach. The efforts of Vladimir I. Lenin to establish communism in Russia upon the overthrow of the tsar in the beginning of the twentieth century necessitated a very different tactic. When the workers did not rise up on their own, Lenin realized that they would need to be led. He created the Communist Party to be the "vanguard of the people" and take charge of the revolution. The result was far from an egalitarian society and much more in line with a totalitarian state, in which members of the Communist Party became the leaders of the Soviet Union, despite their stated commitment to equality.

IN THEIR OWN WORDS
KARL MARX AND FRIEDRICH ENGELS

In short, the Communists everywhere support every revolutionary movement against the existing social and political order of things.

In all these movements, they bring to the front, as the leading question in each, the property question, no matter what its degree of development at the time.

Finally, they labor everywhere for the union and agreement of the democratic parties of all countries.

The Communists disdain to conceal their views and aims. They openly declare that their ends can be attained only by the forcible overthrow of all existing social conditions. Let the ruling classes tremble at a communist revolution. The proletarians have nothing to lose but their chains. They have a world to win.

Proletarians of all countries, unite![16]

The Study of Social and Cultural Borders

Efforts to understand society, culture, and identity have led to several methods of examination—most notably the disciplines of **sociology**, **anthropology**, and **psychology**. These fields of inquiry seek to understand human behavior. Anthropology examines the physical attributes of human beings as well as their social and cultural characteristics. Sociology focuses on people and their relationships to the societies in which they live, and psychology seeks to understand the motivations behind the decisions they make.[17] The writings of Charles Darwin and his theory of evolution in the 1860s played heavily in early conceptualizations of these fields.[18] The notions of evolution and survival of the fittest were groundbreaking ways to consider the plight of humankind.

In the 1940s and 1950s, some sociologists attempted to turn an anthropological understanding of cultural differences into broader, more scientific theories of human behavior. Anthropologists, however, believe that culture is learned and as such needs to be studied in context. In response, they use **ethnography**, the observation and description of people in their environment through in-depth analysis and interaction, focusing on tribal units, their linguistic patterns, and their traditional practices in remote areas to understand cultures.

What these anthropologists want to capture is a better understanding of cultural learning, recognizing that it occurs in a number of different ways. Mostly, a group's beliefs and shared traditions are passed down from one generation to another. A person's rites of passage within a group mark successful transitions in this learning process, known as **enculturation**.[19] These practices, such as rituals surrounding the transition from childhood to adulthood and the acceptance of polygamy as way of life, may be unique to cultural groups and not generally accepted outside of them. The idea that cultural meaning is relative to the environment in which it exists is called **cultural relativism**. The notion here is that culture is situational and should be respected as such.

Writing in the early twentieth century, US anthropologist Margaret Mead believed that a better understanding of others could come from examining their cultural differences without intellectual bias. In her observations about the tribal people of three islands in the western Pacific, she wrote the following:

> If we are to achieve a richer culture, rich in contrasting values, we must recognize the whole gamut of human potentialities, and so weave a less arbitrary social fabric, one in which each diverse human gift will find a fitting place.[20]

Mead examined gender roles in other societies, as well as how children learned social patterns. Her contribution was significant in its effect on scholarly exploration of perception and cultural identification.[21]

Later authors, such as Clifford Geertz, came to understand that individuals ascribe many identities to themselves. He examined not just the ways in which people learn about themselves but also how their political and economic situations—what he called the "hard surfaces of life"—color how culture is defined and understood.[22] Civilizations adapt over time to their "hard surfaces." When people outside the immediate circle of a group embrace their manners, ideas, or identity, **cultural diffusion** occurs. Examples might range from the popularity of ethnic foods, such as sushi, around the world to the use of English as the primary language for communication. This adaptation is not universally welcomed. Indigenous identity is particularly sensitive to these changes, as languages and cultural practices are lost as a result. Estimates suggest that in the last century, 1900 to 2000, 400 languages became extinct and that 50 percent of the world's remaining 6,500 languages will be gone by the end of this century, with some putting that figure as high as 90 percent.[23]

For many years, the perceived purpose of many societies was to create a common culture, such that immigrants to a new place would restructure their identity, or "melt" into a common pot. This emphasis on **assimilation** submerged cultural differences into a broader, dominant culture. Sometimes assimilation was taken to an extreme, driven by inherent

bourgeoisie the owners of the means of production

proletariat the industrial workers

communism a social movement that promotes the communal values of the worker class

sociology a field of study that focuses on people and their relationships to the societies in which they live

anthropology a field of study that examines the physical attributes of human beings as well as their social and cultural characteristics

psychology a field of study that seeks to understand the motivations behind the decisions people make in terms of their cognitive orientation

ethnography the observation and description of people in their environment through in-depth analysis and interaction

enculturation the process by which a society learns its culture

cultural relativism cultural understanding in terms of the environment in which it exists

cultural diffusion the spreading of culture beyond a specific group to be embraced by a wider audience

assimilation the submerging of cultural differences into a broader, dominant culture

In Istanbul, Turkey, a modern young Turkish girl looks at a veiled older woman.

cultural imperialism when one culture is dominated by another culture to the point that the victimized culture is forced to change its cultural practices

biases against those who were different. For example, the children of many first-generation immigrants to the United States in the early twentieth century were forbidden to learn their native languages, as their parents insisted on "English only" to succeed in their new country. Similarly, British colonizers restructured Indian society to adopt British customs, food, and dress.

Assimilation is not always a voluntary process undertaken to gain acceptance. Indigenous peoples often had little or no choice but to adopt the cultural practices and lifestyles of colonial powers. Dominating cultures routinely victimized smaller cultures in a process of **cultural imperialism**. People were frequently forced to abandon time-honored traditions in favor of a more "civilized" course. Nigerian writer Chinua Achebe describes the colonization of his country to the great detriment of the culture of the indigenous people in his 1958 novel *Things Fall Apart*:

> Does the white man understand our custom about land? How can he when he does not even speak our tongue? But he says that our customs are bad; and our own brothers who have taken up his religion also say that our customs are bad. How do you think we can fight when our own brothers have turned against us?[24]

In response to the pressure to integrate into broader societies, many groups have worked to preserve their cultural identity. Instead of melting into the predominant culture, they maintain their unique attributes through ethnic neighborhoods and shops that sell familiar products, as well as places of worship that serve their religions. Difficulties remain in crossing cultural borders, given the reality of multiple identities that may exist at any particular time. Respect for these differences is critical, but there are also broader concerns that may bring people together. The following "Pro/Con" debate on whether indigenous peoples should be educated in their own languages or that of the dominant culture examines the challenges of achieving successful outcomes while respecting cultural differences.

HOW YOU CAN CONNECT

You can better understand your culture and identity by . . .

- interviewing an older family member
- exploring your family roots by researching your genealogical tree
- taking a DNA test
- connecting with groups on campus that reflect your culture
- exploring your religious roots by attending a service

PRO/CON

SHOULD INDIGENOUS PEOPLES BE EDUCATED IN THEIR OWN LANGUAGES?

Pro

Jon Todal

Professor of Sociolinguistics, Sami University College, Guovdageaidnu, Norway. Written for *CQ Global Researcher*, September 2011.

The living conditions of indigenous peoples vary across the world. In some countries they are integrated into society, while in others they are marginalized. Despite these differences, indigenous peoples share many experiences, including the attempt by nation-states to eradicate indigenous languages.

Since the 19th century countries have used schools to achieve monolingualism, or "one state—one language," and all teaching in compulsory education was in the majority language.

As a result, indigenous children struggle more at school than children from the majority population, because they must learn not only their subjects but also a new language. The policy has signaled that indigenous languages are not valued, and such negative school experiences account in part for why indigenous peoples have a lower level of education than majority peoples.

One response among indigenous peoples has been to reject schooling as irrelevant, leading to low levels of education. Another strategy has been to adjust to the schools' values. For example, parents may stop speaking the indigenous language with their children at home so that by the time the children start school they are more on a par with majority children. But this strategy halts the intergenerational transmission of indigenous languages, and the languages become endangered. In other words, both these strategies (rejection and adjustment) have a negative impact on indigenous societies.

A third strategy—to make schools in indigenous areas adjust to the children's language and culture—has produced good results. It is now supported in Scandinavia, for example, where the indigenous Sámi people can receive primary education in Sámi as a separate subject, and they may choose to have Sámi as the language of instruction in other subjects. The level of education among the Sámi is no longer lower than among the majority peoples in Scandinavia, and the Sami language has been strengthened.

Those advocating indigenous peoples receiving education in their own language can find support for their view

Con

Helen Hughes

Emeritus Professor and Fellow, Research School of Asia and the Pacific, Australian National University, Canberra, and Senior Fellow, Centre for Independent Studies Sydney, Australia. Written for *CQ Global Researcher*, September 2011.

Open ended, this is a nonsensical question. However desirable for children to learn to read and write in their mother tongues, in many situations it is impractical. In Papua New Guinea, for example, a developing country with just under 7 million people, it has not been possible to train teachers and develop reading materials in the more than 800 indigenous languages spoken there.

Pretending to do so has contributed significantly to the country's failure of education. After nearly 40 years of independence, education is in crisis, with only about 20 percent of the population literate.

Some languages are dying out—not only in Oceania, but also in the Americas, India, China and many other parts of Asia and Africa—while new ones, such as Bahasa Indonesia, have been evolving. Countries must decide on language teaching that is best for their inhabitants, and this usually means compromises between resources and ideals.

Children must become articulate and literate in the principal language or languages of their country so they can function in its economy and society. They have to be able to qualify for jobs, participate in democratic decision-making and contribute to civil society. In countries made up of disparate groups, a national language or languages can make a contribution to stability, equity and economic and social development.

Fortunately, research on the human brain has demonstrated that children can absorb new languages at very early ages and can absorb several languages simultaneously when very young. Research also shows that linguistic development makes a special contribution to the development of children's brains. Teaching several languages simultaneously in pre-schools that take in children at 3 years of age and (even earlier) has made a multilingual approach to teaching languages possible.

(Continued)

(Continued)

in international conventions. However, these formal rights are not the main issue. The key points are that education in indigenous languages gives children a positive experience of their own culture and also strengthens the traditional indigenous languages. In this way children are better prepared for life both in the wider society and in the indigenous society.

For this reason education in their own language must be an important right for all indigenous peoples.

Equality of opportunity demands quality education from very early years so that children are fully articulate and literate by the end of their primary education in a country's principal language or languages. The extent to which it is sensible to teach mother or traditional tongues in practice depends on a range of factors, including the extent to which such languages are developed and used, a country's resources and parents' wishes. There is no one-size-fits-all model.

Source: Brian Beary, "Saving Indigenous Peoples," *CQ Global Researcher* 5 (2011): 447–472.

Where Do You Stand?

1. Do you think indigenous people should receive instruction in their native language?

2. Does instruction in their native language offer protection for their cultural identity?

3. Does a society have the right to demand that all people speak the dominant language?

Globalization: Homogenization or Hybridization?

Over thousands of years, group identities evolved with little influence from the outside world. Anthropologist John H. Bodley observes that "as recently as 200 years ago, 50 million people continued to live in politically autonomous domestic-scale tribal societies."[25] Different groups controlled large areas of the globe, and external forces such as commercial enterprise did not affect them. Bodley argues that while these tribal groups (more commonly referred to as indigenous peoples) still exist, the commercial world has penetrated and altered their realities.

The impact of globalization on culture and identity has been significant. As sociologist and cultural communications expert John Tomlinson suggests, greater mobility results in a progressive **deterritorialization** of the world that weakens the connection between culture and a particular place.[26] The ability to communicate instantly around the world has rendered the attachment to place less potent. Moreover, many of the issues that affect the peoples of the world, from terrorism to technological innovation, are not limited by its borders. As a result, common cultural experiences emerge.

deterritorialization the weakening of cultural ties to specific locations

Some people are concerned that globalization results in a **homogenization** of culture. A range of cultural activities has been incorporated into a more uniform set of values and practices, primarily Western and specifically American in nature, that threaten cultural diversity and people's ability to maintain their distinctive identities. The pressures to conform and adapt are plentiful and difficult to resist. The same stores, clothes, and services populate shopping centers around the world. KFC and other fast-food establishments are found on main streets from New York to Paris to Doha.

homogenization the incorporation of a range of cultural forms into a uniform set of values and practices

Not everyone shares this concern. In contrast to those who caution against the homogenizing impacts of globalization are analysts who emphasize the resilience of existing cultural forms and their ability to endure the effects of external pressures. They point to the countervailing influence of local customs and cultural practices on these outside forces that has produced a **hybridization** of cultures—a blending that incorporates aspects of different cultures. While the concept of hybridity comes from agrarian roots, where new varieties of plants are created by grafting one plant to another, sociologist Jan Nederveen Pieterse, in his book *Globalization and Culture*, argues that hybridity occurs today due to the mobility of people, their ability to migrate, and the multicultural identities they have developed.[27] This extensive migration, coupled with new forms of communication that provide broader transmission of information and the creation of transnational social networking sites such as Facebook, has an impact on identity. Rather than threatening identity, this exposure simply results in a modification or adaptation as new identities may emerge. The popular *Daily Show* host Trevor Noah, born and raised in South Africa to a black Xhosa mother and white Swiss-German father, an illegal act at the time due to apartheid, represents this hybridization. Well-known golfer Tiger Woods specifically recognizes this fusion, characterizing his identity as "Cablinasian"—a blend of Caucasian, Black, Indian, and Asian.[28]

> **hybridization** a blending of cultures that incorporates different aspects of each culture to create a new entity

Whether globalization is contributing to the homogenization or hybridization of culture, it is clear that it is having a profound impact. A number of leading analysts see globalization as the source of significant cultural conflict, due to its complex and often contradictory components. In his 1999 best-seller, *The Lexus and the Olive Tree*, Pulitzer Prize–winning columnist Thomas Friedman argues that through the development and rapid spread of technology, embodied in the state-of-the-art facility manufacturing Toyota's luxury Lexus automobile, globalization could improve the quality of life for workers who have historically been left behind. At the same time, however, he realizes that the intense desire to protect and preserve individual cultures and identities—symbolized by the ongoing struggle and often violent clashes between Israelis and Palestinians over the ownership of particular olive trees—will persist.

In a more dramatic scenario than Friedman's, political scientist Samuel Huntington projects a future marked by what he terms a "clash of civilizations" (or cultures). In his groundbreaking 1996 work, *The Clash of Civilizations and the Remaking of World Order*, Huntington envisioned global interactions among seven or eight major civilizations—Western, Japanese, Confucian, Islamic, Hindu, Slavic-Orthodox, Latin American, and possibly African.[29] Future conflicts, he argued, were most likely to fall along cultural lines, with the most significant potential for discord between Islam and the West. If not addressed and contained, this conflict could result in a highly contentious global environment where the West would find itself aligned against all other major civilizations.

Huntington's thesis provoked considerable criticism among thinkers who questioned the premise of his argument and the implications of his projections.[30] For some, Huntington went too far in emphasizing the hostility generated by intercultural contact. Others were concerned that he had not underestimated the differences and distinctions among civilizations but had put forward a far too simplistic scenario that was likely to provoke such policies as restricting immigration or imposing restraints on minorities. Efforts by the Trump administration to ban refugees from several primarily Muslim countries have reignited this debate. Similarly, the popularity of extreme nationalist parties across Europe embraces these distinctions as well. Such actions can reinforce existing or latent hostilities. Some have suggested that Huntington's ideas might even be used as a rationale to justify extreme forms of ethnic violence. Nevertheless, Huntington's clash of civilizations argument continues to be an important part of the debate that highlights globalization's evolving and multiple impacts (see Map 8.2).

McDonald's

Globalization's critics love to take aim at the McDonald's restaurant chain, whose global reach extends to 118 countries around the world. They see it as the embodiment of a

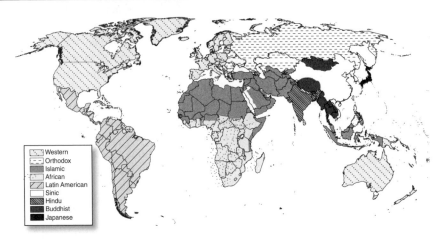

MAP 8.2 ● Clash of Civilizations

Western
Orthodox
Islamic
African
Latin American
Sinic
Hindu
Buddhist
Japanese

Source: THE CLASH OF CIVILIZATIONS AND THE REMAKING OF WORLD ORDER by Samuel P. Huntington. Copyright © 1996 by Samuel P. Huntington. Base Map © Hammond World Atlas Corp. All rights reserved. Reprinted by permission of Georges Borchardt, Inc., for the Estate of Samuel P. Huntington.

Andrey Rudakov/Bloomberg via Getty Images.

A Big Mac hamburger sits on a tray inside a McDonald's fast-food restaurant in Moscow.

dominant US cultural presence and market position across the world—as well as a prime culprit in spreading the consumption of food of questionable nutritional value. However, the ubiquitous McDonald's may bring about more than just hamburgers or the homogenization of culture. Thomas Friedman introduced the idea of a "golden arches theory of conflict prevention," for example, suggesting that countries with McDonald's restaurants (whose presence indicates that these countries are open to global capitalism) are less likely to go to war with one another to avoid the risk of economic disruption.[31]

In his 1996 book on this topic, *Jihad vs. McWorld*, political theorist Benjamin Barber describes two different scenarios to illustrate the integrative and the polarizing tendencies of globalization. *McWorld* symbolizes the connectivity of globalization and its capacity for bringing diverse communities into contact with one another. While this connectivity presents an opportunity for increasing mutual understanding, it is also indicative of globalization's homogenizing tendencies.

In contrast, *jihad* is an Arabic word often identified with the notion of the "holy war" that has motivated al-Qaida. ISIS and other Islamic groups seek to thwart what they perceive to be the threatening dominance of Western values and ideology. As Barber uses the concept, it refers to the resistance of these groups to the perceived cultural uniformity that has come with globalization.[32]

Sociologist George Ritzer uses the term *McDonaldization* to describe the processes that have come to dominate the organization of more and more sectors of production around the world and to impose pressure to adhere to homogenous standards and values. These principles include efficiency, calculability, predictability, and control. McDonald's has been a model of efficiency in its movement of goods from one place to another as well as its ability to capture market share. It has also been a leader in calculability, an emphasis on time and money that delivers a product quickly and cheaply to its customers. One of the hallmarks of McDonald's is its predictability—its products and service are generally the same all over, with the exception of local market adaptation. Finally, McDonald's exerts significant control over how goods are distributed in its restaurants, from drive-thru windows and line service to the appearance of its employees.[33]

Other academics argue that the McDonald's effect noted by Ritzer and other commentators may be somewhat overblown, as it assumes cultural impact to be a one-way street. Political scientist Michael Veseth calls this overemphasis on the homogenizing nature of globalization *globaloney*.[34] In fact, he says, McDonald's must tailor its menus to local tastes and cultural practices in order to retain its competitive position. In India, where eating beef is sacrilege, the Maharaja Mac is a Big Mac made of chicken; in Chile, avocado paste is a standard fixing, with a side of cheese empanadas; and in Japan, you can order a Teriyaki McBurger made of ground pork and teriyaki sauce. McDonald's also serves different purposes in different countries—coffee shop, community gathering location, study hall, or just a place to take the kids. The adaptation of local forms of expression and identity to exposure from outside influences is a process known as **glocalization**.[35]

glocalization the adaptation of local forms of expression and identity to outside influences

Anthropologist Arjun Appadurai has coined the phrase *global scapes* to describe the increasing flows that globalization has released. Global scapes are redefining people's identities.[36] They include the following:

mediascapes: flows of information through the mass media

financescapes: flows of capital

technoscapes: flows of technology

ethnoscapes: flows of people

ideoscapes: flows of ideas

Rather than imposing Western culture and values on others, Appadurai argues, these flows may help invigorate local culture by infusing a broader range of perspectives.

Music and Sport

Music and sport, two elements that often contribute significantly to defining who we are and our relationship to others, are large parts of the global scape that is redefining cultures. Technology has made local sounds global. New recording and sound production technologies have broken down old barriers to transmitting music. While digitization expands opportunities for reproduction and dissemination, the Internet offers a far wider network for exposure than the radio ever did. The ease of streaming and downloading music of all types and genres has been critical. Musicians are able to travel more easily actually and virtually than ever before, bringing new sounds to peoples in different places. This ease of sharing has created a body of world music that captures the diversity of sound from around the world. The music publication *Billboard* provides a weekly list of best-selling world albums. A recent top-ten list included albums from Germany, Ireland, Nigeria, and South Korea (see Table 8.2).

As is the case with other cultural forms, music has been a source of concern for people who fear globalization's homogenizing effects. The international nonprofit organization

TABLE 8.2 ● Billboard's Top Ten World Albums October 20, 2017		
Rank and Artist	**Album**	**Website**
1. BTS	*Love Yourself: Her*	http://bts.ibighit.com/
South Korean K-pop boy band		
2. Celtic Thunder	*Inspirational*	https://www.celticthunder.com/
Irish stage and vocal group		
3. Myrkur	*Mareridt*	https://www.myrkurmusic.com/
Danish musician Amalie Bauun		
4. Belinda Carlisle	*Wilder Shores*	http://www.belindacarlisle.tv/
American singer/songwriter		
5. Mordechai Shapiro	*Machar*	http://www.mordechaishapiro.com/
American Jewish singer		
6. David Maldonado	*Davicas*	http://www.davidmaldonado.com/
American classical/flamenco guitarist		
7. Celtic Woman/ The Orchestra of Ireland	*Voices of Angels*	https://www.celticwoman.com/
Irish music ensemble		
8. Jesse Cook	*Beyond Borders*	http://www.jessecook.com/
Canadian guitarist		
9. Bolbbalgan4	*Red Diary Page.1 (EP)*	http://www.kpopscene.com/bolbbalgan4/
South Korean female K-pop duo		
10. Antibalas	*Where the Gods Are In Peace*	https://antibalas.com/
American Afrobeat band		

Source: Billboard.com and artists' websites.

Global Music Project aims to preserve the uniqueness of different forms of music. Its mission is to promote collaboration and peace through music and cultural awareness.[37] It seeks not only to preserve musical traditions around the world but to share those traditions as well. Its website includes recommended songs from across the globe and provides free downloads. Through artist donations of songs, sponsors, and merchandise sales, the Global Music Project promotes cross-cultural appreciation for music and the unique cultures it represents.

There is little evidence to suggest that greater standardization in production has had a homogenizing effect on music. Instead, it has contributed to a greater degree of diversity.

As particular types of music originating in one locale spread to other places, musicians modify their sounds as a result of their contact with people of other cultures. These modifications enhance the meaning of the music in a way that fits more easily with existing values and experiences.

The introduction and consumption of Afro-Caribbean music in Japan is a case in point. Due to limited contact and communication between Latin America and Japan, Afro-Caribbean music was transmitted largely through the United States and Europe. While some forms such as tango and bolero were favorably received in the 1920s, others such as rumba gained little following. The differences had much to do with the extent to which these different genres resembled Japanese popular music in terms of their beat and tone and how they fit into Japan's value system.[38]

A significant turning point came in 1984 with the creation of the Orquesta de la Luz, a salsa band of Japanese musicians with experience in playing Afro-Caribbean music. Its popularity, both inside Japan and internationally, stemmed largely from its ability to maintain the authenticity of its sound as a distinctively Japanese group. This unique collaboration demonstrated how a local culture can be enriched through its exposure to other cultural forms while simultaneously influencing the composition of those forms.[39] More recently, the popularity of BABYMETAL, a Japanese "girl band" whose three young members combine Japanese pop (J-pop) music with heavy metal, represents another new genre that crosses borders.[40] They have become popular around the world, opening for Lady Gaga in 2014 and the Red Hot Chili Peppers' US tour in 2017, while continuing to enjoy idol status in Japan.

This interplay of the global and local is also reflected in the development of hip-hop, a musical form with global appeal. Originating in the 1970s in the Bronx borough of New York City, hip-hop was based on themes of urban life and evolved into a broader form of expression for young people. In addition to its music, hip-hop incorporates dance, art, and fashion in reflecting a particular outlook and lifestyle. As hip-hop gained in popularity and spread to different parts of the world, it came to take on additional meaning and more varied forms of expression. Hip-hop's themes relating to personal liberation, rebellion, and social justice appealed to masses of youths in far corners of the world.[41] Now a global movement, hip-hop has grown to the point where it has become a culture in and of itself.

As hip-hop spread across the globe, the genre itself underwent considerable transformation. While the message spoke to the experiences of disenfranchised or alienated youth worldwide, each community incorporated its own unique elements to reflect local conditions and circumstances. Different mixes of language and beat give hip-hop in Brazil a different feel from hip-hop in Tanzania. As local attributes distinguish and differentiate the identities of these respective varieties, they also influence the genre in turn.[42] In the case of hip-hop, globalization has yielded glocal hybrids, not Western purebreds.

David Corio/Redferns.

The Notorious B.I.G. performs at Meadowlands, New Jersey, on June 29, 1995.

Similar impacts have flowed from the increasing globalization of sport, another agent of culture whose popularity across borders brings people together. The participation of countries from around the world and the parade of nations that opens the Olympic games demonstrates these connections. Where and how particular games are played can be traced to broader historical patterns. South Asian countries adopted cricket as their national sports pastime from their British colonial occupiers. The Scottish games that originated as a celebration of a hunt with measures of strength and agility, such as "tossing the caber" (throwing a fourteen-foot pole similar to a log end over end) and "throwing the hammer," are now celebrated in "Highland Games" in distant places. The largest gathering of the Scottish clans globally takes place annually in a small town in the mountains of North Carolina, far from Scotland's shores.

The expanding global reach of premier US professional sport leagues goes beyond the traditional diffusion of sports through colonization or immigration. Through the leadership of its commissioner, the National Basketball Association (NBA) has made a concerted effort to penetrate new markets in Europe and beyond to enhance the profitability of the enterprise. In 2016, a record number of 113 international players from forty-one countries and territories held roster spots on NBA teams. The greatest number came from Canada (eleven), followed by France (ten), Brazil (nine), Australia (eight), and Croatia (five).[43] The 2015 finals were broadcast in forty-seven languages to 215 countries.[44]

Marketing techniques have contributed significantly to the growing popularity of this game. They focus largely on promoting key players whose appeal elevates them to the status of cultural icons and place an emphasis on interpersonal rivalries (as opposed to team rivalries). The epic Larry Bird–Magic Johnson duels and the Michael Jordan phenomenon were instrumental in moving the process forward. The role of advertisers was critical. The Michael Jordan brand promoted by Nike was especially effective and has retained its appeal long after his retirement.[45] It even prompted one observer to note the emergence of Jordanscapes (using the Appadurai terminology) in explaining the source of the growing global appeal of the NBA.[46] This marketing strategy has continued with the latest generation of stars, such as LeBron James, Kevin Durant, and Stephen Curry.

China's Yao Ming helped broaden the worldwide appeal of the NBA during his tenure with the Houston Rockets. Although plagued by injuries throughout his career and ultimately forced to retire prematurely in 2011, Yao became a popular hero and an important symbol of China's full-scale emergence on the world stage.[47] The development of Taiwan-born and Harvard-educated Jeremy Lin, a marginal player who had a succession of electrifying performances with the New York Knicks during the 2012 season, contributed further to the expanding Asian connection in the NBA. Now with the Brooklyn Nets, Lin has yet to regain the "Linsanity" that dominated the airwaves in 2012 but has made an impressive comeback.

Major League Baseball (MLB) has also gone global. Broadcasting in 233 countries and territories, its telecasts are retransmitted in seventeen languages.[48] At the start of the 2017 season, non-US players filled 29.8 percent of team rosters, representing nineteen countries and territories.[49] Often touted as a US game, professional baseball has undergone some significant changes. The World Baseball Classic, established in 2009, brings together national teams from across the world and has contributed to the sport's growing popularity in a variety of markets.

Despite its US roots, professional baseball has long been a part of Japan's sports scene. Americans who have played for Japanese teams have often expressed their difficulties in adjusting to a different style of play that emphasizes such Japanese values as group identity, cooperation, and harmony. Tom Davey, who pitched in the Japanese majors, observes the following:

> You need to keep an open mind, nod your head and do what they ask. Maybe I'm not going to do a 300-pitch bullpen, but I'll do the crazy agility drills they have. It's the Japanese Samurai mentality. They can't say, "No, I'm done." You respect it like you respect everything else here.[50]

Similarly, Japan's teams have exhibited some discomfort with their US players—seeking to take advantage of their contributions while not necessarily being interested in having them upstage their local counterparts. This may be understood in terms of the country's homogeneous character and antipathy toward foreigners. Japanese players, on the other hand, are beginning to make their way into the MLB. While a few have enjoyed considerable success (most notably, Ichiro Suzuki and Hideki Matsui), many others who starred in Japan found the transition difficult and failed to live up to expectations.[51] A recent Japanese star to take the United States by storm is Masahiro Tanaka of the New York Yankees. Even as he has been challenged to replicate his achievements, he has pitched opening day for the Yankees since 2015 and was the first Yankees rookie to win the American League Pitcher of the Month Award since its inception in 1979.[52]

The most significant development with respect to the internationalization of the MLB itself has been the infusion of Latin players. While this is not necessarily a new phenomenon, given baseball's longstanding presence in parts of the Caribbean and Central and South America, it has reached impressive proportions. Unlike the NBA, the MLB does not appear to have much interest in establishing franchises overseas. Rather, it has capitalized on and sought to enhance the availability of Latin talent as a means to expand into those markets.[53]

The player "pipeline" between the Dominican Republic, the small Caribbean country that shares the island of Hispaniola with Haiti, and the United States is especially notable. In 2017 there were 93 players from the Dominican Republic on MLB opening-day rosters.[54] All thirty major league clubs have academies in the country that serve as training camps for the purpose of spotting and developing local talent. To prepare the seventeen- to nineteen-year-olds who attend, the academies offer English-language classes and workshops on anger and stress management, as well as basic American culture, etiquette, and protocol.[55] With top prospects commanding hefty signing bonuses and having the potential to land multimillion dollar contracts, baseball has become an important path out of poverty. It has also sometimes become a political headache. The story of Yasiel Puig's defection from Cuba in 2012 to join the Los Angeles Dodgers involves cross-border intrigue that includes underworld smugglers, criminal acts, death, and a great deal of money. These activities resulted in Puig's facing a federal lawsuit in Miami over his role in some of the subsequent actions that took place.[56]

As would be expected, the entry of large numbers of foreign-born players (and even a handful of managers and team executives) is transforming the character and culture of the MLB. Playing styles are more varied, while the management of intercultural relationships and communications has become an important factor in maintaining team chemistry. This diversity is readily apparent not only in terms of the composition of teams but in the makeup of their fan bases. Ballparks now cater to a wider degree of tastes in terms of the foods they offer and the apparel and other items they market, both at home and internationally. For example, churros, a fried dough treat that originated in Spain, can be found at many major-league stadiums.

The globalization of sport is not a phenomenon exclusive to US efforts. In fact, soccer is the most universal sport, even as it has been slow to catch on in the United States. Soccer's progressive spread has been a lengthy and complex process that can be traced all the way back to the time of the Roman Empire. The sport's governing body—the Fédération Internationale de Football Association (FIFA)—oversees its operation and development and has more than 200 national members. FIFA has very successfully promoted the commercialization of the sport, capitalizing on interest in the World Cup, which engages and mobilizes people all over the world as they root for their respective national teams. Premier teams such as Manchester United, Real Madrid, and FC Barcelona have fanatical global fan bases and are readily distinguishable by their jerseys, symbols, and styles of play. The biggest stars, like those of the NBA, are elevated to iconic or cult status.

Kyodo News via Getty Images.

The Refugee Olympic Team marches during the opening ceremony of the Rio de Janeiro Olympics at Maracana Stadium. The International Olympic Committee Executive Board agreed on July 9, 2017, to continue to support refugees by getting them involved in the 2020 Tokyo Olympics.

The same interplay of global and local forces is at work in soccer. Whereas the world's top professional soccer leagues and the center of FIFA power are located in Europe, top players come from all over. This process has had some important and intriguing effects. To begin with, teams in the Global South have suffered from the loss of some of their very best local players to elite teams across Europe in the premier leagues. These players have been lured by high salaries, the promise of broad exposure, and other benefits.[57] National teams competing in the World Cup and other championship events have worked to facilitate the relocation of talented players as a means of recruitment.

The globalization of the game has enabled certain players to attain levels of mobility and wealth that would not be possible otherwise. It has also produced its share of challenges. Soccer has traditionally been an important source of local and national identity. The styles of play of particular clubs may often mirror the cultures of their particular communities, while locals may come to the point where their sense of self is tied closely to the ups and downs of their favorite teams and players. The familiar sight of enthusiastic fans wrapping themselves in the national flag or covering their bodies with paint in their national colors is as important a part of the overall ritual as the incessant sound of the vuvuzela horns.

While potentially a key force in unifying local communities, soccer team loyalty can also serve as a source of conflict when fans of competing teams react in violent ways to the competition on the field. Globalization of the rosters of these teams can also have a significant effect. The increasing racial diversity of many European teams, for example, has resulted in any number of racially tinged taunts and incidents by fans and players alike. In a few cases, it has even led some to question the representative nature and national character of their very own teams.

Conclusion: Identity at the Crossroads

Social and cultural borders can sit on top of and across geographic, political, and economic borders. On any given day, we navigate multiple identities as students, teachers, sons, daughters, workers, and players, but we still find ourselves sharing many commonalities. The world has been drawn closer together in terms of political and economic cooperation as similar interests develop. Cultural integration has created new ground for people to work together. In response to concern over the spread of a common world culture, however, many people across the globe are revisiting their traditional and historical identities. A fear of integration and a perceived need to protect identity raise the potential for conflict. This conflict suggests that Huntington's thesis on the potential clash of civilizations continues to resonate. As we will see in the next chapter, the challenges that face individuals across social and cultural borders emerge from these tensions.

Key Concepts

anthropology 193	bourgeoisie 193	communism 193
assimilation 193	caste system 189	cultural diffusion 193

To Learn More

Books and Other Print Media

Chimamanda Ngozi Adichie, *Americanah* (New York: Alfred Knopf, 2013).

In this novel, the main character moves from a small town in Nigeria to go to school in the capital city of Lagos, then on to the United States for university and work. The story explores how the main character's identity shifts and changes as she moves from place to place.

Allan Bairner, *Sport, Nationalism and Globalization: European and North American Perspectives* (Albany: State University of New York Press, 2001).

Allan Bairner takes stock of the state of sports around the world and how it is affected by the forces of globalization.

Benjamin R. Barber, *Jihad vs. McWorld: Terrorism's Challenge to Democracy* (New York: Ballantine Books, 2001).

In this volume, Benjamin Barber asserts that there are two interdependent forces shaping today's world: religious fundamentalism represented by Jihad, which breaks people apart, and consumer capitalism represented by McWorld, which brings people together.

Katherine Boo, *Behind the Beautiful Forevers: Life, Death, and Hope in a Mumbai Undercity* (New York: Random House, 2012).

This award-winning book explores the real life aspiration of residents of Annawadi, a makeshift settlement on the fringe of luxury hotels near the airport in Mumbai. It captures their hopes and fears, limited by their poverty and lot in life.

Bill Bryson, *I'm a Stranger Here Myself: Notes on Returning to America after Twenty Years Away* (New York: Broadway Books, 2000).

After living in Britain for two decades, Bill Bryson recently moved back to the United States with his English wife and four children. In this novel, he recounts his attempts to reacquaint himself with his own country.

Paul Cuadros, *A Home on the Field* (New York: HarperCollins, 2006).

This book tells the story of how a group of Latino high school boys in Siler City, North Carolina, embraced soccer as a way to overcome the culture clashes they experienced as immigrants. A video documentary series about their experiences, *Los Jets*, is available through NUVOtv.

Dave Eggers, *What is the What: The Autobiography of Valentino Achak Deng* (San Francisco: McSweeney's, 2006).

This book details Valentino Achak Deng's struggles as a refugee, lost boy, and finally resident of the United States, as told to novelist Eggers.

Samuel Huntington, *The Clash of Civilizations and the Remaking of World Order* (New York: Simon & Schuster, 1996).

This widely received and highly controversial book asserts that the greatest threat to peace is the friction between cultural groups.

Sasha Issenberg, *The Sushi Economy: Globalization and the Making of a Modern Delicacy* (New York: Penguin, 2007).

This book details the transformation of sushi from a Japanese street snack to global delicacy in order to demonstrate the power of globalization.

Margaret Mead, *Coming of Age in Samoa: A Psychological Study of Primitive Youth for Western Civilization* (Gloucester, MA: Peter Smith, 1961).

Margaret Mead's psychological study of what it was like in the 1920s for girls growing up in the primitive culture of the Samoan Islands is a classic in scholarly exploration of perception and cultural identification.

Kennedy Odede and Jessica Posner, *Find Me Unafraid: Love, Hope, and Loss in an African Slum* (New York: Harper Collins, 2016).

This is the story of two people, one from Colorado and the other from the largest refugee camp in Kenya, who meet, fall in love, and today collaborate to improve the lives of those trapped in the slums of Kenya.

Pele, *Why Soccer Matters* (New York: Penguin, 2014).

International soccer star Pele, who rose from humble beginnings in Brazil to travel the world as an ambassador for soccer, tells his story and why soccer matters as it crosses borders in the world today.

Jan Nederveen Pieterse, *Globalization and Culture: Global Melange,* 3rd ed. (Lanham, MD: Rowman & Littlefield, 2015).

In this book, Pieterse looks forward to the post-McDonaldization era, where a culture of hybridization has new implications for global challenges and cooperation.

Websites

Center for World Indigenous Studies (CWIS), www.cwis.org

CWIS is a US-based research and education nonprofit focused on the political, social, and economic issues of indigenous peoples worldwide.

Ethnologue: Languages of the World, www.ethnologue.com/web.asp

Ethnologue is a web-based catalogue of the world's 7,106 living languages.

Global Gateway: World Culture & Resources, http://international.loc.gov/intldl/intldlhome.html

This site is maintained by the Library of Congress and includes links to the library's many international collections.

Global Memory Net (GMNet), www.memorynet.org

Supported by the National Science Foundation's International Digital Library program, GMNet is a global digital library aimed at preserving global history, culture, and heritage through its image collections, ranging from antique maps to photos of ethnic groups and places.

United Nations Educational, Scientific and Cultural Organization (UNESCO), en.unesco.org

UNESCO is a specialized agency of the UN that promotes global cooperation through the sharing of education, science, and culture. Its objectives are to strengthen human rights and mutual respect and also to alleviate poverty.

Valentino Achak Deng Foundation, www.vadfoundation.org

The Valentino Achak Deng Foundation is a nonprofit organization dedicated to improving education in South Sudan. Its founder and namesake, Valentino Achak Deng, is the focus of Dave Eggers's semiautobiographical novel *What Is the What.*

Videos

Anthony Bourdain: Parts Unknown (CNN documentary series, 2013–present)

Chef Anthony Bourdain travels the world in this series exploring not only what the locals eat but the culture behind their food. The series includes trips to Brazil, Thailand, Russia, France, India, South Africa, Peru, and Libya, as well as several US destinations—Detroit, the Mississippi Delta, and Los Angeles.

Ballplayer: Pelotero (2011)

A documentary film focusing on the prospects of two Dominican baseball players trying to make it to the major leagues.

China Blue (2005), www.pbs.org/independentlens/chinablue

China Blue is a groundbreaking documentary following the life of seventeen-year-old Jasmine, a worker in a jeans factory in Guangdong, China. It exposes the conditions of laborers in Chinese sweatshops and China's growth as a chief exporter.

"The Danger of a Single Story" (TEDTalks, 2009)

Novelist Chimamanda Adichie tells the story of how she found her authentic cultural voice—and warns that if we hear only a single story about another person or country, we risk a critical misunderstanding.

Ecuador: Dreamtown—Soccer's Ticket Out (2010)

Produced by Frontline/World, this video tells the story of young Ecuadorian soccer players who see the game as their ticket out of poverty.

The Gods Must Be Crazy (1980)

A classic film from South Africa, *The Gods Must Be Crazy* is an allegory about a Bushman and his first experiences with modern civilization and culture.

The Himbas Are Shooting (2012)

The Himba people of Namibia, tired of people making films about them, have made a movie about their tribal lifestyle that includes segments on their social and cultural traditions.

India: A Dangerous Place to Be a Woman (2013)

This British Broadcasting Corporation (BBC) film explores the potential dangers and reality of life for young women in India.

Sabah: A Love Story (2005)

This popular movie is about a Syrian Muslim woman living in Toronto who falls in love with a Canadian man and must come to terms with the subsequent clash of cultures.

"Weird, or Just Different?" (TEDIndia, 2009)

Derek Sivers shows how there is, indeed, a flip side to everything.

9

Challenges to Identity

The Taliban shot me on the left side of my forehead. They shot my friends too. They thought that the bullets would silence us. But they failed.

—Malala Yousafzai, 2013[1]

Learning Objectives

After studying this chapter, you will be able to do the following:

- Understand how religion shapes identity and how that identity impacts the political and social world.

- Define *ethnic conflict* and identify the key areas of conflict today.

- Define a *fragile state*, and explain the role that religious and ethnic conflicts play in destabilizing nation-states.

- Identify methods for resolving these types of conflicts.

Malala was a fourteen-year-old Pakistani schoolgirl when she was fired upon by a Taliban fighter while riding a bus back from a school trip in the Swat region of Pakistan. While a devout Muslim, Malala had spoken out as a young girl against the Taliban's interpretation of Islam that held that women should not be educated. Her father was the head of the school that she attended and supported her beliefs. Her advocacy gained worldwide attention through social media when she was revealed as the author of a blog that appeared on the British Broadcasting Corporation's (BBC's) Urdu website that told about life under the threat of the Taliban. She would subsequently receive the International Children's Peace Prize in 2011 and shared the Nobel Peace Prize in 2014. As a result, Malala became known around the world as the face of young girls who clamored for education. This notoriety made her a target in the conflict between traditional and modern life. The young man who shot her was also Muslim, but they had very different worldviews, and these differences led to this violent act.

After several moves to save her life, Malala was flown to Birmingham, England, for further treatment. Her family settled in this faraway city, and she has never returned home. Aside from the trauma she endured, Malala suffered from homesickness for the Swat Valley and the companionship of her friends. She has since written a book about her experiences and remains an important voice for women and education. She has co-founded a global fund to support education for girls, with priority given to Pakistan, Afghanistan, India, Nigeria, and those countries housing Syrian refugees (Lebanon and Jordan).[2] Malala's story highlights the tensions between modernity and technology that are both bringing people together *and* simultaneously challenging their collective identities, to the point that it divides them. It reminds us of the extremes to which people will go when they believe their identity is being challenged.

Samuel Huntington's argument of an impending clash of civilizations (introduced in Chapter 8) continues to be relevant as trends of integration and disintegration can be seen in several areas. In times of extreme political and economic conditions, people who feel threatened frequently try to protect their identities by returning to their religious or ethnic roots. The rise of religious fundamentalism is a response to this perceived threat. Integration may accentuate ethnic differences as well. Competition for scarce resources can

Malala Yousafzai, the Pakistani advocate for girls education who was shot in the head by the Taliban, speaks at the United Nations (UN) Youth Assembly on July 12, 2013, in New York City. The United Nations declared July 12 "Malala Day," which is also her birthday.

Andrew Burton/Getty Images.

increase tensions between groups. The desire to eliminate the "other" can lead to conflict, civil war, and even **ethnic cleansing**, where one group seeks to eradicate those who are different. Such was the intent of the German effort to exterminate Jews during World War II, the Serbian effort in Bosnia to eliminate Muslims in the early 1990s, the Hutu **genocide** of Tutsis in Rwanda in 1994, and Iraqi attacks against the Kurdish minority under Saddam Hussein, which lasted several decades.

When the artificial boundaries that frequently delineate nation-states disintegrate under pressure, states become very fragile and can fail. Unable to meet the basic needs of their people, shaky governments lose their hold on power and ultimately dissolve into chaos. This failure exacerbates conflict and further erodes identity. Contributing to these failures is the movement of people across borders. To escape conflict, environmental crises, poverty, and social upheavals, groups of people are forced to leave their homelands. **Migration**, whether in times of war or peace, famine or prosperity, creates opportunities for both the dissemination of culture and its breakdown. As people learn about the cultural practices of the new groups they encounter, they begin to forget the old ways; languages are lost, and a cultural heritage dies.

Overcoming differences and working together requires the ability to see integration in a positive light. Religion, ethnic conflict, and fragile states are major forces that can divide people and create clashes over identity. But there are ways to overcome these challenges. Civil society can respect religious laws by recognizing their significance to those who are guided by them. The emergence of truth commissions to reconcile lingering emotions about ethnic conflict and genocide can also provide closure for those who have been most affected by these atrocities. As a result, the ability to move forward for all parties concerned can be greatly facilitated by these simple acts.

The Role of Religion

Throughout history, religion has played a large role in many conflicts. It has been a key factor in people's relationships to one another and their homelands. Some of the earliest known divisions emerged in the fifth century BCE from the philosophical views of Confucius, whose teachings led to the development of Confucianism, and Lao Tzu, whose writings formed the basis of Taoism. Early Christians were pitted against Jews as Christianity was founded in the first and second centuries CE. Religious divisions in India between Hindus and Muslims date to the early 700s and continue today. During the Crusades of the Middle Ages (1095–1291), Christians fought against Muslims for control of lands that both groups considered holy, particularly Jerusalem. In 1920, differences between Protestants and Catholics split Northern Ireland from the rest of the country. Today, the focus is on how religion has driven a backlash against globalization, as different groups seek ways to strengthen their identity through the expression of their beliefs.

The potential for conflict has frequently come from the way in which religion is understood. For example, there are different interpretations of Islam that have divided Muslim followers. Islam is based on the teachings of the prophet Muhammad, who, in the early seventh century, received several revelations that instructed him to be a messenger of God. These messages urged him to teach that there is only one God, to whom all people must commit. Subsequent interpretations of Muhammad's message and disagreements over who should succeed him resulted in a split among Muslims. Two Islamic groups formed—**Sunni** and **Shia**. Sunni Muslims believe that the rightful successor to the Prophet was Abu Bakr, one of his close companions. A smaller group, the Shia, supported the Prophet's son-in-law and cousin, Ali, as the true successor; the group's name in Arabic means "partisans of Ali."[3] Both Sunni and Shia Muslims adhere to the same holy book, the Quran, for their guiding principles; however, the Shia follow a much more literal interpretation of it.

ethnic cleansing when one group forcibly removes another by violence or deportation

genocide the extreme form of ethnic cleansing, where one group seeks to deliberately kill members of another group based solely on their national or ethnic differences

migration the movement of people across borders that reshapes identities, both within states and nations and between them

Sunni Muslims who accept Abu Bakr as the rightful successor to the prophet Muhammad

Shia Muslims who support the prophet's son-in-law and cousin, Ali, as the true successor

Until the twentieth century, these differences were not a major issue. Political conflict within the Islamic world since the 1980s has shaped ruling parties and made the differences between Sunni and Shia more pronounced.[4] The vast majority of Muslims—almost 90 percent—identify themselves as Sunni, and they have frequently been in conflict with Shia authorities. The Iranian revolution in 1979 resulted in Iran being ruled by a Shia majority, which pursued conservative social policies and interpreted globalization as undermining these religious values. In contrast, a Sunni minority ruled Iraq under Saddam Hussein, while the majority of the population considered themselves to be Shia. When the United States overthrew Hussein, the Shia saw an opportunity to regain control of the country. Shia Muslims now lead the government in Iraq, and as a result, Iran and Iraq have more in common politically, a situation that could lead to additional political instability in the region.

Similarly, religious differences in the pursuit of political power have driven unrest in Syria. Syria's leader, Bashar al-Assad, is an Alawite—a member of a Shia Muslim sect that represents a small fraction of the country's population. This accounts, in part, for Iran's continuing support for the regime. Syria's Sunni Muslim majority has long felt marginalized politically and has taken up arms with rebels to overthrow the government in the ongoing conflict there. Shia Muslims from neighboring countries have joined with the regime to defend sacred sites.[5] Despite their varying interpretations of Islam, many are united in their opposition to Western influence. They believe that reliance should be on Islam as a way of life and to provide a legal system for punishment. Based on the writings of the prophet Muhammad, **sharia law** applies broadly to how devout Muslims should live their lives. Thirty-five nations, primarily in the Middle East and sub-Saharan Africa, embrace some form of this religious legal system (see Map 9.1).[6]

Some of these states have based their constitutions on sharia law, including Egypt, Saudi Arabia, Sudan, Afghanistan, Iran, and Pakistan.[7] Others have found themselves internally divided, like Nigeria, where Muslims hold the majority in the northern part of the country and Christians dominate the south. Nigeria's extreme form of sharia law calls for punishments that include stoning and amputation, but Nigeria's Christians do not embrace this system.[8] Such *hadd* punishments in most countries are rarely carried out due to international scrutiny, but the Islamic State of Iraq and Syria (ISIS) has embraced these methods. In December 2014, ISIS published a list of crimes and punishments that would serve "as an explanation and as a warning" to those who lived under the group's control (see Table 9.1).[9]

There are also instances where a family member will murder a relative as an honor killing for alleged adultery or illicit sexual behavior. These executions may even target victims of rape, deemed to have encouraged the crime through their behaviors, or those who have selected marriage partners the family rejects. The perpetrators believe they are acting in accordance with Islam. In 2015, it was reported that 1,096 women were murdered in honor killings in Pakistan alone.[10]

When religious groups use their faith to fuel their nationalistic desires, serious security issues arise. The terrorist organization al-Qaida finds its roots in the Sunni tradition of Islam. Founded by Osama bin Laden in the late 1980s from the remnants of the Muslim resistance to the Soviet takeover of Afghanistan in 1979, al-Qaida was formed to directly combat the increasing role of Western influences on Muslim countries and return those nations to more fundamentalist Islamic regimes.[11] While the death of bin Laden in 2011 weakened the organization, many other groups remain committed to Islamic rule. The Taliban in Afghanistan, Lashkar-e-Taiba in Pakistan, the Abu Sayyaf group in Malaysia and the Philippines, and the Armed Islamic Group in Algeria persist. Since the mid-1990s, al-Qaida has also reached out to groups loyal to the Shia view of Islam, most notably Hezbollah, an Iranian-backed Lebanese militia that has exerted influence across the Middle East. ISIS has built on the divisions among these groups. What started as an

sharia law a legal system that relies on Islam and applies broadly to how Muslims should live their lives; it includes punishments for crimes that may not be acceptable universally

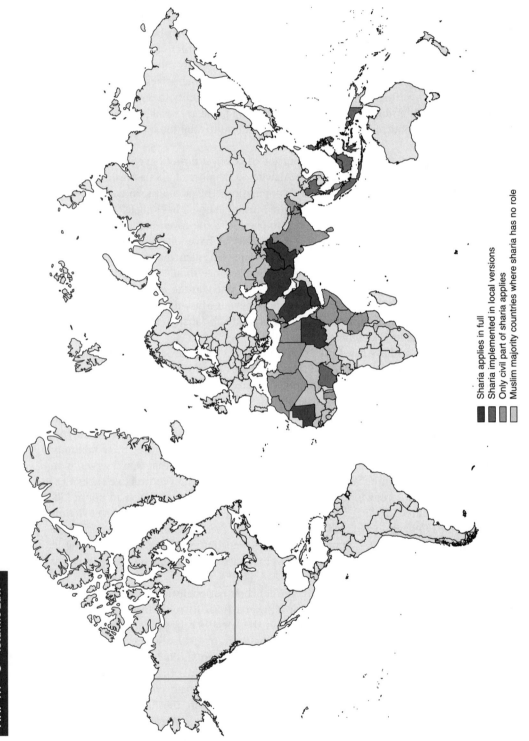

MAP 9.1 ● Islamic Law

Sharia applies in full
Sharia implemented in local versions
Only civil part of sharia applies
Muslim majority countries where sharia has no role

TABLE 9.1 ● ISIS Crime and Punishment	
Crime	**Islamic State Punishment**
Blasphemy (insulting God, the Prophet, the religion)	Death
Acts of homosexuality	
Treason	
Murder	
Slander	80 lashes
Drinking alcohol	
Adultery (if married)	Death by stoning
Adultery (if not married)	100 lashes and exile for a year
Stealing	Amputation of hand
Banditry (theft)	Amputation of hand and foot
Banditry (murder and theft)	Crucifixion

Source: Mary Atkinson and Rori Donaghy, "Crime and Punishment: Islamic State vs. Saudi Arabia," *Middle East Eye*, January 20, 2015, http://www.middleeasteye.net/news/crime-and-punishment-islamic-state-vs-saudi-arabia-1588245666.

Iraqi organization has capitalized on the conflict in Syria, with a focus on fighting the "near enemy" of ruling parties that are not true to Islam, such as the Assad regime in Syria and the Abadi regime in Iraq.[12]

The return to religion as a governing concept is not limited to Islam. While Israel is a secular, democratic state, it is also constituted as a Jewish state based on a general acceptance of Judaism. As Israel has evolved, religious tensions have arisen between secular Jews and those who favor more religious views and practices in state policy. These differing perspectives have created conflict within the Israeli population. For example, in Israel there is compulsory military service, but since the beginnings of the state, ultra-Orthodox, very religious Israeli citizens have been exempted. Some Israelis question this practice, given Israel's ongoing security needs in the troubled region.

Three men who Democratic Forces of Syria fighters claimed were Islamic State fighters sit on a pickup truck while being held as prisoners, near the town of al-Shadadi, in the Hasaka countryside, Syria.

REUTERS/Rodi Said.

Israelis also have different attitudes about territories occupied during the 1967 war with neighboring Arab states. Support for continuing occupation is much greater among more Orthodox Jews, who see these territories as rightfully theirs from biblical times. This demand is supported by the majority of Israelis living in these areas who are Orthodox and see their occupation as a religious mandate.

The role of Christianity in governing across Africa, Europe, and the United States has also been a point of contention. Political parties frequently invoke Christianity as a defining concept, as in the Christian parties that are found across Europe and the emphasis on

Christian values in US political discourse. The center-right European People's Party represents seventy-nine parties from forty-one countries that support Christian democracy and is the largest group in the European parliament.[13] In the Central African Republic (CAR), for several years, fierce fighting has been underway between Christians and Muslims that has pitted neighbor against neighbor, leading the UN to send 12,000 peacekeepers to protect civilians from this sectarian violence in 2014. Despite their efforts, divisions remain, compounded by the harsh realities of a country where the life expectancy is only forty-eight years for men and fifty-one years for women.[14]

In some countries, extremist parties have developed as a backlash to the immigration of minorities. They frequently invoke religion as a cover for their opposition to those who are different. This increase is particularly noticeable where large Muslim immigrant populations are changing the face of communities, most recently in European countries. The Syrian refugee crisis has exacerbated these conflicts and strengthened nationalist parties. These parties (see Table 9.2) have made significant gains in their parliamentary seats and have continued to grow. The success of the Brexit vote that will lead the United Kingdom to disengage from the European Union is another indicator of this growing nationalist sentiment.

Ethnic Conflict

Religious differences have frequently given rise to further divisions along ethnic lines. Ethnicity is a defining principle in identity; it is not only determined by common linguistic and cultural practices but reinforced by religious adherence as well. The lengths to which cultural groups will go to assure their identity may be considerable. The result can be **ethnic conflict** over disputed territories, which can lead to ethnic cleansing, mentioned previously, or the extreme application of this behavior in the form of genocide. The breakup of Yugoslavia in the post–Cold War period and the ethnic conflict that ensued between Serbia and Bosnia illustrates how devastating these conflicts can be.

ethnic conflict when differences in identity are too great to reconcile within state boundaries

TABLE 9.2 ● Nationalist Parties in Europe		
Party	Country	Percentage of the National Vote in Recent Elections
Alternative for Germany	Germany	25% of the vote (2016)
National Front	France	27% of the vote (2016)
Party for Freedom	The Netherlands	10% of the House of Representatives (2016)
Golden Dawn	Greece	6% of the Parliament (2016)
Jobbik	Hungary	20% of the vote (2014)
Sweden Democrats	Sweden	13% of the vote (2014)
Freedom Party	Austria	35% of the vote (2016)
People's Party—Our Slovakia	Slovak Republic	8% of the vote (2016)

Source: "Europe's Rising Far Right: A Guide to the Most Prominent Parties," *New York Times*, December 4, 2016, https://www.nytimes.com/interactive/2016/world/europe/europe-far-right-political-parties-listy.html?_r=0.

WHAT CAN YOU DO WITH INTERNATIONAL STUDIES?

In Between Two Worlds

By Dina Shehata

I was standing behind the register at the restaurant where I worked when a customer walked in to pick up his order. He looked at me and asked, "Was it you who took my order over the phone?" I replied, "Yes," and immediately recognized his confusion. How could a Muslim woman, wearing a hijab, speak English perfectly, without an accent? That was the moment I understood the way many Americans view what it means to be American. To them, I did not fit the mold. The restaurant where I was working is my family's business. It happens to be an Italian restaurant owned by an Egyptian American Muslim family living in the rural South. To me, there is nothing more American than that.

Identifying as both American and Egyptian, along with having opportunities to travel around the world, including one semester in Istanbul, Turkey, to study, has provided me with a unique lens to view the world. It has also propelled my interest in international studies in order to bridge the gap between the Middle East and the United States, a gap that seems to be widening on a daily basis.

I was born in Alexandria, Egypt, and moved to the United States at the age of one. Living in the United States while returning to Egypt during the summers has allowed me to embrace both very different cultures. I speak with no accent in English but have more trouble when speaking in Arabic. On my visits to Egypt, I would constantly be reminded by my family and friends that everyone I encountered automatically knew I wasn't living in Egypt. They said that it showed in the way that I dress, the way that I speak, and sometimes even the way that I think about certain issues. Although my Arabic-speaking capabilities aren't as strong as my English-speaking capabilities, I always feel at home when visiting Egypt. My hijab does not stand out in the majority-Muslim country. I'd never felt truly threatened because of my beliefs, until one memorable day during my undergraduate years at the University of North Carolina at Chapel Hill.

It was a beautiful sunny afternoon with a clear Carolina blue sky, perfect weather for a football game. I was volunteering with the Muslim Student Association, checking bags at one of the entrances to the UNC Chapel Hill football stadium. The policies instructed

Photo courtesy of Dina Shehata.

us to never allow food, drinks, weapons, and so forth into the stadium. It happened quickly, almost as if I had imagined it. As I was checking a man's bag, he looked at me and without hesitation said, "There is something wrong when it's Muslims who are checking your bag."

Before that unforgettable day, I had never encountered such blatant hatred and racism. I had been called offensive names and had experienced never-ending stares, especially because I grew up in the rural South. However, nothing that anyone had said or done had shocked me as much as it did when that man said those words to me.

The following year, on February 10, 2015, the entire world was in shock when three Muslim students were shot and killed by their neighbor in their apartment in what is believed by many to be a hate crime. Deah Barakat was a dental student at the

(Continued)

(Continued)

University of North Carolina at Chapel Hill. His wife of only a few short months, Yusor Abu-Salha, had been accepted to the same dental program and was preparing to join him in the fall of 2015. Yusor's sister, Razan Abu-Salha, was a design student at North Carolina State University and was visiting her sister and brother-in-law on the day of the shooting. I went to school with Deah and Yusor, when I lived in Raleigh briefly to attend a private Islamic school called Al-Iman School. Deah, Yusor, and Razan were known for their dedication to service, always helping those in need, constantly smiling, and being very involved within their community. They will forever be in our hearts and are missed every day.

As I reflect on this tragedy and the incidents I have experienced, which will always be ingrained in my memory, I am motivated to continue my career path within the international studies field. Diversity is said to be championed in the United States but isn't reflected within the political sphere. Today, the United States is more divided than ever. Islamophobia is on the rise. The media, along with some elected officials, play a consistent role in equating Islam to terrorism, and more and more people have bought into anti-Islamic sentiments. It's a difficult time for Muslims living in the West, to say the least. I will continue pursuing my dreams of working in the United Nations to be a voice of reconciliation between my two homes.

For decades, the strong political leadership of communist war hero Josip Broz, also known as Tito, kept together the various ethnic groups that had been brought together under the Yugoslavian flag after World War II. After he died in 1981, the various states began to secede from the country along ethnic lines. The first two of the six states that had been part of Yugoslavia—Slovenia and Croatia—declared their independence in June 1991. Macedonia followed in January 1992, and in April 1992, Bosnia and Herzegovina declared their independence. Montenegro then entered into a federation with Serbia. Serbian nationals claimed a historic relationship to Bosnia and responded to the declaration of independence by its largely Muslim population with attacks that killed an estimated 200,000 people.[15] The leader of Serbia, Slobodan Milosevic, later faced international criminal charges for his part in calling for the genocide, as did military commanders Radovan Karadzic and Ratko Mladic.

Often, the blame for ethnic conflict is attributed to the colonial experience and how states were formed. Colonizers bound traditional groups together by artificial geographical delineations that did not correspond to how these communities lived and worked. While some states, such as India and Indonesia, have been able to overcome their differences and survive with a multitude of ethnic identities, others have not fared as well. This is particularly evident in sub-Saharan Africa, where ethnic differences are exacerbated by other factors, such as the severe lack of basic necessities that pushes groups to rebel against one another.

Tensions have driven violent behavior in the Democratic Republic of the Congo (DRC) and its neighbor, Rwanda, in central Africa. These countries demonstrate the disasters of the colonial experience and the challenges exacerbated by cultural differences in the effort to unite the people under one flag. The Congo area was one of the first places in sub-Saharan Africa to be visited by the Western world. It was ruled by tribal leaders who led kingdoms in low-lying, mineral-rich lands. The Europeans would use this fertile ground for not only the minerals but also the human potential it represented in the form of slaves. In 1885, European powers met and divided their holdings in Africa, giving a major portion of the land to Belgium and, specifically, King Leopold II.[16] Leopold went on to use the land as his personal fiefdom and imposed brutal law on the native people to achieve his economic ends. He divided the country and posted European officials throughout to assure compliance with his demands.

In literature, the depravity of the crimes committed under Leopold's reign are captured by Joseph Conrad's classic novel *The Heart of Darkness*. Written in the early part of the twentieth century, it is based on the brutal actions of Europeans in the Congo. Director

Francis Ford Coppola adapted the book to reflect the violence of the Vietnam War in his 1979 blockbuster *Apocalypse Now*. The film's central character, renegade US military officer Walter E. Kurtz, was styled after one of the most notorious European officials in the Congo, Leon Rom, who made the villagers his personal slaves, cutting off the heads of those who did not obey and displaying them on his property.

The atrocities were so great that Belgium offered to buy the Congo back from Leopold in 1908. It reverted to a Belgian colony, and for the next several years, the Congo enjoyed an uneasy peace and successful economic development. But long-simmering ethnic divisions began to boil after the Congo declared independence from Belgium in 1960. Within a few years, these divisions would spill over into a series of conflicts that persist today.

Complicating the situation were both Hutu and Tutsi Rwandans brought into the Congo by the Belgians to meet labor needs and ease demographic pressure in their home country. They changed the face of the Congo while exacerbating longstanding tensions among the various ethnic groups. The Belgians favored the minority Tutsis, whom they considered genetically superior, due to their larger skull size and lighter skin, relying on the "science" of eugenics—a now discredited practice that stemmed from the Darwinian notion of survival of the fittest. Tutsis were given preferential treatment and dominated the government. In the early 1960s, both countries gained independence from Belgium, but ethnic tensions remained. In Rwanda, decades of delicate political balancing fell apart in 1994 as the Hutus rose up against the minority Tutsis. It is estimated that up to 800,000 people were murdered in just four months. Almost 1.5 million more fled into the Congo, creating large refugee camps that still exist.[17]

Even today, the tensions from both ethnic unrest and a rising refugee population continue to jeopardize the future of the DRC. The delay of elections by President Kabila from 2016 to 2017 has contributed to this continuing instability. One group of those fleeing to the DRC has included refugees from the Lord's Resistance Army (LRA) of Uganda. The virally popular video *KONY 2012*, made by the nonprofit Invisible Children organization, depicts the violence of the LRA and its recruitment of child soldiers. The leader of this army, Joseph Kony, claimed he has a spiritual mission to "purify" the people of Uganda. For the most part, his mission is simply to perpetuate his group, and as a result, his activities have crossed into several regions in central Africa, including the DRC and, more recently, the chaotic South Sudan. While his immediate supporters have faced criminal proceedings at the International Criminal Court in the Netherlands, Kony remains elusive, with just a small band of approximately 200 fighters. Former commanders who have defected have led an effort with American and Ugandan Special Forces to find Kony and destroy the remains of the LRA.[18] The former US ambassador to the United Nations (UN), Samantha Power, suggested that the actions of Boko Haram and their abduction of more than 200 Nigerian schoolgirls in 2014 was inspired by the "monstrous tactics" of the LRA.[19]

Fragile States

Under extreme pressure both politically and economically, nation-states have frequently been destroyed by the turmoil of ethnic conflict. While global conflict on a grand scale has diminished since the Cold War ended, ethnic conflict has become so prevalent that the World Bank estimates that 2 billion people live in countries affected by fragility, conflict, and violence (FCV).[20] South Sudan and the DRC are two of ten nation-states on a list of fragile states and states likely to fail. **Fragile states** are nation-states whose governments can no longer provide political, economic, and social stability.

Two former US government officials, Gerald Helman and Steven Ratner, were the first to use the term *failed states,* now referred to as *fragile states*. They argue that the commitment to self-determination that was an important part of the UN charter adopted at the end of World War II, along with the effort to move beyond colonial relationships, contributed to

fragile states nation-states whose governments can no longer provide political, economic, and social stability

This photo shows a campaign sign displayed by the ruling All Progressives Congress (APC) to show its readiness to defeat Boko Haram Islamists in southwest Nigeria.

a proliferation of states.[21] Many achieved independence without the requisite infrastructure to support it. While some survived on Cold War infusions of cash from the United States and the Soviet Union as a way to preserve their respective spheres of influence, money was not enough. For example, oil-rich Angola found itself in the crosshairs in the mid-1970s as both East and West sought access to its resources. In the post–Cold War era, as the Soviet Union broke up and the United States cut back on international support, these states were particularly challenged to survive.

The Fragile States Index, developed by the Fund for Peace, ranks states on twelve indicators required for stability. The 2017 index included 178 states. Table 9.3 delineates the indicators and the ten most fragile states. The closer each score is to ten, the less stable the state is for that indicator. South Sudan and Somalia are at the top of the list, followed by the Central African Republic (CAR), Yemen, Sudan, Syria, the Democratic Republic of the Congo (DRC), Chad, Afghanistan, and Iraq. As the index demonstrates, population pressures, both from migrations into the country and from people fleeing uncertainty, contribute to the instability of these states. Uneven economic development and the general social decline that accompanies it are also factors. The result is that the governing bodies have no legitimacy; they are not able to provide public services or safety to their people. Human rights abuses abound, external intervention is more likely, and those who have the potential to govern—the elites—cannot agree.

The pursuit of political power has frequently intensified ethnic, clan, and tribal differences. In Zimbabwe, for example, deep divisions remain between the dominant Shona tribe and the minority Ndebele (see Map 9.2). The two groups united in their pursuit of

MAP 9.2 ● Shona and Ndebele Tribal Lands

TABLE 9.3 ● Fragile States Index Data, 2017

	Rank	Total	Security Apparatus	Factionalized Elites	Group Grievance	Economic Decline	Uneven Economic Development	Human Flight and Brain Drain	State Legitimacy	Public Services	Human Rights and Rule of Law	Demographic Pressures	Refugees and IDPs	External Intervention
South Sudan	1st	113.9	10.0	9.7	9.7	10.0	8.9	6.4	10.0	10.0	9.5	9.9	10.0	9.8
Somalia	2nd	113.4	9.4	10.0	8.9	8.9	9.3	9.8	9.3	9.0	9.5	10.0	10.0	9.3
CAR	3rd	112.6	9.0	9.7	9.1	9.1	10.0	7.5	9.7	10.0	9.7	9.0	10.0	9.8
Yemen	4th	111.1	9.8	9.5	9.3	9.3	8.2	7.3	9.7	9.6	9.7	9.3	9.4	10.0
Sudan	5th	110.6	9.0	9.7	10.0	8.5	7.4	8.9	9.8	8.9	9.6	9.3	9.8	9.7
Syria	6th	110.6	9.8	9.9	9.8	8.1	7.7	8.4	9.9	9.2	9.8	8.2	9.8	10.0
DRC	7th	110.0	9.0	9.8	10.0	8.4	8.4	6.6	9.6	9.5	9.8	9.4	10.0	9.5
Chad	8th	109.4	9.4	9.8	8.0	8.5	9.1	8.8	9.1	9.7	9.1	10.0	9.6	8.3
Afghanistan	9th	107.3	10.0	8.6	8.4	8.3	7.5	8.2	9.1	9.9	8.5	9.3	9.8	9.7
Iraq	10th	105.4	10.0	9.6	9.6	6.6	7.3	7.7	9.5	8.2	8.7	8.6	9.9	9.7

Source: The Fund for Peace, Failed States Index, 2017, http://fundforpeace.org/fsi/data.

UNDERSTANDING CROSS-BORDER CONFLICT

HOW CAN INTERNATIONAL STUDIES HELP?

South Sudan: Will the World's Newest Country Survive?

South Sudan was established in 2011 after breaking away from Sudan following a protracted civil war fueled by religious and ethnic divisions (see Map 9.3). The creation of the country, larger than Spain and Portugal combined, brought together former rebels who had fought against one another. The many years of fighting were not easy to overcome and left the country well armed. In December 2013, a civil war broke out when the president of the country, Salva Kiir, a member of the country's larger Dinka ethnic group, accused his deputy, Riek Machar, from the Nuer ethnic group, of an attempted power grab and fired him.

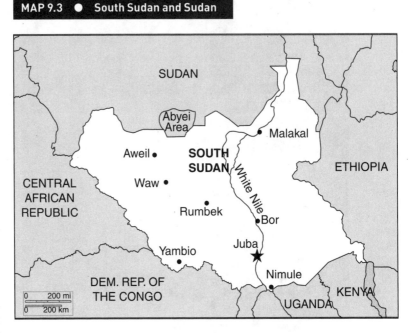

MAP 9.3   ●   South Sudan and Sudan

Despite efforts to broker a peace, these actions divided the army into two factions that have taken the country into chaos. There are extensive oil reserves in South Sudan that account for the majority of the government's revenues, and both sides want control of them. The UN Human Rights Council released a report in February 2017 that found that South Sudan has the largest number of refugees fleeing in Africa, with 1.5 million living outside the country. Of those, 87 percent are women and children, with as many as 36,000 children who are on their own. Within the country, an additional 2 million are internally displaced. The lack of food has reached desperate proportions, with an estimated 47 percent of the population affected, and cholera continues to plague those remaining. The UN has troops on the ground but has not been able to contain the violence due to the size of the country, the lack of infrastructure, and a rainy season that can last up to eight months. The UN has also sought aid from international donors to address the impending humanitarian crisis, but these efforts have been limited in their effect as aid workers have become victims of the ongoing conflict. In 2016, 831 humanitarian access incidents were reported, which included

assaults, ambushes, and armed attacks on workers. These tragedies have led many to conclude that South Sudan may be another failed state.

What is the role of crossing borders in resolving this conflict? How can the cross-disciplinary focus of international studies help?

Questions

- What is the role of geography in this growing crisis?

- What are the political motives behind the leadership dispute?

- What are the economic stakes underlying the conflict?

- What role do social and cultural factors play?

- Can the international community offer any solution?

Source: Office of the United Nations High Commissioner for Human Rights (OHCHR), "Commission on Human Rights in South Sudan," accessed August 21, 2017, http://www.ohchr.org/EN/HRBodies/HRC/CoHSouthSudan/Pages/Index.aspx.

independence, but when faced with sharing power, their differences became more important. Moreover, those who were able to secure power were more concerned with their own personal interests than stability for all. As a result, the state has spun into a downward spiral that has left it as one of the poorest countries in Africa today.

Zimbabwe was formerly part of the larger British colony of Rhodesia; its move for independence was motivated by both racial and ethnic factors. A white minority who declared themselves independent from Great Britain in 1965 initially ruled the country. They were pressured to hold free elections in 1979 by the indigenous majority, and in 1980, current leader Robert Mugabe was elected.[22] Mugabe, from the majority Shona tribe, redistributed the lands previously owned by the white farmers, suppressed the other major ethnic group, the Ndebele, and generally destroyed the country. Corruption, economic mismanagement, and his continued instigation of racial antagonism have marred his leadership. Despite efforts to share power with opposition leader Morgan Tsvangirai, who comes from the Ndebele tribe and previously served as prime minister, the country remains conflicted as Mugabe (age 93 in 2017) continues to hold tightly to power through violence and intimidation by forces loyal to him.

At the extreme, other countries have responded to these types of tensions by simply dividing into separate states. For example, Sudan moved to split into two parts completely, driven by religious differences between the dominant Muslim population to the north and the non-Muslim groups in the south, despite peacekeeping efforts by the UN. Following many years of conflict, South Sudan was recognized as an independent state in July 2011 by the UN. The leader of northern Sudan, Omar al-Bashir, an accused war criminal for the years in which his government engaged in the massacre in the Darfur region, did not accept this division. (See the "Understanding Cross-Border Conflict" feature for more on the challenges faced by this new country.) Some question whether a similar solution will be inevitable in Iraq, as it also remains divided by religious and ethnic differences. The actions of ISIS and its efforts to create an Islamic state that crosses both Iraqi and Syrian borders have furthered divided the country. Will the various groups strive for peaceful coexistence or break into separate states? This is a particularly sensitive case for the Sunni Muslims and the Kurdish ethnic group who have been caught in the crossfire.

South Sudanese refugees fill water jugs at the Al-Nimir refugee camp in Sudan's east Darfur on June 20, 2017. About 400,000 South Sudanese have arrived in Sudan since war erupted in the world's youngest country, according to UNHCR. About 50 percent of them live across ten camps in Sudan, while the rest are scattered in cities and towns.

What Can Be Done?

The challenges created when cultures clash are not easily solved. An initial step toward ending conflict is to recognize that culture and human identity underlie both the problems and their solutions. The early development of languages, practices, and other aspects of the world's diverse cultures was a product of the isolation of groups of people from one another. It is not surprising, then, that a degree of cultural fusion has occurred as transportation and communications have improved, bringing people of various societies into ever more frequent contact. Global cultural differences have decreased substantially since the 1960s in many meaningful ways. Globalization is contributing to these connections as many see themselves in a **multicultural** light, where they relate to several cultural or ethnic identities. The coexistence of different groups, however, is still very much an issue.

multicultural preserving, identifying with, or relating to several cultural or ethnic identities

While religious differences are more readily understood in today's interconnected world, a key question is whether they can coexist. In the United Kingdom, the government allows local sharia councils to rule on Muslim family issues. For example, a Muslim woman may be one of several wives not legally recognized by British law, so she cannot get a civil divorce. The sharia council can grant her a religious divorce, providing for some type of financial restitution and the freedom to marry again.[23] The number of these councils has grown significantly in Great Britain, to around 100 by some estimates; they provide a much-needed service for new immigrants who find themselves and their relationships outside the realm of the official courts.[24] The Law Society of England has drawn up guidelines for lawyers (solicitors) to follow when writing wills to be "sharia compliant" and to be recognized in the official courts.[25] There continues to be some concern that these practices are creating a parallel legal system; however, proponents argue that the procedures perform an important function.

transitional justice the many different types of judicial and nonjudicial actions used to address human rights abuses

Transitional justice offers a way to overcome crimes that have ripped countries apart due to ethnic and religious conflict. It reflects the many different types of judicial and non-judicial actions used to address the fallout that countries must deal with following broad human rights abuses. Formal actions have included criminal trials of some of the most reviled leaders through the International Criminal Court (ICC), which will be introduced in Chapter 10.

An informal way in which ethnic conflicts are moving toward resolution is the development of **truth and reconciliation commissions**. These groups bring together those who have committed the most heinous crimes against one another and seek to develop an understanding that will allow them to let go of their hatred. The effort began in Latin America in the 1980s to address the crimes of military dictators. These commissions have since moved on to South Africa and Rwanda. The Truth and Reconciliation Commission of South Africa formed in 1995 and was the first such commission to include the concept of reconciliation in its mandate.

truth and reconciliation commissions groups formed to bring together those who have suffered under ethnic conflict to resolve their differences and move forward

In Rwanda, these efforts have been very active through a process called **gacaca**, or "justice on the grass."[26] Built on practices that predate the colonial experience, gacaca trials allow people to learn more about what happened to their relatives and provide a framework for healing. More than 2 million people were tried before 12,000 of these community-based courts between 2001 and 2012.[27] The process has now been discontinued, and there is mixed reaction on its successes, due to the political nature of the trials and the types of cases covered.[28] Nevertheless, it remains a model of hope for resolving conflict at the local level.

gacaca an effort in Rwanda dating back to precolonial times when differences were addressed informally through "justice on the grass" to bring healing

The fact remains that people are crossing new borders every day and constantly refining their individual and collective identity. Where your ancestors came from meant something in the past and still matters today. However, the diffusion of cultural practices and accelerated migration are affecting how people define themselves. This definition is becoming less tied to a particular physical space. New ways of interacting with one another are needed that recognize our similarities while appreciating our differences. Former UN secretary-general Kofi Annan observed this in his 2001 Nobel Prize lecture:

Evelyn Hockstein/MCT/MCT via Getty Images.

Jean Claude Gassira, age thirty-eight, stands up to an accusation at a gacaca trial.

People of different religions and cultures live side by side in almost every part of the world, and most of us have overlapping identities, which unite us with very different groups. We can love what we are, without hating what—and who—we are not. We can thrive in our own tradition, even as we learn from others, and come to respect their teachings.[29]

The ability to work together requires new forms of cooperation that transcend traditional borders. Both formal and informal bodies may be called upon to fulfill this role but will require the respect and adherence of the participants to be successful.

Key Concepts

ethnic cleansing 210
ethnic conflict 214
fragile states 217
gacaca 222
genocide 210

migration 210
multicultural 221
sharia law 211
Shia 210
Sunni 210

transitional justice 222
truth and reconciliation
 commissions 222

To Learn More

Books and Other Print Media

Chinua Achebe, *Things Fall Apart* (Portsmouth, NH: Heinemann Educational, 1996).

This classic by Chinua Achebe explores life in a Nigerian village as European colonialists arrive, come to power, and ultimately forever change the social order. Achebe paints a troubled picture of precolonial Nigerian culture on the cusp of its destruction.

Julian Borger, *The Butcher's Trail: How the Search for Balkan War Criminals Became the World's Most Successful Manhunt* (New York: Other Press, 2016).

This is the story of how the perpetrators of Balkan war crimes were captured by an incredible manhunt that took fourteen years.

Joseph Conrad, *Heart of Darkness* (Mineola, NY: Dover, 1990).

This novella, which is Joseph Conrad's most famous work, was first published in 1899 and exposes the darker side of colonization and the cruelty with which the Europeans treated native Africans.

John Esposito, *Unholy War: Terror in the Name of Islam* (New York: Oxford University Press, 2003).

Written in the wake of the 9/11 terrorist attacks, this book offers a solid historical and philosophical account of Islam, jihad, and terrorism.

Adam Hochschild, *King Leopold's Ghost: A Story of Greed, Terror, and Heroism in Colonial Africa* (Boston: Mariner Books, 1999).

This volume details the pursuit of colonial lands by King Leopold II of Belgium, his reign of terror over what are now the DRC and the Republic of the Congo, and its lasting aftermath.

Paul Hopper, *Understanding Cultural Globalization* (Cambridge, UK: Polity Press, 2007).

Paul Hopper explores the various cultural issues brought on by globalization and introduces new critical ways of examining culture.

Latifa, *My Forbidden Face: Growing Up Under the Taliban: A Young Woman's Story* (New York: Miramax Books, 2003).

Latifa recounts her experiences as a young woman growing up in Afghanistan when the Taliban took over, denying the people of Afghanistan basic rights and freedoms and spreading fear.

Dele Olowu and Paulos Chanie, eds. *State Fragility and State Building in Africa: Cases form Eastern and Southern Africa* (Switzerland: Springer International Publishing, 2016).

This book provides several case studies from across Sub-Saharan Africa that have struggled with state fragility and documents their efforts to overcome that status.

Clara Ramirez-Barat and Roger Duthie, eds. *Transitional Justice and Education: Learning Peace* (New York: Social Science Research Council, 2016).

This book from the Social Science Research Council reports the findings of a research project on the relationship of transitional justice and education toward promoting peace.

Malala Yousafzai with Christina Lamb, *I Am Malala: The Girl Who Stood Up for Education and Was Shot by the Taliban* (New York: Little, Brown, 2013).

Malala Yousafzai tells her story in the first person, from her early life in the Swat Valley of Pakistan through her subsequent attack by the Taliban and where she finds herself today.

Websites

BBC, "Religions," www.bbc.co.uk/religion/religions

This website, produced by the BBC, provides an overview of major religions in the world today.

Fragile States Index, http://fundforpeace.org/fsi

The Fund for Peace, a sustainable security nonprofit, publishes the Fragile States Index annually. On the interactive website version, users can explore the world's states and the fund's indicators.

International Rescue Committee (IRC), www.rescue.org

The IRC is an international relief organization that aids people impacted by humanitarian crises across the world.

United Nations High Commissioner for Refugees (UNHCR), www.unhcr.org

The UNHCR was established by the UN General Assembly in 1950 to assist refugees around the world.

Women's Refugee Committee (WRC), http://womens refugeecommission.org/about

A branch of the IRC, the WRC advocates for refugees and internally displaced women and children.

Videos

Apocalypse Now (1979)

This Vietnam War–era movie, based loosely on Joseph Conrad's *Heart of Darkness*, illustrates the psychological damage that can be inflicted by war.

The Devil Came on Horseback (2007)

Based on the book by Brian Steidle, this documentary tells the story of Steidle and his time working for the African Union (AU) as a photographer in Darfur.

Hotel Rwanda (2004)

This is the true story of a hotel manager who offered shelter to refugees during the massacre that occurred in 1994.

KONY 2012 (2012)

A short film created by the group Invisible Children, *KONY 2012* aims to inform the public of the war crimes perpetuated by Uganda's Joseph Kony and the LRA.

My Neighbor My Killer (2009)

This documentary focuses on the process of the gacaca courts, a citizen-based justice system that was put in place in Rwanda after the genocide.

"The Path to Ending Ethnic Conflicts" (TEDGlobal, 2010)

Civil wars and ethnic conflicts have brought incredible suffering, but in the last twenty years, this has decreased. In this talk, Stefan Wolff explains that leadership, diplomacy, and institutional design are our three most effective weapons in waging peace.

Seoul Train (2005)

Seoul Train is a critically acclaimed documentary about North Korean defectors seeking freedom by escaping into China (www.pbs.org/independentlens/seoultrain).

United Nations High Commissioner for Refugees (UNHCR) videos, www.youtube.com/user/unhcr

The UNHCR YouTube channel features hundreds of videos covering just as many topics.

War Don Don (2010)

This documentary film tracks the prosecution of Issa Sesay for war crimes before the Special Court for Sierra Leone.

10

Managing the World
Cooperation at the Global Level

In times of insecurity, when people feel uncertain about their future, when anxieties and fears are promoted and exploited by political populists, old-fashioned nationalists or religious fundamentalists, the success of the UN and the international community lies in our common commitment to our common values.

—UN Secretary-General António Guterres, vision statement, April 4, 2016[1]

Learning Objectives

After studying this chapter, you will be able to do the following:

- Define the terms *intergovernmental organization (IGO)* and *nongovernmental organization (NGO)*, and explain their roles in the international system.

- Define *international law*, and outline its historical development.

- Explain the purpose and basic functions of the United Nations (UN).

- Define the concept of interdependence.

- Explain the function of regional organizations.

- Define the concept of civil society.

- Describe the major activities of the International Criminal Court (ICC) and explain the court's relevance.

A s António Guterres took the helm of the United Nations as secretary-general in 2016, his vison statement recognized the critical function of the organization and the difficulties that lay ahead. In addition to what he expressed in the previous quote, he went on to suggest that "the UN is the institutional expression of the international community, the cornerstone of our international system and the key actor of effective multilateralism."[2] The most serious contemporary problems—poverty, disease, human rights, and environmental concerns—are global in nature and cannot be solved by individual countries alone. Guterres argues that the UN is "uniquely placed to connect the dots" to address peace and security, sustainable development, the protection of human rights, and the delivery of humanitarian assistance.

The barriers to cooperation, however, are the very same borders these issues cross. National borders protect states' interests first and foremost. Economic relationships may frequently dictate behavior, especially when the bottom line is emphasized over the public good. Social and cultural barriers may prevent groups and people from working together when the protection of their identity clashes with the need for cooperation. As a result, the world remains divided on many of the critical issues it must face, and its people must identify new ways to manage their relationships.

Historically, the management of states' behavior toward one another has been addressed through **international law** and the creation of international organizations. As the modern state system emerged in the seventeenth century, there was a need to regulate relationships among countries and identify ways to collaborate. International law developed to formalize operating rules that had been based on customary practices. Organizations were formed through written agreements, as treaties were negotiated to serve the greater good. Philosophically, these organizations grew out of the liberal intellectual tradition we explored in regard to political borders in chapter 4, but they were bound by the nation-states that constituted their membership. As a result, nonstate actors have emerged to provide other ways to work across borders.

international law the regulation of relations among sovereign states emerging from customary practices

People unload Syrian Red Crescent trucks carrying humanitarian aid sent by the United Nations (UN) in the opposition-controlled town of Hamuriye in the Eastern Ghouta region of Damascus, Syria, on April 19, 2016.

Yousef Al-Homs/Anadolu Agency/Getty Images.

intergovernmental organizations (IGOs) formal, international public bodies whose members are nation-states

nongovernmental organizations (NGOs) formal, nonprofit, voluntary organizations whose memberships are composed of individuals organized around specific issues or common concerns

supranational entities international organizations that operate beyond the national boundaries of their members' states

Today, international organizations have become influential actors on the world stage. There are two basic types of international organizations: **intergovernmental organizations (IGOs)**, like the UN, whose members are governments or states, and **nongovernmental organizations (NGOs)**, whose members are individuals. IGOs revolve around three common objectives: (1) to provide a means of cooperation for states, (2) to provide a forum in which decisions on cooperation can be reached and the administrative machinery to carry them out, and (3) to provide multiple channels of communication among governments by offering areas of accommodation and easy access when problems arise.[3] In contrast, NGOs provide a means for cooperation among individuals on issues of common concern. Their strength lies in their ability to communicate their interests without being bound by governmental constraints. The creation of these new **supranational entities**—that is, organizations that exist beyond the boundaries of their member states—has grown exponentially since the end of World War II.

This chapter explores the role of international law and organizations in promoting cooperation and providing effective management at the global level. As the world becomes more interdependent, there is a greater role that IGOs and NGOs can play in addressing the problems facing the international system. The need for regulation of many issues across borders and beyond states' interests requires institutional structures that can both address the problems and represent all interests. IGOs and NGOs may be better suited for this job than nation-states alone. They can provide important structures and forums for essential research and information about global problems.

Defining the Global Order: International Law and Organizations

The evolution of international organizations is directly related to the development of international law, as it established the framework within which international organizations operate. Prior to the seventeenth century, customary practices defined the relations between states. They ranged from rules of engagement on the battlefield that respected noncombatants to accepted practices for ships passing on the high seas. At the beginning of the 1600s, however, changes in the European political system prompted the development of international law in tandem with the sovereign state system to create a framework for cooperation. Concurrent with the Thirty Years' War (1618–1648), European thinkers attempted to address the legal responsibilities among states—what principles should guide behavior and how they would be measured. Of critical importance were the writings of Hugo Grotius.

Hugo Grotius was a Dutchman born in 1583; by the age of sixteen, he had become the lawyer for the Dutch East India Trading Company, the largest trading company of its time. When Grotius was about fifteen, an Italian-born professor of civil law at Oxford named Gentilus published a groundbreaking work called *De Jure Belli* (*Laws of War*), which separated international law from ethics and theology—defining international law as a distinct new branch of law. Intrigued by Gentilus's writings, in 1625 Grotius penned his own monumental piece, *De Jure Belli Ac Pacis—On the Law of War and Peace*.

positivism the theory and development of international law based on the practice of states and the conduct of international relations as evidenced by custom or treaties

Grotius rejected the notion that the principles of the law of nature came directly from divine authority; instead, he argued that these principles should come from universal reason. He believed that the customary practices of nations (*jus gentium*, also called *jus voluntarium*) as they related to one another must guide the law. His distinctions would go on to form the basis of **positivism**—the theory and development of international law based on the practice of states and the conduct of international relations as evidenced by custom or treaties. It would take until the nineteenth century for these concepts to influence behavior.

In the "In Their Own Words" excerpt from his *On the Law of War and Peace*, Grotius details his understanding of this critical distinction between natural and human-made law.

Grotius's book was an important contribution to the evolution of the political order that was emerging. Its successful reception was driven by Grotius's prestigious legal background, combined with recognition from his position with the Dutch East India Trading Company. Over time, his work would be regarded as the first comprehensive basic treatise on international law. The important distinctions he made and the extent to which they would inform the future meant that Grotius is considered to be the father of modern international law.

IN THEIR OWN WORDS
HUGO GROTIUS

Natural right is the dictate of right reason, shewing the moral turpitude, or moral necessity, of any act from its agreement or disagreement with a rational nature, and consequently that such an act is either forbidden or commanded by God, the author of nature. The actions, upon which such a dictate is given, are either binding or unlawful in themselves, and therefore necessarily understood to be commanded or forbidden by God. This mark distinguishes natural right, not only from human law, but from the law, which God himself has been pleased to reveal, called, by some, the voluntary divine right, which does not command or forbid things in themselves either binding or unlawful, but makes them unlawful by its prohibition, and binding by its command.[4]

The Creation of International Organizations

Not long after Grotius's writings, in 1648, a system of independent states developed that depended on a balance of power to keep the peace. At the outset, these new states relied on the relationships that had provided kingdoms with protection for generations: alliances. States were able to maintain a balance of power through the use of force in conjunction with their allies against their enemies. A broader desire for peace to be maintained through a more formal cooperative structure was recognized, and the **Concert of Europe** was formed in 1815. This collaborative group was created to enforce decisions that had been reached at the Congress of Vienna, where the European powers that had defeated Napoleon—Russia, Prussia, Britain, and Austria—gathered to negotiate the peace. The concert formalized the alliances that emerged from the Congress, served as an enforcement mechanism for the agreements that had been made, and sought to promote a cooperative international environment. It hobbled along until the 1870s, undermined early on by the nationalistic tendencies of the member parties.

Concert of Europe a formal collaborative group formed in 1815 to enforce the decisions reached at the Congress of Vienna

A second effort at international cooperation came with the International Peace Conferences of 1899 and 1907. Convened by Russia at the request of Tsar Nicholas II, twenty-six governments gathered to meet in the political capital of the Netherlands, The Hague, to develop a series of agreements to enforce a broader peace and reduce armaments.[5] Most notably, the First Hague Peace Conference, as it came to be known, created a Permanent Court of Arbitration for resolution of conflict among states. The United States sought to push this body to a world court system at the Second Hague Conference but failed. A third conference was scheduled for 1915 but never met due to the outbreak of World War I.

While the conferences may have failed in their broad objectives, they were successful in the creation of public international unions, the first permanent IGOs that addressed practical areas of exchange—communication, transportation, international trade regulation, and

DeAgostini/Getty Images.

The Peace Palace, shown here, is the seat of the International Court of Justice (ICJ) in The Hague, the Netherlands. The ICJ is one of many international organizations designed to facilitate global cooperation.

Kellogg-Briand Pact a multinational pact that outlawed war as a means of conflict resolution

Atlantic Charter a joint declaration by the United States and Great Britain that detailed the position of the two countries relative to World War II and their goals for postwar peace

standards of weight and measure.[6] World War I made it evident that greater international cooperation was needed for global peace as well. Politically, the origins of modern IGOs came from US president Woodrow Wilson's idealism, the negotiated peace in the Treaty of Versailles, and the creation of the League of Nations. President Wilson recognized the need for a new global order as World War I was coming to an end. He elaborated on this vision in his "Fourteen Points" speech to Congress on January 9, 1918: "A general association of nations must be formed under specific covenants for the purpose of affording mutual guarantees of political independence and territorial integrity to great and small states alike."[7] Wilson believed that the creation of a platform for international cooperation was critical to peace going forward.

The Treaty of Versailles of 1919 that negotiated the peace for World War I included the creation of the League of Nations. From the outset, however, its success was limited by the lack of US participation. Though the idea had come from the US president and was included in the peace pact, the US Senate refused to ratify the treaty, favoring an isolationist stance. The League of Nations went forward, without the United States, as the first formal international organization to foster the goals of promoting peace and preventing war. It consisted of a council, assembly, and secretariat. An international court, known as the Permanent Court, was separate from the organization. Membership was by invitation, and headquarters were established in Geneva, Switzerland, in November 1920. The first general assembly of the league held that month had representatives from forty-one nations.

Continued global conflict and the United States' failure to join the organization weakened the League of Nations. The United States subsequently tried to lend its support through its backing of the **Kellogg-Briand Pact**. Introduced to the United States in 1927 by Aristide Briand, the French foreign minister, as a proposed treaty between the two countries, US president Calvin Coolidge and secretary of state Frank B. Kellogg wanted to expand its scope as a general pact against war. The final document was signed by fifteen countries in 1928 and subsequently ratified by sixty-two states to outlaw war as a means of conflict resolution.[8] Such assistance was too little, too late for the League of Nations. With no way to enforce Kellogg-Briand, its signatories saw armed aggression by the Japanese in Manchuria and the Italians in Ethiopia, followed by Hitler and the Nazi party's emergence in Germany in the early 1930s. The actions of these belligerent states ultimately undermined both the League of Nations and the Kellogg-Briand Pact.

The outbreak of World War II and the early cooperation between the United States and Great Britain resulted in the creation of the **Atlantic Charter**. A joint declaration detailing the position of the two countries regarding the growing conflict and a desire for peace, it laid the foundation for the conception of the UN following the end of the war. The United States realized that its strategy of disengagement had failed it between the world wars and that the evolving world order after World War II would require it to take an active role. A series of meetings among the Allies, beginning in 1942 and culminating in San Francisco in 1945, led to the creation of the United Nations.

The United Nations

While aspirations were high for the newly formed United Nations, the political nature of the international system after World War II limited the UN and frustrated the efforts of founding secretary-general Trygve Lie of Norway (1946–1952). In response to the political order that emerged, as well as compromises made in the finalization of the founding UN Charter, five states—the United States, United Kingdom, France, China, and Russia—received special status as permanent members of the Security Council, the policymaking body of the UN (see Figure 10.1). Ten additional seats were allocated for nonpermanent members that represent geographical diversity and rotate every two years. The permanent members have a veto power that ensures that any policy considered by the group that is not in a country's interest can be overridden by a negative vote. The Security Council requires nine affirmative votes to take action, and the Big Five permanent members have frequently used their veto power—the Soviet Union especially as the Cold War evolved. It used its veto power seventy-nine times in the first ten years of the UN's existence, compared to France, which used it twice, and China, which used it only once.[9]

UN secretary-general Dag Hammarskjöld of Sweden (1953–1961) established the character of the organization by professionalizing the Secretariat—the body that runs the UN day-to-day business under the secretary-general's stewardship—and moving the UN forward as an institution of peace. Known for his "quiet diplomacy," Hammarskjöld fostered the idea of UN presence as a method of preventing conflict. During his second five-year term, to which the General Assembly had appointed him unanimously, he died in a plane crash while on a diplomatic mission in Africa. He was posthumously awarded the Nobel Peace Prize in 1961 for his contributions.

The General Assembly is the representative body of the UN. All states that have ratified the UN Convention are members of this body. The General Assembly supervises UN activities, can decide on financial matters, and elects the nonpermanent members of the Security Council and the secretary-general, with the recommendation of the Security Council. It may also play a role in amending or revising the charter. Despite its broad membership, the General Assembly lacks policymaking power. Only the Security Council has this authority. Nevertheless, the UN remains the most universal forum for the consideration of critical issues confronting the global system today.

Other organs of the UN include the Economic and Social Council (ECOSOC), which prepares studies and reports on economic and social concerns. ECOSOC consists of fifty-four members, elected by the General Assembly for three-year terms, with eighteen national members elected each year. Their influence is broadly felt through their administration of the majority of the human and financial resources of the UN, which include fourteen specialized agencies, eight functional commissions, and five regional commissions.[10] The following list of the commissions illustrates their breadth and depth:[11]

ECOSOC Functional Commissions

- Statistical Commission
- Commission on Population and Development
- Commission for Social Development
- Commission on the Status of Women
- Commission on Narcotic Drugs
- Commission on Crime Prevention and Criminal Justice
- Commission on Science and Technology for Development
- United Nations Forum on Forests

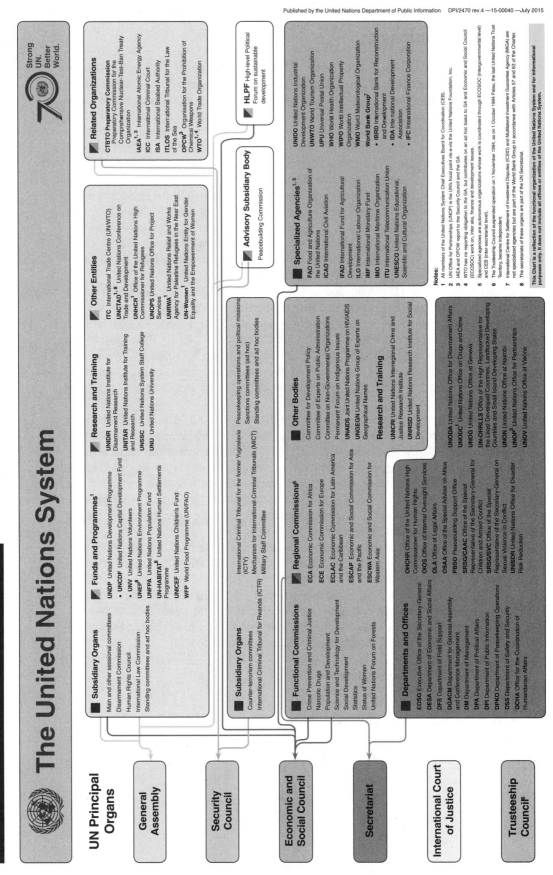

Published by the United Nations Department of Public Information   DPI/2470 rev.4 —15-00040 —July 2015

FIGURE 10.1 ● United Nations Organizational Chart

The United Nations System

70 Strong UN. Better World.

UN Principal Organs

General Assembly

Security Council

Economic and Social Council

Secretariat

International Court of Justice

Trusteeship Council[6]

■ Subsidiary Organs

Main and other sessional committees
Disarmament Commission
Human Rights Council
International Law Commission
Standing committees and ad hoc bodies

■ Funds and Programmes[1]

UNDP United Nations Development Programme
 • UNCDF United Nations Capital Development Fund
 • UNV United Nations Volunteers
UNEP[6] United Nations Environment Programme
UNFPA United Nations Population Fund
UN-HABITAT[6] United Nations Human Settlements Programme
UNICEF United Nations Children's Fund
WFP World Food Programme (UN/FAO)

■ Research and Training

UNIDIR United Nations Institute for Disarmament Research
UNITAR United Nations Institute for Training and Research
UNSSC United Nations System Staff College
UNU United Nations University

■ Other Entities

ITC International Trade Centre (UN/WTO)
UNCTAD[1, 8] United Nations Conference on Trade and Development
UNHCR[1] Office of the United Nations High Commissioner for Refugees
UNOPS United Nations Office for Project Services
UNRWA[1] United Nations Relief and Works Agency for Palestine Refugees in the Near East
UN-Women United Nations Entity for Gender Equality and the Empowerment of Women

---

■ Subsidiary Organs

Counter-terrorism committees
International Criminal Tribunal for Rwanda (ICTR)
International Criminal Tribunal for the former Yugoslavia (ICTY)
Mechanism for International Criminal Tribunals (MICT)
Military Staff Committee
Peacekeeping operations and political missions
Sanctions committees (ad hoc)
Standing committees and ad hoc bodies

■ Advisory Subsidiary Body

Peacebuilding Commission

■ Functional Commissions

Crime Prevention and Criminal Justice
Narcotic Drugs
Population and Development
Science and Technology for Development
Social Development
Statistics
Status of Women
United Nations Forum on Forests

■ Regional Commissions[8]

ECA Economic Commission for Africa
ECE Economic Commission for Europe
ECLAC Economic Commission for Latin America and the Caribbean
ESCAP Economic and Social Commission for Asia and the Pacific
ESCWA Economic and Social Commission for Western Asia

■ Other Bodies

Committee for Development Policy
Committee of Experts on Public Administration
Committee on Non-Governmental Organizations
Permanent Forum on Indigenous Issues
UNAIDS Joint United Nations Programme on HIV/AIDS
UNGEGN United Nations Group of Experts on Geographical Names

Research and Training

UNICRI United Nations Interregional Crime and Justice Research Institute
UNRISD United Nations Research Institute for Social Development

---

■ Departments and Offices

EOSG Executive Office of the Secretary-General
DESA Department of Economic and Social Affairs
DFS Department of Field Support
DGACM Department for General Assembly and Conference Management
DM Department of Management
DPA Department of Political Affairs
DPI Department of Public Information
DPKO Department of Peacekeeping Operations
DSS Department of Safety and Security
OCHA Office for the Coordination of Humanitarian Affairs

OHCHR Office of the United Nations High Commissioner for Human Rights
OIOS Office of Internal Oversight Services
OLA Office of Legal Affairs
OSAA Office of the Special Adviser on Africa
PBSO Peacebuilding Support Office
SRSG/CAAC Office of the Special Representative of the Secretary-General for Children and Armed Conflict
SRSG/SVC Office of the Special Representative of the Secretary-General on Sexual Violence in Conflict
UNISDR United Nations Office for Disaster Risk Reduction

UNODA United Nations Office for Disarmament Affairs
UNODC[1] United Nations Office on Drugs and Crime
UNOG United Nations Office at Geneva
UN-OHRLLS Office of the High Representative for the Least Developed Countries, Landlocked Developing Countries and Small Island Developing States
UNON United Nations Office at Nairobi
UNOP[2] United Nations Office for Partnerships
UNOV United Nations Office at Vienna

■ Related Organizations

CTBTO Preparatory Commission Preparatory Commission for the Comprehensive Nuclear-Test-Ban Treaty Organization
IAEA[1, 3] International Atomic Energy Agency
ICC International Criminal Court
ISA International Seabed Authority
ITLOS International Tribunal for the Law of the Sea
OPCW[3] Organisation for the Prohibition of Chemical Weapons
WTO[1, 4] World Trade Organization

■ HLPF High-level Political Forum on sustainable development

■ Specialized Agencies[1, 5]

FAO Food and Agriculture Organization of the United Nations
ICAO International Civil Aviation
IFAD International Fund for Agricultural Development
ILO International Labour Organization
IMF International Monetary Fund
IMO International Maritime Organization
ITU International Telecommunication Union
UNESCO United Nations Educational, Scientific and Cultural Organization
UNIDO United Nations Industrial Development Organization
UNWTO World Tourism Organization
UPU Universal Postal Union
WHO World Health Organization
WIPO World Intellectual Property Organization
WMO World Meteorological Organization
World Bank Group[7]
 • IBRD International Bank for Reconstruction and Development
 • IDA International Development Association
 • IFC International Finance Corporation

Notes:

1 All members of the United Nations System Chief Executives Board for Coordination (CEB).
2 UN Office for Partnerships (UNOP) is the UN's focal point vis-à-vis the United Nations Foundation, Inc.
3 IAEA and OPCW report to the Security Council and the GA.
4 WTO has no reporting obligation to the GA, but contributes on an ad hoc basis to GA and Economic and Social Council (ECOSOC) work on, inter alia, finance and development issues.
5 Specialized agencies are autonomous organizations whose work is coordinated through ECOSOC (intergovernmental level) and CEB (inter-secretariat level).
6 The Trusteeship Council suspended operation on 1 November 1994, as on 1 October 1994 Palau, the last United Nations Trust Territory, became independent.
7 International Centre for Settlement of Investment Disputes (ICSID) and Multilateral Investment Guarantee Agency (MIGA) are not specialized agencies but are part of the World Bank Group in accordance with Articles 57 and 63 of the Charter.
8 The secretariats of these organs are part of the UN Secretariat.

This Chart is a reflection of the functional organization of the United Nations System and for informational purposes only. It does not include all offices or entities of the United Nations System.

ECOSOC Regional Commissions

- Economic Commission for Africa (ECA)

- Economic and Social Commission for Asia and the Pacific (ESCAP)

- Economic Commission for Europe (ECE)

- Economic Commission for Latin America and the Caribbean (ECLAC)

- Economic and Social Commission for Western Asia (ESCWA)

The International Court of Justice (ICJ) is the legal branch of the UN and is composed of fifteen judges elected by the General Assembly and Security Council for nine-year terms. There cannot be more than one judge from any country. Member states involved in a case must agree to the court's authority before it hears the case. It is also limited in its judgments, as it has no coercive power, such as fines or jail sentences, to enforce its decisions. As a result, it depends on nation-states to voluntarily comply with its rulings. The ICJ pronouncement in the case of *Nicaragua v. the United States* is considered a critical landmark in this regard.[12]

In 1984, Nicaragua came before the ICJ charging the United States with interfering in its internal affairs. Nicaragua's ruling party—the Marxist Sandinistas—estimated that the United States had provided supplies to an opposition force of more than 10,000 troops— the Contras—along Nicaragua's border with Honduras. The Contras were deemed responsible for laying mines in Nicaragua's harbors using materials supplied by the United States. The United States would not agree to the case being heard by the court, but the court went ahead anyway—extending its compulsory jurisdiction, a right the United States had supported since the creation of the ICJ in 1946. The case was considered, and in 1986, the United States was found guilty of violating the sovereignty of Nicaragua. The court ordered that the United States pay reparations of $300 million to Nicaragua. The United States refused to abide by the decision, however, arguing that it did not accept the court's jurisdiction in this case because of its historical relationship with Latin America and Nicaragua specifically. As a result, full compliance with ICJ decisions went from 80 percent in the period of 1946 to 1987 to 60 percent from 1987 to 2004.[13]

In recent years, the ICJ has become much more active as the number of cases it considers has increased significantly. In 2017, the court had seventeen cases pending that ranged from armed activities in the Territory of the Congo (*Democratic Republic of the Congo v. Uganda*) to certain Iranian assets (*Islamic Republic of Iran v. United States of America*).[14] Two of the contentious cases before the court (i.e., cases that must be submitted by states) involved questions of borders: land boundary in the northern part of Isla Portillos (*Costa Rica v. Nicaragua*) and sovereignty over Pedra Branca/Pulau Batu Puteh, Middle Rocks, and South Ledge (Malaysia/Singapore).[15]

Finally, in terms of the organs of the UN, the Trusteeship Council was established to administer trust territories that existed when the UN was created to facilitate their transition to independence. The council's members were the five permanent members of the Security Council. The work of this body from its original charge was completed in 1994. It remains available to meet should a need arise.

Since its origins in the post–World War II period, the UN has grown considerably— from 51 founding members to 193 today. However, the permanent members of the Security Council have resisted expanding their membership. Given their growing influence in the international system politically and economically, Germany and Japan have actively sought this distinction. Brazil and India have also argued for inclusion, based on their increasing global status and geographic location as part of the Global South. Another approach for changing the membership has been to simply expand the number of nonpermanent members of this group. Any of these actions would require amending the UN Charter, which is a very onerous process. Two-thirds of all members of the General Assembly must adopt and ratify the amendment, and all permanent members of the Security Council must be on board. Attaining such a level of comprehensive agreement is highly unlikely.

Interdependence and Regional Intergovernmental Organizations

As the UN emerged from the trials and tribulations of World War II, its most critical objective was peace. Other international organizations that developed were influenced by functional considerations—the need to cooperate on many different levels. These organizations have become more critical as countries find themselves increasingly interdependent. Their reliance on one another, particularly in economic terms, has created new structures to facilitate cooperation. International relations scholars Robert Keohane and Joseph Nye describe this relationship as one of **complex interdependence**, where states have come to realize how sensitive and vulnerable they are in relation to others.[16] In this context, *sensitivity* refers to how quickly changes in one country may affect another, while *vulnerability* explores the range of options available for response and their cost. To strengthen state relationships in this regard, one response has been the creation of regional organizations.

complex interdependence the interdependent relationship that exists between states, such that variation in one state's behavior significantly affects the other state

Regional organizations are composed of nation-states based on their geographical proximity and common interests. Some of the more broad-based associations that have followed from the UN example include the Organization of American States (OAS), the Arab League, the African Union (AU), and the Association of Southeast Asian Nations (ASEAN). The charter of the OAS, the world's oldest regional organization (dating from the First International Conference of American States in 1889 and formalized in 1948), is reflective of the broad objectives of these types of organizations. Article 2 of the OAS Charter identifies the following "essential purposes":

a. To strengthen the peace and security of the continent;

b. To promote and consolidate representative democracy, with due respect for the principle of nonintervention;

c. To prevent possible causes of difficulties and to ensure the pacific settlement of disputes that may arise among the Member States;

d. To provide for common action on the part of those States in the event of aggression;

e. To seek the solution of political, juridical, and economic problems that may arise among them;

f. To promote, by cooperative action, their economic, social, and cultural development;

g. To eradicate extreme poverty, which constitutes an obstacle to the full democratic development of the peoples of the hemisphere; and

h. To achieve an effective limitation of conventional weapons that will make it possible to devote the largest amount of resources to the economic and social development of the Member States.[17]

Similar language can be found in the operating principles of other regional bodies.

Regional organizations have also been created for very specific purposes. These include modern-day alliances, like the North Atlantic Treaty Organization (NATO), which was formed for security purposes after World War II and today includes a broad range of states from both Eastern and Western Europe and the United States. Similarly, economic needs have brought states together; perhaps the best-known organization in this regard is the European Union (EU), introduced in chapter 6.

Through a series of multilateral treaties, the EU has expanded to become a major regional power. It is integrated on multiple levels, including a common passport and currency—the euro. Today, twenty-eight of Europe's forty-nine countries are members of the EU (see Table 10.1), an association of states that has developed its own parliament, laws, and coordinated trade policies. Five countries are candidate members: Albania, Macedonia, Montenegro, Serbia, and Turkey. Their candidacy has forced the EU to look more closely at itself and the practices of its member states. A critical issue has been the extent to which the membership can be more broadly defined. The EU requires member states to adhere to a set of economic policies. There is some concern that these measures are so strict that they deny membership to states that may be fundamentally different culturally from longstanding members of the EU.

Even current member states have questioned the capacity of the organization to sustain necessary levels of cooperation, in light of the difficulties of reconciling divergent national interests. The June 2016 British referendum favoring withdrawal from the EU, Brexit, was sobering. The negotiations will be complicated, but it is anticipated that the

TABLE 10.1 ● European Union Members, 2017

Country	Entry	Country	Entry
Austria	1995	Italy	1957
Belgium	1957	Latvia	2004
Bulgaria	2007	Lithuania	2004
Croatia	2013	Luxembourg	1957
Cyprus	2004	Malta	2004
Czech Republic	2004	Netherlands	1957
Denmark	1973	Poland	2004
Estonia	2004	Portugal	1986
Finland	1995	Romania	2007
France	1957	Slovakia	2004
Germany	1957	Slovenia	2004
Greece	1981	Spain	1986
Hungary	2004	Sweden	1995
Ireland	1973	United Kingdom	1973

Source: European Union, "EU Member Countries," https://europa.eu/european-union/about-eu/countries_en https://europa.eu/european-union/about-eu/countries_en.

actual separation should occur by the summer of 2019.[18] The 2017 French elections raised similar issues as Marine Le Pen, the National Front party leader, ran on a platform of reasserting French nationalism and leaving the EU. Her resounding loss to centrist candidate Emmanuel Macron, who won with 66.1 percent of the vote, has provided some stability.[19] Similar populist movements in other EU member states, including Austria, Germany, Italy, and The Netherlands may have an impact in the future.[20] Despite these challenges, the EU remains the model for economic integration, one not easily duplicated by other regional bodies.

TURNING POINT
JUNE 23, 2016

Brexit

Wiktor Szymanowicz/Barcroft Im/Barcroft Media via Getty Images.

Hundreds of pro-EU supporters gather on Whitehall to protest the process of Britain's leaving the European Union and demonstrate against Prime Minister Theresa May's vision of Brexit, on the first anniversary of the EU referendum, June 23, 2017, in London, England.

What?

On June 23, 2016, voters across the United Kingdom (England, Wales, Scotland, and Northern Ireland) went to the polls to cast their ballots on a referendum calling for their country to leave the EU—Brexit, short for "British exit." While a hotly contested and divisive campaign, the result was not widely anticipated and sent shockwaves across the continent and global financial markets. Adding to the complexity was the breakdown of the vote; while the decision is binding on all parts of the UK, the majority of voters in Scotland and Wales favored remaining in the EU. This fueled speculation that Brexit could impact the future of the UK itself, especially with respect to Scotland, where it reinvigorated support for moving toward independence.

Why?

Some believed that this step was inevitable, as the British have never been entirely comfortable with their

membership and status with the EU since joining the body then known as the European Community in 1973. This was reflected in the decision to opt out of the eurozone, the nineteen-member group that adopted the euro as a common currency in 1999. The more recent concerns that prompted the referendum stemmed from longstanding concerns relating to membership fees and the encompassing nature of EU economic and financial regulations. The passion evident throughout the campaign, however, was driven largely by the EU's expansive immigration policy and pressures to accommodate significant numbers of Syrian refugees. Net migration in the UK stood at 330,000 per year, with 188,000 coming from outside the EU. This raised fundamental questions regarding the future of British sovereignty and identity, which ultimately swayed the outcome of the vote.

How?

Following the referendum, British prime minister David Cameron, who strongly favored remaining in the EU, resigned and was replaced by Theresa May. Ironically, May also supported the pro-EU position but immediately moved forward to lay the foundation for the exit. It will take an estimated two years to complete the rather complex process. In addition to managing the withdrawal, new agreements and arrangements will be necessary across a range of foreign policy, national security, finance, and trade issues as Britain begins to chart its new course. Everyday matters affecting the lives of individual citizens, such as visas to live or work in EU countries, health cards to permit medical care for ill travelers, and the design of automobile license plates, will also require fine tuning.

Will It Make a Difference over Time?

The immediate fallout was substantial. Global financial markets wobbled, many British companies fretted openly about the loss of existing and future markets, the

British currency lost value, and there were dire warnings about the pending implosion of the British economy and the collapse of the European Union. As the shock subsided, reactions moderated, and the focus shifted to the "nuts and bolts" of proceeding with the exit strategy. There is little question that the vote has transformed the futures of Britain and the EU in terms of their orientations, perspectives, outlooks, and policies. The magnitude of these changes is difficult to determine just yet and will be influenced by how well the exit negotiations proceed and by the abilities of both Britain and the EU to adjust internally and externally to the new reality. The process was complicated even further by the political uncertainties in Britain following the snap election in June 2017, which significantly weakened the mandate of the May government.

What Do You Think?

Is this truly a turning point for Britain and the European Union? Will the anticipated effects materialize? Are the parties likely to be strengthened or weakened by the turn of events? To help you get started in framing your views, you might want to take a look at the following resource:

Alex Hunt and Brian Wheeler, "Brexit: All You Need to Know about the UK Leaving the EU," *BBC News*, June 13, 2017, http://www.bbc.com/news/uk-politics-32810887.

Nongovernmental Organizations

When lost boy Valentino Achak Deng, whom we met at the outset of chapter 8, fled civil war–torn Sudan in the late 1980s, he was helped along the way in his journey to the United States by NGOs. Organizations like the International Committee of the Red Cross provided basic necessities for the boys and girls who found their way to refugee camps in Kenya. The International Rescue Committee (IRC) facilitated the relocation of many of these young people to safe havens, with many of them ending up in the United States. Both organizations continue to work closely with refugees of war, famine, and environmental disasters all over the world. Their operations are funded by voluntary contributions from both individuals and countries.

Such NGOs, the other broad type of international organization, are the fastest-growing entities in the world today. Their ability to bring together people driven by common interests on specific issues gives them great flexibility. Frequently, they are best situated to perform some of the functions of IGOs when the IGOs' member states are stymied by their own interests, lack the necessary expertise, or are unable or unwilling to cooperate. Increasingly, the spread of information about events around the world, such as the Syrian crisis, has brought the plight of distant nations into the collective psyche, and it is NGOs that have responded.

The history of NGOs is tied to the development of individual activism on critical issues. Today, we sometimes use the term **civil society** to describe these actors. The World Bank offers a good definition of civil society that is commonly accepted: "the wide array of non-governmental and not-for-profit organizations that have a presence in public life, expressing the interests and values of their members or others, based on ethical, cultural, political, scientific, religious or philanthropic considerations."[21] One of the first international NGOs was the Anti-Slavery Society, which had its origins in England but came to America in 1833 with the founding of the American Anti-Slavery Society in Philadelphia.[22] Its ranks expanded rapidly in the United States, supported by the abolitionist movement, as the group's membership grew to more than 250,000 in just five years.[23] By 1874, there were thirty-two similar organizations with international linkages. Over the next forty years, NGOs grew steadily, with 1,083 reported in 1914 at the outset of World War I.

NGOs developed rapidly in the post–World War II period, as the UN Charter explicitly recognized them as contributing bodies to the work of ECOSOC. As a result, by the mid-1970s, NGOs were significant actors in the field of international development. This trend has continued as the participation by NGOs and, specifically, civil society organizations

civil society
nongovernmental groups and organizations that represent the interests and values of their members in public life

(CSOs) in World Bank–funded projects increased from 21 percent in fiscal year 1990 to an estimated 88 percent in fiscal year 2015.[24] In 2013, the adoption of the World Bank Group Strategy included the Strategic Framework for Mainstreaming Citizen Engagement in World Bank Group–Supported Operations, with the goal of having beneficiary feedback in 100 percent of its financed projects by 2018.

Today, the UN recognizes more than 4,900 NGOs as having consultative status to ECOSOC.[25] This status gives NGOs the ability to participate in UN international conferences on a broad range of issues, such as gender, sustainable development, small arms, and human rights.[26] The UN Education, Scientific and Cultural Organization (UNESCO) uses three criteria to distinguish the different types of NGOs in its civil society network: country or region of origin, field of activity, and organizational type. This last category can include anything from academic groups, such as the American Anthropological Association, to representatives of indigenous people, such as the Aboriginal and Torres Strait Islander Commission from Australia (see Figure 10.2).[27]

FIGURE 10.2 ● Types of Nongovernmental Organizations

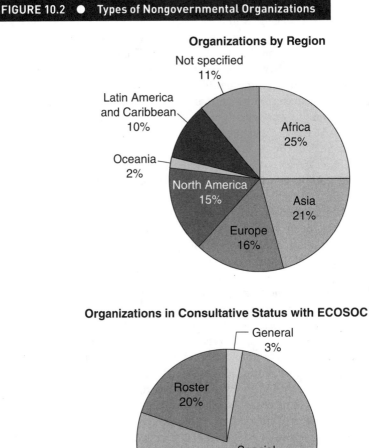

Organizations by Region

Not specified 11%
Latin America and Caribbean 10%
Oceania 2%
North America 15%
Europe 16%
Asia 21%
Africa 25%

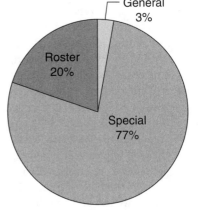

Organizations in Consultative Status with ECOSOC

General 3%
Roster 20%
Special 77%

Fields of Activity

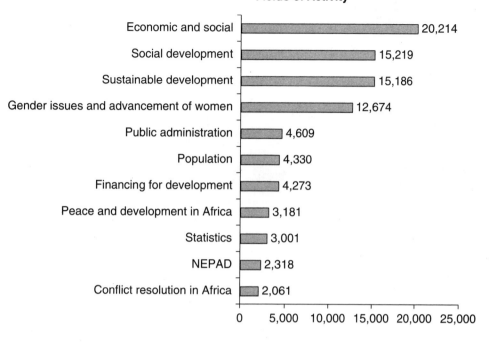

Field	Value
Economic and social	20,214
Social development	15,219
Sustainable development	15,186
Gender issues and advancement of women	12,674
Public administration	4,609
Population	4,330
Financing for development	4,273
Peace and development in Africa	3,181
Statistics	3,001
NEPAD	2,318
Conflict resolution in Africa	2,061

Organization Types

Type	Value
Nongovernmental organization	29,935
Association	2,615
Indigenous peoples organizations	2,529
Academics	1,526
Foundation	1,298
Others	899
Disability, development, and rights organizations	795
Private sector	790
Institution	435
Intergovernmental organization	400
Local government	240
Media	197
Cooperative	142
Open-ended working group on ageing	136
Trade union	100

Source: Information is from United Nations NGO Branch, Department of Economic and Social Affairs, "Integrated Civil Society Organizations System," http://esango.un.org/civilsociety/login.do.

STRINGER/AFP/Getty Images.

Staff from the International Red Cross and from the Syrian Red Crescent are seen in the embattled city of Aleppo as efforts were underway to evacuate rebel fighters and their families from rebel-held areas on December 15, 2016.

We can think about NGOs today in terms of their political advocacy, economic and development activities, environmental actions, and humanitarian interests. An example of a political-advocacy NGO would be Amnesty International. Formed in 1961, it promotes the political freedoms of citizens, regardless of their country's orientation. Its annual report has become an important part of the human rights dialogue. Economic development work is carried out by a broad range of NGOs, from religious-based groups, such as Catholic Relief or Lutheran World Services, to large operations that subcontract with national governments, such as CARE International, which works in more than ninety countries to address global poverty.[28]

Many environmental NGOs are well known, ranging from the World Wildlife Fund, which promotes conservation of nature, to some of the more politically active organizations, such as Greenpeace and the Sea Shepherd Conservation Society. The Sea Shepherd organization's mission to preserve marine wildlife, particularly to prevent the harvesting of whales by Japanese whalers, has been captured in the Animal Planet television series *Whale Wars*. Humanitarian NGOs seek to provide direct services to those in need. For example, Médecins Sans Frontières—Doctors Without Borders—works in more than sixty countries all over the world in response to health threats from violence, poor medical care, and natural disasters (see Map 10.1).

The Evolution of the United Nations and Civil Society

The UN was formed in response to the horrific tragedies of World War II, which saw tremendous loss of life and territorial devastation; its founding premise was to promote peace. In keeping with its organizing principles, its objective in intervening in conflict was simply to maintain and enforce agreements among previously warring parties. Forces would be formed with soldiers from member states to act as peacekeepers. The famous blue helmets they would wear and the clear labeling of their support vehicles was to keep them out of harm's way as they provided an important service. In the post–Cold War world, however, the UN has been called upon for a broader mission—to be a peacemaker. In the early 1990s, UN peacekeeping forces frequently found themselves in positions that required armed intervention, a response well outside the mandate of their mission; yet the circumstances demanded more aggressive action, if only for the survival of the troops deployed. For example, with the breakup of the Soviet Union and Yugoslavia, new states sought assistance from the UN to protect their independence. In 2017, the UN had sixteen peacekeeping missions throughout the world, as shown in Map 10.2. As of March 31, 2017, 124 countries contributed military and police personnel to support a peacekeeping workforce consisting of 84,533 troops and military observers, 11,944 police, 4,784 international civilian personnel, 9,474 local civilian staff, and 1,577 UN volunteers.[29]

In 1992, the UN responded to the need to enhance its organizational capabilities in this area by creating the Department of Political Affairs (UNDPA) to coordinate peacemaking and preventive diplomacy. Headed by the undersecretary-general for political affairs, today this organization has more than 250 staff at UN headquarters in New York and supervises more than 1,700 personnel in Africa, Asia, and the Middle East. The activities

MAP 10.1 ● **Doctors Without Borders/Médecins Sans Frontières Operations**

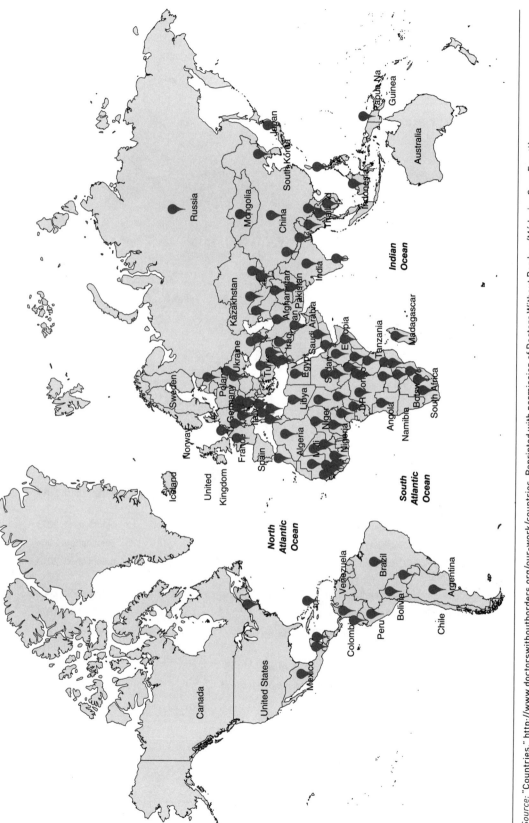

Source: "Countries," http://www.doctorswithoutborders.org/our-work/countries. Reprinted with permission of Doctors Without Borders/Médecins Sans Frontières.

In some sixty countries around the world, Médecins Sans Frontières (MSF) saves lives by providing medical aid where it is needed most—in armed conflicts, epidemics, natural disasters, and other crisis situations. Many contexts call for a rapid response employing specialized medical and logistical help, but MSF also runs longer-term projects designed to tackle health crises and support people who cannot otherwise access health care.

MAP 10.2 ● United Nations Peacekeeping Missions, 2017

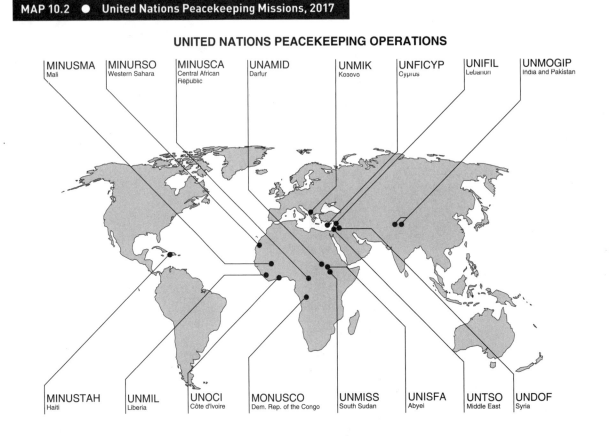

UNITED NATIONS PEACEKEEPING OPERATIONS

MINUSMA — Mali
MINURSO — Western Sahara
MINUSCA — Central African Republic
UNAMID — Darfur
UNMIK — Kosovo
UNFICYP — Cyprus
UNIFIL — Lebanon
UNMOGIP — India and Pakistan

MINUSTAH — Haiti
UNMIL — Liberia
UNOCI — Côte d'Ivoire
MONUSCO — Dem. Rep. of the Congo
UNMISS — South Sudan
UNISFA — Abyei
UNTSO — Middle East
UNDOF — Syria

MINURSO	United Nations Mission for the Referendum in Western Sahara	established: 1991
MINUSCA	United Nations Multidimensional Integrated Stabilization Mission in the Central African Republic	established: 2014
MINUSMA	United Nations Multidimensional Integrated Stabilization Mission in Mali	established: 2013
MINUSTAH	United Nations Stabilization Mission in Haiti	established: 2004
MONUSCO	United Nations Organization Stabilization Mission in the Dem. Republic of the Congo	established: 2010
UNAMID	African Union-United Nations Hybrid Operation in Darfur	established: 2007
UNDOF	United Nations Disengagement Observer Force	established: 1974
UNFICYP	United Nations Peacekeeping Force in Cyprus	established: 1964
UNIFIL	United Nations Interim Force in Lebanon	established: 1978
UNISFA	United Nations Interim Security Force for Abyei	established: 2011
UNMIK	United Nations Interim Administration Mission in Kosovo	established: 1999
UNMIL	United Nations Mission in Liberia	established: 2003
UNMISS	United Nations Mission in South Sudan	established: 2011
UNMOGIP	United Nations Military Observer Group in India and Pakistan	established: 1949
UNOCI	United Nations Operation in Côte d'Ivoire	established: 2004
UNTSO	United Nations Truce Supervision Organization	established: 1948

Source: The United Nations, http://www.un.org/Depts/Cartographic/map/dpko/P_K_0.pdf.

of this organization have shifted the UN even further from peacekeeping and peace-making to **peacebuilding**.[30] In conjunction with humanitarian NGOs, the UN sets up elections, reorganizes police forces, provides relief services, and participates in any other activities needed to create a viable state. It tracks global political developments, advises both the UN secretary-general and peace envoys in the field on the best courses of action to attain peace, and provides service to states directly in the electoral process.

Reasserting its mission for 2016–2019, the UNDPA has pledged "to promote the search for—and assist countries to reach inclusive political solutions as the key to—preventing or reducing conflicts and acts of political violence, while ensuring long lasting solutions that reduce human suffering around the world." The strategic goals for the UNDPA to realize this mission are as follows: (1) strengthening international peace and security through inclusive prevention, mediation, and peacebuilding processes; (2) deepening and broadening partnerships within the UN and beyond; and (3) fit for the future—ensuring organizational effectiveness (see Figure 10.3).[31] The Peacebuilding Commission of the UN, which includes the Peacebuilding Commission, the Peacebuilding Fund, and the Peacebuilding Support Office, was established in 2010 to support these efforts. These organizations work together to assist countries emerging from conflict, to reduce the risk of relapse, and to lay the foundation for sustainable peace and development.[32]

Japanese 63rd troop personnel arrive at Juba airport to take part in UN peacekeeping activities, including rescue operations, in Juba, South Sudan, on November 21, 2016.

peacebuilding the UN, in conjunction with humanitarian NGOs, organizes elections, reorganizes police forces, provides relief services, and participates in any other activities that are needed to create a viable state

HOW YOU CAN CONNECT

You can gain a greater appreciation of the challenges of global governance by . . .

- joining the Model UN Club at your school
- visiting the UN building in New York City
- watching a live feed from UN Web TV
- joining a chapter of an NGO on your campus
- volunteering for an NGO

One of the greatest challenges for the UN in these efforts is the fact that UN staff are outsiders to the conflicts they address. Many question their right to intervene, as well as their capacity to bring about a lasting peace. NGOs can sometimes bridge the gap between the UN and the local people. They are frequently better situated than the UN to provide many of the services needed. They operate closer to the people, at a grassroots level, and can be more nimble in their response to humanitarian crises. Political unrest in North Africa and the Middle East—the Arab Spring, which included Tunisia, Morocco, Egypt,

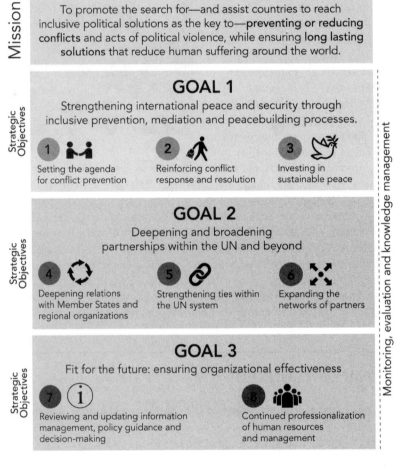

FIGURE 10.3 ● UN Department of Political Affairs Strategic Plan

United Nations Department of Political Affairs
STRATEGIC PLAN
2016–2019

Mission
To promote the search for—and assist countries to reach inclusive political solutions as the key to—**preventing or reducing conflicts** and acts of political violence, while ensuring **long lasting solutions** that reduce human suffering around the world.

GOAL 1
Strengthening international peace and security through inclusive prevention, mediation and peacebuilding processes.

1 Setting the agenda for conflict prevention
2 Reinforcing conflict response and resolution
3 Investing in sustainable peace

GOAL 2
Deepening and broadening partnerships within the UN and beyond

4 Deepening relations with Member States and regional organizations
5 Strengthening ties within the UN system
6 Expanding the networks of partners

GOAL 3
Fit for the future: ensuring organizational effectiveness

7 Reviewing and updating information management, policy guidance and decision-making
8 Continued professionalization of human resources and management

Strategic Objectives

Monitoring, evaluation and knowledge management

Source: United Nations Department of Political Affairs, "Strategic Plan, 2016–2019," November 20, 2015, http://www.un.org/undpa/sites/www.un.org.undpa/files/2016%20Annual%20Appeal%20Strategic%20Plan%20leaflet.pdf.

Libya, and Syria—led UN secretary-general Ban Ki-moon to emphasize the important role NGOs can play for countries in transition.[33] In a meeting with representatives of the NGO community in October 2011, the secretary-general cited their efforts in disarmament and sustainable development as examples of successes where partnerships with the UN had been significant. He noted that civil society's engagement with the creation of new governments would be critical:

> There can be no success without a healthy civil society. Please, do your part. Help these women's groups, social media activists, human rights defenders and others to take their rightful place in society—in government, in parliament, in every public institution.[34]

PRO/CON
IS THE UN STILL AN EFFECTIVE AGENCY FOR INTERNATIONAL CHANGE?

Pro

Peter Yeo, President, Better World Campaign. Written for *CQ Researcher*, June 2016.

Seventy years after its creation, the United Nations is more relevant and needed than at any time in its history to advance U.S. national security priorities while fostering burden-sharing among nations.

Peace and stability remain at the core of the institution's efforts as they did when President Harry S. Truman signed its charter, with peacekeepers constituting the world's largest deployed military force. However, the kinds of conflict they take on are much different than the brutality the world feared after World War II.

Today's peacekeepers operate in terrorist hotbeds like Mali and in nations wracked by civil war like South Sudan. Their presence often means the difference between life and death. A 2013 study found that deploying large numbers of U.N. peacekeepers "dramatically reduces civilian killings." A Columbia University study found that, in the post–Cold War era, deploying U.N. peacekeepers reduces by half the hazard that a country will slide back into all-out war. As former Joint Chiefs of Staff Chairman Mike Mullen noted, peacekeepers "help promote stability. . . . Therefore, the success of these operations is very much in our national interest."

Yet, some of the U.N.'s value is hidden in the stories that don't make the front pages — or perhaps the stories it prevents from happening. Take its delivery of vaccines: They are one of the most cost-effective ways to save the lives of children, improve health and ensure long-term prosperity in developing countries.

Immunizations have saved more children than any other medical intervention in the last 50 years. The U.N. is a leader in this field, vaccinating 58 percent of the world's children. As a result, polio is close to being eradicated, and vaccines for measles, diphtheria, tetanus and pertussis save some 2.5 million lives each year.

Similarly, as the Zika virus affects thousands of pregnant women throughout the Americas, the U.N. is on the front lines: The World Health Organization is coordinating the international response; the U.N. Population Fund is providing voluntary contraception and family planning; UNICEF is helping affected families.

Con

U.S. Rep. Mike Rogers, R-Ala.; Sponsor, Restore American Sovereignty Act. Written for *CQ Researcher*, June 2016.

According to its charter, the United Nations can take action on a wide range of issues confronting humanity in the 21st century, from peace and security, climate change, sustainable development, human rights, disarmament and terrorism to gender equality and food production. As noble as its mission sounds, the U.N. has lost its way and become an ineffective and bloated international organization.

The United States funds 22 percent of the U.N.'s operations, significantly more than any other member state. Despite relying on American taxpayer dollars, recent U.N. actions go directly against the interests and values of our nation. The proposed U.N. Arms Treaty is a threat to our Second Amendment rights, and the Law of the Sea Treaty directly infringes upon American sovereignty. Recently, the U.N. Human Rights Council condemned Israel with five resolutions, but human rights abusers like China were never mentioned. The United Nations cannot balance its broad mission with so many member nations.

Another aspect the U.N. fails in is as an international peacekeeper. The world is more dangerous than ever. With North Korea, China and Iran provoking America and its allies, national security is at the forefront of my mind. We need a deliberative body that acts quickly and forcefully to neutralize threats across the world.

However, the United Nations Security Council, tasked with this exact job, remains gridlocked. Its sanctions against North Korea after that country's most recent provocations amount to nothing more than a slap on the wrist.

When Syrian President Bashar al-Assad began using chemical weapons against his owns citizens, the Security Council was inactive in a response. Russia, led by President Vladimir Putin, continues to ignore internationally recognized nuclear treaties. Yet, as one of the five permanent council members, Russia remains unpunished.

(Continued)

(Continued)

The U.N. is not a perfect institution, and U.S. involvement will remain essential to continue reforms and ensure improvement. Yet, as global crises become more complex, so too do the work and reach of the U.N. Today more than ever, no single country can resolve the world's most pressing challenges. By working with the U.N., we don't have to go it alone.

Many people have tried to prescribe a fix for the U.N. I won't do that. Former U.N. Ambassador Jeane Kirkpatrick was once asked why the United States didn't leave the U.N. She responded that it's not worth the trouble.

I disagree. I have introduced H.R. 1205, the Restore American Sovereignty Act, that would remove the United States from the United Nations. When American taxpayers pay for an organization that actively works against them, I think it's time we step up and move on.

Source: Reed Karaim, R. "Reforming the U.N.," *CQ Researcher* 26 (June 24, 2016): 553–576. http://library.cqpress.com.

Where Do You Stand?

1. What role should the UN play in resolving conflicts within and between countries?

2. Should the UN expand its membership to be a more effective organization?

The concept of civil society has evolved in this regard over time. The end of the Cold War and the forces of globalization that emerged afterward prompted social movements around the world that were particularly influenced by the engagement of civil society.[35] No longer restricted by borders, these groups were able to appeal across territorial boundaries to garner support for their cause. They were particularly influential in the changes that took place in Central Europe as countries such as Czechoslovakia and Poland crafted new identities for themselves. As a result, the inclusion of civil society is more important than ever in creating peaceful coexistence in today's world.

What, then, is the role for the UN going forward? Is the UN still a relevant body in today's globalized world? The "Pro/Con" feature addresses this issue and the effectiveness of the organization.

The Expansion of International Law and the International Criminal Court

Concurrent with the growth of UN activities, the post–Cold War period has also been marked by the progressive expansion of international law. The broadening of the concepts of the rule of law and the means for enforcement through the creation of more binding statutes has resulted in more cases going to the ICJ than ever before. While case decisions made by the court do not constitute precedents in the same way that they do in the US court system, they do inform how the law is applied in the future. Most notably, the development of international criminal law has followed this pattern.

Within just decades of the Nazi atrocities of World War II, the world would learn of Rwandans and Serbians actively committing acts of genocide. At first, the UN responded with the creation of ad hoc courts to address the crimes on an international basis. By 1994, there was a growing international consensus that the time had come for a permanent international criminal court. Based on the Nuremberg war crime trials of Nazis and the ad hoc courts, the International Law Commission of the UN drafted a statute calling for the creation of the International Criminal Court (ICC).

In 1998, the UN General Assembly adopted the ICC Rome Statute, which details the governing principles of the court. Citing sovereign national interests, the United States has never ratified the statute and has chosen not to participate in ICC cases. However, international support is widespread. By 2002, enough states (sixty) had ratified the statute to make the ICC a fully functioning institution. Today, more than 120 countries are signatories. The ICC has been critical to a new level of attention given to violations of the Geneva Conventions, which outline the rules of war and engagement, as well as to the Universal Declaration of Human Rights. Since ratification, the court has considered twenty-three cases and has issued six verdicts, with nine people found guilty and one acquitted. These actions have ignited some criticism. In 2017, the African Union called for the mass withdrawal of its member states from the ICC, arguing that Africans have been the only ones prosecuted so far. South Africa and Burundi have indicated they will withdraw, while Nigeria and Senegal have rejected the nonbinding resolution. This lack of support, as well as the court's limited enforcement capabilities, raises the question as to whether the ICC can be truly effective in deterring crimes against humanity.

Conclusion: Compliance and Enforcement

Despite the reluctance of states to formally commit to some far-reaching agreements, such as the jurisdiction of the ICC, there are broad areas of agreement on the laws governing the seas, outer space, and the Antarctic. Treaties are the instruments of global cooperation and may be bilateral or multilateral. Since World War II, agreement and compliance have been found in major multilateral international treaties that involve the global commons and seek to protect the "common heritage of man." There are more than 560 multilateral treaties deposited with the UN secretary-general, and the number continues to grow. The following list includes some of the most important, along with the dates they were first passed and their functions:

1959: Antarctic Treaty—governs the protection of the Antarctic

1968: Nuclear Non-Proliferation Treaty (NPT)—prevents the spread of nuclear weapons and promotes the goal of nuclear disarmament

1979: Moon and Other Celestial Bodies Agreement—governs the activities of states on the moon and other bodies in outer space

1982: UN Convention on the Law of the Sea—governs territorial claims to the oceans and rules on the high seas

1992: UN Framework on Convention on Climate Change—seeks cooperation on the prevention of climate change

1994: UN Convention to Combat Desertification—seeks agreement to assist those in dry areas and prevent further destruction

1996: Comprehensive Nuclear Test-Ban Treaty—bans nuclear testing on earth for both military and civilian purposes

It may take member states of IGOs years to negotiate treaties and accords like these that govern specific areas. These treaties then still require ratification from the signatories to go into force. For any IGO, the greatest limiting factor can, in fact, be its member states.

The United States is noteworthy in this regard. For example, in the treaties that have been negotiated to cover the Law of the Sea and to enact a Comprehensive Nuclear Test-Ban Treaty, the United States has signed the relevant treaties, but the US Senate has not ratified them, citing "national interests." In these cases, domestic issues drive international decisions, and states put their own perceived national self-interest ahead of the greater global good. These barriers are porous, however, as countries like the United States may still generally abide by the principles of the agreements, even if they do not ratify them.

Clearly, the increasing severity of global issues that defy national boundaries, such as poverty, infectious disease, and human rights, requires cooperation on the global level. The evolution of international law and its role in regulating the international arena, coupled with the activism of IGOs and NGOs, is critical. The extent to which they can help states overcome their differences will have a significant impact on the well-being of not only the planet but also the people who live here. The effectiveness of these organizations in addressing some of the challenges that face the international system is explored next in Chapter 11.

Key Concepts

Atlantic Charter   230
civil society   237
complex interdependence   234
Concert of Europe   229

intergovernmental organizations (IGOs)   228
international law   227
Kellogg-Briand Pact   230

nongovernmental organizations (NGOs)   228
peacebuilding   243
positivism   228
supranational entities   228

To Learn More

Books and Other Print Media

Rye Barcott, *It Happened on the Way to War* (New York: Bloomsbury USA, 2011).

This book tells the story of a college student's journeys, which resulted in his creation of the NGO Carolina for Kibera (which helps a slum in Nairobi, Kenya), as well as his experiences as a US Marine.

Victoria Bernal and Inderpal Grewal, eds., *Theorizing NGOs: State, Feminisms, and Neoliberalism* (Durham, NC: Duke University Press, 2014).

This edited volume explores the role of NGOs in promoting women's issues.

Carla Del Ponte, *Madame Prosecutor: Confrontations with Humanity's Worst Criminals and the Culture of Impunity* (New York: Other Press, 2009).

In these memoirs, Del Ponte recounts her role as the International Criminal Tribunal's chief prosecutor for the former Yugoslavia and Rwanda, bringing justice to those who had committed acts of genocide in those countries.

Paul Diehl and Brian Frederking, eds., *The Politics of Global Governance: International Organizations in an Interdependent World*, 5th ed. (Boulder, CO: Lynne Rienner, 2015).

This edited volume takes a broad look through many different lenses at the activities of international organizations

Linda Fasulo, *An Insider's Guide to the UN*, 3rd ed. (New Haven, CT: Yale University Press, 2015).

This popular book from news correspondent Linda Fasulo includes candid remarks from UN diplomats and in-depth examinations of issues confronting the UN today.

Leymah Gbowee, *Mighty Be Our Powers: How Sisterhood, Prayer, and Sex Changed a Nation at War* (New York: Beast Books, 2011).

In this harrowing memoir, 2011 Nobel laureate Leymah Gbowee recalls Liberia's civil war and how she led a group of women in healing and reconciliation, protest, and peacebuilding. She details the critical role Liberian women played in brokering peace and empowering their sisters in other West African nations.

Monica Krause, *The Good Project: Humanitarian Relief NGOs and the Fragmentation of Reason* (Chicago: University of Chicago Press, 2014).

This book explores the decision-making processes at NGOs and the extent to which they are project driven.

Wangari Muta Maathai, *Unbowed* (New York: Knopf, 2006).

Unbowed is the memoir of the late Nobel laureate Wangari Muta Maathai, who established the Green Belt Movement in Kenya. Maathai fought not only for the environment but also for women's rights and democracy.

Samantha Power, *"A Problem From Hell": America and the Age of Genocide* (New York: Basic Books, 2013).

Former Balkan war correspondent Samantha Power explores why American leaders continue to tolerate genocide, drawing on interviews with top officials, declassified documents, and her own experiences in the field.

David Scheffer, *All the Missing Souls: A Personal History of the War Crimes Tribunals* (Princeton, NJ: Princeton University Press, 2011).

From a US-centric view, David Scheffer writes about the Rwandan genocide and Srebrenica massacre; his role in establishing criminal tribunals for war crimes in the Balkans, Cambodia, Sierra Leone, and Rwanda; and the subsequent creation of the ICC.

Mark Schuller, *Killing with Kindness: Haiti, International Aid, and NGOs* (New Brunswick, NJ: Rutgers University Press, 2012).

Anthropologist Mark Schuller examines the role of NGOs in the rebuilding of Haiti after the 2004 coup and 2010 earthquake, focusing on the challenges of externally funded organizations and internal operations. He characterizes the processes and outcomes as "trickle-down imperialism."

Websites

Green Belt Movement, www.greenbeltmovement.org

The official website of the Green Belt Movement features information on its tree planting, advocacy, and community empowerment programs.

International Criminal Court (ICC), www.icc-cpi.int

The ICC investigates and tries individuals charged with genocide, war crimes, and crimes against humanity.

International Criminal Tribunal for Rwanda (ICTR), www.unictr.org

The ICTR was created in 1994 by the UN to seek resolution to serious violations of humanitarian law that occurred in Rwanda. The website features a daily journal and proceedings and a database of cases brought to the tribunal.

Union of International Associations (UIA), www.uia.org

The UIA is a Brussels-based institute that documents and researches international organizations and publishes the *Yearbook of International Organizations* and the *Encyclopedia of World Problems and Human Potential*.

United Nations (UN), www.un.org

The main website for the UN features information on peace and security, development, human rights, humanitarian affairs, and international law, as well as publications, databases, maps, and other documents and information on internships and employment.

Videos

I Came to Testify (2011), www.pbs.org/wnet/women-war-and-peace/full-episodes/i-came-to-testify

This film explores the story of sixteen women prisoners of the Serbs during the war in the Balkans in the 1990s who testified against their captors in an international court of law.

The International Criminal Court (2013), http://www.films.com/ecTitleDetail.aspx?TitleID=33449&r=SR

This documentary explores the day-to-day operations of the court through the activities of chief prosecutor Luis Moreno-Ocampo.

International Law and Global Governance (2011), http://meridian.films.com/ecTitleDetail.aspx?TitleID=23790

This series discusses the role of international law in the global system and explores the interaction between domestic and international law.

Pray the Devil Back to Hell (2008), www.pbs.org/wnet/women-war-and-peace/full-episodes/pray-the-devil-back-to-hell

This documentary focuses on the role of women in the peacemaking process in Liberia who protested against the war crimes of former dictator Charles Taylor.

United Nations Association Film Festival (UNAFF), www.unaff.org

UNAFF is an international documentary film festival focusing on human rights, the environment, women's issues, health, and other topics. The website contains links to past festivals and their featured films.

United Nations Videos, www.youtube.com/user/united nations

The official YouTube channel of the UN features daily videos and messages from the secretary-general, as well as special videos on a range of topics, including disarmament, the Sustainable Development Goals (SDGs), and peacemaking.

UN: Last Station Before Hell (2015), http://www.films.com/ecTitleDetail.aspx?TitleID=112960

This video explores the changing definition of international security and the difficulties faced by UN peacekeeping missions through field investigations and interviews with key decision makers.

UN Web TV: The United Nations Live & On Demand, http://webtv.un.org

The UN Web TV channel, available 24 hours a day, includes both live coverage of meetings and events and prerecorded videos and documentaries.

The Whistleblower (2010)

This popular movie tells the story of peacekeeping in postwar Bosnia from the perspective of a female police officer from Nebraska who worked as a contractor there. It is based on a true story.

Challenges to Cooperation

Overcoming poverty is not a gesture of charity. It is an act of justice. It is the protection of a fundamental human right, the right to dignity and a decent life. While poverty persists, there is no true freedom.

—Nelson Mandela, Trafalgar Square, London, February 3, 2005[1]

Learning Objectives

After studying this chapter, you will be able to do the following:

- Explain the origins of the Millennium Development Goals (MDGs) and the Sustainable Development Goals (SDGs), what they are designed to measure, and their successes and failures in addressing poverty worldwide.

- Identify the main health-related challenges facing the world, and describe the steps being taken to address them.

- Define *human rights*, identify the primary areas of concern worldwide, and explain the different ways in which they are approached.

- Define the term *global governance*, and describe the role that international regimes can play.

N elson Mandela's address to the Global Campaign for Action against Poverty was a call for the younger generation to become leaders in reconciling the great disparity between those who have and those who have not. The global needs of those in extreme poverty are critical, as they are the most elementary in nature—adequate food, shelter, safe water to drink, and basic medical care. The ability to address these fundamental issues requires cooperation at the highest level across borders, putting humanity first. Jean-Jacques Rousseau's eighteenth-century philosophical notion of a social contract emphasizes the mutual obligation of people to one another. If we subscribe to the social contract, we must accept responsibility for our global neighbors and leave no one behind.

International organizations have been able to meet people's urgent needs in certain instances, but are limited by their size and the diversity of their members' interests. All too often, the self-interests of states drive their responses and limit their willingness to cooperate. Nongovernmental organizations (NGOs) have stepped in when they can, but their efforts are constrained by resources and a lack of coordination. Some scholars have gone so far as to say that there should be a system of **global governance**, where international cooperation is regulated on a grand scale using both existing organizations, such as the UN, and new regulatory mechanisms. There are also ways for individuals to act collectively to make a difference by exercising their global citizenship.

global governance voluntary international cooperation to manage transnational issues through a system of governance agreed to by all interested parties

The United Nations has led the most sustained cooperative effort to address global inequality over the last two decades. When UN secretary-general Kofi Annan came into office in 1997, he vowed to revitalize the UN to make it more responsive to the world that had evolved since its creation. Toward the end of his first term, in April 2000, he issued a Millennium Report titled *We the Peoples: The Role of the United Nations in the 21st Century*. The report called on member states to commit themselves to an action plan for ending poverty and inequality, improving education, reducing the number of people suffering from HIV/AIDS, safeguarding the environment, and protecting people from deadly conflict and violence.[2] While introducing the report at a press conference, Annan noted, "If the United Nations does not attempt to chart a course for the world's peoples in the first decades of the new millennium, who will?"[3]

Nelson Mandela speaks at the Make Poverty History rally at Trafalgar Square in London. Make Poverty History is a coalition of more than 220 charities, campaigns, trade unions, faith groups, and celebrities.
Fred Duval/FilmMagic.

The report formed the basis of the Millennium Declaration adopted by heads of state at the Millennium Summit, held at UN headquarters in September 2000. The document identified eight **Millennium Development Goals (MDGs)** that sought to improve the lives of people all over the globe by 2015, as follows:

1. Eradicate extreme hunger and poverty.

2. Achieve universal primary education.

3. Promote gender equality and empower women.

4. Reduce child mortality.

5. Improve maternal health.

6. Combat HIV/AIDS, malaria, and other diseases.

7. Ensure environmental sustainability.

8. Develop a global partnership for development.[4]

The evaluation of these goals at the completion of the term indicated both successes and failures. Despite significant progress in many areas, the poorest and most vulnerable were still left behind. In particular, gender inequality persists, large gaps between the richest and the poorest and between urban and rural areas still exist, the poor are the most affected by climate change and environmental degradation, conflict remains the greatest threat to human development, and millions of people go hungry and live in extreme poverty.[5]

In response, the UN constructed a new set of seventeen objectives, the **Sustainable Development Goals (SDG)**, to guide global initiatives until 2030. They can be organized into three broad categories: ending poverty, reducing inequality, and protecting the environment. The first six goals address the most basic needs: food, health, clean water, and equal access for all. The next six goals (7–12) focus on actions that will reduce inequality, from access to energy, economic growth, infrastructure, and safe human settlements to sustainable patterns of consumption and production. The final five goals (13–17) emphasize protecting the earth from climate change, supporting conservation, and promoting a peaceful global environment that can facilitate cooperation. A closer look at the progress made thus far in relation to three broad areas addressed by the goals—poverty, disease, and human rights—demonstrates the critical needs as well as the road blocks that limit cooperation.

Poverty

Continuing the key focus of the MDGs, the number one goal of the SDGs is ending poverty. **Poverty** refers to the want of food, as well as access to clean water, shelter, health care, education, employment, and general well-being. A critical factor underlying political conflict and economic disparity, poverty defines social distinctions and can undermine cultures, as large groups of people are forced to be on the move in response to conflict, natural disasters, and the most basic needs of food and water. The World Bank estimates that 10 percent of the global population live on less than $1.90 per day.[6] Hunger is felt by 11 percent of the global population.[7] One in ten people lack access to safe water, and one in three people lack access to a toilet.[8]

Poverty prevents many people from being able to appreciate the broader issues of the world in which they live. Writing in 1943, psychologist Abraham Maslow argued that individuals experience five levels of needs that affect their motivation and participation in

SUSTAINABLE DEVELOPMENT GOALS

Goal 1. End poverty in all its forms everywhere

Goal 2. End hunger, achieve food security and improved nutrition, and promote sustainable agriculture

Goal 3. Ensure healthy lives and promote well-being for all at all ages

Goal 4. Ensure inclusive and equitable quality education and promote lifelong learning opportunities for all

Goal 5. Achieve gender equality and empower all women and girls

Goal 6. Ensure availability and sustainable management of water and sanitation for all

Goal 7. Ensure access to affordable, reliable, sustainable, and modern energy for all

Goal 8. Promote sustained, inclusive, and sustainable economic growth, full and productive employment, and decent work for all

Goal 9. Build resilient infrastructure, promote inclusive and sustainable industrialization, and foster innovation

Goal 10. Reduce inequality within and among countries

Goal 11. Make cities and human settlements inclusive, safe, resilient, and sustainable

Goal 12. Ensure sustainable consumption and production patterns

Goal 13. Take urgent action to combat climate change and its impacts*

Goal 14. Conserve and sustainably use the oceans, seas, and marine resources for sustainable development

Goal 15. Protect, restore, and promote sustainable use of terrestrial ecosystems, sustainably manage forests, combat desertification, and halt and reverse land degradation and halt biodiversity loss

Goal 16. Promote peaceful and inclusive societies for sustainable development, provide access to justice for all, and build effective, accountable, and inclusive institutions at all levels

Goal 17. Strengthen the means of implementation and revitalize the Global Partnership for Sustainable Development

Source: United Nations, "70/1. Transforming Our World: The 2030 Agenda for Sustainable Development," resolution adopted by the General Assembly, September 25, 2015, http://www.un.org/ga/search/view_doc.asp?symbol=A/RES/70/1&Lang=E.

*Acknowledging that the United Nations Framework Convention on Climate Change is the primary international, intergovernmental forum for negotiating the global response to climate change.

society (see Figure 11.1).[9] The first level consists of physiological needs—the need for food and water. Once these most basic needs are met, the second level can be considered—safety needs, ranging from the creation of shelter to be protected from the elements to more complex notions of security from conflict and crime. The third level expands the individual's relationship to others, as love and belongingness become important. At the fourth level, individuals become conscious of their place in society and relationship to others—esteem needs. Only once these levels have been reached can the final level, the need for self-actualization, be realized. Because many of the people of the world are still struggling at the first levels of Maslow's hierarchy, they are unable to achieve their full potential.

The activities associated with achieving the SDGs seek to move people up this pyramid. The most recent report on the SDGs (in 2016) notes some improvements to date in realizing the goals and the challenges that will continue.[10] Sub-Saharan Africa faces the greatest difficulties, as more than 40 percent of its working population lives on less than $1.90 per day.[11]

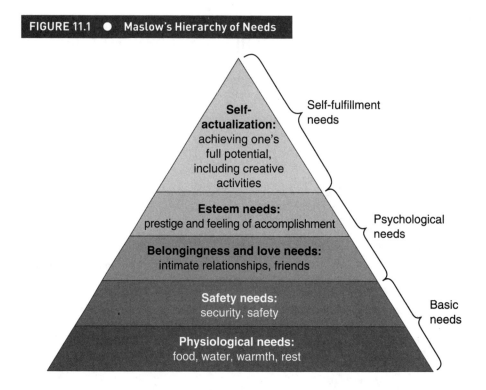

FIGURE 11.1 ● Maslow's Hierarchy of Needs

(See Figure 11.2.) Globally, young people (ages 15–24) are most likely to be among the working poor, with 16 percent living below the poverty line, compared to 9 percent of working adults. Goal 2 of the SDGs calls for zero hunger. Despite decreases in the percentage of the global population that suffers from hunger (from 15 percent in 2000 to 11 percent in 2016), more than 50 percent of the adult population in sub-Saharan Africa faces moderate or severe food insecurity, followed by South Asia at 25 percent.[12] Lack of access to sufficient nutritious food worldwide has resulted in an estimated 158.6 million children—or one in four—under the age of five having stunted growth.

The accessibility of water and sanitation compound these limits on food availability.[13] Goal 6 of the SDGs calls for clean water and sanitation. While access to improved drinking water sources has improved globally, from 82 percent in 2000 to 91 percent in 2015, more than 600 million people still use unimproved sources or surface water. Similarly, upgraded sanitation has increased, from 50 percent in 2000 to 68 percent in 2015, but 2.4 billion people still face challenges, including 946 million who have no access to any facilities. This lack of sanitation facilities can have a direct impact on the water quality of an area.

Education is critical to addressing these issues, identified in Goal 4 of the SDGs.[14] While there have been improvements globally, there were still 59 million primary-age children and 63 million adolescents who did not attend school in 2013, primarily coming from rural areas. There were 757 million adults unable to read and write, with women representing two-thirds of that group. Of particular concern is the extent to which students are acquiring fundamental skills in reading and math. Data from thirty-eight developed countries indicate that 75 percent of young people are attaining some minimum proficiency, while only five of twenty-two developing countries are attaining similar successes.[15]

Given these inequities, how are the world's most powerful political and economic actors responding to meet the challenges of global poverty? What are the implications of these policies for the United States or the European Union (EU)? How well are they responding to these critical differences?

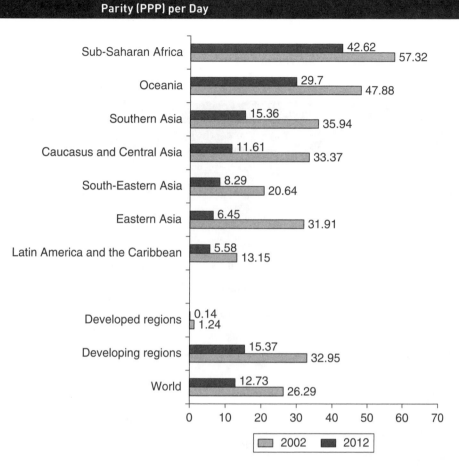

FIGURE 11.2 ● Proportion of Population Living below $1.90 Purchasing Power Parity (PPP) per Day

Source: United Nations, Department of Economic and Social Affairs Statistics Division, "Goal 1: End Poverty in All Its Forms Everywhere," *Sustainable Development Goals Overview.*

In 2004, the US Congress created the Millennium Challenge Account to address some of these concerns. Administered by the **Millennium Challenge Corporation (MCC)**, this organization provides economic assistance to countries based on their ability to meet political, economic, and social performance standards. A matrix of measures identifies twenty-one different indicators used to determine eligibility for US assistance (see Table 11.1).

A list of countries that have met targets is generated annually, and funds are appropriated to them through one of two types of grants: compact and threshold. The compact grants are relatively large and given to countries that clearly meet the eligibility criteria. Threshold grants are smaller and awarded to those nearing the standards but needing a bit more time to reach them. To date, the MCC has approved more than $10 billion in compact and threshold programs that support projects all over the world in a broad range of areas:

- Agriculture and irrigation
- Transportation (roads, bridges, ports)
- Water supply and sanitation

Millennium Challenge Corporation (MCC) an organization created by the US Congress to administer economic assistance to developing countries in response to the MDGs

- Access to health
- Finance and enterprise development
- Anticorruption initiatives
- Land rights and access to education[16]

TABLE 11.1 ● Millennium Challenge Corporation Country Selection Indicators		
Indicator	**Category**	**Source**
Access to Credit Indicator	Economic Freedom	International Finance Corporation
Business Start-Up Indicator	Economic Freedom	International Finance Corporation
Child Health Indicator	Investing in People	Columbia/Yale
Civil Liberties Indicator	Ruling Justly	Freedom House
Control of Corruption Indicator	Ruling Justly	World Bank/Brookings Institution
Fiscal Policy Indicator	Economic Freedom	International Monetary Fund (IMF)
Freedom of Information Indicator	Ruling Justly	Freedom House, Center for Law and Democracy
Gender in the Economy Indicator	Economic Freedom	World Bank
Girls' Primary Education Completion Rate Indicator	Investing in People	UNESCO
Girls' Secondary Education Enrollment Ratio Indicator	Investing in People	UNESCO
Government Effectiveness Indicator	Ruling Justly	World Bank/Brookings Institution
Health Expenditures Indicator	Investing in People	World Health Organization
Immunization Rates Indicator	Investing in People	WHO/UNICEF
Inflation Indicator	Economic Freedom	International Monetary Fund (IMF)
Land Rights and Access Indicator	Economic Freedom	International Fund for Agricultural Development (IFAD) International Finance Corporation
Natural Resource Protection	Investing in People	Columbia/Yale
Political Rights Indicator	Ruling Justly	Freedom House
Primary Education Expenditures Indicator	Investing in People	UNESCO
Regulatory Quality Indicator	Economic Freedom	World Bank/Brookings Institution
Rule of Law Indicator	Ruling Justly	World Bank/Brookings Institution
Trade Policy Indicator	Economic Freedom	The Heritage Foundation

Source: Millennium Challenge Corporation, "Selection Indicators," https://www.mcc.gov/who-we-fund/indicators.

The inventory of compact and threshold recipients shows the breadth of this program (see Table 11.2).

As an example of how these programs work, the MCC signed a compact with Niger for $437 million in July 2016 to bolster the agricultural sector of the country.[17] Niger is one of the least developed countries in the world, and 80 percent of its population relies on agriculture to make a living. The objectives of the compact are to provide greater access to irrigation, to improve roads, and to create a better infrastructure for the agricultural marketplace, the second largest export sector of the country. In Central America, as part of its first compact with El Salvador for $461 million, the MCC funded the Northern Transnational Highway, linking the mountains of El Salvador with the Honduran border to the east and Guatemala to the west. This critical roadway through rugged terrain has increased enrollment in schools, has made it easier for people to get to work, and has promoted trade.[18]

The EU countries were instrumental in the formulation and adoption of the **2030 Agenda for Sustainable Development** that lays out the SDGs.[19] As a group, they provide more than 50 percent of all global development aid. The EU has detailed specific responses for all seventeen goals, with funding mechanisms developed through its Agenda for Change.[20] Specifically, its Development Cooperation Instrument has an allocated budget of 19.6 billion euros, or more than $21 billion dollars, for the 2014–2020 period. These funds are allocated across three broad areas—by geographic distribution across forty-seven countries (11.8 billion euros), thematic interests of promoting global public good and civil society (7 billion euros), and the more recently established Pan-African Programme (845 million euros).

TABLE 11.2 ● Compact and Threshold Grant Recipients

Compact Grant Recipients	Threshold Grant Recipients
Armenia	Albania
Benin	Burkina Faso
Burkina Faso	Guyana
Cape Verde	Honduras
El Salvador	Indonesia
Georgia	Jordan
Ghana	Kenya
Honduras	Kyrgyz Republic
Indonesia	Liberia
Jordan	Malawi
Lesotho	Moldova
Madagascar	Niger
Malawi	Paraguay
Mali	Peru
Moldova	Philippines
Mongolia	Rwanda
Morocco	Sao Tome and Principe
Mozambique	Tanzania
Namibia	Timor-Leste
Nicaragua	Uganda
Philippines	Ukraine
Senegal	Zambia
Tanzania	
Vanuatu	
Zambia	

Source: Millennium Challenge Corporation, "Countries & Country Tools," www.mcc.gov/pages/countries.

Global Health and the Threat of Disease

Another critically important part of the SDGs is attention to global health, particularly the spread of infectious disease. Goal 3 seeks to "ensure healthy lives and promote well-being for all at all ages." Women are the most affected in the poorest countries, having very limited access to health care. The gap between rich and poor is most profound in the area of maternal health. Almost all women in developed countries receive skilled health care when delivering a child, while such care is far from universal in developing countries. Maternal death rates remain high, as 830 women die every day from preventable causes related to pregnancy and childbirth, with 99 percent of those deaths occurring in developing countries.[21] The goal of the SDGs is to reduce the global maternal mortality ratio (i.e., how many women die related to pregnancy and childbirth) to 70 per 100,000 births. As of 2015, this ratio was 239 per 100,000 live births in developing countries, compared to 12 per 100,000 live births in developed countries.

2030 Agenda for Sustainable Development a document adopted by world leaders that came into force on January 1, 2017, and outlines the seventeen SDGs

The global transmission of diseases across borders has never been greater, and many of the issues we have examined up to this point have contributed to this trend. From environmental challenges to technological innovation that facilitates travel, political unrest that forces migration, and the economic imperative for trade, all these factors have moved people and diseases rapidly around the world. There is a global fear of **pandemics**, the spread of diseases across a wide geographical area and to a large population. These kinds of concerns are not new and go back at least as far as the Black Death, a result of the bubonic plague in the 1300s thought to have killed more than 30 percent of the population in Europe. Concerns that are more recent have revolved around severe acute respiratory syndrome (SARS), which affected 8,000 people and resulted in 750 deaths during a 2003 outbreak.[22] Similar fears are raised periodically by recurrent outbreaks of the avian and swine flus as well. The spread of the Ebola virus disease (EVD) in 2014 heightened a sense of urgency to find solutions to these deadly diseases. The way in which Zika, a mosquito-borne virus identified in gorillas in Uganda in 1947, crossed from animals to humans, across Africa, to Asia, to Latin America, and then to the United States shows that there are no borders when it comes to disease.

pandemics the widespread outbreak of diseases

Other critical diseases targeted by the SDGs include HIV/AIDS and malaria, which were specific aims of the previous MDGs and continue to be of grave concern. There has been progress as the number of new cases of HIV/AIDS has declined, but the total of those living with HIV continues to rise. It is estimated that 36.7 million people are currently living with HIV/AIDS, with 1.8 million of them being children under the age of fifteen.[23] The creation of drugs that can alter the course of the disease, as well as drugs that can prevent the transfer of the disease during childbirth, has been significant. The number of people living with HIV on antiretroviral therapy has increased, from fewer than 1 million in 2000 to 18.2 million in 2016. However, the costs associated with the medications, as well as the lack of effective distribution networks, have often kept these drugs from those with the greatest need. The developing world has suffered the most, with sub-Saharan Africa remaining the region most affected; 66 percent of all new HIV infections in 2015 occurred there.

A baby suffering from malnutrition is photographed at the pediatric department of Malakal Teaching Hospital, where medical staff from the International Committee of the Red Cross (ICRC) work with children suffering from conditions such as malaria, malnutrition, diarrhea, tuberculosis (TB), and kala azar. The hospital serves three conflict-affected states in the northern regions of South Sudan.

Tom Stoddart/Getty Images.

While the spread of HIV/AIDS has received considerable public attention, it is just one small part of the threat. Of particular concern to many people around the world is malaria, a mosquito-borne illness, which can be successfully curtailed with the right medications and equipment. According to the World Health Organization, almost half of the world's population is at risk of exposure to malaria.[24] There were approximately 212 million cases of malaria and 429,000 deaths in 2015. Sub-Saharan Africa faces the greatest challenge in this area as well, with 90 percent of the new cases and 92 percent of the deaths.

One of the most visible responses to fight the spread of malaria has been the provision of mosquito nets to people living in vulnerable areas to protect them while they sleep. The NothingButNets campaign is a grassroots movement sponsored by the Bill & Melinda Gates Foundation and a broad range of organizations around the world to solicit $10 donations to purchase an insecticide-treated mosquito bed net, transport it to Africa, and educate people on how to use it.[25] Partners includes the National Basketball

UNDERSTANDING CROSS-BORDER CONFLICT

HOW CAN INTERNATIONAL STUDIES HELP?

Ebola: Health Crisis in West Africa

Ebola virus disease (EVD) is a viral ailment that has passed from wild animals to the human population in Central and West Africa. It is characterized by a sudden onset of fever, subsequent internal and external bleeding, and a quick death. It has a fatality rate of 90 percent. In June 2014, an epidemic of the disease spread to three countries—Guinea, Sierra Leone, and Liberia—with 350 confirmed deaths and probable deaths of almost 600. It takes only one infected person to spread the disease through a village. Due to this rapid transmission, immediate action is required, but there are few doctors in the regions where the outbreaks have occurred. There are not sufficient health-care treatment facilities where doctors, like the Doctors Without Borders group, can treat victims. They also must take extreme precautions that include wearing protective suits.

Liberia responded by closing its borders and halting trade with Guinea, the source of the initial outbreak, as well as neighboring states Sierra Leone and Senegal. But the disease had already crossed into the country. As a result, the Liberian leadership was criticized for not taking the threat seriously enough.

An effective response requires cooperation across borders to reach those who are infected and to prevent the disease from spreading. Because of EVD's rapid transmission, digital mappers around the world have worked together to trace outbreaks. One nonprofit group, Map International, is providing the infectious disease protective suits needed for doctors to respond. The disease remains on the move, showing up in the Democratic Republic of the Congo (DRC) in 2017. The effort to find a cure is ongoing, with recent successes from an experimental vaccine in Guinea.

What is the role of crossing borders in resolving this crisis? How can the cross-disciplinary focus of international studies help?

MAP 11.1 • The Ebola Crisis in West Africa

2014 Ebola outbreak in West Africa—Outbreak distribution map

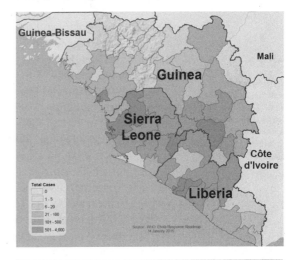

Source: Centers for Disease Control and Prevention, "2014 Ebola OutbreakinWestAfrica—OutbreakDistributionMap,"https://www.cdc.gov/vhf/ebola/outbreaks/2014-west-africa/distribution-map.html.

Questions

- What is the role of geography in this growing crisis?
- Do political factors affect efforts to contain the virus?
- What are the economic implications?
- Do social and cultural factors play a role here?
- Can the international community offer any solution?

Source: AllAfrica, "Liberia: Ebola 'Politics': Urey, Presidency Spar Over Sirleaf's Travel," April 7, 2014, http://allafrica.com/stories/201404071639.html.

Association (NBA) outreach initiative NBA Cares, the People of the United Methodist Church, the Major League Soccer (MLS) outreach initiative MLS WORKS, the Union for Reform Judaism, and Junior Chamber International. They work in conjunction with several UN partners to reach the affected areas.

Critical to all these efforts is the World Health Organization (WHO), which has exercised leadership in this area.[26] The WHO is a specialized agency of the UN; it was created in 1948 to improve the health of people globally. For a large entity governed by 193 member states, it can be difficult to service the diversity of global health needs. As a result, NGOs have been critical to much of the hands-on assistance rendered for global health. Most notable in this regard is the development of the civil society initiative of the WHO, which recognizes the necessity of NGOs in the successful delivery of health care. There are 206 NGOs that enjoy official relations with the WHO.[27] These include a broad range of international associations, federations, societies, and unions, as well as more popularly known groups such as Oxfam, Save the Children, Rotary International, and World Vision International.

Human Rights

Freedom from poverty and disease is essential to the general well-being of the world and is a fundamental human right. Amnesty International, an NGO that focuses on the protection of **human rights**, offers the following definition: "basic rights and freedoms entitled to all people regardless of nationality, sex, national or ethnic origin, race, religion, language, or other status."[28] The 1948 Universal Declaration on Human Rights outlines the international community's commitment. This document remains the defining accord for the protection of human rights around the world and covers a broad range of these rights, emphasizing the personal, legal, cultural, and educational obligations of humans to one another. It was a special interest of former US first lady Eleanor Roosevelt, who believed that respect for human rights was fundamental. Speaking to the UN in 1958, she noted, "Without concerted citizen action to uphold them close to home, we shall look in vain for progress in the larger world."[29]

The transparency that has come with the spread of technology has resulted in people all over the world having firsthand knowledge of the physical and mental abuses that occur in some countries. There is greater exposure and global response to human rights because there is nowhere to hide. Anyone with access to the Internet can view videos of abuses, from factory workers toiling in unsafe conditions to violent suppression of political acts. Pictures of refugees caught in the middle of combat can go viral in a matter of moments, and the whole world is watching. The Syrian regime's use of chemical weapons to regain control and the consequent suffering of the victims has spurred global outrage, but the ability to prevent such acts is limited.

The greatest difficulties arise in how to address human rights from a global perspective. The efforts to develop **universal norms** for behavior, as delineated in the Universal Declaration, are inhibited by culturally **relative norms** that are unique to various societies, dictated by their religion, traditional practices, level of development, and acceptable criminal punishments. For example, the rights of women are of critical concern to human rights advocates; however, some religious groups define these rights in terms that are very different from what might be acceptable to others. National interests and practices more frequently drive behavior.

The continuing controversy over dress requirements and practices of Muslim women in Europe illustrates the tensions between religious practices and implied universal norms. There are two types of Muslim veils—the burka, a traditional full-body cover worn by Muslim women in public, and the niqab, which covers all of the face except for the eyes. France was the first to pass legislation in 2010 that bans the wearing of these covers, imposing a 150-euro fine and requiring offenders to attend a "French citizenship course" to learn about the "values of the French republic."[30] French leadership argued that such a ban was needed for security and in keeping with French secular policies that limit religious expression. In the five years since the law passed, the French Interior Ministry reported that it made 1,623 stops and issued 1,545 fines to 908 women. Several are repeat offenders,

human rights the fundamental rights and freedoms based on the premise that all people are inherently equal and must be treated as such, regardless of their nationality or ethnic origin, race, religion, language, or other status

universal norms human rights as delineated in the Universal Declaration that most countries can agree on

relative norms rights that are unique to an individual society, dictated by its religion, cultural practices, level of development, and acceptable criminal punishments

including one woman fined thirty-three times.[31] More recently, efforts by French beaches to ban the burkini, a swimsuit that completely covers the wearer except for the face, hands, and feet, has reignited the debate. Critics argue that this step is a direct attack on the French Muslim population. Similar bans on the burka and niqab can be found in the Netherlands, Belgium, Bulgaria, Switzerland, and Italy.[32]

Acceptable criminal punishments also vary greatly.[33] In Singapore, medically supervised caning, where an offender is stripped and beaten for a number of strokes, depending on the offense, is legal. The caning of an American student in Singapore for writing graffiti in a public place garnered consider-

Australian model Mecca Laalaa wears an Islamic swimsuit by Muslim fashion designer Aheda Zanetti at the Islamic Sport & Swimwear shop in Sydney, Australia. The burkini was marketed as the first two-piece Muslim swimwear for women and has attracted customers from North America, Europe, and across the Middle East.

able international attention and brought this practice to the global stage. Another form of punishment, stoning, is used in many states, including Saudi Arabia, Sudan, Pakistan, Iran, Yemen, Somalia, Sudan, the United Arab Emirates, and Nigeria. The offender is buried in a hole covered with soil, then pummeled by stones and sticks until death. In 2008, a thirteen-year-old Somali girl was stoned to death by fifty participants and with 1,000 onlookers. Her crime? She had been raped by three men, and in seeking help from authorities, she was accused of adultery and sentenced to death.[34]

In Sudan, conversion from Islam to Christianity is punishable by death. The 2014 case of the Sudanese woman sentenced to death for "apostasy"—the abandoning of the Islamic faith—to marry a Christian man from South Sudan became a global issue. While her sentence was ultimately overturned due to this scrutiny, she faced death threats against herself and her two children and ultimately sought refuge at the US embassy in Khartoum. Gay rights are also a controversial issue in some countries (see Map 11.2). Despite the growing acceptance of same-sex marriages in many Western countries (twenty-two as of 2016), there are ten countries where homosexual acts can be punished by death (ranging from Afghanistan to Nigeria) and sixty-five countries where homosexual acts are illegal.[35]

Women and girls are particularly vulnerable to human rights violations. Goal 5 of the SDGs recognizes the dangers to women and girls globally and the prevalence of discriminatory laws and practices. At the most basic level is the constitutional guarantee for equality between women and men. While 143 countries include such provisions, 52 countries have not made this commitment.[36] Traditional rituals may dictate behavior that is hard to overcome. Female genital mutilation (FGM), a procedure that stems from cultural practices and intentionally alters female genital organs, is a common occurrence in many parts of Africa and some countries in Asia and the Middle East. It is a violation of not only women but children as well, as the practice is generally carried out on minors. Despite legal mandates in thirty countries to stem FGM, as well as international conventions that explicitly recognize the practice as a violation of human rights, it continues.[37] The WHO estimates that more than 200 million girls and women in thirty countries across Africa and the Middle East have undergone this procedure.[38]

Legal protection against rape is also woefully inadequate. Equality Now, an NGO dedicated to promoting legal solutions to protect the human rights of women and girls, surveyed eighty-two legal jurisdictions in 2014 and 2015 on this issue. They found exceptions around the world:

- Rape by a husband is legal in at least ten jurisdictions (Ghana, India, Indonesia, Jordan, Lesotho, Nigeria, Oman, Singapore, Sri Lanka, and Tanzania).

- A perpetrator of rape can escape punishment by marrying the victim in nine jurisdictions (Bahrain, Iraq, Jordan, Kuwait, Lebanon, Palestine, the Philippines, Tajikistan, and Tunisia).

- Exemption from punishment can be avoided by reaching a "settlement" in twelve jurisdictions (Belgium, Croatia, Iraq, Jordan, Kazakhstan, Lebanon, Palestine, Nigeria, Romania, Russia, Singapore, and Thailand).

- Rape is addressed as an issue of morality versus violent crime in fifteen jurisdictions (Afghanistan, Belgium, China, India, Indonesia, Jordan, Luxembourg, the Netherlands, Nigeria, Pakistan, Palestine, Peru, Singapore, Taiwan, and Yemen).[39]

Equality Now also examined sex trafficking and found that while 134 countries have criminal laws to prohibit it, there are an estimated 20.9 million adults and children who are bought and sold into various forms of sexual, forced, or bonded labor.[40]

MAP 11.2 ● The State of Gay Rights around the World

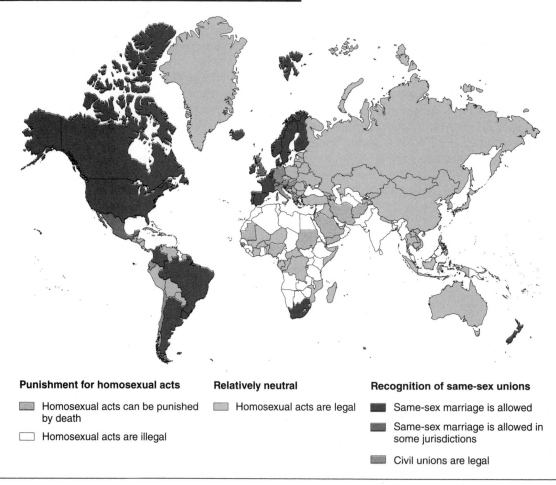

Punishment for homosexual acts

- Homosexual acts can be punished by death
- Homosexual acts are illegal

Relatively neutral

- Homosexual acts are legal

Recognition of same-sex unions

- Same-sex marriage is allowed
- Same-sex marriage is allowed in some jurisdictions
- Civil unions are legal

Source: Darla Cameron and Bonnie Berkowitz, "The State of Gay Rights around the World," Washington Post, updated June 14, 2016, https://www.washingtonpost.com/graphics/world/gay-rights.

WHAT CAN YOU DO WITH INTERNATIONAL STUDIES?

One Student's Journey to Address Human Trafficking by Establishing Her Own NGO

Jillian Mourning, Founder of All We Want is LOVE (Liberation of Victims Everywhere)

International studies opened up a world of culture, understanding, interest, and compassion. I switched after one year at UNC Charlotte from biology to international studies, and it was one of the best decisions I have made to date. I coupled the IS major with German and minored in Holocaust, genocide, and human rights (HGHR). In pursuing my areas of concentration, I had the opportunity to study abroad in Germany and to explore my passion for Holocaust studies. I visited multiple camps and memorials not only in Germany but in Poland, the Netherlands, and the Czech Republic. During my travels, I developed a great interest in human rights abuses and injustices in addition to the Holocaust. I witnessed trafficking and prostitution throughout Europe and was deeply affected. I explored the issue of human trafficking and sexual slavery for my senior thesis.

Two years post-graduation, I decided to do additional research to better understand human trafficking at the local level. Realizing how little North Carolina was doing to address trafficking in terms of awareness and education, specifically in Charlotte, I had a desire to work toward helping educate others about one of the largest human rights abuses of our time. Having been a victim of sexual abuse, I found a way to use a negative situation in my life and my educational experiences to get a conversation going and make a difference. I founded a nonprofit organization called All We Want is LOVE (Liberation of Victims Everywhere) in 2012 and began an amazing, challenging, exhausting, and very rewarding journey. In the few years since, the organization has spoken at more than 100 schools around the country to educate students on human trafficking, hosted conferences for law enforcement and health care, and facilitated projects to provide safe houses with necessities, as well

Photo courtesy of Jillian Mourning.

as donation drives around various holidays for extra items. We have also started a twice-per-week program with Title I elementary school students on issues that create vulnerabilities for human trafficking. We provide those students with an outlet for talking about tough issues and offer them a new pair of shoes upon completion. Many of the children cannot play sports due to a lack of proper shoes. This leaves them with a considerable amount of unsupervised time in the afternoons, when they might become engaged in activities that could threaten their personal security.

My interests and activities led me to begin a master's program in the spring of 2014 with the United Nations–mandated University for Peace. I have completed my coursework and am now working on my thesis that combines my passion for Holocaust studies and sexual violence education. I am exploring sexual violence in the Holocaust compared to modern-day genocide, specifically Darfur, through film and media. My goal is to teach at a college or university about human rights abuses, including but not limited to the Holocaust and human trafficking. I hope to spark an interest in students about the conflicts that fill our world and to encourage them to work toward finding solutions for the human rights injustices of our time.

The differences in the way in which human rights are interpreted is a sensitive subject for less developed countries, as they have argued that more rigorous standards are applied to them, particularly in terms of worker rights. They note that the wealthier countries of the world faced circumstances similar to theirs 100 years ago or more. As a result, they often utilized sweatshops and child labor and violated safety standards in their industrialization efforts, just as developing countries sometimes do now. Today, there are international

A supervisor holds an Apple iPad as he checks an employee's badge during roll call at a Pegatron factory in Shanghai, China, on April 15, 2016. This is the realm in which the world's most profitable smartphones are made, part of Apple's closely guarded supply chain.

regulations that govern these areas, and there is a cost associated with compliance. Demands in many developing countries for labor, as well as the willingness of workers to tolerate inequities, have exacerbated these tensions.

The controversy surrounding the production of Apple products in China illustrates this problem. Foxconn, a Taiwan-based manufacturing giant that assembles many of Apple's electronic products in China, was cited in 2010 for unsafe conditions, inadequate pay, and forced overtime, which placed pressure on workers. These circumstances came to light when eighteen attempted or committed suicide. More recently, in 2016, China Labor Watch found that Pegatron, a major Apple supplier employing almost 100,000 workers in mainland China, has engaged in similar workplace practices.[41] This includes a new scheme that employs "interns"—young workers ages seventeen to eighteen who come to the factories to gain experience and find themselves on the production lines of the latest iPhones. They are working overtime up to eighty hours per month, equivalent to full-time employees, despite Chinese laws that prohibit interns from extra work. Still, there are Chinese vocational students who are willing to accept these conditions as a way to get ahead or are forced by their parents to work to help support their families.

The specific institution that regulates these activities is the International Labour Organization (ILO), which sets the standards for the global workplace. Founded in 1919 after World War I in an effort to create greater equality for working people, the ILO became a specialized agency of the UN in 1946.[42] It is the only "tripartite" organization of the UN, bringing together government representatives, employers, and workers to improve labor conditions around the world. Not all states agree with these principles, however, and compliance can be difficult to assure.

Given the limitations on the effectiveness of international public organizations, the role of NGOs has grown in protecting the rights of individuals. Many NGOs seek to monitor the progress of states in protecting the human rights of their citizens. Human Rights Watch works to give voice to those who are oppressed, publishing more than 100 reports and briefings on conditions in ninety countries.[43] Freedom House is another NGO that advocates for human rights and serves as an international watchdog to assure democratic freedoms.[44] Their *Freedom in the World* annual report offers comparative data on global political rights and civil liberties for 195 countries and fourteen territories. It is widely used around the world to monitor freedom and human rights generally.

What Can Be Done?

There is a real and immediate need for effective leadership that can guide governments, corporations, international organizations, and other institutions to work jointly to promote international cooperation. All too frequently, national leaders focus on their own short-term interests and not on broader, global, long-term concerns. IGOs have also struggled to keep pace with the rapid changes transforming the world. They have failed to redefine their core competencies vis-à-vis the emerging capacities of the private sector and NGOs. Their structure and the interests of their member states frequently limit IGOs. The extent to which they are able to work together to address the really critical issues confronting the world today may well require some system of international cooperation that goes beyond national boundaries.

While the term *global governance* may sound like global government, in fact, it refers to the "management of transnational issues through voluntary international cooperation," according to Hakan Altinay, senior fellow at the Brookings Institution and the founding director of the Open Society Foundation in Turkey.[45] It has been a successful strategy for the administration of many functional areas in the international system, from simple travel accords and practices to more complicated arenas, such as the environment. Nevertheless, the concept can be problematic for different groups around the world.

Global Governance Watch, a joint project of the American Enterprise Institute (AEI, a conservative public policy think tank in Washington, DC) and the Federalist Society for Law and Public Policy Studies (also a conservative organization for legal reformers), argues that the movement toward global governance is a threat to national sovereignty. These groups focus on monitoring the transparency and accountability of both IGOs and NGOs and the extent to which these organizations are influencing domestic political outcomes.[46] They are particularly concerned with the interface between global action and national interests in four areas: international organizations, business and human rights, European institutions, and global political Islam. The views of the Trump administration, including its lack of support for global institutions, reinforce this position.

Given these limitations, what other approaches can be used to address global issues? The concept of international regimes describes one way in which groups have worked together outside traditional frameworks.[47] **International regimes** refer to cooperation among states based on custom and practice, without formal agreement. They represent other avenues that can be pursued when states are unable to reach agreement on steps to address particular issues or situations through formal procedures that already exist, and when international organizations are not capable of generating acceptable solutions.

international regimes
cooperation among states based on custom and practice, without formal agreement

International regimes have been particularly prominent in relationship to the environment, frequently establishing lines of cooperation that later translate into formal agreements. The Convention on International Trade in Endangered Species of Wild Fauna and Flora, entered into force in 1975, is one example where common concerns about wildlife brought interested parties together for conservation. Today, 183 countries voluntarily agree to comply with the framework of this convention to provide protection to 35,000 animal species and plant specimens.[48]

Individuals can also play a role as they exercise their rights as global citizens. The interdependence of the international system and the way technology has transformed the connectedness between people across the planet require new institutions that can respond to these challenges. The knowledge people have of others around the globe and the conditions in which they exist creates a global human empathy that returns to Rousseau's concept of a social contract. In the age of Facebook, Instagram, Twitter, and YouTube, people can put pressure on their own governmental institutions to act in response to human rights abuses.

Photo by Scott Olson/Getty Images.

Demonstrators protest President Donald Trump's decision to exit the Paris climate change accord on June 2, 2017, in Chicago, Illinois.

transnational advocacy
networks (TANs) networks
that provide opportunities
for cooperation and
collaboration for people
across borders to channel
their influence in the
international arena

Margaret Keck and Kathryn Sikkink refer to the associations of like-minded people who come together on global issues as **transnational advocacy networks (TANs)**.[49] These networks provide opportunities for cooperation and collaboration across borders to channel influence in the international arena. They take some of the issues of greatest concern, such as human rights and the environment, back to the people who are most affected to bring about change that is not constrained by national boundaries. The Occupy Wall Street movement is an example of a TAN. It originated in the United States and spread to more than 100 US cities and 1,500 cities around the world to protest the structure of the international economy, which it saw as disproportionally favoring the richest 1 percent of the world's population.[50] A similar response to President Trump's rejection of the Paris Agreement on Climate Change has invigorated individuals and state and local governments to take a stand in opposition to the Trump administration's stance.

Managing the world and the many issues confronting it will require cooperation. Global issues cross international borders, and it will be incumbent on people of different nationalities to work together to solve them. The SDGs offer goals to strive for, and there has been some success. Innovative and dynamic partnerships between and among governments, NGOs, the private sector, and IGOs will be necessary to address the challenges ahead. You will also need to consider your own contributions to this process. Chapter 12 offers you a guide as to how you can participate.

Key Concepts

To Learn More

Books and Other Print Media

Laurie Garrett, *Betrayal of Trust: The Collapse of Global Public Health* (New York: Hyperion, 2001).

Best-selling author Laurie Garrett exposes global public health issues that could give rise to a potential disaster, including the outbreak of EVD in the DRC (then Zaire) and the deterioration of health care in the former Soviet Union.

Nicholas D. Kristof and Sheryl WuDunn, *Half the Sky: Turning Oppression into Opportunity for Women Worldwide* (New York: Knopf, 2009).

This book takes a critical look at the continued disparities and oppression faced by women around the world.

Somaly Mam, *The Road of Lost Innocence: The True Story of a Cambodian Heroine* (New York: Spiegel & Grau, 2009).

Sold into sexual slavery at age twelve, Mam uncovers the dark world of human trafficking in Southeast Asia and her transformation into a leader in the fight against it.

Peter Manzel, Charles C. Mann, and Paul Kennedy, *Material World: A Global Family Portrait* (New York: Sierra Club Books, 1994).

This book unwraps the contents of peoples' homes from around the world to uncover what they value and cherish most.

Dambisa Moyo, *Dead Aid: Why Aid Is Not Working and How There Is a Better Way for Africa* (New York: Farrar, Straus and Giroux, 2009).

This *New York Times* best-seller challenges the way in which aid has been given to African nations and suggests an alternative model.

Nina Munk, *The Idealist: Jeffrey Sachs and the Quest to End Poverty* (New York: Doubleday, 2013).

This book looks at the relationship between the ideas of Jeffrey Sachs, whose best-seller, *The End of Poverty*, has been very influential in the fight against poverty, and how these ideas have actually played out in Africa.

Sonia Shah, *Pandemic: Tracking Contagions, from Cholera to Ebola and Beyond* (New York: Farrar, Straus and Giroux, 2016).

Prizewinning journalist Sonia Shah explores the origins of contagions and their transmission to understand the new diseases challenging the world today.

Rordan Wilkinson and Jennifer Clapp (eds.), *Global Governance, Poverty and Inequality* (New York: Routledge, 2010).

This book looks at the role global governance can play in addressing poverty.

Websites

Bill & Melinda Gates Foundation, http://www.gatesfoundation.org

The Gates Foundation supports global development and global health through foundation grants in countries around the world.

Doctors Without Borders (Médecins sans Frontières), www.doctorswithoutborders.org

The group's official website features information about its work, including press releases, blog posts, and videos.

Food and Agriculture Organization of the United Nations (FAO), www.fao.org

The FAO is a specialized agency of the UN focusing on food security in developed and developing countries alike. Its website contains a wealth of information, including the FAO Food Price Index, descriptions of its key programs, and statistical databases.

Human Rights Watch, www.hrw.org

Human Rights Watch is an independent NGO dedicated to defending human rights and reporting on violations.

International Labour Organization (ILO), www.ilo.org

The ILO is a specialized agency of the UN that is dedicated to the protection of workers' rights around the world.

"On the Ground," http://kristof.blogs.nytimes.com

The online version of Nicholas Kristof's *New York Times* op-ed column discusses an array of global policy issues.

UN World Food Programme (WFP), www.wfp.org

The WFP is the agency of the UN that deals with matters related to food aid and assistance. Its website features information about hunger and countries with chronic hunger problems.

World Health Organization (WHO), www.who.int

The WHO is a specialized agency of the UN dedicated to global public health, providing coordination of effort and services.

Videos

Born into Brothels (2004)

This documentary explores the world of Sonagachi, the red-light district of Calcutta, India, and the children who live there.

Don't Panic: How to End Poverty in 15 Years (2015), http://www.films.com/ecTitleDetail.aspx?TitleID=127774&r=SR

This video offers a statistical evaluation of the progress on poverty to date and how the world can move forward.

Flip Your Thinking on AIDS in Africa (2007), www.ted.com/talks/emily_oster_flips_our_thinking_on_aids_in_africa.html

Through an economics lens, Emily Oster reexamines our knowledge about HIV/AIDS in Africa and reorients our strategy in battling the disease.

Global Health and Human Development (2011)

This short video offers an overview of the UN Human Development Index and the 2015 MDGs through the work of Australia's Nossal Institute for Global Health in one community in Ghana.

How Mr. Condom Made Thailand a Better Place (2010), www.ted.com/talks/mechai_viravaidya_how_mr_ condom_made_thailand_a_better_place.html

Mechai Viravaidya discusses the successes of family planning and child mortality reduction programs in Thailand and the role of condoms in raising Thailand's standard of living.

Lost in Lebanon (2017)

This film follows the lives of four Syrian refugees as they seek a new life in Lebanon to escape the humanitarian crisis of the Syrian conflict.

The Perfect Famine (2003), http://www.bullfrogfilms .com/catalog/l3tpf.html

This short documentary focuses on the conditions that caused famine in Malawi.

"Unlock the Intelligence, Passion, Greatness of Girls" (2012), www.ted.com/talks/leymah_gbowee_unlock_ the_intelligence_passion_greatness_of_girls.html

In this TED Talk, Nobel laureate Leymah Gbowee speaks about how we can transform the world by empowering girls.

"The Worst Place on Earth to Be a Woman": Healing the Eastern Congo (2012), https://www.youtube.com/ watch?v=qTQerPA5jF4

This is a short report on HEAL Africa, an organization that helps women healing from injuries sustained from rape and assault in the DRC.

MAKEPOVERTYHISTORY

12

Connecting to the World
Where Do You Go from Here?

Studying abroad adds another level to your college experience. . . . It is so important today to have a solid understanding of different cultures, and I think sending students abroad is an easy way to set up our generation to be a more globally minded society.

—Emily O'Hara, "Become Global Minded," studyabroad.com, 2011[1]

Learning Objectives

After studying this chapter, you will be able to do the following:

- Understand what it means to study abroad and the range of opportunities available.

- Identify the types of international careers available in the private sector, in government, and in intergovernmental organizations (IGOs) and nongovernmental organizations (NGOs).

- Understand the opportunities for advanced academic study available to graduates with international studies backgrounds.

N ot that long ago, only the wealthy and powerful had the means to become citizens of the world. The technological revolutions in travel and communications have opened up this possibility to more and more people. Interacting with others whose backgrounds and customs are different from our own is not an easy task. It can lead to embarrassing or uncomfortable moments. If you found yourself sitting down to a meal in another country, staring at an undesirable-looking local delicacy you were expected to consume, would you risk insulting your hosts by refusing to taste it? Remember Sudanese lost boy Valentino Achak Deng's discomfort in the opening to Chapter 8 as he sat down to an unfamiliar meal. If you were visiting a country where modest types of clothing are the custom, would you wear shorts? Before traveling to another country, are you likely to familiarize yourself with the gestures that are considered disrespectful or profane? These questions relate directly to the challenge of going beyond our comfort zones to engage more directly with the world in which we live.

To work and operate effectively in a global environment, you will be called upon to demonstrate levels of political, economic, and cultural sophistication. Critical thinking, communication, language, collaboration, and technology skills will be indispensable.[2] International studies programs and courses can help provide you with the requisite tools. To be more fully prepared, however, it is best to experience the world even as you are learning about it. This was clearly evident in the journey of Emily O'Hara, who provided the opening quote to this chapter; her study abroad program in England gave her opportunities to encounter unfamiliar circumstances and practices over the course of her travels.[3]

This chapter lays out the practical elements that should accompany your academic studies for a fuller understanding of the world. It identifies some of the hands-on experiences that are at your disposal as you move through your undergraduate studies, such as work and study abroad, service learning, and internships. It also addresses how you might think about and prepare for a career in international service.

International Studies beyond the Classroom

Study abroad offers students opportunities to expand their horizons and appreciations. Many of our students have reported that the study abroad experience was the highlight of their undergraduate education, and some have gone so far as to suggest that it was truly life

study abroad to attend an educational institution in another country

Peace Corps volunteer Marya Cota-Wilson teaches students how to garden in Costa Rica.

Paul Conklin/Getty Images.

altering, in terms of thinking about future plans and careers. These experiences expose students to a particular foreign culture, while giving them the opportunity to make important contacts and forge lasting relationships with people they encounter along the way. They may also provide a base for additional travel during periods when classes are not in session. It is important to select a program that fits with both your interests and your academic needs. Living arrangements (apartment, dorm, or host family), instructional language, curriculum or course options available to foreign students, and thematic focus vary. A desirable and safe location is often a high priority.

Study abroad programs and exchanges are the most common ways to study the world beyond the classroom. The 2016 annual report of the Institute of International Education, *Open Doors 2016*, showed that the total number of American students studying abroad has more than tripled over the past two decades. While European countries remain the most popular destinations, China and a number of other developing and emerging economies now account for nearly half of the top twenty-five sites (see Figure 12.1). But while more Americans are studying abroad, the trend is for shorter stays. The majority (63.1 percent) choose programs offered either in the summer session or during midwinter break, rather than a full semester abroad.[4]

These numbers represent a very small percentage of students enrolled on US campuses; only 313,415 studied abroad during the 2014–2015 academic year. This was a mere 1.6 percent of total students enrolled at US higher education institutions that year. Overall, only an estimated 10 percent of US undergraduates study abroad at some point over the course of their degree program.[5] Students choose not to go abroad for many different reasons: their program of study does not allow time for or require an international experience, students lack resources, they do not see its advantages, or their parents do not support it. Together, these factors keep the overall numbers relatively low. At the same time, the US overseas connections continue to be enhanced by the considerable number of international students on US campuses. In the 2015–2016 academic year, the total passed the threshold of 1 million as it reached 1,043,839 students, up 7.1 percent from the previous year. International students now account for around 5 percent of total enrollments at US colleges and universities.[6]

FIGURE 12.1 ● Host Regions of US Study Abroad Students

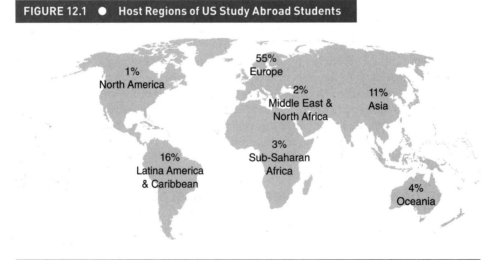

Source: Data from Institute of International Education, Open Doors, 2016, *Open Doors Report on International Educational Exchange*, https://www.iie.org/Research-and-Insights/Open-Doors/Fact-Sheets-and-Infographics/Infographics/US-Study-Abroad-Data.

For students enrolled in international studies programs, study abroad or some alternative international experience is essential in gaining an appreciation of the world's complexity and the challenges of operating effectively within it. Unfortunately, even some of the most committed students may not have the time or resources to participate beyond a few weeks. But the impact of short-term programs can be enhanced by intensive immersion into another culture as well as thoughtful preparation for and reflection on the experience. This is usually provided by the several pre- and post-departure class sessions that are a part of most of these programs, where students complete readings and assignments (as they would in a more traditional class) and engage in a thorough debriefing upon their return, where they consider what they have gained and learned from the course.

Many employers have come to look favorably on the study abroad experience in terms of the knowledge and skills that it may foster in prospective employees. It might even tip the balance in a hiring decision. Personnel managers often see experience living and studying abroad as an indicator of such traits as initiative and adaptability.[7]

Most universities offer many options and have a study abroad office or designated adviser to assist with the selection process. In many cases, programs originate from the school itself, and students are usually eligible to enroll in those offered by other accredited institutions. There are also some highly regarded private companies that organize and administer programs for academic credit. These tend to be rather expensive. A study abroad adviser can ensure that such an experience is reputable and that its academic credits are transferable.

Exchange agreements are the most cost-effective alternatives. These formal arrangements enable students to enroll at foreign universities for the same tuition as they would pay at home. Given the price advantage and the fact that the flow of incoming and outgoing students between the partner institutions must be relatively balanced, spaces in these programs are often limited. Familiarity with the range of opportunities and a prompt application can help you secure an available slot.

exchange agreements arrangements that enable students to study abroad at foreign universities for the same tuition that they would pay to the home institution

While not all study abroad programs center around learning another language, many students use the experience to enhance this skill. The ability to communicate effectively in a different language is a critical requirement for many international careers. Employers view linguistic competency very favorably, and it could well prove the key determinant in landing a position. By sequencing your study abroad experience with your advanced language training, you can hone your skills through ongoing communication with native speakers. Given critical shifts in the global political and economic arenas, languages such as Arabic and Chinese are in particularly high demand. While these languages may be challenging to master, time spent on becoming proficient may pay off in terms of expanding employment prospects.

If you cannot participate in a formal study program, there are other ways to sample the world. There are companies that advertise on campus, offering relatively inexpensive international airfares to students. Check with the study abroad or student affairs office to help determine the reputation and reliability of these firms. Once abroad, you can usually find reasonable accommodations at youth hostels or other budget rooming houses. Foreign travel of any sort is useful in learning to adjust to unfamiliar circumstances and to interact in a setting where the language is different and local customs seem strange. It might also prove valuable in assisting with decisions regarding the languages you study, the courses you take, or the career you choose to pursue.

Even if you cannot go abroad, you can increase your international awareness right at home by visiting a local international grocery store, attending an ethnic festival, enjoying food from another country, or viewing a foreign film. While not the same as traveling or studying abroad, these experiences can be enlightening. The challenge is greater in less cosmopolitan areas, but today a foreign country is just a click away with a laptop or smartphone at hand.

A Dong Supermarket in Westminster's Little Saigon in Southern California has a former South Vietnam flag and an American flag draped in the front windows.

service learning programs that combine classroom education with opportunities that engage students directly in service activities

internships positions that offer practical training in workplace settings

Globalization has brought the world closer to home. Opportunities have expanded for communicating with diverse communities, working with agencies or nongovernmental organizations (NGOs) with an international agenda, volunteering to assist immigrant groups, or joining in global projects and activities, either locally or abroad. These are commonly referred to as **service learning** opportunities, as they engage students in situations that they have become aware of through their classroom studies. Real-life experiences are a critical part of any undergraduate education. They have also become increasingly important to employers in evaluating job applicants.

In addition to increasing marketability, service learning and internships offer the chance to develop important job-related skills. Although **internships** often do not pay, they provide practical training in a professional setting and the opportunity to observe actual workplace processes and practices. Interns perform clerical tasks—they run errands, make copies of documents, file papers, and answer the phones. In return, companies or agencies train them to become involved in more meaningful activities. For any internship to be worthwhile, it must offer a reasonable degree of professional engagement. Thus, before accepting a position, students need to check to ensure that they will have some chance to partake in non-clerical activities related directly to the mission of the organization. The relationships forged with supervisors, clients, and customers may also open doors to future employment.

HOW YOU CAN CONNECT

You can gain international experience by . . .

- traveling independently
- participating in a formal study abroad program
- acquiring an internship in another country
- interacting with students on campus who come from other countries
- volunteering with international organizations or groups within your community

---

An internship can be time-consuming, but it can also be very rewarding and illuminating. Here is one student's view of her work with a local nonprofit that hosted international visitors on formal exchange visits:

A Nonprofit Experience

My internship at International House has been one of my best career moves yet. I gained insight into the professional realm of non-profits, experience in event

> coordination and planning, and knowledge about a variety of cultures from all over the world. . . . It helped to develop my professional persona . . . and helped renew my passion for culture and showed me that being able to relate to the world from different cultural perspectives will always be an asset.[8]
>
> —Kristina Bergan

Kristina would go on to observe that the internship was the highlight of her undergraduate experience as she gained insights about a variety of cultures and peoples from her encounters with visiting officials from Brazil, Tajikistan, Taiwan, and elsewhere.

Because many academic institutions have only limited resources to support internships, students are often responsible for identifying their own opportunities. Planning should begin well in advance. You might start by meeting with your academic adviser and visiting the university career center. The study abroad office or adviser should have information on overseas programs. Be sure to exhaust every potential resource to identify possibilities, including faculty, family members, and even friends and acquaintances. Do not forget your own backyard. Larger communities, especially those located in or near major metropolitan centers, have numerous organizations and enterprises with international connections and interests. Many schools allow students to receive academic credit for their internships. In these cases, a set number of hours will need to be completed, and interns are likely to be responsible for keeping a journal of their activities or completing some other type of written assignment.

International Career Opportunities

Your coursework in international studies and experience with the international community will give you more in-depth knowledge of particular issue areas and a fuller appreciation of the diversity of perceptions and interests across the world. What are you likely to do with this information? How are you going to put your interests to work? Perhaps most important, what can you do with a background in international studies? A range of options and numerous resources can help you answer these questions and further enhance your global skills and competencies.

HOW YOU CAN CONNECT

You can begin to prepare for a career in the international field by . . .

- visiting your campus career center, attending career-related workshops, and talking to your professors

- investigating possible options for advanced study after graduation that will provide you with the knowledge and skills you will need to build your credentials

- pursuing opportunities to gain hands-on volunteer or work experiences during your undergraduate years to help identify your particular interests

- interacting with people from other countries and cultures in your own community and visiting or studying in other countries if possible

A job in the global workplace could take you anywhere in the world that needs your talents. At the same time, rapid advances in technology will lead to the creation of innovative types of jobs that will demand new or enhanced knowledge and skills. While most students enter international studies programs knowing that they wish to pursue some sort of global career, not many know exactly what that means in practical terms or have a sense of how to go about it. Despite the ups and downs of the job market, the number of positions in the international field is likely to grow, and there will be opportunities to apply your training in a variety of ways.

Students considering international studies (and their parents) frequently express concern about its **employability quotient**—its ability to prepare them for work in the real world. Questions relating to jobs and careers are both advisable and appropriate. International studies curricula generally incorporate many of the liberal arts and offer training that may open any number of paths to employment. The pursuit of an international studies degree in conjunction with study of a particular academic discipline (e.g., anthropology, economics, geography, history, political science)—either as a second major, minor, or track—can be a good way to go to enhance your marketability in a specific area.

International studies programs offer strong intellectual preparation in their own right and prepare students for careers that transcend traditional borders. For the most part, these programs have a rigorous set of academic requirements that include direct international experience or exposure and intermediate or advanced foreign language competency. This package can go a long way in providing students with an important competitive edge. Despite only limited prior training related directly to the position she was offered, one of our recent graduates reported that she secured a job with a large French oil company due to her research skills and language fluency, as well as the significant on-the-ground experience she acquired while studying abroad.

Most international studies curricula also promote the development of effective written and oral communication capabilities. International studies helps students develop **transferable skills** that they may apply broadly and that a range of prospective employers will value. These include writing and research and the ability to communicate across languages and cultures. The types of courses that generally comprise international studies programs also tend to challenge students in ways that require them to tap into skills that are critical to success in the twenty-first century workplace. Dubbed the four *C*s, these include critical thinking, communication, collaboration, and creativity.[9] Together, they make international studies graduates attractive job candidates with a set of core competencies that is useful in a variety of settings.

International studies students may find employment in government, nonprofit organizations, business, law, media, education, international program administration, or the military—depending on their interests, skills, and experiences. Our graduates have gone on to work with refugee resettlement agencies and other humanitarian organizations. They have found positions in public relations, health, teaching, law, student services, and translation services. Some have sharpened their skills to pursue careers in journalism, filmmaking, and photography. Graduates who have entered the business world have worked for airlines, automobile companies, banks, and textile manufacturers in their international divisions. Others have taught English in Japan and South Korea and English as a second language to immigrants at US high schools and community colleges. Still others have secured employment with the US government in diplomatic, military, and intelligence capacities. Our students from abroad have returned home to work for their governments or nonprofit organizations.

US Department of State

Many students are attracted to international studies with an eye toward a career in diplomacy. For US students, this may mean a position with the Foreign Service of the

---

employability quotient the extent to which a course of study provides sufficient preparation for gainful employment

transferable skills talents and abilities that may be applied to a range of settings and job environments

US Department of State. Aspiring **Foreign Service Officers (FSOs)** may choose from among five career paths—political, economic, management, consular, and public diplomacy. FSOs engage in interesting and rewarding careers, but the selection process is extremely rigorous. It begins with a written Foreign Service examination and continues with a series of other interviews and screenings for those who score high enough to move forward. It is estimated that no more than 20 to 25 percent of those taking the exam pass during any given year, with far fewer finally receiving an offer of employment.[10] Candidates must be prepared to serve in any capacity anywhere in the world, representing and defending all existing policies of the United States.

NurPhoto/Contributor.

Ukrainian president Petro Poroshenko (right) and US secretary of state Rex Tillerson (left) speak during a joint media conference following their meeting in Kiev, Ukraine, on July 9, 2017.

Foreign Service Officers (FSOs) diplomats employed by the US Department of State

Many other jobs besides being an FSO advance the diplomatic mission. The Department of State offers a comprehensive online guide to career opportunities, including information on the application process.[11] Successful candidates generally possess a broad base of knowledge and specialized expertise in some aspect of international affairs. Foreign language fluency is not required at entry, but coming in with a high level of proficiency can lead to a more desirable posting.

Other US Government Positions

Many federal departments and agencies—even those with primarily domestic agendas—have goals that are best served by employees with international sensitivities and perspectives. There are all sorts of options. For students focusing on international business and finance, the Departments of Commerce and Treasury have positions dealing with trade, investment, and other economic policy matters. Through its Foreign Agricultural Service, the US Department of Agriculture (USDA) has a network of offices across the world to promote export opportunities and global food security. The Departments of Education, Energy, Justice, and Labor also have internationally oriented jobs. Any number of executive agencies and commissions may also be worth pursuing. These include the US Agency for International Development (USAID), the Drug Enforcement Administration, the Environmental Protection Agency, the Export-Import Bank, the Federal Communications Commission, the General Services Administration, and the Office of the US Trade Representative. Each of these organizations has its own procedures for recruiting and hiring.

International studies students also look to careers related to defense and security. For some, the path may be through the military. The Department of Defense has a wide variety of jobs of both a military and a civilian nature. In addition, many federal departments and agencies have their own intelligence units and personnel. The Central Intelligence Agency, the Federal Bureau of Investigation, and the National Security Agency (NSA) are particularly desirable possibilities for those interested in this field. The Department of Homeland Security is also worth serious consideration. Best known as the guardian of airline security through its Transportation Security Administration, the department is actually a large and complex organization that pursues an overall task of strengthening the country's defense against terrorism. As in the case of the Foreign Service, these intelligence-based positions are highly competitive and can be difficult to attain. Candidates with prior experience, substantive background, and foreign language skills (especially in those languages that are considered of critical strategic importance) will have an advantage.[12]

Job seekers interested in the legislative branch of government may be encouraged to know that the number of employees with international expertise on Capitol Hill has greatly increased since 2001. More and more members of the US Congress find themselves engaged in foreign and defense policy and look to round out their staffs with experts. In addition, dozens of the approximately 250 committees and subcommittees in the US Senate and the House of Representatives seek staff with expertise in international affairs. There is no single recruiting or hiring process for these jobs, and they are difficult to secure. Personal contacts from previous partisan political involvement or prior internships may be particularly important to making these types of connections.[13]

Moreover, state governments (and even some local ones) have needs for people with expertise related to immigration, trade, and other sorts of international issues that are of increasing importance to them. Some state governments even have offices abroad to promote economic development opportunities. Washington State is a case in point, with more than $86 billion in exports (the country's third largest number, behind California and New York) and more than 100,000 residents working for foreign-owned firms. The state employs a number of foreign trade representatives to further local business interests in European, Asian, and Latin American markets. It also operates offices in China, India, Japan, Mexico, and some European countries. In addition, periodic overseas business missions by state officials and business executives are sponsored to encourage investment by foreign companies.[14]

Peace Corps a US government agency that sends volunteers to assist other countries, to promote friendship and mutual understanding

Volunteering with the **Peace Corps** is good preparation for these positions. Many of our students have taken this route, completing a two-year commitment to service abroad on behalf of the US government. Established in 1961, the Peace Corps dispatches people to work at the grassroots level in such areas as education, community development, health, agriculture, and engineering. Some of these positions require specialized skills. For the most part, however, the organization casts a wide net in terms of its recruitment. Today, close to 7,000 volunteers operate in sixty-three countries, with the greatest concentration in Africa and Latin America. Since its creation, the Peace Corps has sent more than 220,000 to 140 host countries.[15] Living conditions are often quite basic, and the financial arrangements are modest.

The opportunities described here require US citizenship, but international studies programs in the United States also prepare foreign students for government careers

The Peace Corps.

Community health volunteer Michelle Joffe is pictured with her primary school students at an orphanage in Uganda as they celebrate the installation of a new water well. Michelle received both her undergraduate and graduate degrees from Tulane University.

back home. The paths to these jobs are unique to each country. Quite often, these students come from families that have been involved in government service or political activity. For some of our African students, in particular, these experiences have resulted in significant personal dramas and uncertainties as political circumstances in their countries have changed. For example, we have hosted students from the Democratic Republic of Congo (DRC), Liberia, and Sudan whose nations and families have endured considerable instability and conflict. Of course, prevailing sociopolitical conditions will influence their prospects for government service or political activism. For one of our former students, a lost boy from

Sudan whose village was ravaged by war, the easing of violence (along with the financial support he secured from contacts he made in the United States) enabled him to travel home to build a school to replace the one that had been destroyed.

International Organizations

International organizations engaged in a range of activities across the globe number in the thousands. Students with interests in economics and finance should take a look at inter-governmental organizations (IGOs) such as the International Monetary Fund (IMF), the World Bank, or similar bodies operating at the regional level. An advanced degree is often a prerequisite for these jobs, in which case an entry-level position at another, more general organization may be a better place to start.

We occasionally hear from international studies students that their dream job would be one with the United Nations (UN). To be sure, working for the UN can be a particularly good fit. The entry-level Young Professionals Programme is for those interested in working for the Secretariat, the organization's administrative arm. Applicants must submit to a competitive exam to determine their initial eligibility. An Associate Experts Programme attracts candidates interested in working on projects designed to assist developing countries, and there are other opportunities to work directly for the UN agencies, funds, and programs that operate across the world. Jobs are apportioned geographically to ensure representation across all member states. An internship program open to advanced undergraduate and graduate students is also in place. The UN has a comprehensive job portal that advertises career opportunities.[16]

NGOs may offer more options than IGOs. These groups cover the full range of global issues. They frequently operate on a nonprofit basis, so salaries are modest. Today, there are well over 60,000 international NGOs.[17] While organizations such as Amnesty International and Greenpeace (two particularly well-known NGOs) seek to convey information and bring atten-tion to matters of global significance, their primary mission is to advocate for change in policies and practices related to their areas of concern. These organizations can be found across a broad political spectrum. The World Association of Non-Governmental Organizations (WANGO) provides consider-able information about the work of many groups at www.wango.org and lists NGOs associated with the UN. A good number of NGOs work toward enhancing development across the Global South and provide unique and rewarding, if highly challenging, experi-ences. The Global Volunteer Network (GVN) Foundation, for example, works to alleviate poverty by partnering with local organiza-tions to complete specific community-based projects. In addition to its staff, the GVN has interns from around the world who volunteer for six-month tours to assist with the implementation of these projects.[18]

In George Square in Glasgow, supporters of Amnesty International, Oxfam Scotland, and the Scottish Refugee Council form a giant human chain to mark World Refugee Day and to also mark the start of the Refugee Festival Scotland.

Andrew Milligan/PA Images via Getty Images.

Private Sector

For an ever-increasing number of companies, doing business—even if it is primarily in one country—involves global connections. Although international studies majors may lack aca-demic credentials in marketing or finance, employers value their broad liberal arts training and sensitivity to the nuances of interacting with clients and partners from other backgrounds and cultures. As one hiring manager has put it, "All major hiring companies need global citizens. Global sensitivities, global perspective, global insight, along with the maturity and a capacity for risk-taking, are exactly the skills every major organization is looking for—in every industry."[19] Quite often, the most important tools required for success in the workplace are acquired on the job itself. Technical training may be provided in-house, and the company may support advanced education to promote professional development.

International studies can provide a path to any number of other careers in the private sector, such as banking and other financial services, translating, journalism and other media, travel and tourism, public relations, and law. With so many industries and interest groups actively involved in efforts to influence legislation (many in and around Washington, DC), moreover, a position as a political lobbyist is also a possibility. Lobbyists engage in a variety of activities to secure favorable responses from legislators on matters of importance to the organizations they represent.

This brief review of some career options merely scratches the surface. It is never too early, however, to begin thinking about how your choice of a program of study will significantly impact your future. Finding the path that best meets your needs and suits your talents will probably be a challenge. Given the complex and competitive nature of the job market, it is important to be proactive and to start early in considering the types of positions that might interest you. This process requires time and energy, and you can enhance it considerably by seeking out professors, academic advisers, career services, and other campus resources. As noted earlier, internships can offer real-world experience related to possible fields of interest and add to your credentials. Even if you do not really have a clue at this point, you might spend some time considering your interests and how they might translate into a prospective career path. This would be useful in guiding decisions with respect to the courses you take, the types of internships you might pursue, the additional languages you learn, and the destination for your study abroad experience.

Educational Options

A liberal arts education is an approach to learning that is intended to prepare students to deal with the complexity and diversity of the world in which they live. In addition to offering broad knowledge across an array of subjects and academic disciplines, it also provides the opportunity to gain in-depth knowledge in a specific area of interest.[20] Like other liberal arts majors, international studies may not necessarily provide a direct route to a career in the field without training beyond the undergraduate level. A liberal arts degree prepares you for graduate school, business school, law school, journalism school, or other professional degrees.

Graduate Programs in International Affairs

Some students entering international studies programs express an interest in pursuing a career in teaching and research. The path to becoming a faculty member at a four-year college or university can be a lengthy one. In most cases, a doctorate (usually a PhD) is required for a full-time position. This takes approximately four to six years of study beyond the undergraduate level and includes the writing of a dissertation, a book-length original research project on a particular issue or problem. Your professors can provide you with details as to the nature of the process. A growing number of part-time faculty are teaching classes at many institutions, and these jobs, as well as those at community colleges, may be open to candidates with a master's degree (generally attainable within a two-year period). Teaching languages, history, or social studies at the secondary or even primary level is also a possibility. Certification is usually required and may be secured in combination with many undergraduate majors by taking the appropriate education courses. While an advanced degree is generally not mandatory for teaching secondary or primary school, it is highly recommended and is often necessary to progress professionally and to command higher salaries.

In addition to providing the necessary credential to secure a faculty position at a college or university, a PhD (doctor of philosophy) also qualifies you to work as a researcher or analyst for the government or some privately funded policy institutes (often referred to as **think tanks**). PhD programs are generally organized by discipline, such as anthropology, geography, foreign language, history, or political science. There are also a few interdisciplinary doctoral programs in international/global studies.[21]

think tanks privately funded research- and policy-oriented institutes

In some cases, students may be admitted directly to a PhD program when they finish their undergraduate studies. They earn their master's degree once they complete the requisite number of classes and requirements along the way. In other instances, students may choose to enroll in a particular institution to acquire their master's and then seek entrance to a PhD program elsewhere to continue with their studies. The standardized Graduate Record Examination (GRE) is often required as part of the admissions process. As you evaluate prospective programs, pay particular attention to financial support for both first-year and continuing students and the procedures for assisting graduates in their search for employment.

Most agencies, and even some companies, looking for employees with international knowledge and awareness will welcome individuals with master's-level training. A discipline-based program offering internationally oriented coursework and training will generally provide preparation of an academic nature. It is designed to further understanding of the theories, concepts, and issues that form the basis of the respective disciplines.

The number of master's-level programs that focus on preparing you for a professional career in the field of international affairs is growing. These tend to be interdisciplinary in character and may closely resemble the structure of your undergraduate international studies program. They focus more on training that can be applied directly to work situations and may often include requirements, tracks, or courses relating to policy analysis, program administration, and foreign language proficiency. In the past, these types of programs were geared mainly toward students seeking diplomatic or other types of government careers. More recently, many programs have extended their curricula to accommodate students with more diverse career interests and aspirations.

A good place to begin learning about these possibilities is the Association of Professional Schools of International Affairs (APSIA). Its thirty-seven members and thirty-one affiliates are among the more interesting and highly regarded programs from around the world (see Table 12.1).[22] In addition to standard classroom work, many also offer opportunities to acquire practical experience along the way. Although it is certainly no guarantee, a broadly constructed and professionally oriented master's degree in international or public affairs could go a long way toward enhancing your employability in the field.

Business School

Given the growing networks that connect the global marketplace, it is certainly appropriate for international studies students to consider careers in management, marketing, finance, or accounting via the business school route. Hiring managers in both the private and public sector may see a master of business administration (MBA) degree as a particularly desirable, if not required, credential. Business school curricula include a heavy dose of quantitatively based courses, and this prompts some undergraduate international studies programs to include required courses in economics or math and statistics as preparation. If you find

TABLE 12.1 ● Association of Professional Schools of International Affairs: Member Schools	
Institution	**Degree Offered or School**
American University	School of International Service
Carleton University	Norman Paterson School of International Affairs
Columbia University	School of International and Public Affairs
Duke University	Sanford School of Public Policy
George Washington University	Elliott School of International Affairs
Georgetown University	Edmund A. Walsh School of Foreign Service
Georgia Institute of Technology	Sam Nunn School of International Affairs
Graduate Institute of International and Development Studies	The Graduate Institute, Geneva
Harvard University	John F. Kennedy School of Government
IE University (Spain)	School of International Relations
Johns Hopkins University	Paul H. Nitze School of Advanced International Studies
Korea University	Graduate School of International Studies
MGIMO University	Moscow State Institute of International Relations
National University of Singapore	Lee Kuan Yew School of Public Policy
Pennsylvania State University	School of International Affairs
Princeton University	Woodrow Wilson School of Public and International Affairs
Ritsumeikan University	Graduate School of International Relations
Sciences Po (Paris)	Master in International Affairs
Seoul National University	Graduate School of International Studies
St. Petersburg State University	School of International Relations
Stockholm School of Economics	Stockholm School of Economics
Syracuse University	The Maxwell School
Texas A&M University	Bush School of Government & Public Service
Tufts University	The Fletcher School of Law and Diplomacy
University of California, San Diego	Graduate School of International Relations and Pacific Studies
University of Denver	Josef Korbel School of International Studies
University of Maryland	School of Public Policy
University of Michigan	Gerald R. Ford School of Public Policy
University of Minnesota	Hubert H. Humphrey Institute of Public Affairs

Institution	Degree Offered or School
University of Pittsburgh	Graduate School of Public and International Affairs
University of Southern California	Master of Public Diplomacy
University of St. Gallen	Master of Arts in International Affairs and Governance
University of Texas at Austin	Lyndon B. Johnson School of Public Affairs
University of Toronto	Munk School of Global Affairs
University of Washington	Henry M. Jackson School of International Studies
Yale University	The Whitney and Betty MacMillan Center
Yonsei University	Graduate School of International Studies

Source: Association of Professional Schools of International Affairs, "Member Directory," 2017, http://www.apsia.org/graduate-schools-programs/member-directory.

yourself considering business school, some undergraduate courses in economics and business-related fields will allow you to determine your interest level and the suitability of this type of graduate degree. Some graduate programs may require the completion of a few prerequisite undergraduate courses, while others do not. Many schools use the standardized Graduate Management Admissions Test (GMAT) as part of the application process, and an MBA degree generally requires two years of full-time study.

As globalization has transformed the fundamental nature and character of business across the world, graduate business schools have internationalized their curricula. In addition to new courses, they may also provide opportunities for overseas experiences. Some programs devoted exclusively to international business offer interdisciplinary degrees that are separate from the MBA. The Master of International Business (MIB) programs at the University of South Carolina and through the Fletcher School of Tufts University, the Thunderbird School of Global Management affiliated with Arizona State University, and the combined online/residency Master of Arts in International Business and Policy at Georgetown University are among the most noteworthy. These programs offer broader if less technical curricula and emphasize proficiency in foreign language and cross-cultural communication.

Law School

A good number of our students over the years have chosen to attend law school and to pursue careers in international law. Whether you are drawn to the business and commercial side, immigration issues, or political and humanitarian problems, a law degree (JD, or juris doctor) may serve you well in seeking a position related to international affairs in government or the private sector. Although international studies may not necessarily provide direct preparation through coursework, it does develop the kinds of reasoning and problem-solving skills you need to be successful in the legal field.

Law schools consider applicants from all majors and tend to favor those with broad interests and experiences. A key factor in the admissions decision will be your score on the LSAT, the Law School Admission Test, which assesses reading and reasoning skills. It generally takes three years of full-time study to complete most programs. If possible, sample a law course or two at the undergraduate level to get a sense of the type of study and work that is involved, both in law school and beyond. While most standard law school curricula include few if any courses devoted exclusively to international law, there are joint or dual programs that will grant you both a law degree and a master's degree in international affairs.[23]

WHAT CAN YOU DO WITH INTERNATIONAL STUDIES?

My Journey

By Leah Gardner, International Studies Graduate, United States

I am passionate about design. As a high school student, I honed my skills in painting, entering my work in competitions and for display at galleries. Wanting to put my skills to practical use, I applied and was accepted to a five-year interior architecture program. I learned how to draft and use AutoCAD, render images with traditional and digital media, and apply the elements and principles of design. In my fourth year, I studied abroad at Yonsei University in Seoul, South Korea.

I had traveled to other countries before, but South Korea was unlike any other place that I had visited. By the end of my four months there, I was in love with the city of Seoul, and it was absolutely heart-wrenching for me to leave. A year later, I graduated with my degree in interior architecture, but instead of finding a job in my field, I took up a teaching position at a private academy in Seoul. I was thrilled to be back in this wonderful city!

I immersed myself as much as possible into Korean life. I picked up a bit of the language; experimented with the food; and started following their music, movies, and television media. Most of all, I found myself paying more and more attention to politics. A short distance from this cosmopolitan city is North Korea. Civilian protection drills became a part of my life. The military and police were ever-present, honing their skills and conducting training exercises. I even visited the Demilitarized Zone (DMZ) to learn more about it. The Korean people put great time and energy into local and national politics, and I guess that energy rubbed off on me.

Most of all, I was heavily influenced by interacting with my students. Never before had I felt so connected to myself and other people than during the time I spent with them. I was proud of them for being such demand-

Leah Gardner

ing students and proud of myself for contributing to their education. Over time, it became clear to me that I was not destined for a career in design, and I needed to redefine my focus to international studies.

I returned to the United States for the express reason of entering a graduate program. I chose a master of international studies degree because it is designed to give students the skills needed for a successful career. I was also attracted to the fact that a student could specialize in practically any aspect of international studies—international education, regional or global politics, economics, and more. When I first started, I had a loose idea of what I wanted to do, but after getting my feet wet, I knew I wanted to specialize in sustainable development. Studying international studies has been exhilarating for me, and I feel that same connected feeling that I did during my time in Seoul. I know I made the right choice.

I now work on a US Agency for International Development (USAID) project that is addressing public health issues in the developing world, focusing on population, disease, and nutrition. I look forward to my future, and I am glad I started my journey.

Conclusion: Where Do You Go from Here?

As globalization transforms how we live, it forces each of us to consider our relationship to the world and our responsibility for sustaining it. International studies courses and programs can help you think more clearly as borders shift.[24] First, they foster an appreciation of the multiple perspectives that guide perceptions and visions across the world. Recognition of this diversity of approaches can build understanding of the wide array of political, economic, and cultural systems that dot the planet, while suggesting commonalities of interests both within and across them. Second, international studies puts forward a view of the world as an increasingly interconnected set of systems while emphasizing the interdependence of people living within them. This view serves to advance a truly global perspective.[25] Finally, international studies focuses on global issues that transcend state jurisdictions. These issues cross traditional borders and require joint responses.[26]

The pursuit of international studies helps students develop **intercultural competence**— that is, an ability to understand other customs and practices and to communicate effectively and appropriately with people whose backgrounds and interests are different from their own. Opportunities to connect and network are readily available through LinkedIn, Twitter, Facebook, and other professional and social media. Intercultural competence is critical to developing the perspectives that are necessary to tackle the problems affecting our planet. As international educator Darla Deardorff cautions, however, there is not a quick fix that can be accomplished in one semester or over the course of an undergraduate education. Rather, it is a lifelong process.[27]

Everything local is global, and everything global is local. This simple statement belies the challenges of confronting a changing world, where borders are shifting and interests are often difficult to define. We hope this book has helped you consider your place in this world and has helped you chart a path for where you will go from here.

intercultural competence
the ability to communicate effectively with people from different backgrounds and with different interests

Key Concepts

To Learn More

Books and Other Print Media

Stacie Nevadomski Berdan, *Go Global: Launching an International Career Here or Abroad* (SNB Media, 2011).

This innovative resource, published by an international careers author and consultant, also comes in digital format and is available for downloading. It contains recommendations for acquiring the skills and experiences that will help in launching an international career and incorporates suggestions and anecdotes from practitioners. It also offers opportunities to interact personally with the author, who has other resource materials related to the subject available through her website: stacieberdan.com.

Laura E. Cressey, Barrett J. Helmer, and Jennifer E. Steffensen, *Careers in International Affairs*, 9th ed. (Washington, DC: Georgetown University Press, 2014).

This is a comprehensive review of the array of jobs and career paths for those interested in international affairs. It includes chapters on opportunities available through the federal government, international organizations, banking, business, consulting, nonprofits, and research institutes. Useful information relating to strategies that might be employed in navigating the international affairs job market is also included.

Steven T. Duke, *Preparing to Study Abroad: Learning to Cross Cultures* (Sterling, VA: Stylus, 2014).

This is a useful read for students preparing for their study abroad experience. It offers important insight into how to maximize the development of cross-cultural skills and appreciations.

Maia Gedde, *Working in International Development and Humanitarian Assistance: A Career Guide* (New York: Routledge, 2015).

This provides a general introduction to the field and offers hands-on advice on how to identify potential jobs and various career options.

Harry W. Kopp and John K. Naland, *Career Diplomacy: Life and Work in the US Foreign Service*, 3rd ed. (Washington, DC: Georgetown University Press, 2017).

This is an insider's guide to the Foreign Service that is of great use for those looking to pursue a diplomatic career within the US government.

Jeffrey S. Lantis and Jessica DuPlaga, *The Global Classroom: An Essential Guide to Study Abroad* (Boulder, CO: Paradigm, 2010).

Jeffrey Lantis and Jessica DuPlaga's book is particularly useful reading prior to selecting a particular study abroad program. It offers insight on how to choose the right program and suggests steps that can be taken to get the most out of the experience. Worksheets are included to assist the reader in addressing the recommendations included in the text.

Sherry L. Mueller and Mark Overmann, *Working World: Careers in International Education, Exchange and Development,* 2nd ed. (Washington, DC: Georgetown University Press, 2014).

This is a valuable reference for job seekers. Much of the book is devoted to a listing of resources that may be of use in identifying potential employers and employment opportunities and learning more about different career paths that are available.

Donovan Russell, *Choosing a Career in International Development: A Practical Guide to Working in the Professions of International Development* (College Station, TX: VBW Publishing, Inc., 2013).

This book offers valuable information and advice for students interested in pursuing careers in the field of international development and humanitarian assistance. Although self-published, it contains useful material that comes from the author's extensive experiences in the field over many decades.

Richard Slimbach, *Becoming World Wise: A Guide to Global Learning* (Sterling, VA: Stylus, 2010).

Slimbach's focused and informative guidebook offers tips for those considering the many paths to acquiring first-hand global experience, ranging from participation in formal study abroad programs to individually organized travel tours. Particularly useful are the recommendations as to how to maximize the intellectual and personal benefits of an international experience.

Websites

There are many web-based search engines that are available to assist with internship, study abroad, advanced education, employment, and career opportunities.

Association of Professional Schools of International Affairs (APSIA), www.apsia.org/member-schools

For students looking to become familiar with schools offering advanced professional training related to careers in international affairs, APSIA is the gateway to this information. Links to each of its member and affiliate institutions are included.

Go Abroad, www.goabroad.com, www.goabroad.com/intern-abroad, www.goabroad.com/volunteer-abroad, www.goabroad.com/teach-abroad, www.goabroad.com/study-abroad

Students interested in exploring a broad range of options for gaining international experience may access Go Abroad and its related sites. These have been developed by international educators and focus on linking students with international opportunities.

Idealist, www.idealist.org

Idealist focuses on nonprofit and volunteer opportunities at home and abroad. It also list prospective jobs and internships.

The International Partnership for Service Learning and Leadership, www.ipsl.org

This nonprofit organization offers information on earning academic credit for volunteer service abroad through its programs.

International Volunteer Programs Association, www.volunteerinternational.org

The International Volunteer Programs Association, an alliance of NGOs that sponsor international volunteer and internship exchanges, provides listings of programs.

Internships.com, www.internships.com

This website identifies a broad range of international internship opportunities.

NGO Global Network, www.ngo.org

This site is the home for NGOs associated with the UN.

Rutgers University, Political Science Department, Careers in International Relations, http://polisci.rutgers.edu/undergraduate/careers/59-undergraduate/undergraduate-program/180-careers-in-international-relations

This particularly useful and comprehensive review of career options in international affairs has been prepared by Roy Licklider and Edward Rhodes of the Department of Political Science at Rutgers University.

United Nations (UN) Job Opportunities, https://careers.un.org/lbw/Home.aspx

This site allows you to explore career opportunities with the UN.

US Department of State Government Careers, www.careers.state.gov

This is the source for jobs offered by the Department of State. For all jobs offered by the US government, see www.usajobs.gov.

The Washington Center for Internships and Academic Seminars, www.twc.edu

The Washington Center provides internships and seminars for students in Washington, DC.

World Association of Non-Governmental Organizations (WANGO), www.wango.org

Those with a particular interest in working for NGOs will find considerable information on this website.

Videos

Council on International Educational Exchange (CIEE) Teach Abroad, (YouTube Channel), www.youtube.com/user/cieeteachabroad

The official YouTube channel for CIEE Teach Abroad hosts videos about getting teaching jobs worldwide and experiences of previous employees.

Global Civics (2012), http://www.youtube.com/watch?v=JPOfhSbI7QQ

This video features interviews with people from five continents regarding their views and attitudes relating to civic responsibility in a global age.

Idealist (YouTube Channel), www.youtube.com/user/idealist

The official YouTube channel for Idealist.org showcases career profiles in a variety of fields, including policy, social work, volunteering, advocacy, and the environment.

Peace Corps (YouTube Channel), www.youtube.com/user/peacecorps

The official YouTube channel for the Peace Corps features videos about becoming a volunteer.

University for Peace (UPEACE), https://www.youtube.com/playlist?list=PLDBB71CC80334D682

The United Nations' University for Peace offers a series of nine short videos that present valuable information on career opportunities within the UN.

• Notes •

Chapter 1

1. Douglas Adams, *The Hitchhiker's Guide to the Galaxy* (New York: Harmony Books, 1979).

2. Theodore Levitt, "The Globalization of Markets," *Harvard Business Review,* May–June 1983, 92–102.

3. Colin Hay and David Marsh, eds., *Demystifying Globalization* (London: Macmillan, 2002); David Held and Anthony McGrew, eds., *Governing Globalization: Power, Authority, and Global Governance* (Basingstoke, UK: Palgrave, 2002), quoted in Luke Martell, "The Third Wave in Globalization Theory," *International Studies Review* 9, no. 2 (2007): 173–196.

4. International Monetary Fund, *Staff Studies for the World Economic Outlook* (Washington, DC: International Monetary Fund, 1997), 79.

5. Brink Lindsey, *Against the Dead Hand: The Uncertain Struggle for Global Capitalism* (New York: John Wiley & Sons, 2002), 63.

6. Martell, "The Third Wave," 173–196.

7. Pietra Rivoli, *The Travels of a T-Shirt in the Global Economy* (Hoboken, NJ: John Wiley, 2005).

8. Colin Hay and David Marsh, eds., *Demystifying Globalization* (Basingstoke, UK: Palgrave, 2002), quoted in Martell, "The Third Wave."

9. Martell, "The Third Wave," 186.

10. Thomas Friedman, *The Lexus and the Olive Tree* (New York: Farrar, Straus and Giroux, 1999).

11. Statistic Brain, "Job Outsourcing Statistics," accessed August 25, 2016, www.statisticbrain.com/outsourcing-statistics-by-country.

12. Tata, "Tata Consultancy Services," www.tata.com/company/profile/Tata-Consultancy-Services; Infosys, "About Us," www.infosys.com/about/Pages/index.aspx; Wipro, "About Wipro," www.wipro.com/about-wipro.

13. International Monetary Fund, "World Economic Outlook Database," April 2016, www.imf.org/external/pubs/ft/weo/2016/01/weodata/index.aspx.

14. Lester R. Brown, *The Twenty-Ninth Day* (New York: Norton, 1978).

15. Mihaly Csikszentmihalyi, *Finding Flow: The Psychology of Engagement in Everyday Life* (New York: Basic Books, 1997).

16. Raintree Nutrition, Inc., "Rainforest Facts," last updated December 21, 2012, http://www.rain-tree.com/facts.htm#.V78-SPkrLX4.

17. "Hillary Clinton and Katy Perry Attend Star-Studded UNICEF Snowflake Ball," *Look to the Stars: The World of Celebrity Giving,* December 5, 2016, https://www.looktothestars.org/news/16099-hillary-clinton-and-katy-perry-attend-star-studded-unicef-snowflake-ball.

18. "Bono," *ONE,* accessed August 19, 2017, https://www.one.org/us/person/bono.

19. Geoffrey Stokes, "Global Citizenship," *Ethos* 12, no. 1 (2004): 20.

20. United Nations, Department of Economic and Social Affairs, Population Division, *International Migration Report 2015,* http://www.un.org/en/development/desa/population/migration/publications/migrationreport/docs/MigrationReport2015_Highlights.pdf.

21. Seyla Benhabib, "Borders, Boundaries, and Citizenship," *PS: Political Science & Politics* 38, no. 4 (2005): 673.

22. Megha Satyanarayana, "Site Enables Anyone to Use Small Loans to Change Lives a World Away," *Charlotte Observer,* July 22, 2007, 1D.

23. Nigel Dower, *An Introduction to Global Citizenship* (Edinburgh, UK: Edinburgh University Press, 2003), 35–49.

24. Oxfam, *Education for Global Citizenship: A Guide for Schools* (London: Oxfam, 2006), 3, www.oxfam.org.uk/education/gc/files/education_for_global_citizenship_a_guide_for_schools.pdf.

25. Stokes, "Global Citizenship," 21–22.

26. Dower, *An Introduction to Global Citizenship,* 31–32.

27. Ibid., 127–128.

28. Chris Armstrong, "Global Civil Society and the Question of Global Citizenship," *Voluntas: International Journal of Voluntary and Nonprofit Organizations* 17, no. 4 (2006): 348–356, www.springerlink.com.

29. Quoted in Dower, *An Introduction to Global Citizenship*, 81.

Chapter 2

1. Jeffrey D. Sachs, "Weapons of Mass Salvation," *Economist* (October 24, 2002), www.economist.com/node/1403544.

2. Garrett Hardin, "The Tragedy of the Commons," *Science* 62, no. 3859 (1968): 1243–1248.

3. Ibid.

4. Quoted in John C. Derbach, *Agenda for a Sustainable America* (Washington, DC: Environmental Law Institute, 2009), 6.

5. "Our Common Future, Chapter 2: Towards Sustainable Development," *Our Common Future: Report of the World Commission on Environment and Development*, 1987, www.un-documents.net/ocf-02.htm.

6. Ellen Bailey, "Eratosthenes of Cyrene," EBSCO*host*, 2006, available from Middle Search Plus, Ipswich, MA.

7. Amy Witherbee, "Ptolemy," EBSCO*host*, 2006, available from Middle Search Plus, Ipswich, MA.

8. E. Badertscher, "Baron Alexander von Humboldt," EBSCO*host*, 2007, available from Middle Search Plus, Ipswich, MA.

9. US Geological Survey, "Geographic Information Systems," February 22, 2007, egsc.usgs.gov/isb/pubs/gis_poster.

10. National Snow and Ice Data Center, "View NSIDC Data on Virtual Globes: Google Earth," accessed July 9, 2012, nsidc.org/data/virtual_globes.

11. Alexander Von Humboldt, *Cosmos: A Sketch of the Physical Description of the Universe,* vol. 2, trans. E. O. Otte (New York: Harper and Brothers, 1850), 351–352.

12. David Smith, "Humanitarian Crisis as World's Largest Refugee Camp Declared Full," *Guardian,* June 10, 2011, www.guardian.co.uk/world/2011/jun/10/humanitarian-crisis-refugee-camp-declared-full.

13. "Kenya Aims to Halve Size of Dadaab Refugee Camp by End-2016," *Star* (Kenya), June 27, 2016, http://www.the-star.co.ke/news/2016/06/27/kenya-aims-to-halve-size-of-dadaab-refugee-camp-by-end-2016_c1376409; Deborah Bloom, Hilary Clarke, and Farai Sevenzo, "Kenya to Appeal Court Block on Closure of World's Largest Refugee Camp," *CNN*, February 17, 2017, http://www.cnn.com/2017/02/09/africa/kenya-dadaab-refugee-camp/index.html.

14. Norwegian Refugee Council, *Global Estimates 2015: People Displaced by Disasters*, July 2015, http://www.internal-displacement.org/assets/library/Media/201507-globalEstimates-2015/20150713-global-estimates-2015-en-v1.pdf.

15. James Hollifield and Idean Salehyan, "Environmental Refugees," Wilson Center, December 21, 2015, https://www.wilsoncenter.org/article/environmental-refugees.

16. US Census Bureau, "International Programs: International Data Base World Vital Events," accessed August 19, 2017, http://www.census.gov/population/international/data/idb/worldvitalevents.php.

17. Population Reference Bureau, "2016 World Population Data Sheet," 2016, http://www.prb.org/pdf16/prb-wpds 2016-web-2016.pdf.

18. "India's Still-Growing Population Threatens 'Ungovernable Mess,'" *The National*, UNDP Human Development Reports, 2010, hdr.undp.org/en/reports/global/hdr2010/news/mpi/title,20594,en.html.

19. Worldometers, "India Population (Live)," accessed August 3, 2017, http://www.worldometers.info/world-population/india-population; Internet World Stats, "The World Population and the Top Ten Countries with the Highest Population," accessed August 3, 2017, http://www.internetworldstats.com/stats8.htm.

20. Chris Buckley, "China Ends One-Child Policy, Allowing Families Two Children," *New York Times*, October, 29, 2015, http://www.nytimes.com/2015/10/30/world/asia/china-end-one-child-policy.html?_r=0.

21. Alan Greenblatt, "The Graying Planet: Will Aging Populations Cause Economic Upheaval?" *CQ Global Researcher* 5, no. 6 (2012), http://library.cqpress.com/cqresearcher/document.php?id=cqrglobal2011031500

22. US Census Bureau, "International Programs," June 8, 2012, www.census.gov/ipc/www/idb/groups.php.

23. Changing Minds, "Maslow's Hierarchy," 2012, changing minds.org/explanations/needs/maslow.htm.

24. Yves Charbit, *Economic, Social and Demographic Thought in the XIXth Century: The Population Debate from Malthus to Marx* (Dordrecht and London: Springer, 2009), 13.

25. David Biello, "Another Inconvenient Truth: World's Growing Population Poses a Malthusian Dilemma," *Scientific American*, 2009, www.scientificamerican.com/article.cfm?id=growing-population-poses-malthusian-dilemma.

26. Food and Agriculture Organization of the United Nations, *The State of Food Insecurity in the World 2015: Meeting the 2015 International Hunger Targets* (Rome: Food and Agriculture Organization of the United Nations, 2015), http://www.fao.org/3/a-i4646e/i4646e04.pdf.

27. Food and Agriculture Organization of the United Nations, "Crop Prospects and Food Situation," June 2016, http://www.fao.org/3/a-i5710e.pdf.

28. Food and Agriculture Organization of the United Nations, "Hunger Portal," 2012, www.fao.org/hunger/en.

29. Integrated Food Security Phase Classification, "Evidence and Standards for Better Food Security Decisions," 2017, http://www.ipcinfo.org/ipcinfo-home/en.

30. Food and Agriculture Organization of the United Nations, "Crop Prospects and Food Situation," June 2016, http://www.fao.org/3/a-i5710e.pdf.

31. World Food Programme, *The World Food Programme Year in Review 2015*, http://documents.wfp.org/stellent/groups/public/documents/communications/wfp284681.pdf?_ga=1.231653724.2104839375.1489184066.

32. Food and Agriculture Organization of the United Nations, "The November FAO Food Price Index Nearly Unchanged from October," 2011, www.fao.org/worldfoodsituation/wfs-home/foodpricesindex/en.

33. World Trade Organization, "Agriculture Negotiations: Backgrounder: Update Phase 2: Food Security," October 10, 2002, www.wto.org/english/tratop_e/agric_e/negs_bkgrnd18_ph2foodsecurity_e.htm.

34. Food and Agriculture Organization of the United Nations, "Weighing the GMO Arguments: Against," 2003, www.fao.org/english/newsroom/focus/2003/gmo8.htm.

35. Union Carbide Corporation, Bhopal Information Center, "The Incident, Response, and Settlement," 2012, http://www.bhopal.com/UCC-Response-Efforts-to-Tragedy

36. World Wildlife Fund, "Overview: Deforestation," accessed August 19, 2017, http://www.worldwildlife.org/threats/deforestation.

37. World Wildlife Fund, "Overview: Soil Erosion and Degradation," accessed August 19, 2017, http://www.worldwildlife.org/threats/soil-erosion-and-degradation.

38. Jacopo Parigiani and Samantha Spooner, "2015 Is the Year of Soils," *Mail & Guardian Africa*, January 9, 2015, http://mgafrica.com/article/2015-01-08-2015-is-the-year-of-soil-10-reasons-why-every-african-should-care.

39. United Nations Convention to Combat Desertification, "Desertification Land Degradation and Drought—Some Global Facts & Figures," accessed August 19, 2017, http://www.unccd.int/Lists/SiteDocumentLibrary/WDCD/DLDD%20Facts.pdf.

40. "The Water Crisis," *Water.org*, accessed August 19, 2017, http://water.org/our-impact/water-crisis.

41. "Egypt, Ethiopia and Sudan Sign Deal to End Nile Dispute," *BBC*, March 23, 2015, http://www.bbc.com/news/world-africa-32016763.

42. US Environmental Protection Agency, "Greenhouse Gas Emissions: Overview of Greenhouse Gases," accessed August 21, 2017, https://www.epa.gov/ghgemissions/overview-greenhouse-gases.

43. Rebecca Lindsey, "No Surprise, 2015 Sets New Global Temperature Record," January 19, 2016, https://www.climate.gov/news-features/featured-images/no-surprise-2015-sets-new-global-temperature-record; Oliver Milman, "Nasa: Earth Warming at a Pace Unprecedented in 1,000 Years," *Guardian*, August 30, 2016, https://www.theguardian.com/environment/2016/aug/30/nasa-climate-change-warning-earth-temperature-warming; Justin Gillis, "Earth Sets a Temperature Record for the Third Straight Year," *New York Times*, January 18, 2017, https://www.nytimes.com/2017/01/18/science/earth-highest-temperature-record.html.

44. "What Is the Kyoto Protocol and Has It Made Any Difference?" *The Guardian*, March 11, 2011, https://www.theguardian.com/environment/2011/mar/11/kyoto-protocol.

45. See COP 21, http://www.cop21.gov.fr/en, and Center for Climate and Energy Solutions, "Outcomes of the U.N. Climate Change Conference in Paris," December 2015, http://www.c2es.org/international/negotiations/cop21-paris/summary.

46. Mark Landler and Jane Perlez, "Rare Harmony as China and U.S. Commit to Climate Deal," *New York Times*, September 3, 2016, http://www.nytimes.com/2016/09/04/world/asia/obama-xi-jinping-china-climate-accord.html?_r=0.

47. Brad Plumer, "The U.S. Won't Actually Leave the Paris Deal Anytime Soon," *New York Times*, June 7, 2017, https://www.nytimes.com/2017/06/07/climate/trump-paris-climate-timeline.html?_r=0.

48. Coral Davenport, "Nations, Fighting Powerful Refrigerant That Warms Planet, Reach Landmark Deal," *New York Times*, October 15, 2016, http://www.nytimes.com/2016/10/15/world/africa/kigali-deal-hfc-air-conditioners.html?_r=0.

49. Tatiana Schlossberg, "English Village Becomes Climate Leader by Quietly Cleaning Up Its Own Patch," *New York Times*, August 21, 2016, http://www.nytimes.com/2016/08/22/science/english-village-becomes-climate-leader-by-quietly-cleaning-up-its-own-patch.html?_r=0.

50. US Environmental Protection Agency, "Advancing Sustainable Materials Management: 2013 Fact Sheet," June 2015, https://www.epa.gov/sites/production/files/2015-09/documents/2013_advncng_smm_fs.pdf.

51. United Nations Environment Programme, "Illegally Traded and Dumped E-Waste Worth up to $19 Billion Annually Poses Risks to Health, Deprives Countries of Resources, Says UNEP Report," *UNEP News Centre*, May 12, 2015, http://www.unep.org/newscentre/illegally-traded-and-dumped-e-waste-worth-19-billion-annually-poses-risks-health-deprives-countries; "Report Highlights Growing Global E-waste Problem," *Deutsche Welle*, May 13, 2015, http://www.dw.com/en/report-highlights-growing-global-e-waste-problem/a-18448012.

52. United Nations Environment Programme, "Urgent Need to Prepare Developing Countries for Surge in E-Wastes," 2010, https://unu.edu/media-relations/releases/urgent-need-to-prepare-developing-countries-for-surge-in-e-wastes-un.html

53. United Nations Environment Programme, "Environment and E-Waste in India," accessed August 21, 2017, http://staging.unep.org/resourceefficiency/Home/Business/SectoralActivities/ICT/ProjectsActivities/EnvironmentandEWasteinIndia/tabid/101142/Default.aspx.

54. Habitat for Humanity, "ReStore Resale Outlets," 2012, www.habitat.org/restores/default.aspx?tgs=Ni85LzIwMTEgMTE6NDU6MjUgQU0%3d.

55. Mike Ozanian, "Professor Identifies Cancer-Causing Chemicals in Artificial Turf," *Forbes*, March 28, 2016, http://www.forbes.com/sites/mikeozanian/2016/03/28/professor-identifies-cancer-causing-chemicals-in-artificial-turf/#72df210e7fdd.

56. Martin Medina, "The Informal Recycling Sector in Developing Countries: Organizing Waste Pickers to Enhance Their Impact," *GridLines,* October 2008, https://openknowledge.worldbank.org/handle/10986/10586

57. Ibid.

58. International Labour Organization, *Women and Men in the Informal Economy: A Statistical Picture*, 2nd ed. (Geneva: International Labour Office, 2013), 48, http://www.ilo.org/wcmsp5/groups/public/---dgreports/---stat/documents/publication/wcms_234413.pdf.

Chapter 3

1. "Mark Zuckerberg's Commencement address at Harvard," *Harvard Gazette*, May 25, 2017, http://news.harvard.edu/gazette/story/2017/05/mark-zuckerbergs-speech-as-written-for-harvards-class-of-2017.

2. Thomas L. Friedman, *The World Is Flat* (New York: Farrar, Straus and Giroux, 2007), 5.

3. Abdi Latif Dahir, "Cameroon's Government Is Calling Social Media a New Form of Terrorism," *Quartz Africa*, November 18, 2016, https://qz.com/840118/cameroons-government-is-reacting-to-online-criticism-by-calling-social-media-a-new-form-of-terrorism.

4. Friedman, *The World Is Flat*, 50–200.

5. Internet World Stats, *World Internet Usage and Population Statistics*, www.internetworldstats.com/stats.htm.

6. Ibid.

7. James Burke, *Connections* (Boston: Little, Brown, 1978), quoted in J. Michael Adams and Angelo Carfagna, *Coming of Age in a Globalized World: The Next Generation* (Sterling, VA: Kumarian Press, 2006), 19.

8. Charles More, *Understanding the Industrial Revolution* (London and New York: Routledge, 2000), 98.

9. Engineering Toolbox, "Power and Horsepower in Electrical Motors," www.engineeringtoolbox.com/electrical-motor-horsepower-d_653.html.

10. Thomas Savery, *The Miner's Friend; or, an Engine to Raise Water by Fire, Described: And of the Manner of Fixing it in Mines . . .* (London: S. Crouch, 1827), 26.

11. "U.S. International Air Passenger and Freight Statistics," Office of the Assistant Secretary for Aviation and International Affairs, US Department of Transportation, June 2016, https://www.transportation.gov/sites/dot.gov/files/docs/mission/office-policy/aviation-policy/278521/us-international-air-passenger-and-freight-statistics-report-june-2016.pdf.

12. "World Car Market: The Top 100 Countries Ranking in 2016," *Focus2Move*, March 5, 2017, http://focus2move.com/world-car-market.

13. Norihiko Shirouzu, "Train Makers Rail Against China's High Speed Designs," *Wall Street Journal*, November 17, 2010, http://online.wsj.com/article/SB10001424052748704814204575507353221141616.html#ixzz16i7pfQjy.

14. Clara Moskowitz, "Earth's Beauty From Space: Q&A With 'Space Clown' Guy Laliberte," *Space.com*, June 28, 2011, www.space.com/12088-photos-earth-space-gaia-guy-laliberte.html.

15. Virgin Galactic, "Our Vehicles," accessed August 19, 2017, http://www.virgingalactic.com/human-space-flight/our-vehicles.

16. Susan Montoya Bryan, "Virgin Galactic's Branson Says Kutcher Is 500th Customer to Put Down Deposit for Space Ride," Associated Press, March 20, 2012, http://news.yahoo.com/virgin-galactics-branson-says-kutcher-500th-customer-put-122015438.html.

17. "Richard Branson Unveils Virgin Galactic's New Spaceship Named VSS *Unity* by Professor Stephen Hawking," Virgin Galactic, February 19, 2016, http://www.virgingalactic.com/updates.

18. Sarah Fecht, "Elon Musk Wants to Put Humans on Mars by 2025," *Popular Science*, June 2, 2016, http://www.popsci.com/elon-musk-wants-to-put-humans-on-mars-by-2025.

19. Ria Misra, "A SpaceX Rocket Just Exploded at Cape Canaveral," *Gixmodo*, September 1, 2016, http://gizmodo.com/report-a-spacex-falcon-rocket-just-exploded-on-the-lau-1786042146.

20. Thomas H. White, "Electric Telegraph Development and Morse Code," *United States Early Radio History*, http://earlyradiohistory.us/sec002.htm.

21. Anna Robertson, Steve Garfinkel, and Elizabeth Eckstein, "Radio in the 1920s," *Chicago Radio Show 1924*, http://xroads.virginia.edu/~ug00/3on1/radioshow/1920radio.htm.

22. Michael R. Ward, "Rural Telecommunications Subsidies Do Not Work," University of Texas at Arlington, www.uta.edu/faculty/mikeward/JRAP.pdf.

23. Pew Research Center, "Mobile Fact Sheet," January 12, 2017, http://www.pewinternet.org/fact-sheet/mobile; Christian de Looper, "For the First Time Ever, Most U.S. Households Use Only Wireless Phones," *Digital Trends*, May 4, 2017, https://www.digitaltrends.com/mobile/most-households-now-wireless.

24. ITU, "Statistics 2017: Country ICT Data, Mobile-Cellular Subscriptions," accessed August 21, 2017, http://www.itu.int/en/ITU-D/Statistics/Pages/stat/default.aspx.

25. ITU, "Statistics 2017: Global and Regional ICT Data, Mobile-Cellular Subscriptions," accessed August 21, 2017, http://www.itu.int/en/ITU-D/Statistics/Pages/stat/default.aspx.

26. Gary Wolf, "Steve Jobs: The Next Insanely Great Thing," *Wired*, 1996, www.wired.com/wired/archive/4.02/jobs_pr.html.

27. Sean P. Larkin, "The Age of Transparency: International Relations Without Secrets," *Foreign Affairs* 95, no. 3 (2016, May/June): 136–146.

28. Emerson T. Brooking and P.W. Singer, "War Goes Viral: How Social Media Is Being Weaponized across the World," *Atlantic*, November 2016, https://www.theatlantic.com/magazine/archive/2016/11/war-goes-viral/501125.

29. J. M. Berger, "Tailored Online Interventions: The Islamic State's Recruitment Strategy, "*CTC Sentinel*, October 2015, 8:10, 19-23. https://www.ctc.usma.edu/posts/tailored-online-interventions-the-islamic-states-recruitment-strategy.

30. "Types of Search Engine Providers in China in 2014," http://www.slideshare.net/incitezchina/china-search-engine-market-overview-2015.

31. Brooking and Singer, "War Goes Viral."

32. Ibid.

33. Joshua Keating, "The U.S. Government's Anti-ISIS Account Is Full of Tabloid Garbage," *Slate*, May 12, 2015, http://www.slate.com/blogs/the_slatest/2015/05/12/the_u_s_government_s_anti_isis_twitter_account_is_full_of_tabloid_garbage.html.

34. Rick Sterling, "How US Propaganda Plays in Syrian War," *consortiumnews.com*, September 23, 2016, https://consortiumnews.com/2016/09/23/how-us-propaganda-plays-in-syrian-war; Tyler Durden, "Government Trolls Are Using Psychology-Based Influence Techniques on Youtube, Facebook and Twitter," *zerohedge.com*, July 2, 2015, http://www.zerohedge.com/news/2015-07-02/government-trolls-are-using-psychology-based-influence-techniques-youtube-facebook-a.

35. Leo Benedictus, "Invasion of the Troll Armies: From Russian Trump Supporters to Turkish State Stooges," *Guardian*, November 6, 2016, https://www.theguardian.com/media/2016/nov/06/troll-armies-social-media-trump-russian.

36. Ben Westcott, "Duped by Fake News Story, Pakistani Minister Threatens Nuclear War with Israel," *CNN*, December 26, 2016, http://www.cnn.com/2016/12/26/middleeast/israel-pakistan-fake-news-nuclear.

37. Sarah Gordon and Richard Ford, *Cyberterrorism?* Symantec White Paper, 2003, www.symantec.com/avcenter/reference/cyberterrorism.pdf.

38. WikiLeaks, "What Is WikiLeaks?" accessed August 19, 2017, https://wikileaks.org/What-is-Wikileaks.html.

39. WikiLeaks, "DNC Email Archive," July 22, 2016, https://wikileaks.org/dnc-emails; "EU Military Ops against Refugee Flows," February 17, 2016, https://wikileaks.org/eu-military-refugees; "Turkey: Ruling Party Still Working Out Article 301 Differences," August 30, 2011, https://wikileaks.org/plusd/cables/08ANKARA714_a.html.

40. "Edward Snowden Biography," *Biography.com*, http://www.biography.com/people/edward-snowden-21262897#awesm=~oEUIejQ0zrP59L.

41. Intelligence Community Assessment, "Assessing Russian Activities and Intentions in Recent US Elections," January 6, 2017, https://www.intelligence.senate.gov/sites/default/files/documents/ICA_2017_01.pdf.

42. Rebecca R. Ruiz and Mark Landler, "Robert Mueller, Former F.B.I. Director, Is Named Special Counsel for Russia Investigation, *New York Times*, May 17, 2017, https://www.nytimes.com/2017/05/17/us/politics/robert-mueller-special-counsel-russia-investigation.html?_r=0.

43. Oren Dorrell, "Europe Targeted in Russia Hacks," *USA Today*, January 9, 2017, 1A–2A.

44. Eric Auchard and Bate Felix, "French Candidate Macron Claims Massive Hack as Emails Leaked," *Reuters*, May 6, 2017, http://www.reuters.com/article/us-france-election-macron-leaks-idUSKBN1812AZ.

45. Adam Segal, "How China Is Preparing for Cyberwar," *Christian Science Monitor*, March 20, 2017, http://www.csmonitor.com/World/Passcode/Passcode-Voices/2017/0320/How-China-is-preparing-for-cyberwar.

46. Gary J. Schmitt, "Waging War in Zero and Ones," *Wall Street Journal*, February 28, 2016, http://www.aei.org/publication/waging-war-in-zeros-and-ones; David E. Sanger and William J. Broad, "Hand of U.S. Leaves North Korea's Missile Program Shaken," *New York Times*, April 18, 2017, https://www.nytimes.com/2017/04/18/world/asia/north-korea-missile-program-sabotage.html?_r=0.

47. SAP StreamWork, "SAP Customer, All for One, Keeps Projects Rolling Around the Clock, Around the Globe," November 8, 2011, sapstreamwork.com/news-blog/sap-customer-all-one-keeps-projects-rolling-around-clock-around-globe.

48. Infosys, About Us—History, https://www.infosys.com/about/Pages/history.aspx.

49. Sid Arora, "Companies Are Moving Away from Bangalore, India's Largest IT Hub," *Diplomat*, July 25, 2016, http://thediplomat.com/2016/07/companies-are-moving-away-from-bangalore-indias-largest-it-hub.

50. Infosys, Product Categories, https://www.infosys.com/products-and-platforms.

51. "E-commerce Share of Total Global Retail Sales from 2015 to 2021," *Statista*, accessed May 26, 2017, https://www.statista.com/statistics/534123/e-commerce-share-of-retail-sales-worldwide; "Global Net Revenue of Amazon.com from 2014 to 2016, by Segment (in Billion U.S. Dollars)," *Statista*, accessed May 26, 2017, https://www.statista.com/statistics/672747/amazons-consolidated-net-revenue-by-segment.

52. Elizabeth Weise, "With Amazon, Chinese Sellers Are Skipping the Middleman," *USA Today*, January 27, 2017, 2B; "What Is Alibaba?" *The Wall Street Journal*, accessed May 26, 2017, http://projects.wsj.com/alibaba.

53. "Getting Started with Bitcoin," *Bitcoin.org*, accessed August 19, 2017, https://bitcoin.org/en/getting-started.

54. "What Is Bitcoin?, *CNN*, accessed May 25, 2017, http://money.cnn.com/infographic/technology/what-is-bitcoin.

55. Jethro Mullen, "Hackers Steal Bitcoins Worth Millions in Attack on Exchange," *CNN*, August 3, 2016, http://money.cnn.com/2016/08/03/technology/bitcoin-exchange-bitfinex-hacked.

56. Alec MacFarlane, "Why the Massive Cyberattack Won't Make the Hackers Rich," *CNN*, May 17, 2017, http://money.cnn.com/2017/05/17/technology/wannacry-ransomware-bitcoin-cyberattack.

57. Marisa Urgo, *Al-Shabaab's Exploitation of Alternative Remittance Systems (ARS) in Kenya,* June 11, 2009, www.orgsites.com/va/asis151/JIEDDO_J2_OSAAC_Al-Shabaabs_Exploitation_of_Alternative_Remittance_Systems_in_Kenya.pdf.

58. Nima Elbagir, "Kenya Mall Attack: Four Accused of Having Role in Bloody Siege," *CNN World,* http://www.cnn.com/2013/11/04/world/africa/kenya-mall-attack.

59. Lauren Silveira, "4 Technologies Helping Us to Fight Corruption," *World Economic Forum*, April 18, 2016, https://www.weforum.org/agenda/2016/04/4-technologies-helping-us-to-fight-corruption.

60. Darren Boyle, "US Freezes Kim Jong-un's Assets for Human Rights Abuses and Brands North Korea 'Among the World's Most Repressive Countries' for Executions, Torture and Forced Labor in Prison Camps," *Daily Mail*, July 7, 2016, http://www.dailymail.co.uk/news/

article-3678333/US-freezes-Kim-Jong-s-assets-human-rights-abuses-brands-North-Korea-world-s-repressive-countries-executions-torture-forced-labor-prison-camps.html.

61. "Most Famous Social Network Sites Worldwide as of August 2017, Ranked by Number of Active Users (in Millions)," *Statista*, August 2017, https://www.statista.com/statistics/272014/global-social-networks-ranked-by-number-of-users.

62. Farhad Manjoo, "Social Media's Globe-Shaking Power, *New York Times*, November 16, 2016, https://www.nytimes.com/2016/11/17/technology/social-medias-globe-shaking-power.html?_r=0.

63. Carla Marshall, "Top Vine Stars & Most-Watched Vine Creators: June 2016 Leaderboard," *TubularInsights*, July 23, 2016, http://tubularinsights.com/top-vine-stars.

64. Kia Kokalitcheva, "Snapchat Unveils Video-Recording Sunglasses," *Fortune*, September 23, 2016, http://fortune.com/2016/09/24/snapchat-video-sunglasses.

65. "Translate," *TED*, accessed May 29, 2017, https://www.ted.com/participate/translate.

66. Melissa Pandika, "Could Nanotechnology End Hunger?" *OZY*, August 2, 2016, http://www.ozy.com/fast-forward/could-nanotechnology-end-hunger/70771.

67. Joost Reek, "5 Ways Nanotechnology Can Tackle Climate Change," *World Economic Forum*, July 15, 2015, https://www.weforum.org/agenda/2015/07/5-ways-nanotechnology-can-tackle-climate-change.

68. Sandhya Venkatachalam, "3 Ways Artificial Intelligence Will Change the World for the Better," *World Economic Forum*, May 29, 2017, https://www.weforum.org/agenda/2017/05/artificial-intelligence-will-change-the-world-heres-how.

69. Rem Rieder, "Single-Topic Website Puts Plight of Refugees in Global Spotlight," *USA Today*, March 8, 2016, 2B.

70. Jessica Dineen, "UNICEF Teams Up with Google to Fight Zika," Unicef USA, accessed August 21, 2017, https://www.unicefusa.org/stories/unicef-teams-google-fight-zika/30035.

71. "International Rescue Committee: Refugee Crisis," accessed August 21, 2017, https://www.google.org/our-work/crisis-response/irc-refugee-crisis.

72. See Infosys Foundation, https://www.infosys.com/infosys-foundation/about.

Chapter 4

1. Parag Khanna, "How Megacities Are Changing the Map of the World," *TED2016*, February 2016, https://www.ted.com/talks/parag_khanna_how_megacities_are_changing_the_map_of_the_world; World Policy Institute, "Talking Policy: Parag Khanna on Connectography," *World Policy Blog*, May 13, 2016, http://www.worldpolicy.org/blog/2016/05/13/talking-policy-parag-khanna-connectography.

2. North Atlantic Treaty Organization, "Warsaw Summit Communique," press release no. 100, July 9, 2016, http://www.nato.int/cps/en/natohq/official_texts_133169.htm?selectedLocale=en.

3. Thucydides, *The History of the Peloponnesian War*, Rex Warner, trans. (Baltimore: Penguin Books, 1972), 400–408.

4. Joseph S. Nye Jr., *Understanding International Conflicts*, 7th ed. (New York: Longman, 2008), 2–4.

5. Ibid., 3.

6. Niccolo Machiavelli, *The Prince*, 2nd ed. (New York: W. W. Norton, 1992), 46.

7. Michael Duffy, "The Causes of World War One," *firstworldwar.com*, August 22, 2009, www.firstworldwar.com/origins/causes.htm.

8. Michael Duffy, "Archduke Franz Ferdinand's Assassination, 28 June 1914," *firstworldwar.com*, August 22, 2009, www.firstworldwar.com/source/harrachmemoir.htm.

9. Woodrow Wilson, "The Fourteen Points," in *Classics of International Relations*, 3rd ed., ed. John A. Vasquez (Englewood Cliffs, NJ: Prentice Hall, 1996), 38.

10. Hans Morgenthau, *Politics among Nations: The Struggle for Power and Peace* (New York: Knopf, 1948).

11. Michelle Nichols, "UN: Crimes against Humanity in South Sudan," *Huffington Post*, May 8, 2014, http://www.huffingtonpost.com/2014/05/08/south-sudan-crimes-against-humanity_n_5290164.html; "Why South Sudan Is Still at War," *Economist*, October 4, 2016, http://www.economist.com/blogs/economist-explains/2016/10/economist-explains-0; "UN: South Sudan on Brink of Ethnic Civil War," *Al Jazeera*, December 14, 2016, http://www.aljazeera.com/news/2016/12/south-sudan-brink-ethnic-civil-war-161214104548897.html.

12. North Atlantic Treaty Organization, "NATO's Role in Afghanistan," 2012, www.nato.int/cps/en/natolive/topics_8189.htm.

13. Rebecca Kaplan, "White House: U.S. Will Have 9,800 Troops in Afghanistan after 2014," *CBS News*, May 27, 2014, http://www.cbsnews.com/news/white-house-u-s-will-have-9800-troops-in-afghanistan-after-2014; Nake M. Kamrany, "How to End Afghanistan War: Negotiate with Taliban," *Huffington Post*, June 8, 2014, http://www.huffingtonpost.com/nake-m-kamrany/how-to-end-afghanistan-wa_b_5469838.html.

14. Ahmed Mengli and F. Brinley Bruton, "Obama's Afghanistan Legacy: What Trump Faces in America's Longest War," *NBC News*, January 19, 2017, http://www.nbcnews.com/storyline/president-obama-the-legacy/obama-s-afghanistan-legacy-what-trump-faces-america-s-longest-n708331; Melanie Garunay, "An Update on Our Mission in Afghanistan," *The White House*, July 6, 2016, https://obamawhitehouse.archives.gov/blog/2016/07/06/update-our-mission-afghanistan.

15. Greg Botelho, "5 Predictions Revisited: Iraq's Troubles Are Years in the Making, Experts Say," *CNN*, http://www.cnn.com/2014/06/11/world/meast/iraq-predictions-revis ited; Tim Lister, "ISIS: The First Terror Group to Build an Islamic State?" *CNN*, http://www.cnn.com/2014/06/12/world/meast/who-is-the-isis; Amir Hassanpour, "The Kurdish Experience," *MER 189*, Middle East Research and Information Project, July/August 1994, http://www.merip.org/mer/mer189/kurdish-experience.

16. Emily Anagnostos, "Iraq Situation Report: January 6-11, 2017," *Institute for the Study of War*, January 11, 2017, http://www.understandingwar.org/backgrounder/iraq-situation-report-january-6-11-2017; Helene Cooper, "U.S. to Send 600 More Troops to Iraq to Help Retake Mosul from ISIS," *New York Times*, September 28, 2016, https://www.nytimes.com/2016/09/29/world/middleeast/obama-troops-iraq.html?_r=0.

17. "Syrian Civil War Fast Facts," *CNN*, December 22, 2016, http://www.cnn.com/2013/08/27/world/meast/syria-civil-war-fast-facts; Andrew Osborn and Alexander Winning, "Putin and Trump Agree to Try to Rebuild U.S.-Russia Ties, Cooperate in Syria," *Reuters*, January 28, 2017, http://www.reuters.com/article/us-usa-trump-putin-idUSKBN15C0SK; Patrick Wintour, "Russia in Power-Broking Role as Syria Peace Talks Begin in Astana," *Guardian*, January 23, 2017, https://www.theguardian.com/world/2017/jan/22/russia-syria-talks-astana-kazakhstan-.

18. Armed Conflict Location and Event Data Project (ACLED), "Egypt—November 2016 Update," November 2016, http://www.crisis.acleddata.com/egypt-november-2016-update.

19. Danielle Renwick and Claire Felter, "Colombia's Civil Conflict," *CFR Backgrounders*, Council on Foreign Relations, January 11, 2017, http://www.cfr.org/colombia/colombias-civil-conflict/p9272.

20. Public Radio International, "A Peace Agreement Brings a Civil War to an End in Colombia," *Agence France-Presse*, August 25, 2016, https://www.pri.org/stories/2016-08-25/peace-agreement-brings-civil-war-end-colombia; Raf Sanchez, "Colombia's President Juan Manuel Santos Wins Nobel Peace Prize for Efforts to End Civil War," *Telegraph*, October 7, 2016, http://www.telegraph.co.uk/news/2016/10/07/colombias-president-juan-manuel-santos-wins-nobel-peace-prize-fo.

21. Brad Lendon, "Is Kim Jong Un 'the World's Most Dangerous Man'?" *CNN*, December 29, 2016, http://www.cnn.com/2016/12/28/asia/north-korea-kim-jong-un-year-end-lookahead.

22. US Department of the Treasury, "Iran Sanctions," 2012, www.treasury.gov/resource-center/sanctions/programs/pages/iran.aspx.

23. "Iran Nuclear Deal: Key Details," *BBC*, January 16, 2016, http://www.bbc.com/news/world-middle-east-33521655.

24. Steven Lee Myers and Ellen Barry, "Putin Reclaims Crimea for Russia and Bitterly Denounces the West," *New York Times*, March 18, 2014, http://www.nytimes.com/2014/03/19/world/europe/ukraine.html?_r=0.

25. Paul Coyer, "The Crisis of Russian-American Relations and America's Failed Russia Policy," *Forbes*, October 15, 2016, http://www.forbes.com/sites/paulcoyer/2016/10/15/the-crisis-of-russian-american-relations-and-americas-failed-russia-policy/#3964f9c14762; Eric Lipton, David E. Sanger, and Scott Shane, "The Perfect Weapon: How Russian Cyberpower Invaded the U.S.," *New York Times*, December 13, 2016, https://www.nytimes.com/2016/12/13/us/politics/russia-hack-election-dnc.html?rref=collection%2Fnewseventcollection%2Frussian-election-hacking&action=click&contentCollection=politics&region=rank&module=package&version=highlights&contentPlacement=1&pgtype=collection&_r=0.

26. Shi Yinhong, "China's Complicated Foreign Policy," European Council on Foreign Relations, March 31, 2015, http://www.ecfr.eu/article/commentary_chinas_complicated_foreign_policy311562.

27. Bob Savic, "Behind China and Russia's 'Special Relationship,'" *The Diplomat*, December 7, 2016, http://thediplomat.com/2016/12/behind-china-and-russias-special-relationship.

28. Raymond Kuo, "Can Trumpian Triangular Diplomacy Work?" *The Diplomat*, January 6, 2017, http://thedip lomat.com/2016/12/behind-china-and-russias-special-relationship.

29. Nicholas Onuf, *World of Our Making: Rules and Rule in Social Theory and International Relations* (Columbia: University of South Carolina Press, 1989).

30. J. Ann Tickner, *Gendering World Politics: Issues and Approaches in the Post–Cold War Era* (New York: Columbia University Press, 2001).

Chapter 5

1. Nuclear Threat Initiative, "Former Senator Sam Nunn Remarks at the Foreign Policy Association's Andrew Carnegie Distinguished Lecture on Conflict Prevention Honoring David Hamburg, " March 21, 2016, http://www.nti.org/analysis/speeches/former-senator-sam-nunn-remarks-foreign-policy-associations-andrew-carnegie-distinguished-lecture-conflict-prevention-honoring-david-hamburg.

2. Robert John, "Behind the Balfour Declaration: Britain's Great War Pledge to Lord Rothschild," *Journal of Historical Review* 6, no. 4 (Winter 1985–1986), accessed through Institute of Historical Review, www.ihr.org/jhr/v06/v06p389_John.html.

3. Jimmy Carter Library & Museum, "The Camp David Accords," 2012, www.jimmycarterlibrary.gov/documents/campdavid.

4. Middle East Research and Information Project, "Oslo Accords," 2012, www.merip.org/palestine-israel_primer/oslo-accords-pal-isr-prime.html.

5. Israel Palestine Center for Research and Information, "Camp David 2000 until Today: A Review of the Lessons Learned in the Ten Years Since the Camp David Summit," October 19, 2010, www.ipcri.org/IPCRI/Videos/Entries/2010/10/19_Camp_David_2000_Until_Today__Pini_Meidan_and_Nabeel_Shaath.html.

6. Sharon Otterman, "Middle East: The Road Map to Peace," Council on Foreign Relations, February 7, 2005, www.cfr.org/middle-east/middle-east-road-map-peace/p7738.

7. William Booth and Ruth Eglash, "Kerry's Nine-Month Quest for Middle East Peace Ends in Failure," *Washington Post*, April 29, 2014, https://www.washingtonpost.com/world/middle_east/kerrys-nine-month-quest-for-middle-east-peace-ends-in-failure/2014/04/29/56521cd6-cfd7-11e3-a714-be7e7f142085_story.html?utm_term=.57785a1476b8.

8. Nina Tannenwald, "Stigmatizing the Bomb: Origins of the Nuclear Taboo," *International Security* 29, no. 4 (2005, Spring): 5–49.

9. Arms Control Association, "U.S.-Russian Nuclear Arms Control Agreements at a Glance," April 1, 2014, https://www.armscontrol.org/factsheets/USRussia NuclearAgreementsMarch2010; US Department of State, "Diplomacy in Action: New START," December 1, 2016, https://www.state.gov/t/avc/newstart.

10. Joby Warrick, "More Than 1,400 Killed in Syrian Chemical Weapons Attack, U.S. Says," *Washington Post*, August 30, 2013, https://www.washingtonpost.com/world/national-security/nearly-1500-killed-in-syrian-chemical-weapons-attack-us-says/2013/08/30/b2864662-1196-11e3-85b6-d27422650fd5_story.html?utm_term=.e0d98d505486; Russell Goldman, "Syria's Chemical Weapons Have Been Destroyed. So, Why Do Chlorine Gas Attacks Persist?" *New York Times*, August 11, 2016, http://www.nytimes.com/2016/08/12/world/middleeast/syria-chlorine-gas-attack.html; Jared Malsin, "Assad's Regime Is Still Using Chemical Weapons in Syria," *Time*, September 14, 2016, http://time.com/4492670/syria-chemical-weapon-aleppo-assad-regime.

11. Nuclear Threat Initiative, "North Korea," October 2016, http://www.nti.org/learn/countries/north-korea.

12. Lyser Doucet, "Iran Nuclear Deal: Turning Point or Transformation?" *BBC*, July 22, 2015, http://www.bbc.com/news/world-middle-east-33624217.

13. Usha Sahay and Alexander Pearson, "Fact Sheet: Iran's Nuclear and Ballistic Missile Programs," Center for Arms Control and Non-Proliferation, December 2013, http://armscontrolcenter.org/publications/fact-sheets/fact_sheet_irans_nuclear_and_ballistic_missile_programs; Washington Institute for Near East Policy, "Assessing the Iran Nuclear Agreement and the Washington Institute's June 24 Policy Statement," August 4, 2015, http://www.washingtoninstitute.org/policy-analysis/view/assessing-the-iran-nuclear-agreement-and-the-institutes-iran-study-group-ju.

14. Carol Morello, "Assessing the Iran Nuclear Deal One Year after It Was Reached," *Washington Post*, July 13, 2016, https://www.washingtonpost.com/world/national-security/assessing-the-iran-nuclear-deal-one-year-after-it-was-reached/2016/07/13/cf3de73a-4828-11e6-acbc-4d4870a079da_story.html?utm_term=.5e2c11129245.

15. Information Clearing House, "For Sale: West's Deadly Nuclear Secrets," *Sunday Times,* January 5, 2008, www.informationclearinghouse.info/article19006.htm.

16. US Department of State, "Annex of Statistical Information," *Country Reports on Terrorism 2016*, (College Park, MD: National Consortium for the Study of Terrorism and Responses to Terrorism, 2017), http://www.state.gov/j/ct/rls/crt/2016/272241.htm.

17. US Department of State, Bureau of Counterterrorism, "State Sponsors of Terrorism," *Country Reports on Terrorism 2016* (Washington, DC: Bureau of Counterterrorism, 2017), https://www.state.gov/j/ct/rls/crt/2016/272235.htm; US Department of State, "Rescission of Cuba as a State Sponsor of Terrorism," May 29, 2015, https://www.state.gov/r/pa/prs/ps/2015/05/242986.htm.

18. Cindy C. Combs, *Terrorism in the Twenty-First Century* (Upper Saddle River, NJ: Prentice Hall, 2012), 20–21.

19. Rachel Clarke, "Colombia: 52 Years of War, 220,000 Dead, Now Peace," *CNN*, August 25, 2016, http://www.cnn.com/2016/08/25/americas/colombia-farc-peace-deal-explainer.

20. Marc Sageman, "The Next Generation of Terror," *Foreign Policy,* February 19, 2008, www.foreignpolicy.com/articles/2008/02/19/the_next_generation_of_terror.

21. Paul Haven, "Next Generation in Disarray?" *The Charlotte Observer,* June 10, 2006.

22. "White House Advisor: Bomb Plot Highlights AQAP as Cancer," *CBS News,* May 8, 2012, www.cbsnews.com/8301-505263_162-57429767/wh-adviser-bomb-plot-highlights-aqap-as-cancer; Backgrounder: Council on Foreign Relations, "Al-Qaeda in the Arabian Peninsula," June 19, 2015, http://www.cfr.org/yemen/al-qaeda-arabian-peninsula-aqap/p9369; Yara Bayoumy, "How Saudi Arabia's War in Yemen Has Made al Qaeda Stronger—and Richer," *Reuters,* April 8, 2016, http://www.reuters.com/investigates/special-report/yemen-aqap.

23. Zachary Laub and Jonathan Masters, "Al-Qaeda in the Islamic Maghreb," Backgrounders: Council on Foreign Relations, March 27, 2015, http://www.cfr.org/terrorist-organizations-and-networks/al-qaeda-islamic-maghreb-aqim/p12717; Christopher S. Chivvis and Andrew Liepman, "North Africa's Menace: AQIM's Evolution and the U.S. Policy Response," RAND Corporation, 2013, http://www.rand.org/pubs/research_reports/RR415.html.

24. Olivier Guitta, "The Re-emergence of AQIM in Africa," *Al Jazeera,* March 20, 2016, http://www.aljazeera.com/indepth/opinion/2016/03/emergence-aqim-africa-160320090928469.html; Corinne Dufka, "Confronting Mali's New Jihadist Threat," *New York Times,* May 9, 2016, http://www.nytimes.com/2016/05/10/opinion/confronting-malis-new-jihadist-threat.html?_r=0; Caleb Weiss, "Al Qaeda Has Launched More Than 100 Attacks in West Africa in 2016," *FDD's Long War Journal,* June 8, 2016, http://www.longwarjournal.org/archives/2016/06/over-100-al-qaeda-attacks-in-west-africa-since-beginning-of-the-year.php.

25. United States Institute of Peace, "The Jihadi Threat 2: Whither the Islamic State?" December 12, 2016, http://www.usip.org/publications/2016/12/11/the-jihadi-threat-2-whither-the-islamic-state; "ISIS Fast Facts," *CNN,* November 1, 2016, http://www.cnn.com/2014/08/08/world/isis-fast-facts; Zachary Laub, "The Islamic State," Backgrounders: Council on Foreign Relations, August 10, 2016, http://www.cfr.org/iraq/islamic-state/p14811.

26. Tim Lister, et.al., "ISIS Goes Global: 143 Attacks in 29 Countries Have Killed 2,043," *CNN,* September 1, 2016, http://www.cnn.com/2015/12/17/world/mapping-isis-attacks-around-the-world.

27. Kevin Liptak, "US Says 75% of ISIS Fighters Killed," *CNN,* December 14, 2016, http://www.cnn.com/2016/12/14/politics/white-house-isis-numbers.

28. Jonathan Masters, "Al-Shabab," Backgrounders: Council on Foreign Relations, March 13, 2015, http://www.cfr.org/somalia/al-shabab/p18650; "Who Are Somalia's al-Shabab?" *BBC News,* December 9, 2016, http://www.bbc.com/news/world-africa-15336689; Mohsin Ali and Sebastien Billard-Arbelaez,"Al-Shabab Attacks in Somalia (2006–2016)," *Al Jazeera,* August 31, 2016, http://www.aljazeera.com/indepth/interactive/2016/08/al-shabab-attacks-somalia-2006-2016-160830110231063.html.

29. Mohammed Aly Sergie and Toni Johnson, "Boko Haram," Backgrounders: Council on Foreign Relations, March 5, 2015, http://www.cfr.org/nigeria/boko-haram/p25739; Vladimir Duthiers, Faith Karimi, and Greg Botelho, "Boko Haram: Why Terror Group Kidnaps Schoolgirls, and What Happens Next," *CNN,* May 2, 2014, http://www.cnn.com/2014/04/24/world/africa/nigeria-kidnapping-answers; Edward Delman, "The World's Deadliest Terrorist Organization," *Atlantic,* November 18, 2015, http://www.theatlantic.com/international/archive/2015/11/isis-boko-haram-terrorism/416673; Helene Cooper, "Boko Haram and ISIS Are Collaborating More, U.S. Military Says," *New York Times,* April 20, 2016, http://www.nytimes.com/2016/04/21/world/africa/boko-haram-and-isis-are-collaborating-more-us-military-says.html?_r=0.

30. See US Department of State, *Country Reports on Terrorism 2015* (Washington, DC: Bureau of Counterterrorism and Countering Violent Extremism, 2016), http://www.state.gov/j/ct/rls/crt/2015/index.htm.

31. Preparatory Commission for the Comprehensive Nuclear Test Ban Treaty Organization, "Status of Signature and Ratification," accessed August 19, 2017, https://www.ctbto.org/the-treaty/status-of-signature-and-ratification.

32. Thomas Risse-Kappen, "Democratic Peace-Warlike Democracies? A Social Constructivist Interpretation of the Liberal Argument," in *Peace Studies: Critical Concepts in Political Science*, ed. Matthew Evangelista (New York: Routledge, 2005), 78.

Chapter 6

1. Hernando de Soto, *The Mystery of Capital: Why Capitalism Triumphs in the West and Fails Everywhere Else* (New York: Basic Books, 2000), 2.

2. International Monetary Fund, "Subdued Demand: Symptoms and Remedies," *World Economic Outlook*, October 2016, http://www.imf.org/external/pubs/ft/weo/2016/02/pdf/text.pdf.

3. David N. Balaam and Bradford Dillman, *Introduction to International Political Economy* (Boston: Longman, 2011), 58–60.

4. Adam Smith, 1776, quoted in Helen Joyce, "Adam Smith and the Invisible Hand," *+plus magazine*, March 1, 2001, http://plus.maths.org/issue14/features/smith.

5. Paul Kennedy, *The Rise and Fall of Great Powers* (New York: Random House, 1987).

6. Vince Crawley, "Marshall Plan for Rebuilding Europe Still Echoes after 60 Years," *America.gov*, www.america.gov/st/washfile-english/2007/May/20070521163245MVyelwarC7.548159e-02.html; Barry Eichengreen and Marc Uzan, "The Marshall Plan," *Economic Policy* 7, no. 14 (April 1992): 13–54, 59–75.

7. Immanuel Wallerstein, "The Rise and Demise of the World Capitalist System: Concept for Comparative Analysis," *Comparative Studies in Society and History* 16, no. 4 (September 1974): 387–415.

8. Andre Gunder Frank, *Capitalism and Development in Latin America* (New York: Monthly Review Press, 1967).

9. Andre Gunder Frank, *Latin America: Underdevelopment or Revolution* (New York: Monthly Review Press, 1969), 4.

10. Joseph E. Stiglitz, *Making Globalization Work* (New York: W. W. Norton, 2007).

11. OPEC, "Brief History," www.opec.org/opec_web/en/about_us/24.htm; US Department of Energy, "Crude Oil Production, OPEC, the Persian Gulf, and the United States," Fact #296, December 1, 2003, www1.eere.energy.gov/vehiclesandfuels/facts/2003/fcvt_fotw296.html.

12. Geoffrey Kemp and Robert Harkavy, *Strategic Geography and the Changing Middle East* (Washington, DC: Brookings Institution, 1997).

13. Spencer L. Davidson, "The U.S. Should Soak Up That Shower of Gold," *Time*, December 16, 1974, 41.

14. Robert O. Keohane and Joseph S. Nye, *Power and Interdependence: World Politics in Transition* (Boston: Little, Brown, 1977).

15. Lester Thurow, *Head to Head: The Coming Economic Battle among Japan, Europe, and America* (New York: William Morrow, 1991).

16. US Department of Commerce, *Survey of Current Business* 54, no. 1 (January 1974) and no. 7 (July 1974).

17. US Census Bureau, "Foreign Trade: Trade in Goods with Japan," www.census.gov/foreign-trade/balance/c5880.html#1990.

18. EUROPA: Gateway to the European Union, europa.eu.

19. BRICS Ministry of External Relations, *Economic Data and Trade Statistics*, http://brics.itamaraty.gov.br/about-brics/economic-data.

20. Simon Tisdall, "Has the Brics Bubble Burst?" *Guardian*, March 27, 2016, https://www.theguardian.com/business/2016/mar/27/brics-bubble-burst-brazil-russia-india-china-south-africa.

21. International Monetary Fund, *World Economic Outlook Database*, October 2016, https://www.imf.org/external/pubs/ft/weo/2016/01/weodata/index.aspx.

22. Ibid.

23. Ministry of Commerce, People's Republic of China, "Statistics of FDI in China in January-December 2015," January 22, 2016, http://english.mofcom.gov.cn/article/statistic/foreigninvestment/201602/20160201260821.shtml.

24. Ministry of Commerce, People's Republic China, "Brief Statistics on China's Import & Export in December 2015," January 22, 2016, http://english.mofcom.gov.cn/article/statistic/BriefStatistics/201603/20160301265939.shtml; United States Census Bureau, "Trade in Goods

with China," accessed August 19, 2017, http://www .census.gov/foreign-trade/balance/c5700.html; Kan Yue and Kevin Honglin Zhang, "How Much Does China's Exchange Rate Affect the U.S. Trade Deficit?" *The Chinese Economy*, accessed August 21, 2017, http://www.tand fonline.com/doi/pdf/10.2753/CES1097-1475460605.

25. "Tholons 2016 Top 100 Outsourcing Destinations: Rankings and Executive Summary," *Tholons*, http:// www.tholons.com/TholonsTop100/pdf/Tholons_ Top_100_2016_Executive_Summary_and_Rankings. pdf, January 29, 2016; Tata Consultancy Services, "About Us," http://www.tcs.com/about/corp_facts/ Pages/default.aspx; Infosys, "About Us," https://www .infosys.com/about/Pages/fact-file.aspx; Tata Motors, "Company Profile," 2016, http://www.tatamotors. com/about-us/company-profile; Vanessa Able, "Tata Nano: The Car That Was Just Too Cheap," *Guardian*, February 3, 2014, https://www.theguardian.com/ commentisfree/2014/feb/03/tata-nano-car-cheap- poor-safety-rating.

26. Steffi Joseph, "IT/ITES (BPO) Industry," *Shine.com*, accessed August 19, 2017, http://info.shine.com/ industry/it-ites-bpo/11.html; "Job Overseas Outsourcing Statistics," *Statistic Brain*, accessed August 19, 2017, www.statisticbrain.com/outsourcing-statistics-by- country.

27. International Monetary Fund, *World Economic Database*, October 2016.

28. Roger Cohen, "The World Is Upside Down," *New York Times*, June 2, 2008, www.nytimes.com/2008/06/01/ opinion/01iht-edcohen.1.13366689.html.

29. The G-7 members include Canada, France, Germany, Italy, Japan, the United Kingdom, and the United States. Data are from International Monetary Fund, *World Economic Outlook Database*, October 2016.

30. World Bank, *Poverty Overview*, http://www.worldbank .org/en/topic/poverty/overview.

31. International Monetary Fund, *World Economic Outlook Database*, October 2016.

32. National Highway Traffic Safety Administration, "Part 583 American Automobile Labeling Act (AALA) Reports," 2016, https://www.nhtsa.gov/part- 583-american-automobile-labeling-act-reports.

33. International Monetary Fund, *World Economic Outlook Database*, October 2016; Europa, *Eurostat Unemployment Statistics*, updated June 2017, http:// ec.europa.eu/eurostat/statistics-explained/index.php/ Unemployment_statistics.

34. International Monetary Fund, *World Economic Outlook Database*, October 2016.

35. Ibid.

36. "What is the Deficit?" accessed August 19, 2017, www.usgovernmentdebt.us/us_deficit; "Debt Clock," accessed August 19, 2017, www.usgovernmentdebt.us.

37. US Department of the Treasury, Office of International Affairs, "Major Foreign Holders of Treasury Securities," http://ticdata.treasury.gov/Publish/mfh.txt.

38. OPEC, *Annual Statistical Bulletin*, 2016 edition, http:// www.opec.org/opec_web/static_files_project/media/ downloads/publications/ASB2016.pdf.

39. US Energy Information Administration, Office of Energy Statistics, US Department of Energy "Monthly Energy Review: July 2017" (Washington, DC: Office of Energy Statistics, 2017), http://www.eia.gov/ totalenergy/data/monthly/pdf/mer.pdf; US Energy Information Administration, US Department of Energy, "Official Energy Statistics from the US Government," September 2016,.

40. Russell Flannery, "Forbes China 30 Under 30: Meet 30 Young Entrepreneurial Disruptors in China," *Forbes*, March 17, 2013, http://www.forbes.com/sites/ russellflannery/2013/03/11/forbes-china-30-under- 30-meet-30-young-entrepreneural-disruptors-in- china/#11dce60a173a.

41. International Labour Organization, "ILO Says Forced Labour Generates Annual Profits of US$150 Billion," May 20, 2014, http://www.ilo.org/global/about-the-ilo/ newsroom/news/WCMS_243201/lang--en/index.htm.

42. US Department of State, *Trafficking in Persons Report* (Washington, DC: US Department of State, June 2016), http://www.state.gov/documents/organization/ 258876.pdf.

43. See Piece & Co., http://www.pieceandco.com.

Chapter 7

1. Peter Vanham, "Davos Leaders Agree: Share More Wealth, or Face the Consequences," World Economic Forum Annual Meeting, January 20, 2017, https:// www.weforum.org/agenda/2017/01/davos-leaders- agree-we-should-share-more-of-the-worlds-wealth-or- face-the-populist-consequences.

2. Oxfam International, "An Economy for the 99%," January 2017, https://www.oxfam.org/sites/www.oxfam .org/files/file_attachments/bp-economy-for-99-percent- 160117-summ-en.pdf.

3. Montreal WSF 2016 Collective, "World Social Forum," September 25, 2015, https://fsm2016.org/wp-content/uploads/2015/11/One-pager-EN.pdf.

4. Joseph E. Stiglitz, *Globalization and Its Discontents* (New York: W. W. Norton, 2002).

5. World Trade Organization, "The Multilateral Trading System—Past, Present and Future," accessed August 21, 2017,https://www.wto.org/english/thewto_e/whatis_e/inbrief_e/inbr01_e.htm.

6. Robert Wright, "Shipping's Size Obsession Could Be Ending, Study Finds," *Financial Times*, March 8, 2016, https://www.ft.com/content/255d9394-e47a-11e5-a09b-1f8b0d268c39?mhq5j=e3.

7. World Trade Organization, press release, March 23, 2009, www.wto.org/english/news_e/pres09_e/pr554_e.htm; World Trade Organization, press release, March 26, 2010, www.wto.org/english/news_e/pres10_e/pr598_e.htm; World Trade Organization, press release, April 12, 2017, https://www.wto.org/english/news_e/pres17_e/pr791_e.htm.

8. World Trade Organization, "Dispute Settlement: The Disputes," accessed August 19, 2017, https://www.wto.org/english/tratop_e/dispu_e/dispu_status_e.htm.

9. Catholic Relief Services, "CRS Fair Trade: What's the Difference Between Fair Trade and Free Trade?" accessed August 21, 2017, http://wm.p80.ca/Org/Org179/Images/Economic%20Justice/How-is-Fair-Trade-Different.pdf; Global Envision, "Free Trade v. Fair Trade," October 26, 2005, http://www.globalenvision.org/library/15/834; Chris Woodford, "Fair Trade," *Explainthatstuff*, last updated August 5, 2017, http://www.explainthatstuff.com/fairtrade.html.

10. Joseph E. Stiglitz, *Making Globalization Work* (New York: W. W. Norton, 2006), 120–124.

11. OECD, *Trade in Counterfeit and Pirated Goods: Mapping the Economic Impact*, 2016. http://www.keepeek.com/Digital-Asset-Management/oecd/governance/trade-in-counterfeit-and-pirated-goods_9789264252653-en#.WBzJwC0rLX4#page3.

12. James McBride and Mohammed Aly Sergie, "NAFTA's Economic Impact," Council on Foreign Relations, January 24, 2017, http://www.cfr.org/trade/naftas-economic-impact/p15790; Knowledge @ Wharton, "NAFTA's Impact on the U.S. Economy: What Are the Facts?" September 6, 2016, http://knowledge.wharton.upenn.edu/article/naftas-impact-u-s-economy-facts; M. Angeles Villarreal and Ian F. Fergusson, "The North American Free Trade Agreement," Congressional Research Service, February 22, 2017, https://fas.org/sgp/crs/row/R42965.pdf; Kimberly Amadeo, "Do NAFTA's 6 Pros Outweigh Its 6 Cons?" *The Balance*, February 13, 2017, https://www.thebalance.com/nafta-pros-and-cons-3970481.

13. Global Exchange, "FTAA," 2011, www.globalexchange.org/resources/FTAA.

14. World Trade Organization, "About the WTO—a Statement by the Director-General," 2012, www.wto.org/english/thewto_e/whatis_e/wto_dg_stat_e.htm.

15. Russ Kuykendall, "Going Local in a Global World: Principled Free Trade, Mercantilism, and Environmental Protectionism," October 27, 2011, www.cardus.ca/policy/article/2936.

16. Richard McCormack, "Anti-Free Trade Lobby Is Completely Ignored by U.S. Senators," *Manufacturing & Technology News* 18, no. 12 (July 29, 2011), www.manufacturingnews.com/news/11/0729/KoreaFTA.html.

17. PressTV, "Malaysian Anti-Free Trade Activists Protest FTA Deals with the US," December 5, 2011, www.presstv.ir/detail/213930.html.

18. Lydia Depillis, "Everything You Need to Know About the Trans Pacific Partnership," *Washington Post*, December 11, 2013, http://www.washingtonpost.com/blogs/wonkblog/wp/2013/12/11/everything-you-need-to-know-about-the-trans-pacific-partnership; Kevin Granville, "This Was the Trans-Pacific Partnership," *New York Times*, November 11, 2016, http://www.nytimes.com/interactive/2016/business/tpp-explained-what-is-trans-pacific-partnership.html?_r=0; "TPP: What Is It and Why Does It Matter?" *BBC*, November 22, 2016, http://www.bbc.com/news/business-32498715.

19. Office of the United States Trade Representative, "U.S. Objectives, U.S. Benefits in the Transatlantic Trade and Investment Partnership: A Detailed View," March 2014, http://www.ustr.gov/about-us/press-office/press-releases/2014/March/US-Objectives-US-Benefits-In-the-TTIP-a-Detailed-View; Kimberly Amadeo, "Transatlantic Trade and Investment Partnership (TTIP)," *Balance*, September 8, 2016, https://www.thebalance.com/transatlantic-trade-and-investment-partnership-ttip-3305582; Tim Wallace, "EU's TTIP Trade Deal with the US Has Collapsed, Says Germany," *Telegraph*, August 28, 2016, http://www.telegraph.co.uk/business/2016/08/28/eus-ttip-trade-deal-with-the-us-has-collapsed-says-germany.

20. Martin D. D. Evans and Viktoria Hnatkovska, "International Capital Flows, Returns and World Financial Integration" (First draft), September 23, 2005,

www.georgetown.edu/faculty/evansm1/wpapers_files/globalv1.pdf.

21. Robert E. Scott, "US Current Account Deficit Improves in 2007 Despite Rising Oil Prices," Economic Policy Institute, March 26, 2008, www.epi.org/publication/indicators_intlpict_20080326; C. Fred Bergsten, "The Current Account Deficit and the US Economy," *Peterson Institute for International Economics*, February 1, 2007, https://piie.com/commentary/testimonies/current-account-deficit-and-us-economy.

22. "The *Fortune* 2016 Global 500," 2016, http://beta.fortune.com/global500/list; Statistics Times, "List of Countries by Projected GDP," October 21, 2016, http://statisticstimes.com/economy/countries-by-projected-gdp.php.

23. "Global 500 2013," 2013, http://fortune.com/global500/2013/royal-dutch-shell-plc-1.

24. "Business Digest: Around the Nation and World," *Charlotte Observer,* February 24, 2006, 3D.

25. See "About Lenovo," https://www.lenovocareers.com/about.html.

26. John Ross, "China's Global Companies: Strengths and Weaknesses," June 26, 2011, www.china.org.cn/opinion/2011-06/26/content_22855094.htm; "Chinese Automobile Industry and Sales of Chinese Cars Abroad," *Facts and Details*, 2008, factsanddetails.com/china.php?itemid=361&catid=9&subcatid=61; Matt Gasnier, "World: How the Chinese Are Setting Themselves up for Success," April 20, 2014, http://bestsellingcarsblog.com/2014/04/20/world-how-the-chinese-are-setting-themselves-up-for-success-part-5-mature-markets; Helena Soderpalm and Mia Shanley, "China's Geely Cars Think Big with Volvo Makeover," *Reuters*, May 17, 2016, http://www.reuters.com/article/us-autos-geely-design-idUSKCN0Y81C3; Haval, "Haval Tula Plant Breaks Ground, Expected to Go into Production in Late 2017," October 10, 2015, http://www.haval-global.com/news_detail-2176.html.

27. Michael Arria, "H&M Has a New Labor Plan: It Looks a Lot Like All the Others," *Truthout*, October 23, 2015, http://www.truth-out.org/news/item/33357-h-m-has-a-new-labor-plan-it-looks-a-lot-like-all-the-others; "H&M: Living Wage Coming to Textile Workers by 2018," *Huffington Post*, November 25, 2013, http://www.huffingtonpost.com/2013/11/25/hm-living-wage_n_4337474.html.

28. Connor Jones, "University to Implement Anti-Sweatshop Regulation," United Students Against Sweatshops, March 22, 2012, http://usas.org/tag/dsp/

29. Eduardo Porter, "Dividends Emerge in Pressing Apple over Working Conditions in China," *New York Times,* March 6, 2012, www.nytimes.com/2012/03/07/business/dividends-emerge-in-pressing-apple-over-working-conditions-in-china.html; Shai Oster, "Inside One of the World's Most Secretive iPhone Factories," *Bloomberg*, April 24, 2016, http://www.bloomberg.com/news/features/2016-04-24/inside-one-of-the-world-s-most-secretive-iphone-factories.

30. David Meyer, "Google Makes Short-Lived Return to China," *Fortune*, March 28, 2016, http://fortune.com/2016/03/28/google-china-firewall; Kaveh Waddell, "Why Google Quit China and Why It's Heading Back," *Atlantic*, January 19, 2016, http://www.theatlantic.com/technology/archive/2016/01/why-google-quit-china-and-why-its-heading-back/424482; Eva Dou, "China's Xi Jinping Opens Tech Conference With Call for 'Cyber Sovereignty,'" *Wall Street Journal*, November 16, 2016, http://www.wsj.com/articles/chinas-xi-jinping-opens-tech-conference-with-call-for-cyber-sovereignty-1479273347.

31. Jana Honke, Nicole Kranz, Tanja A. Borzel, and Adrienne Heritier, "Fostering Environmental Regulation? Corporate Social Responsibility in Countries with Weak Regulatory Capacities," Basel Institute of Governance, SFB-Governance Working Paper Series, no. 9, February 2008.

32. Martin Khor, "The Double Standards of Multinationals," *Guardian,* June 25, 2010, www.guardian.co.uk/commentisfree/cif-green/2010/jun/25/double-standards-multinationals-ecological-disasters; Odisu Terry Andrews, "The Nigerian State, Oil Multinationals and the Environment: A Case Study of Shell Petroleum Development Company (SPDC)," *Journal of Public Administration and Policy Research* 7, no. 2 (March 2015): 24–28, http://www.academicjournals.org/journal/JPAPR/article-full-text-pdf/3F5BE7F51539.

33. Organization for Economic Cooperation and Development, "Multilateral Agreement on Investment: Documentation from the Negotiations," accessed August 21, 2017, http://www.oecd.org/daf/mai/intro.htm.

34. GM Media, "About GM China," http://media.gm.com/media/cn/en/gm/company.html; "Fiat Chrysler CEO Says He'd Only Merge With These 3 Automakers," *Fortune*, April 15, 2016, http://fortune.com/2016/04/15/fiat-chrysler-vw-ford; Groupe Renault, "Our Alliance With Nissan: Together Stronger," https://group.renault.com/en/our-company/a-group-an-alliance-and-partnerships/our-alliance-with-nissan; J. Weston

Phippen, "Car Manufacturers and Ride-Sharing Apps Become Friends, *The Atlantic*, May 24, 2016, http://www.theatlantic.com/international/archive/2016/05/toyota-uber/484220.

35. Kelsey Mays, "The 2016 Cars.com American-Made Index, *Cars.com*, June 28, 2016, https://www.cars.com/articles/the-2016-carscom-american-made-index-1420684865874; Steven Peters, "50 Most American Cars," *Wallst.com*, June 30, 2016, http://247wallst.com/special-report/2016/06/30/most-american-cars; Frank Dubois, *2016 Kogod Made in America Auto Index*, 2016, http://kogodbusiness.com/reports/auto-index. The American Automobile Labeling Act ratings are based on the origin of parts and point of assembly.

36. "Forex Volumes in June Hit Above $5 Trillion A Day," *Fortune*, July 14, 2016, http://fortune.com/2016/07/14/forex-volumes-june-brexit.

37. International Monetary Fund, "Factsheet—the IMF at a Glance," October 3, 2016, http://www.imf.org/en/About/Factsheets/IMF-at-a-Glance; International Monetary Fund, "IMF Support for Low-Income Countries," October 3, 2016, http://www.imf.org/en/About/Factsheets/IMF-Support-for-Low-Income-Countries.

38. Oxfam International, "2011 Review of Conditionality and the Design of Fund-Support Programs," 2011, www.oxfam.org/sites/www.oxfam.org/files/oxfam-imf-conditionality-submission.pdf; Alliance Sud, "The IMF's Lending Conditions: Slight Corrections," January 10, 2013, http://www.alliancesud.ch/en/politics/development-policy/imfs-lending-conditions-slight-corrections; Jeffrey Griffiths and Konstantinos Todoulos, "Conditionality Yours: An Analysis of the Policy Conditions Attached to IMF Loans," European Network on Debt and Development, April 2014, http://eurodad.org/files/pdf/533bd19646b20.pdf.

39. World Bank, "World Bank Group Support Tops $61 Billion in Fiscal Year 2016," press release, July 12, 2016, http://www.worldbank.org/en/news/press-release/2016/07/12/world-bank-group-support-tops-61-billion-in-fiscal-year-2016.

40. World Bank, "Projects and Operations: Country Strategies," last updated June 12, 2017, http://www.worldbank.org/en/projects-operations/country-strategies; World Bank, "Bangladesh: Proposed Country Partnership Framework FY 2016–2020," October–November 2015, http://documents.worldbank.org/curated/en/573241468188929633/pdf/100526-WP-P153756-PUBLIC-Box393236B-Bangladesh-Draft-CPF-FY-2016-2020-Executive-Summary.pdf.

41. United Nations, "We Can End Poverty: Millennium Development Goals and Beyond 2015," accessed August 21, 2017, http://www.un.org/millenniumgoals/bkgd.shtml; Millennium Project, "What They Are," 2006, www.unmillenniumproject.org/goals/index.htm; World Bank, "Millennium Development Goals," accessed August 21, 2017, http://www5.worldbank.org/mdgs; World Bank, "Sustainable Development Goals: Keeping Citizens at the Center," January 28, 2016, https://live.worldbank.org/sustainable-development-goals-keeping-citizens-at-center.

42. African Development Bank Group, "Land Desalinated in Senegal for Food Self-Sufficiency: Tackling the Sea," accessed August 19, 2017, http://www.afdb.org/en/projects-and-operations/selected-projects/project-to-support-local-small-scale-irrigation-papil; "Lake Turkana Wind Farm Project: The Largest Wind Farm Project in Africa," accessed August 21, 2017, https://www.afdb.org/en/projects-and-operations/selected-projects/lake-turkana-wind-power-project-the-largest-wind-farm-project-in-africa-143.

43. Paul Krugman, *The Return of Depression Economics and the Crisis of 2008* (New York: W. W. Norton, 2009), 139–164; Anup Shah, "Global Financial Crisis 2008," *Global Issues,* January 15, 2009, www.globalissues.org/print/article/768.

44. Krugman, *Return of Depression Economics,* 165–180.

45. International Monetary Fund, *Global Financial Stability Report,* April 2010, www.imf.org/external/pubs/ft/gfsr/index.htm.

46. Krugman, *Return of Depression Economics,* 77–100; "Thailand: The Crisis Starts," *BBC News*, November 26, 1997, http://news.bbc.co.uk/1/hi/special_report/1997/asian_economic_woes/34487.stm.

47. Institute of International Finance, "November 2016 Capital Flows to Emerging Markets," November 2, 2016, https://www.iif.com/publication/capital-flows-emerging-markets-report/november-2016-capital-flows-emerging-markets; Rudolf Bems and Luis A. V. Catao, "IMF Survey: Emerging Markets Show More Resilience to Capital Flow Cycle," *IMF News*, April 6, 2016, https://www.imf.org/en/News/Articles/2015/09/28/04/53/sores040616b.

48. US Department of the Treasury, "Financial Regulatory Reform: A New Foundation," June 17, 2009, www.treasury.gov/initiatives/Documents/FinalReport_web.pdf.

49. Group of 20, "What is the G20 and How Did This International Forum Begin?" 2012, https://www.g20.org/Webs/G20/EN/G20/FAQs/faq.html; "G20 Members," http://g20.org.tr/about-g20/g20-members.

50. Caitlin Byrne, "China's G20 Summit Was Big on Show but Short on Substance," *Guardian*, September 5, 2016, https://www.theguardian.com/world/2016/sep/06/chinas-g20-summit-was-big-on-show-but-short-on-substance.

Chapter 8

1. Dave Eggers, *What is the What: The Autobiography of Valentino Achak Deng* (San Francisco: McSweeney's, 2006), 175.

2. Ibid., 175.

3. "Quote of the Day: Culture Shock," *Ellen* [TV show], October 16, 2012. http://www.ellentv.com/2012/10/16/quote-of-the-day-culture-shock.

4. Marshall Segall, Pierre R. Dasen, John W. Berry, and Ype H. Poortinga, *Human Behavior in Global Perspective: An Introduction to Cross-Cultural Psychology,* 2nd ed. (Needham Heights, MA: Allyn & Bacon, 1999), 33.

5. UNESCO, "Universal Declaration on Cultural Diversity," November 2, 2001, http://portal.unesco.org/en/ev.php-URL_ID=13179&URL_DO=DO_TOPIC&URL_SECTION=201.html.

6. Ida Magli, *Cultural Anthropology: An Introduction* (Jefferson, NC: McFarland, 2001), 21.

7. Manning Nash, *The Cauldron of Ethnicity in the Modern World* (Chicago: The University of Chicago Press, 1989), 1.

8. Adam Kuper, *Culture: The Anthropologists' Account* (Cambridge, MA: Harvard University Press, 1999), 5–9.

9. Matthew Arnold, *Culture and Anarchy,* 3rd ed. (New York: Macmillan, 1882), www.library.utoronto.ca/utel/nonfiction_u/arnoldm_ca/ca_titlepage.html#search.

10. Commonwealth, "Member Countries," accessed August 19, 2017, http://thecommonwealth.org/member-countries.

11. Sarah Crowe and Rajat Madhok, "Gaining Ground on the Millennium Development Goals, with Equity, in Nepal," United Nations Children's Fund, September 24, 2010, www.unicef.org/mdg/nepal_56213.html.

12. Julie McCarthy, "The Caste Formerly Known as 'Untouchables' Demands a New Role in India," *NPR*, August 13, 2016, http://www.npr.org/sections/goatsandsoda/2016/08/13/489883492/the-caste-formerly-known-as-untouchables-demands-a-new-role-in-india.

13. Tania Branigan, "Millions of Chinese Rural Migrants Denied Education for Their Children," *Guardian*, March 14, 2010, www.guardian.co.uk/world/2010/mar/15/china-migrant-workers-children-education.

14. John Sudworth, "Counting the Cost of China's Left-Behind Children," *BBC*, April 12, 2016, http://www.bbc.com/news/world-asia-china-35994481.

15. "China's Cities: The Great Transition," *Economist*, May 22, 2014, http://www.economist.com/news/leaders/21599360-government-right-reform-hukou-system-it-needs-be-braver-great.

16. Karl Marx and Friedrich Engels, *Manifesto of the Communist Party,* trans. Samuel Moore, Marx/Engels Selected Works, Vol. One (Moscow: Progress Publishers, 1969), 98–137, https://www.marxists.org/archive/marx/works/1848/communist-manifesto/ch04.htm.

17. Kuper, *Culture,* 15–16.

18. Chris Jenks, *Culture,* 2nd ed. (London: Routledge, 2005), 30.

19. Marvin Harris, *The Rise of Anthropological Theory: A History of Theories of Culture* (New York: Thomas Y. Croswell, 1968), 11.

20. Margaret Mead, *Sex and Temperament in Three Primitive Societies* (New York: Morrow Quill Paperbacks, 1963), 322.

21. Her psychological study of what it was like in the 1920s for girls growing up in the primitive culture of the Samoan Islands remains a classic in this regard. See Margaret Mead, *Coming of Age in Samoa: A Psychological Study of Primitive Youth for Western Civilization* (Gloucester, MA: Peter Smith, 1961).

22. Clifford Geertz, *The Interpretation of Cultures* (New York: Basic Books, 1973), 30.

23. Rachel Nuwer, "Languages: Why We Must Save Dying Tongues," *BBC Future*, June 6, 2014, http://www.bbc.com/future/story/20140606-why-we-must-save-dying-languages.

24. Chinua Achebe, *Things Fall Apart* (London: Heinemann, 1958), 124.

25. John H. Bodley, *Anthropology and Contemporary Human Problems,* 5th ed. (Lanham, MD: Altamira Press, 2008), 6.

26. John Tomlinson, *Globalization and Culture* (Chicago: University of Chicago Press, 1999), 27–31.

27. Jan Nederveen Pieterse, *Globalization and Culture: Global Melange* (Lanham, MD: Rowman & Littlefield, 2004), 87.

28. Ibid., 95.

29. Samuel P. Huntington, *The Clash of Civilizations and the Remaking of World Order* (New York: Simon & Schuster, 1996).

30. Huntington, *The Clash of Civilizations? The Debate,* 2nd ed. (New York: Council on Foreign Relations, 2010).

31. Thomas L. Friedman, *The Lexus and the Olive Tree* (New York: Random House, 2000), 248.

32. Benjamin R. Barber, *Jihad v. McWorld: How Globalism and Tribalism are Reshaping the World* (New York: Random House, 1996).

33. George Ritzer, *McDonaldization: The Reader* (Thousand Oaks, CA: Sage, 2002), 16–19.

34. Michael Veseth, *Globaloney: Unraveling the Myths of Globalization* (Lanham, MD: Rowman & Littlefield, 2005), 121–143.

35. Roland Robertson, *Globalization: Social Theory and Global Culture* (Thousand Oaks, CA: Sage, 1992), 173–174.

36. Arjun Appadurai, *Modernity at Large: Cultural Dimensions of Globalization* (Minneapolis: University of Minnesota Press, 1996), 48.

37. See "Global Music Project," globalmusicproject.org.

38. Maria del Carmen de la Peza, "Music and Globalization: The Impact of Latin American Music in Japan," *Intercultural Communication Studies* 15, no. 1 (2006): 168–173.

39. Ibid.

40. "Artists: Babymetal," *Billboard*, accessed August 19, 2017, http://www.billboard.com/artist/5938492/babymetal.

41. Martha Diaz, "The World Is Yours: A Brief History of Hip-Hop Education," Steinhardt School of Culture, Education, and Human Development, New York University, 2012, http://www.academia.edu/1088920/The_World_IS_Yours_A_Brief_History_of_Hip-Hop_Education.

42. H. Samy Alim, "How Hip-Hop Culture is Changing the Wor(l)d," *UCLA Newsroom,* January 23, 2007, http://newsroom.ucla.edu/stories/h-samy-alim_hip-hop.

43. "NBS Rosters Feature Record 113 International Players from 41 Countries and Territories," *NBA.com*, October 25, 2016, http://pr.nba.com/nba-rosters-international-players-2016-17.

44. Jonathan Vanian, "How the NBA Finals Are Beamed across the Globe without Hiccups," *Fortune*, June 16, 2015, http://fortune.com/2015/06/16/nba-broadcast-finals-globe.

45. Walter LaFeber, *Michael Jordan and the New Global Capitalism* (New York: W. W. Norton, 1999).

46. David L. Andrews et al., "Jordanscapes: A Preliminary Analysis of the Global Popular," *Sociology of Sport Journal* 13 (1996), 428–457.

47. Chih-ming Wang, "Capitalizing the Big Man: Yao Ming, Asian American, and the China Global," *Inter-Asia Cultural Studies* 5, no. 2 (2004), 263–278.

48. "MLB: International," *MLB.com,* http://mlb.mlb.com/mlb/international/mlbi_index.jsp.

49. Bill Baer, "29.8% of Players on 2017 Opening Day Rosters Born outside the U.S., Setting New Record," *NBCSports,* April 3, 2017, http://mlb.nbcsports.com/2017/04/03/29-8-of-players-on-2017-opening-day-rosters-born-outside-the-u-s-setting-new-record.

50. Quoted in Paul White, "American, Japanese Players Adapt to New Surroundings," *USA Today,* April 11, 2007, http://usatoday30.usatoday.com/sports/baseball/2007-04-11-japan-cultureshock_n.htm.

51. For a broad discussion on this topic, see Michael Lewis and William Londo, *Studies on Asia: An Interdisciplinary Journal of Asian Studies Series III* 3, no. 2 (Fall 2006) [Special issue on baseball and *besuboro* in Japan and the United States].

52. "Masahiro Tanaka Named the American League Pitcher of the Month," *MLB.com*, press release, June 3, 2014, http://mlb.mlb.com/news/article.jsp?ymd=20140603&content_id=78018736&vkey=pr_mlb&c_id=mlb.

53. Leonard Koppett, "The Globalization of Baseball: Reflections of a Sports Writer," *Indiana Journal of Global Legal Studies* 8, no. 1 (2000): 81–84.

54. Baer, "29.8% of Players."

55. Enrique Rojas, "Baseball Academies Thrive in the Dominican Republic," *ESPN*, July 1, 2015, http://www.espn.com/blog/onenacion/post/_/id/710/baseball-academies-thrive-in-the-dominican-republic.

56. "From Cuba to the Majors: Yasiel Puig's Harrowing Story," *Miami Herald*, April 20, 2014, http://www.miamiherald.com/news/local/community/miami-dade/article1963115.html.

57. Veseth, *Globaloney,* 102.

Chapter 9

1. "The Full Text: "Malala Yousafzai Delivers Defiant Riposte to Taliban Militants with Speech to the UN General Assembly," *Independent,* July 12, 2013, http://www.independent.co.uk/news/world/asia/the-full-text-malala-yousafzai-delivers-defiant-riposte-to-taliban-militants-with-speech-to-the-un-general-assembly-8706606.html.

2. Malala Yousafzai, *I Am Malala: The Girl Who Stood Up for Education and Was Shot by the Taliban,* with Christina Lamb (New York: Little, Brown, 2013); see also http://www.malala.org.

3. "Religions: Sunni and Shi'a," *BBC,* August 19, 2009, http://www.bbc.co.uk/religion/religions/islam/subdivisions/sunnishia_1.shtml.

4. George Mason University's History News Network, "What Is the Difference Between Sunni and Shiite Muslims—and Why Does It Matter?" February 22, 2011, hnn.us/articles/934.html.

5. Daniel Burke, "Syria Explained: How it Became a Religious War," *CNN.com,* September 4, 2013, http://religion.blogs.cnn.com/2013/09/04/syrian-wars-got-religion-and-that-aint-good.

6. Sarah Glazer, "Sharia Controversy: Is There a Place for Islamic Law in Western Countries?" *CQ Global Researcher* 6, no. 1 (2012): 1–28.

7. Ibid.

8. "Nigeria: Facts and Figures," *BBC News,* April 17, 2007, news.bbc.co.uk/2/hi/africa/6508055.stm.

9. Rori Donaghy and Mary Atkinson, "Crime and Punishment: Islamic State vs. Saudi Arabia," *Middle East Eye,* January 20, 2015 (updated October 13, 2015), http://www.middleeasteye.net/news/crime-and-punishment-islamic-state-vs-saudi-arabia-1588245666.

10. "Pakistan Honour Killing on the Rise, Report Reveals," *BBC News,* April 1, 2016, http://www.bbc.com/news/world-asia-35943732.

11. Jayshree Bajoria and Greg Bruno, "Backgrounder: al-Qaeda (a.k.a. al-Qaida, al-Qa'ida)," Council on Foreign Relations, August 29, 2011, www.cfr.org/terrorist-organizations/al-qaeda-k-al-qaida-al-qaida/p9126.

12. Daniel L. Byman, "Testimony: Comparing Al Qaeda and ISIS: Different Goals, Different Targets," *Brookings,* April 29, 2015, https://www.brookings.edu/testimonies/comparing-al-qaeda-and-isis-different-goals-different-targets.

13. "European People's Party: History," accessed August 19, 2017, http://www.epp.eu/about-us/history.

14. "Central African Republic Country Profile," *BBC News,* November 21, 2016, http://www.bbc.com/news/world-africa-13150040.

15. Robert Hayden, "Serbian and Croatian Nationalism and the Wars in Yugoslavia," *Cultural Survival,* March 19, 2010, www.culturalsurvival.org/ourpublications/csq/article/serbian-and-croatian-nationalism-and-wars-in-yugoslavia.

16. Josh Kron, "Conflict in Congo," CQ *Global Researcher* 5 (April 5, 2011): 157–182.

17. Ibid.

18. Kevin Maurer, "Joseph Kony's Former Bodyguards Are Now Helping US Troops Hunt Him," *Daily Beast,* May 14, 2016, http://www.thedailybeast.com/articles/2016/05/14/joseph-kony-s-former-bodyguards-are-now-helping-u-s-troops-hunt-him.html.

19. "What Ever Happened to African Warlord Joseph Kony?" *News.com.au,* June 12, 2014, http://www.news.com.au/world/africa/what-ever-happened-to-african-warlord-joseph-kony/story-fnh81gzi-1226951404637.

20. World Bank, "Fragility, Conflict and Violence Home: Overview," last updated April 10, 2017, http://www.worldbank.org/en/topic/fragilityconflictviolence/overview.

21. Gerald B. Helman and Steven R. Ratner, "Saving Failed States," *Foreign Policy* 89 (Winter 1992–1993): 3–20, www.jstor.org/stable/1149070.

22. US Central Intelligence Agency, "Zimbabwe," *World Factbook,* July 15, 2017, https://www.cia.gov/library/publications/the-world-factbook/geos/zi.html.

23. Glazer, "Sharia Controversy."

24. Zoie O'Brien, "Theresa May Forced to Defend Views on Sharia Law as She Prepares to Enter No. 10," *Sunday Express,* July 13, 2016, http://www.express.co.uk/news/uk/688662/Theresa-May-Sharia-Law-inquiry-Prime-Minister-leader-conservative-party-downing-street.

25. John Bingham, "Islamic Law Is Adopted by British Legal Chiefs," *Telegraph,* March 22, 2014, http://www.telegraph.co.uk/news/religion/10716844/Islamic-law-is-adopted-by-British-legal-chiefs.html.

26. Jina Moore, "Truth Commissions: Can Countries Heal after Atrocities?" *CQ Global Researcher* 4 (January 2010): 1–24.

27. Laura Seay, "Rwanda's Gacaca Courts Are Hailed as a Post-Genocide Success. The Reality Is More

Complicated," *Washington Post*, June 2, 2017, https://www.washingtonpost.com/news/monkey-cage/wp/2017/06/02/59162/?utm_term=.52140efe998d.

28. Human Rights Watch, "Justice Compromised: The Legacy of Rwanda's Community-Based Gacaca Courts," May 31, 2011, https://www.hrw.org/report/2011/05/31/justice-compromised/legacy-rwandas-community-based-gacaca-courts.

29. Kofi Annan, "Nobel Lecture," Oslo, Norway, December 10, 2001, http://www.nobelprize.org/nobel_prizes/peace/laureates/2001/annan-lecture.html.

Chapter 10

1. Antonio Guterres, "Challenges and Opportunities for the United Nations," United Nations, April 4, 2016, http://www.un.org/pga/70/wp-content/uploads/sites/10/2016/01/4-April_Secretary-General-Election-Vision-Statement_Portugal-4-April-20161.pdf

2. Ibid.

3. Leroy Bennett and James K. Oliver, *International Organizations: Principles and Issues,* 7th ed. (New York: Prentice Hall, 2002), 3.

4. Hugo Grotius, "Chapter 1: On War and Right," in *On the Law of War and Peace (De Jure Belli ac Pacis),* Book I, trans. A. C. Campbell (London: 1814), www.constitution.org/gro/djbp_101.htm.

5. International Committee of the Red Cross, "Final Act of the International Peace Conference. The Hague, 29 July 1899," www.icrc.org/ihl.nsf/INTRO/145?OpenDocument.

6. Thomas R. Van Dervort, *International Law and Organization: An Introduction* (Thousand Oaks, CA: Sage, 1998), 19.

7. Woodrow Wilson, "The Fourteen Points," in *Classics of International Relations*, 3rd ed., ed. John A. Vasquez (Upper Saddle River, NJ: Prentice Hall, 1996), 40.

8. US Department of State, Office of the Historian, "Milestones 1921–1936: The Kellogg-Briand Pact, 1928," accessed August 19, 2017, https://history.state.gov/milestones/1921-1936/kellogg.

9. Tarik Kafala, "The Veto and How to Use It," *BBC News,* September 17, 2003, news.bbc.co.uk/2/hi/middle_east/2828985.stm.

10. United Nations Economic and Social Council, "About ECOSOC," accessed August 19, 2017, www.un.org/en/ecosoc/about.

11. United Nations Economic and Social Council, "Subsidiary Bodies of ECOSOC," accessed August 19, 2017, http://www.un.org/en/ecosoc/about/subsidiary.shtml.

12. "Case Concerning the Military and Paramilitary Activities in and against Nicaragua (*Nicaragua v. United States of America*) (Merits)," Judgment of June 27, 1986, accessed August 21, 2017, http://www.icj-cij.org/files/case-related/70/6505.pdf.

13. Dana Neacsu, "The International Court of Justice Research Guide," Arthur W. Diamond Law Library Research Guides, Columbia University, February 4, 2015, http://library.law.columbia.edu/guides/International_Court_of_Justice.

14. United Nations, International Court of Justice, "Pending Cases," accessed August 21, 2017, http://www.icj-cij.org/en/pending-cases.

15. Ibid.

16. Robert Keohane and Joseph Nye, *Power and Interdependence,* 2nd ed. (Glenview, IL: Scott, Foresman, 1989), 12–13.

17. Organization of American States, "Charter of the Organization of American States: Chapter 1: Nature and Purposes," 2017, http://www.oas.org/en/sla/dil/inter_american_treaties_A-41_charter_OAS.asp#Chapter_I.

18. Alex Hunt and Brian Wheeler, "Brexit: All You Need to Know about the UK Leaving the EU," *BBC News,* April 25, 2017, http://www.bbc.com/news/uk-politics-32810887.

19. "Macron Wins French Election," *Wall Street Journal,* May 7, 2017, http://www.wsj.com/livecoverage/frelect.

20. CNN Staff, "Will Europe Ride the Populist Wave? A Visual Guide," May 5, 2017, http://www.cnn.com/2017/03/15/europe/populism-in-european-elections-visual-guide.

21. World Bank, "Defining Civil Society," last updated July 22, 2013, http://web.worldbank.org/WBSITE/EXTERNAL/TOPICS/CSO/0,,contentMDK:20101499~menuPK:244752~pagePK:220503~piPK:220476~theSitePK:228717,00.html.

22. "Chapter 5: Deepening Democracy at the Global Level," *Human Development Report,* 2002, hdr.undp.org/en/media/chapterfive1.pdf; Louis Ruchames, ed., "The American Anti-Slavery Society," *The Abolitionists: A Collection of their Writing* (New York: Putnam, 1963), 78.

23. Ruchames, "The American Anti-Slavery Society," 78.

24. World Bank, "Civil Society," accessed August 19, 2017, http://www.worldbank.org/en/about/partners/civil-society.

25. United Nations NGO Branch, Department of Economic and Social Affairs, "Consultative Status with ECOSOC and Other Accreditations," accessed August 21, 2017, http://esango.un.org/civilsociety/displayConsultativeStatusSearch.do?method=search&sessionCheck=false.

26. Ibid.

27. United Nations NGO Branch, Department of Economic and Social Affairs, "Basic Facts about ECOSOC Status," accessed August 19, 2017, http://csonet.org/?menu=100.

28. CARE, "Where We Work," accessed August 19, 2017, http://www.care-international.org/where-we-work.

29. United Nations, United Nations Peacekeeping, "About Us," accessed August 19, 2017, http://www.un.org/en/peacekeeping/about.

30. Karen Mingst and Margaret P. Karns, *The United Nations in the 21st Century,* 3rd ed. (Boulder, CO: Westview, 2007), 103.

31. United Nations, United Nations Department of Political Affairs, "Strategic Plan 2016–2019," November 20, 2015, http://www.un.org/undpa/sites/www.un.org.undpa/files/2016%20Annual%20Appeal%20Strategic%20Plan%20leaflet.pdf.

32. United Nations, United Nations Peacebuilding Commission, "Mandate of the Peacebuilding Commission," accessed August 21, 2017, http://www.un.org/en/peacebuilding/mandate.shtml.

33. UN News Centre, "Ban Stresses Role of NGOs in Helping Transitional Countries Build Institutions," October 26, 2011, http://www.un.org/apps/news/story.asp?NewsID=40206

34. Ibid.

35. Mary Kaldor, "Five Meanings of Global Civil Society," in Manfred B. Steger, *The Global Studies Reader,* 2nd ed. (New York: Oxford University Press, 2015).

Chapter 11

1. "In Full: Mandela's Poverty Speech," *BBC News,* February 3, 2005, http://news.bbc.co.uk/2/hi/uk_news/politics/4232603.stm.

2. Kofi Annan, *We the Peoples: The Role of the United Nations in the 21st Century*, Millennium Report of the Secretary-General of the United Nations, 2000, www.un.org/millennium/sg/report.

3. "We the Peoples: Press Conference," press release no. SG/SM/7342, Secretary-General of the United Nations, April 3, 2000, https://www.un.org/press/en/2000/20000403.sgsm7342.doc.html.

4. United Nations, "We Can End Poverty: Millennium Development Goals and Beyond 2015," accessed August 19, 2017, https://www.un.org/millenniumgoals.

5. United Nations, *The Millennium Development Goals Report 2015,* 2015, https://www.un.org/millennium-goals/pdf/MDG_Gap_2015_E_web.pdf

6. World Bank, "Strategic Themes," January 31, 2012, http://go.worldbank.org/3ZPR01N4I0.

7. United Nations, Sustainable Development Knowledge Platform, "Sustainable Development Goal 2," accessed August 19, 2017, https://sustainabledevelopment.un.org/sdg2.

8. "The Water Crisis," *Water.org,* http://water.org/water-crisis/water-sanitation-facts.

9. Abraham H. Maslow, "A Theory of Human Motivation," *Psychological Review* 50 (1943): 370–396, quoted in Christopher D. Green, *Classics in the History of Psychology,* accessed August 19, 2017, psychclassics.yorku.ca/Maslow/motivation.htm.

10. United Nations, *The Sustainable Development Goals Report 2016,* 2016, https://unstats.un.org/sdgs/report/2016.

11. Ibid.

12. United Nations, Department of Economic and Social Affairs, Statistics Division, "Goal 2: Zero Hunger," accessed August 19, 2017, https://unstats.un.org/sdgs/report/2016/Goal-02.

13. United Nations, Department of Economic and Social Affairs, Statistics Division, "Goal 6: Clean Water and Sanitation," accessed August 19, 2017, https://unstats.un.org/sdgs/report/2016/goal-06.

14. United Nations, Department of Economic and Social Affairs, Statistics Division, "Goal 4: Quality Education," accessed August 19, 2017, https://unstats.un.org/sdgs/report/2016/Goal-04.

15. Ibid.

16. Millennium Challenge Corporation, "About MCC," accessed April 14, 2017, www.mcc.gov/pages/about.

17. Millennium Challenge Corporation, "Q&A with MCC Resident Country Director for Niger Kristin Penn: Bolstering Niger's Agricultural Sector," May 22, 2017, https://www.mcc.gov/blog/entry/blog-052217-qa-kristin-penn-niger.

18. Millennium Challenge Corporation, "In El Salvador, a Highway to Education, Opportunity and Prosperity," accessed August 19, 2017, https://www.mcc.gov/our-impact/story/story-111915-el-salvador-highway-brings-education-prosperity.

19. European Commission, "European Development Policy," accessed August 19, 2017, https://ec.europa.eu/europeaid/policies/european-development-policy_en.

20. European Commission, "The Sustainable Development Goals," accessed August 19, 2017, https://ec.europa.eu/europeaid/policies/sustainable-development-goals_en.

21. World Health Organization, "Maternal Mortality," November 2016, http://www.who.int/mediacentre/factsheets/fs348/en.

22. "Severe Acute Respiratory Syndrome (SARS)," *A.D.A.M. Medical Encyclopedia,* February 28, 2013, https://www.ncbi.nlm.nih.gov/pubmedhealth/PMHT0024856.

23. "Global Statistics: The Global HIV/AIDS Epidemic," *HIV.gov,* https://www.hiv.gov/hiv-basics/overview/data-and-trends/global-statistics.

24. World Health Organization, "10 Facts on Malaria," December 2016, http://www.who.int/features/factfiles/malaria/en.

25. NothingButNets, "About Us," accessed August 19, 2017, http://www.nothingbutnets.net/new/about-us.html?referrer=http://www.nothingbutnets.net.

26. World Health Organization, "About WHO," accessed August 19, 2017, http://www.who.int/about/en.

27. World Health Organization, "English/French List of 206 Non-State Actors in Official Relations with WHO Reflecting Decisions of the 140th Session of the Executive Board, January 2017," 2017, http://www.who.int/about/collaborations/non-state-actors/non-state-actors-list.pdf?ua=1.

28. Amnesty International USA, "About Us," accessed August 19, 2017, www.amnestyusa.org/research/human-rights-basics.

29. Eleanor Roosevelt Papers Project, George Washington University, "Quotations by Eleanor Roosevelt," accessed August 19, 2017, https://www2.gwu.edu/~erpapers/abouteleanor/er-quotes/

30. Lorena Galliot, "Wearing Full Islamic Veil Could Land Women in 'Citizenship' School," *France24,* May 19, 2010, www.france24.com/en/20100518-france-full-islamic-veil-burqa-niqab-ban-citizenship-courses-alliot-marie.

31. Jake Cigainero, "Five Years into Ban, Burqa Divide Widens in France," *Deutsche Welle,* April 10, 2016, http://www.dw.com/en/five-years-into-ban-burqa-divide-widens-in-france/a-19177275.

32. Alice Foster, "Where in the World are the Burka and Niqab Banned?" *Express,* December 7, 2016, http://www.express.co.uk/news/world/652842/Burka-Niqab-Islamic-Face-veil-Ban-UK-Fine-France-Belgium-Netherlands-Europe-Muslim-dress.

33. Megan Palin, "World's Most Extreme Punishments," *News.com.au,* October 25, 2016, http://www.news.com.au/world/worlds-most-extreme-punishments/news-story/e2aa343de293208e336765a415a2c072.

34. United Nations, "Somalia: UNICEF Speaks Out against Stoning Death of 13-Year-Old Rape Victim," November 4, 2008, http://www.un.org/apps/news/story.asp?NewsID=28809#.WSxvduvysvA.

35. Darla Cameron and Bonnie Berkowitz, "The State of Gay Rights around the World," *Washington Post,* June 14, 2016, https://www.washingtonpost.com/graphics/world/gay-rights.

36. United Nations, Economic and Social Council, *Progress towards the Sustainable Development Goals: Report of the Secretary-General,* June 3, 2016, http://www.un.org/ga/search/view_doc.asp?symbol=E/2016/75&Lang=E.

37. Center for Reproductive Rights, "Female Genital Mutilation (FGM): Legal Prohibitions Worldwide," December 11, 2008, https://www.reproductiverights.org/document/female-genital-mutilation-fgm-legal-prohibitions-worldwide.

38. World Health Organization, "Female Genital Mutilation," 2016, http://www.who.int/reproductivehealth/topics/fgm/prevalence/en.

39. Equality Now, "The World's Shame: The Global Rape Epidemic," February 2017, http://www.equalitynow.org/sites/default/files/EqualityNowRapeLawReport2017_Single%20Pages.pdf.

40. Equality Now, "End Sex Trafficking," accessed August 19, 2017, http://www.equalitynow.org/issues/end-sex-trafficking.

41. China Labor Watch, "Apple Making Big Profits but Chinese Workers' Wage on the Slide," August 24, 2016, http://www.chinalaborwatch.org/upfile/2016_08_23/Pegatron-report%20FlAug.pdf.

42. International Labour Organization, "About the ILO," accessed August 19, 2017, www.ilo.org/global/about-the-ilo/lang--en/index.htm.

43. Human Rights Watch, "About," accessed August 19, 2017, https://www.hrw.org/about.

44. Freedom House, "About Us," accessed August 19, 2017, www.freedomhouse.org.

45. Hakan Altinay, "Global Governance: A Work in Progress," *YaleGlobal,* January 26, 2010, http://yaleglobal.yale.edu/state-global-governance-audit.

46. Global Governance Watch, "About Global Governance Watch," accessed August 19, 2017, http://www.globalgovernancewatch.org/about.

47. Stephen Krasner, *International Regimes* (Ithaca, NY: Cornell University Press, 1983).

48. Convention on International Trade in Endangered Species of Wild Fauna and Flora, "What Is CITES?" accessed August 19, 2017, www.cites.org/eng/disc/what.php.

49. Margaret Keck and Kathryn Sikkink, *Activists beyond Borders: Advocacy Networks in International Politics* (Ithaca, NY: Cornell University Press, 1998).

50. Occupy Wall Street, "About," accessed August 19, 2017, http://occupywallst.org/about.

Chapter 12

1. Emily O'Hara, "Become Global-Minded," *studyabroad.com*, July 25, 2011, http://www.studyabroad.com/articles/study-abroad-testimonials.aspx.

2. Marcelo M. Suarez-Orozco, "Wanted: Global Citizens," *Educational Leadership* 64, no. 7 (April 2007): 58–62.

3. O'Hara, "Become Global-Minded."

4. Institute of International Education, "Fast Facts," *Open Doors 2016,* November 14, 2016, http://www.iie.org/Research-and-Publications/Open-Doors/Data/Fast-Facts#.WEWZkbIrLX4.

5. Ibid.

6. Ibid.

7. Jeffrey S. Lantis and Jessica DuPlaga, *The Global Classroom* (Boulder, CO: Paradigm, 2010), 95.

8. Kristina Bergan, "A Non-Profit Experience," (paper submitted to fulfill requirements for internship at International House, UNC Charlotte, May 2009).

9. National Education Association, "Preparing 21st Century Students for a Global Society: An Educators Guide to the Four Cs," 2012, http://www.nea.org/assets/docs/A-Guide-to-Four-Cs.pdf; Craig D. Jerald, "Defining a 21st Century Education," Center for Public Education, July 2009, http://www.centerforpubliceducation.org/Learn-About/21st-Century/Defining-a-21st-Century-Education-Full-Report-PDF.pdf.

10. Tamar Lewin, "Rarely Win at Trivial Pursuit? An Embassy Door Opens," *New York Times,* December 17, 2006, http://www.nytimes.com/2006/12/17/weekinreview/17lewin.html.

11. US Department of State, "Careers Representing America," www.careers.state.gov. Also see Lisa Kubiske, "Careers in the US Foreign Service," in *Careers in International Affairs*, 9th ed., ed. Laura E. Cressey, Barrett J. Helmer, and Jennifer E. Steffensen (Washington, DC: Georgetown University Press, 2014), 77–86.

12. Nicole Melcher, "The US Government: Careers in Executive Branch Agencies," in *Careers in International Affairs*, 9th ed., ed. Laura E. Cressey, Barrett J. Helmer, and Jennifer E. Steffensen (Washington, DC: Georgetown University Press, 2014), 63–107.

13. Brent Woolfork, "Careers on Capitol Hill," in *Careers in International Affairs*, 9th ed., ed. Laura E. Cressey, Barrett J. Helmer, and Jennifer E. Steffensen (Washington, DC: Georgetown University Press, 2014), 86–93.

14. Washington State Department of Commerce, *Choose Washington,* 2016, http://choosewashingtonstate.com; US Department of Commerce, International Trade Administration, "Washington: Exports, Jobs, and Foreign Investment," February 2016, https://www.trade.gov/mas/ian/statereports/states/wa.pdf.

15. Peace Corps, "Fast Facts," last updated September 30, 2016, https://www.peacecorps.gov/news/fast-facts.

16. See https://careers.un.org/lbw/Home.aspx for a review of UN career information and actual job openings.

17. Union of International Associations, "Frequently Asked Questions," http://www.uia.org/faq; also see Taylor Stager, "Careers in Development Agencies," in *Careers in International Affairs*, 9th ed., ed. Laura E. Cressey, Barrett J. Helmer, and Jennifer E. Steffensen (Washington, DC: Georgetown University Press, 2014), 93–101.

18. Global Volunteer Network Foundation, www.gvnfoundation.org.

19. Kevin Gill, global director of staffing for Honeywell, quoted by Bill Clabby in "Proving That Study Abroad Is Worth It—Conclusions from Research on Real Benefits of the Experience," (presentation at CIBER Short-Term

Study Abroad Conference, Provo, UT, 2009), http://marriottschool.byu.edu/conferences/ciberstsa/presentations.

20. Association of American Colleges and Universities, "What is Liberal Education?" 2014, www.aacu.org/leap/What_is_liberal_education.cfm.

21. Rutgers University offers a PhD (as well as an MS) in global affairs on its Newark campus through its Division of Global Affairs. The Global and International Studies Program at the University of California Santa Barbara, which had previously offered a global emphasis as part of PhD programs of participating departments, now has a standalone PhD in global studies. The Jackson School of the University of Washington offers a cross-disciplinary PhD in international studies that incorporates intensive area studies, and Old Dominion University also offers a PhD that is somewhat interdisciplinary in character. For more information, see http://dga.newark.rutgers.edu/phd-program-73-total-credits; http://www.global.ucsb.edu/phd; https://jsis.washington.edu/programs/graduate/phd; http://catalog.odu.edu/graduate/collegeofartsletters/internationalstudies/#doctorofphilosophy-internationalstudies. Indiana University and the University of Wisconsin–Madison offer global studies minors in conjunction with disciplinary PhD programs. See http://www.indiana.edu/~intlweb/graduate/gsminor.shtml; http://global.wisc.edu/minor.

22. See the APSIA website: www.apsia.org.

23. There are many options, given the increasing popularity of these types of programs across the United States. A few examples include Georgetown, American, and George Washington universities in the DC area; Columbia, Seton Hall, and Boston universities in the Northeast; Florida State University, the University of Florida, and the University of Virginia in the South; Marquette University, the University of Chicago, and the University of Denver in the Midwest; Stanford University, the University of Southern California, and the University of San Diego in the West. See https://www.law.georgetown.edu/academics/academic-programs/graduate-programs/degree-programs/dual-master; https://www.wcl.american.edu/admiss/jdma; https://elliott.gwu.edu/joint-degrees/ma-jd; https://sipa.columbia.edu/academics/dual-degree-programs/columbia-dual-degree-programs; https://www.shu.edu/academics/jd-ma-diplomacy.cfm; http://www.bu.edu/academics/law/programs/jdma-ir; http://www.law.fsu.edu/academic-programs/joint-degree-programs/international-affairs-and-law; https://polisci.ufl.edu/graduate/ma-programs/jdma-joint-degree-program; http://www.law.virginia.edu/html/academics/govt.htm; https://law.marquette.edu/programs-degrees/joint-degree-programs; http://www.law.uchicago.edu/joint-degrees; http://www.du.edu/korbel/programs/masters/dual.html; https://law.stanford.edu/education/degrees/joint-degrees-within-stanford-university/law-and-international-policy-studies; https://dornsife.usc.edu/sir/joint-professional-degree-programs; https://www.sandiego.edu/law/academics/jd-programs/concurrent-degrees.

24. Robert G. Blanton, "Surveying International Studies Programs: Where Do We Stand?" *International Studies Perspectives* 10, no. 2 (2009): 224–240; Marijke Breuning and John Ishiyama, "International Studies Programs: For What Purpose and For Whom?" *International Studies Perspectives* 5, no. 4 (November 2004): 400–402; Marijke Breuning and John Ishiyama, "Marketing the International Studies Major: Claims and Content of Programs at Primarily Undergraduate Institutions in the Midwest," *International Studies Perspectives* 8, no. 1 (February 2007): 121–133; Jeanne A. K. Hey, "Can International Studies Research Be the Basis for an Undergraduate International Studies Curriculum?" *International Studies Perspectives* 5, no. 4 (November 2004): 395–399; James C. Hendrix, "Globalizing the Curriculum," *Clearing House* 71, no. 5 (May–June 1998): 305–309; Heidi H. Hobbs, Harry I. Chernotsky, and Darin H. Van Tassell, "International Studies and the Global Community: Transforming the Agenda," in Robert A. Denemark, ed., *The International Studies Encyclopedia*, vol. 7 (Hoboken, NJ: Wiley-Blackwell, 2010), 4598–4609; Ann Kelleher, "Does International Studies Have a Common Core? An Analysis of Seventy-Three Curriculum Programs," (presentation at the annual meeting of the International Studies Association, Honolulu, HI, March 4, 2005).

25. Robert G. Hanvey, "An Attainable Global Perspective," *Theory Into Practice* 21, no. 3 (1982), reprinted in Patrick O'Meara, Howard D. Mehlinger, and Roxana Ma Newman, eds., *Changing Perspectives on International Education* (Bloomington: Indiana University Press, 2001), 244–279.

26. Maryann Cusimano Love, *Beyond Sovereignty: Issues for a Global Agenda* (Belmont, CA: Thomson Higher Education, 2007).

27. Darla K. Deardorff, "The Identification and Assessment of Intercultural Competence as a Student Outcome of Internationalization at Institutions of Higher Education in the United States," (EdD thesis, North Carolina State University, 2004).

• Index •